*A Salute to Courage*

**Washington, Lafayette, and Tench Tilghman at Yorktown**

ARTIST: CHARLES WILLSON PEALE

COURTESY OF THE MARYLAND COMMISSION ON ARTISTIC PROPERTY, STATE HOUSE, ANNAPOLIS

# A
# SALUTE
# TO
# COURAGE

*The American Revolution as Seen
Through Wartime Writings of Officers
of the Continental Army and Navy*

*Edited by* DENNIS P. RYAN

*from documents provided by
The Daughters of the Cincinnati*

*Foreword by Richard B. Morris*

*New York*   COLUMBIA UNIVERSITY PRESS   *1979*

**Library of Congress Cataloging in Publication Data**
Main entry under title:

A Salute to courage.

   Produced by the Daughters of the Cincinnati.
   1. United States—History—Revolution, 1775–
1783—Sources.   2. United States—History—
Revolution, 1775–1783—Personal narratives.
I. Ryan, Dennis P., 1943–     II. Daughters of the Cincinnati.
E203.S15      973.3      78-9775
ISBN 0-231-04230-2

769715

$C$

COLUMBIA UNIVERSITY PRESS
NEW YORK    GUILDFORD, SURREY

6001728801

*TO*
*THOSE PATRIOTIC MEN AND WOMEN*
*WHOSE SELFLESS DEDICATION AND SACRIFICES*
*DURING THE AMERICAN REVOLUTION*
*WON FOR US OUR CHERISHED FREEDOM*

# Contents

CHAPTER ONE     THE CALL TO ARMS: BOSTON, CANADA, NEW YORK, NEW JERSEY, APRIL 1775–MARCH 1777

CHAPTER TWO    VICTORY AT SARATOGA, DEFEAT IN PENNSYLVANIA,
1777–1778

CHAPTER THREE     THE WAR IN THE NORTH: INDIANS, BATTLES AND SKIRMISHES, MUTINY, AND CONSPIRACY, 1778–1781

### EPILOGUE    THE FINAL DAYS

# Illustrations

Portraits and other illustrations held in private hands unless otherwise noted in captions.

## MAPS

# Foreword

THIS IS A BOOK of many tales told by valiant men. The tellers provide an on-the-spot view of the campaigns of the American Revolution, that epochal and extended conflict exacting from its participants courage, conviction, and sacrifice. What distinguishes the stories from so many others is that they were told by men who were line officers of the Continental army, most of them not famous like George Washington and Nathanael Greene—although they are here, too—but chiefly men of lesser rank—ensigns, lieutenants, captains, and colonels.

Through the diligent research and investigative skills of their descendants, the line officers now have a chance to give their side of the story. The Daughters of the Cincinnati, who proudly claim descent from these line officers, have searched attics, ransacked old cupboards and bureaus, and pressed their search in local manuscript repositories from all over the original Thirteen States. These persistent and inspired sleuths turned up diaries, orderly books, journals, and bundles of letters, many never before known to be extant, and it is from this cache that the story is told. Indeed, what makes *A Salute to Courage* a significant and distinctive contribution to the glorious story of the American Revolution is the fact that so much of this material has never before appeared in print, and much else has been buried in relatively obscure or specialized journals, unavailable to the general reader.

The letters, diaries, and journals herein excerpted bear witness to the moments of great heroism as well as to incidents of desertion, mutiny, and despondency. For seven years and even longer, the line officers stayed with their companies and regiments, giving some kind of permanence to a largely phantom army, whose privates enlisted for short terms and were impatient to return to hearth and home. With their men, the line officers shared almost unbelievable privations, starving, freezing, suffering from disease and wretched medical care, and often going payless. We share their moments of despair as well as their episodes of exultation.

The book carries an impact of immediacy. We are with the officers from the beginning at Lexington to the evacuation of British troops from New York City. "I was the last man on the neck," writes Benjamin Gould about the retreat from Breed's Hill. Two days before Christmas, Jacob Cheesman, from the frozen encampment before Quebec, writes that now is not the time to return home and put his hand to the plow again, "expetially now When my Country Calls Loudly for assistance." Eight days later he fell in battle. Cheesman is but one of many whose deeds are recorded in this book. Others suffered imprisonment and degradation in noisome jails like the New York Sugar House. They quickly found that they were fighting not only a war for independence against Redcoats but also a civil war against neighbors, friends, and even close of kin. "The troubels of a Sivel War are Grat," bemoaned William Greenleaf, whose home was burned to the ground by the British on their march to Concord. Throughout one detects a recurrent note of intense loneliness and aching for loved ones, often never to be seen again.

During the darkest days of the war the Continental line officers kept the faith. They were sustained by the conviction that they were fighting not only for their nation's independence but also for their own freedom and that of their children and their children's children. For their sustained commitment a grateful nation salutes them.

RICHARD B. MORRIS

*Columbia University*
*July 1978*

# Preface

A *Salute to Courage* is a tribute to officers who served in the American Revolution. It is a collection of excerpts from their correspondence, diaries, journals, and orderly books, which shows some of the inside story of the winning of the eight-year conflict. The materials have been collected by and this book produced for the Daughters of the Cincinnati, a patriotic society founded in 1894 by women descendants of officers of the Continental army and navy.

The Society, in instituting projects to further the knowledge of the Revolutionary War, is thereby fulfilling one of its basic reasons for existing. Its constitution states, in part:

WHEREAS: an investigation of the incidents of the war and of efforts of individuals, through the private correspondence and papers of the participants, must tend to throw new light upon the history of that eventful period, and must be fraught with interest and benefit to us all. . . . The objects of this Society shall be:

. . . To advance and encourage investigation and study of the history of the Revolution, its causes and results, and to instill in the minds of the rising generation a knowledge of, and reverence for, the spirit and patient, unswerving determination which successfully carried on the struggle for liberty against overwhelming force and Old World prejudice.

In order to fulfill this objective, the Society's Board of Managers appointed a committee from the membership to collect the wartime writings of as many officers as possible on the Society's roster of ancestors. It was the Society's desire to increase the knowledge of the long war for America's independence, in a book containing details having human interest appeal that reveal daily problems and many of the vicissitudes of army life that could not be better told than by the officers themselves. The Board of Managers also desired that portraits of the officers be included in the book. Most of those selected are privately owned and have not been seen by the general public.

A great effort was made to avoid as much as possible secondary sources and previously published eyewitness accounts of the Revolution. Some of the manuscripts were found in the libraries of historical societies, public libraries, and state archives, or were obtained from the descendants who had inherited them. Others required endless correspondence and patient detective work to locate.

It is regretted that it was not possible to include a manuscript by every officer-ancestor on the roster of the Daughters of the Cincinnati, and that many interesting diaries, orderly books, and journals had to be abridged because of their length. It is also regretted that original material from some geographical areas was scarce. This was particularly true in the South, which has suffered through two major wars during which many courthouses and homes were burned. For example, when the British entered Savannah in

December 1778, they destroyed numerous documents. A few were rescued by Captain John Milton, who escaped with them to Charleston. When the British advanced northward, Milton finally took them to Annapolis. Thus some of the important documents were saved.

After many manuscripts had been found by the Book Committee, it commissioned a specialist on the American Revolution, Dr. Dennis P. Ryan of New York University, associate editor of *The Papers of William Livingston,* to make a selection from our collected manuscripts, and to transcribe and annotate them for publication. As editor he has achieved this goal admirably.

For the end of the book the Committee supplied from the Society's official files a list of the 459 officers on the Society's roster, giving the places and dates of their births, marriages, and deaths, and their wives' places and dates of birth and death. All this data has been verified by professional genealogists. Discrepancies with other standard sources can be checked by writing to our Society.

An important activity of the Society is its scholarship program, which was started in 1910. In the past twenty-five years it has awarded over eight hundred grants to daughters of officers in the United States Armed Forces. This financial aid has made it possible for them to attend the colleges of their choice.

One of the objectives stated in the constitution of the Daughters of the Cincinnati is: "To gather and preserve carefully documents and relics relating to the Revolutionary period." Therefore, one of the preservation projects of the Society has been to contribute to the collection and maintenance of authentic furnishings for Yorktown's Moore House, where the articles of capitulation were prepared for Lord Cornwallis' surrender.

The precedent which inspired a group of women descendants of line officers of America's Revolutionary War to establish this Society was the founding of the Society of the Cincinnati in May 1783 by Continental Line officers. The Society of the Cincinnati is a military, benevolent, social, and non-political order. The preamble to that Society's "Institution," written by Major General Henry Knox, Brigadier General Edward Hand, Brigadier General Jedediah Huntington, and Captain Samuel Shaw at Verplanck Mansion, New York,* stated the reasons for forming such a society:

It having pleased the Supreme Governor of the Universe, in the disposition of human affairs, to cause the separation of the colonies of North America from the domination of Great Britain, and, after a bloody conflict of eight years, to establish them free, independent and sovereign States, connected, by alliances founded on reciprocal advantage, with some of the great princes and powers of the earth.

To perpetuate, therefore, as well the remembrance of this vast event, as the mutual friendships which have been formed under the pressure of common danger, and, in many instances, cemented by the blood of the parties, the officers of the American Army do hereby, in the most solemn manner, associate, constitute and combine themselves into one SOCIETY OF FRIENDS, to endure as long as they shall endure, or any of their eldest male posterity, and, in failure thereof, the collateral branches who may be judged worthy of becoming its supporters and Members.

The officers of the American Army having generally been taken from the citizens of

---

*Verplanck Mansion, built 1730–40 by Gulian Verplanck at Fishkill, New York, is now known as "Mt. Gulian." It was the headquarters of Baron von Steuben in 1783. It is being reconstructed by various Society of the Cincinnati state societies and by other patriotic societies and individuals. This Dutch Colonial homestead, sixty miles north of New York City, overlooking the Hudson River, is open to the public several times a week.

America, possess high veneration for the character of that illustrious Roman, Lucius Quintus Cincinnatus; and being resolved to follow his example, by returning to their citizenship, they think they may with propriety denominate themselves THE SOCIETY OF THE CINCINNATI.

The following principles shall be immutable and form the basis of the Society of the Cincinnati:

An incessant attention to preserve inviolate those exalted rights and liberties of human nature, for which they have fought and bled, and without which the high rank of a rational being is a curse instead of a blessing.

An unalterable determination to promote and cherish, between the respective States, that union and national honor so essentially necessary to their happiness, and the future dignity of the American empire.

To render permanent the cordial affection subsisting among the officers. This spirit will dictate brotherly kindness in all things, and particularly, extend to the most substantial acts of beneficence, according to the ability of the Society, towards those officers and their families, who unfortunately may be under the necessity of receiving it. . . .*

It is the shared opinion of the Daughters of the Cincinnati and the Editor that there is a significant message to be derived from these worthy objectives. May the convictions that motivated the heroic officers of the War for Independence to make such tremendous personal sacrifices be a recurrent reminder that our freedom was dearly bought and that the retaining of it will be assured only if we cherish this freedom enough to live as if we were on the verge of losing it.

THE BOOK COMMITTEE

Adelaide B. Adams
Gabrielle M. Bielenstein
Pamela Brinton, Chairman
Virginia B. Clarke
Jane H. Liddell
Marie D. Powers, Vice-Chairman
Helen H. Weist
*Daughters of the Cincinnati*

* Bryce Metcalf (Vice-President General), Original Members and Other Officers Eligible to the Society of the Cincinnati, Introduction, p. 1 and ch. 1, p. 1.

# Acknowledgments

A PROJECT OF this scope is the work of many minds and hands. We would like to express our gratitude to those whose assistance made this book possible.

Of inestimable importance in its development has been the interest, advice, and enthusiasm of the renowned historian, Dr. Richard Brandon Morris, professor emeritus of American history at Columbia University. His expert guidance was a major contribution to the entire project.

The Book Committee was very fortunate in its choice of editor, Dr. Dennis Ryan, adjunct assistant professor at New York University and associate editor of *The Papers of William Livingston,* a project of the New Jersey Historical Commission. He brought not only a thorough knowledge of the American Revolution but also a specialized skill in weaving our manuscripts into a chronological narrative with explanatory notes and identifications. His keen mind and his cooperation made working with him a pleasure.

We appreciate and honor, in memoriam, the dynamic leadership of the previous editor, Dr. Catherine Snell Crary. She was a professor of American history whose brilliant mind and scholarly guidance during the first months accelerated the momentum of the project. Although temporarily curtailed by her tragic death from cancer in 1974, the collecting and editing process has continued unabated.

Our special thanks go to Mr. Bernard Gronert of Columbia University Press for his sustained interest and assistance.

We are very grateful to the members of the Society who participated in this project:

Adelaide B. Adams, chairman of research, traveled many miles to follow historical clues, mastered technical difficulties in libraries and archives, and transcribed with care and accuracy almost illegible eighteenth-century manuscripts.

Gabrielle M. Bielenstein brought orderly scholarship, valuable assistance, and cohesiveness to the committee. Her various abilities were indispensable.

Pamela Brinton, our excellent chairman, raised funds and integrated the talents of the group. Her cheerful perseverance helped us through our difficulties until the book's successful completion.

Virginia B. Clarke initiated during her presidency the idea of collecting, identifying, and annotating portraits of officers on our roster and sparked the subsequent development of the present volume.

Jane H. Liddell has consistently and enthusiastically taken part in every facet of the production of this book. Her zealous persistence assured that every element would express the spirit of patriotism that inspired our ancestors. Her academic activities resulted in obtaining the services of Dr. Catherine S. Crary and Dr. Dennis P. Ryan.

Marie D. Powers' constant interest and executive abilities as president provided the direction needed for the production of this book. With her husband, John M. Powers, she made possible the fine reproductions of the portraits, many of which are in private hands.

Helen H. Weist recorded all our meetings. Her numerous skills, coupled with her constant good humor, remained a bulwark throughout.

Many members and friends of our Society helped in typing, research, filing, genealogical work, checking, etc. Without such help this work would have been considerably delayed. They are: Nannie P. T. Carlton, Barbara O. de Zalduondo, Dorothy C. Hauck, Elizabeth G. Hayward, Florence P. Hohenstein, Louis H. Hollister, Elizabeth D. Mallard, Elizabeth N. Nicholson, Anne B. H. Plumb, Michelle B. Putnam, Lucy V. G. Ralston, Phyllis M. Rhinelander, Caroline C. Seymour, Mary Elizabeth G. Shallow, Fairchild B. Smith, William Earl Dodge Stokes, Jr., Janet R. Whitman, and Pamela S. Williamson.

The following individuals and organizations were helpful in providing copies of manuscripts and valuable help while we searched for documents, and in graciously granting permission for publication: Robert E. Banta, director of libraries, State University of New York, Plattsburgh; Timothy F. Beard, assistant librarian of Local History and Genealogical Information, New York Public Library; James R. Bentley, manuscript librarian, The Filson Club; Edmund Berkeley, Jr., curator of manuscripts, University of Virginia Library; Patricia L. Bodak, reference archivist, Yale University Library; Nancy C. Boles, curator of manuscripts, Maryland Historical Society; Alfred N. Brandon, librarian, New York Academy of Medicine; Paul I. Chestnut, assistant curator for reader services, Duke University Library; Alexander P. Clark, curator of manuscripts, Princeton University Library; Howson W. Cole, curator of manuscripts, Virginia Historical Society; Winifred Collins, manuscript librarian, Massachusetts Historical Society; Diane Corrigan, curator, James Morris Library; Thomas J. Dunnings, Jr., curator of manuscripts, New–York Historical Society; Thomas R. Gaffney, acting director, Maine Historical Society; Sue A. Gillies, reference librarian, and James A. Gregory, librarian, New–York Historical Society; Thompson R. Harlow, director, Connecticut Historical Society; Josephine L. Harper, manuscript curator, State Historical Society of Wisconsin; Lilla M. Hawes, director, Georgia Historical Society; John Hawkes, owner of Washington-McDougall correspondence; James J. Heslin, director, New–York Historical Society; Codman Hislop, chairman, Hawkes Papers Committee, Union College; John D. Kilbourne, director of Anderson House Museum, Society of the Cincinnati; Margaret Klapthor, Smithsonian Institution; Albert T. Klyberg, director, Rhode Island Historical Society; Jean R. McNiece, assistant librarian of Manuscript and Archives Department, and John Miller, chief of American History Division, New York Public Library; James E. Mooney, director, Historical Society of Pennsylvania; Anne M. Murphy, director of libraries, Fordham University; Mardel Pacheco, assistant to curator of manuscripts, Princeton University Library; Natalie B. Perry, director, Wilton Historical Society; Peter Parker, librarian, Historical Society of Pennsylvania; Howard H. Peckham, former director, William L. Clements Library; Rutherford D. Rogers, university librarian, Yale University Library; Mattie U. Russell, curator of manuscripts, Duke University Library; Faye Simkin, executive officer, New York Public Library, The Research Libraries; Brigadier General E. H. Simmons, director of History and Museums Division, United States Marine Corps; Don R. Skemer, manuscript librarian, New Jersey Historical Society; Charles R. Smith, historian, History and Museums Division, United States Marine Corps; Louis L. Tucker, director, Massachusetts Historical Society; Carolyn A. Wallace, librarian, Southern Historical Collection, University of North Carolina; Howard W. Wiseman, curator, New Jersey Historical Society.

THE BOOK COMMITTEE
OF THE DAUGHTERS
OF THE CINCINNATI

# Editorial Guidelines

THIS DOCUMENTARY WORK is divided into four chapters and an epilogue, with a genealogical appendix that gives a complete list of all officers on the roster of the Daughters of the Cincinnati with dates of births, deaths, and marriages. Portraits of many of the officers who are either mentioned or who are the authors of the manuscripts printed are also included. The chapters follow the ebb and flow of the American Revolution through the documentary materials selected. Chapter 1 follows the newly formed American army from Lexington Green through the siege of Boston, the Canadian disaster, and the fight for New York City. The descriptions of the retreat through New Jersey are followed by accounts of the great victories at Trenton and Princeton, which helped to sustain the patriot through the long winter encampment at Morristown. Chapter 2 depicts the campaigns on the two major battle fronts of 1777: New York State and the hills and fields of the area in and around Philadelphia. The victory at Saratoga compensated for the bloody defeats at Brandywine and Germantown. Both campaigns are vividly portrayed in the diaries and letters. However, there was little to cheer the soldiers and officers in the infamous winter encampment at Valley Forge. The upsurge in confidence gained by the Americans at the Battle of Monmouth in June 1778 provides an appropriate end to the chapter. Chapter 3 encompasses the war in the north from 1778 to the end of 1781. Indian warfare, the Sullivan expedition, the battles of Connecticut Farms and Springfield,

Arnold's conspiracy, and the mutiny of the Pennsylvania and New Jersey lines are but some of the many challenges that the officers in the north had to survive. Chapter 4 shifts the focus to the war in the south between the invading British army under General Sir Henry Clinton and Lord Cornwallis against the outnumbered collection of Continental soldiers and officers and southern militiamen. The long series of depressing defeats, often caused by acute shortages of supplies, was obliterated by the stirring siege and ultimate victory of Washington's army at Yorktown. The letters of the officers also reveal that after Yorktown the armies in the north and south not only had to continue their vigilance to keep the British within their urban enclaves but also had to fight new enemies—boredom, fatigue, and intense longing to be with loved ones. The end of the war did come in 1783, and the chapter concludes with General Nathanael Greene's address to troops to help prepare them for the difficult transition to civilian life. The epilogue, compiled by The Daughters of the Cincinnati, contains memorable messages and accounts of the emotional scenes in General George Washington's farewell to his officers and to a grateful nation.

All chapters contain a brief introductory comment that interprets the documents and events described. Headnotes to each document provide the context in which the manuscript was written and furnish other helpful information. Footnotes are brief and intended not to interfere with reader interest and continuity. Only archaic terms not found in a standard dictionary are defined. They will identify those individuals for whom information is available. Dates of officers were compiled from standard reference sources. Any discrepancy with the roster of ancestors reflects the fact that biographical and genealogical research often depends on meagre or contradictory sources. Officers are usually identified only once in the volume, and they are given their rank and regiment at the time of that service. The reader seeking further information on the service of officers in the American Revolution is advised to consult Francis B. Heitman, *Historical Register of the Officers of the Continental Army during the War of the Revolution, April 1775 to December 1783* (Washington, D.C., 1893). In general, footnotes avoid lengthy historical discussion.

The footnotes furnish the manuscript collection and repository of the document as well as a physical description of the type of document: autograph letter signed (ALS), autograph document (AD), contemporary copy, autograph copy, and typescript copy. Whenever possible, the original manuscript has been used. Printed letters, journals, diaries, orderly books, and typescript copies have been used when the original manuscript was not extant or available. In these cases, bibliographical information is noted. Long diaries, journals, and orderly books have been selectively extracted. In no case has a letter been extracted when the complete manuscript was available to the editor.

It is the sincere wish of the editor that the vibrance, vitality, and candor of these eighteenth-century writings be preserved, without major alterations. The text of each document has been rendered into print as faithfully as possible, consonant with modern scholarly editorial standards. Superscript letters have been lowered to the line and the thorn (þ) has been replaced with "th." Errors in punctuation and spelling have not been corrected. Each sentence begins with a capital letter and ends with a period, question mark, or exclamation point, and any changes from the orig-

inal text have been made silently as necessary, while preserving the author's intent. The dash, a popular eighteenth-century device, has been silently omitted when superfluous or replaced with the appropriate punctuation when used at the end of a sentence. When material deleted by the writer adds additional or significant information, the canceled word or passage has been placed before the word that replaced it and enclosed in angle brackets (<>). Otherwise, the words crossed through by the author have been silently omitted by the editor. The ellipsis has been used only in instances where printed or typescript versions of manuscripts have been employed and material was excluded from that version. The dateline of a letter has been placed to the right above the text of the document regardless of its position on the manuscript. For journals, diaries, and orderly books, the dateline has remained immediately before the entry when that was the case in the original. In other instances, the dateline is placed to the right above the entry. All datelines have been italicized. When a dateline does not appear on the manuscript itself, it appears above the headnote introducing the document. The extended complimentary close has been brought up with the final line of text. Finally, if the manuscript is mutilated or illegible, square brackets ([]) are used to indicate the missing material. If the word is conjectural, it is placed within the square brackets.

These documents reflect love of country, bravery, firmness, and tenacity. They reveal the variety of conditions and situations that confronted the Continental army officers and that tested their belief in the new nation and the principles for which they were fighting. That these men persevered with such determination is testimony to their patriotism. The Daughters of the Cincinnati and the editor believe this documentary work is a fitting salute to their courage.

DENNIS P. RYAN

*A Salute to Courage*

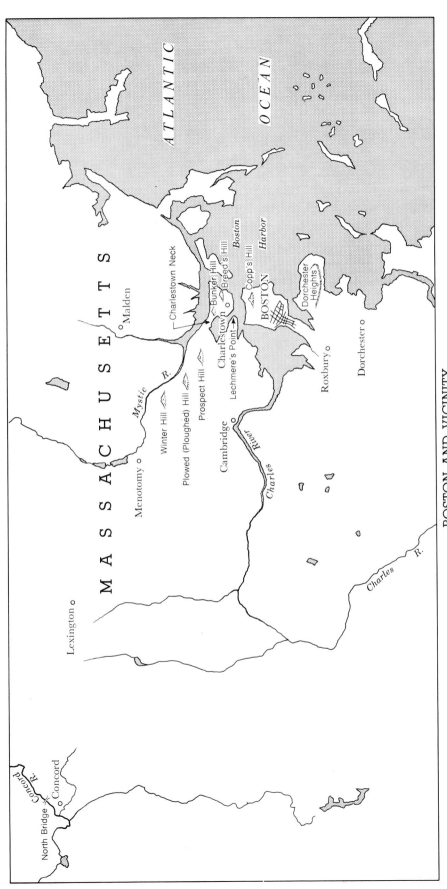

BOSTON AND VICINITY

# CHAPTER ONE

# The Call to Arms:
# Boston, Canada, New York, New Jersey

∞∞∞∞∞∞∞∞∞∞∞∞∞∞∞∞∞

*April 1775–March 1777*

T HE VIOLENT CLASH between British regulars and American minutemen that took place at Lexington and Concord inspired concerned men to take up arms in 1775 to defend America. The exhilaration over routing the British at Concord was shortly superseded by the sobering demands of recruitment and supply, construction of emplacements around Boston, and finally the bloody bayonet warfare on Breed's Hill. By July 1775 the young army was fast becoming familiar with the many hazards of challenging the greatest land and naval power in the world.

The successful capture of Fort Ticonderoga in May 1775 emboldened the American army to invade Canada. A serious lack of cohesion between the many units and leaders participating and the delayed start of the expedition hampered its effectiveness from its commencement. The army made a valiant but unsuccessful siege on Quebec on December 31, 1775, which resulted in the death of many brave officers, the capture and imprisonment of hundreds of soldiers, and the bleak prospect of a long, cold winter before the city's walls. Despite the arrival of a relief

force in April 1776, the tired, sick, and defeated force left Canada in June 1776. The failures and errors of the campaign would eventually persuade many officers to accept temporary setbacks to gain ultimate victory.

With the departure of the British army by sea from Boston in March 1776, George Washington astutely perceived that the war would shift to the Middle Colonies, and New York in particular. Efforts to defend New York City required more men and supplies to complete the network of forts and obstructions to resist British attack. However, the arrival in July of the massive invasion force led by General Sir William Howe and transported by the awesome naval forces of Lord Admiral Richard Howe created grave apprehensions within the Continental army. The Battle of Long Island in August 1776 was a British victory that was achieved as much by overwhelming numbers as by shrewd tactics and strategy. During the next two months, Washington demonstrated brilliant leadership by avoiding a pitched battle with the British, thus enabling him to survive despite the British seizure of New York City and the fall of Fort Lee and Fort Washington.

The retreat through New Jersey was a somber experience for the Continental army and its officers. Men deserted, refused to re-enlist, and took protection from the British army. The fortunes of the Americans seemed to ebb further with each town they passed through. Only the lack of boats and the haughty condescension and want of vigor of the British and Hessian generals saved Washington and his decimated army encamped on the Pennsylvania shore of the Delaware River.

The surprise assault on the Hessian barracks at Trenton and the bloody victory at Princeton buoyed the hopes of the American people and their fighting men. Defeat had turned to victory, and the tired army moved to the safety of their winter encampment at Morristown. By 1777 the Continental officers and their troops had been challenged in far-flung battlefields and had been sustained by their patriotism, their skill in battle, and their patience with the multifarious problems of army service.

# WILLIAM GREENLEAF TO JONATHAN BUCK

O N APRIL 18, 1775, General Thomas Gage (c.1719–87), commander of the British troops in America, ordered 700 men under Lieutenant Colonel Francis Smith (1723–91) to seize the arms of Massachusetts citizens at Concord. The raid was to be a surprise, but Paul Revere's ride warned the people of Lexington and, on the morning of April 19, 1775, more than 70 minutemen under Captain John Parker (1729–75) clashed with the advancing British units. Eight Americans died. When the redcoats arrived at Concord, they engaged the provincial forces at the North Bridge, and lives were lost on both sides. A British relief column met their own retreating men under Smith at Lexington. By the time the exhausted British units reached Charlestown, 73 men of the force of 1,500 soldiers had fallen, victims of American vigilance and courage.

The success of the irregular units at Lexington and Concord played an important part in the formation of the American Continental, or regular, army and gave rise to a flood of protest in the thirteen colonies. Pride in the courage of the minutemen and shock at the spilling of blood during the British attack is evident in the letter of William Greenleaf (1724–1803) to a friend, written only days after the first battles of the American Revolution. Greenleaf would join the call to arms, serving from May 1775 to June 3, 1783. This lengthy service was remarkable for a man in his fifties. His prose was awkward, but he did articulate the rising spirit of American patriotism that helped to form an American army.

*Haverhill 29 of Aprill 1775*

Dear Frind

I Send You thees Shirt Lins just to Let You No My Famaly are all Well thanks to God. The Hous I Lived In is Burnt by fier. I Lost Everey thing In the Seler With about 40 bushels of Hey & Intier Corn With a forth Part of Housel furnituer to the Whol about 8 or 9 Hund. Pound. Squier Whits & Lads Wit Dunkins Slitheres Warehouse's & Shops are all Burnt down. God Grant We May Lay Righteousnes thereby the troubels of a Sivel War are Grat. There Went from Boston about Eighteen Hundred Men to Concord by the Way fierd on about twenty of Ouer Men that Was asembled at Lexentown to Watch the Moshen about the [grean] of the Morning Kild & Wond. Eight then Proseded to Cunkered & destroy'd about 50 Bls of flower Nockt the town goods of [        ] a few Canon as Sun as the Pepol New the afor they fel on them & Kild about three Hundred & the Enemy Maid a dishonarebel Retret behaving Lick Savg. I Wold tel You Mor but am in Hast. The Liberty Partey at New yorck as Sun as they Heard the Nues Ros & tuck the fort With fifteen Hundred arms 2 Provision Vessels bound for boston & are In persut of the third that got out.[1] This Nues arived at the Camp Yesterday by a Post. There is a grait deal Mor God Give us Suckses is I Hop the Prayer of all His Peopel. Fare Well

WM: GREENLEAF

ALS, William Heath Papers, Massachusetts Historical Society, Boston.

[1] This riot occurred on April 23, 1775.

# BENJAMIN GOULD NARRATIVE

## *April 19, 1775–June 19, 1775*

THE VICTORIES at Lexington and Concord resulted in the confining of the British forces to Boston. A two-month stalemate was created when the British retained access to the sea and the Americans massed their forces on land at Cambridge. An American council of war on June 15, 1775, ordered Massachusetts and Connecticut units to fortify Breed's Hill on Charlestown Neck. An active participant in this effort was Benjamin Gould (1751–1841), who served as a minuteman, a private in Colonel Moses Little's (1724–98) Massachusetts Battalion, and then as an ensign in the Twelfth Continental Regiment. Gould's narrative describes the American action against the retreating British on April 19 and the efforts to dig entrenchments on Breed's Hill in the face of severe cannonading from British ships. Although written years later, Gould's narrative of the events of the beginning of the Revolutionary War vividly depicts those crucial moments.

On the 19th of April, 1775, we were informed by an express from Salem that the enemy had marched out of Boston for Concord. About thirty of us started off to meet them, which we did near Menotomy meeting-house. Not thinking of their flank-guard, we aimed at the main body; we were attacked by them, but drove them in. We had several killed and wounded; I was slightly. Followed them to Charlestown.

I enlisted soon after in Capt. John Baker's company,[1] Col. Moses Little's regiment, and marched to Cambridge. On the seventeenth of June was ordered on guard at Lechmere's Point. Lt. Col. Asa Whitcomb commanded the guard.[2] After the battle had been commenced some time, the guard was ordered on to reinforce the troops, upon the hill, but when we got on the neck, met them there retreating, but kept on until we met General Putnam,[3] who spoke to Col. Whitcomb and he retreated. While on the neck, the ship that was in Charles River fired upon us[4] and the floating batteries came up Mystic River within small-arms shot of us, and Col. Whitcomb took me in front of him a little to his left, when we halted. It placed me in a situation for them to take aim. I think it was the first shot that struck the breech of my gun as I held it in my hand, the second struck the ground close to my feet, the third came into the hole and made it deeper. I turned my eye to the guard and found them retreating. I was the last man on the neck. As I retreated I slipped through the fence on the right hand, seeing the ground more favorable to cover me from their fire. When I had gotten about a rod I saw the flash of their cannon. I dropped to the ground, and the ball passed over my back, and struck the ground a little distance beyond me. I then returned to the guard, and found they had all got safe back. A few days after, I was on guard on Plought. and as I was relieving the sentries, they fired at us, and a ball struck me, but happened to strike something hard and flattened, and I picked it up.

Original manuscript in private hands; typescript copy in Miscellaneous Manuscripts, New-York Historical Society, New York City.

[1] Captain John Baker (1733–1815) of Little's Massachusetts Battalion.
[2] Colonel Asa Whitcomb (1719–1804) of Massachusetts.
[3] Colonel Israel Putnam (1718–90) of the Third Connecticut Regiment was appointed major general in the Continental army June 19, 1775.
[4] Probably H.M.S. *Lively*.

# SAMUEL BLACHLEY WEBB TO JOSEPH WEBB

## *June 19–20, 1775*

ON JUNE 16–17, 1775, the principal American fortification was erected on Breed's Hill, and an auxiliary one was built on Bunker Hill. When the British learned of these activities, they attacked with infantry, marines, and artillery. The events of June 17, 1775, are usually referred to as the Battle of Bunker Hill, but the main engagement occurred on adjacent Breed's Hill. The American positions there proved untenable against the British onslaught. General Sir William Howe's (1729–1814) forces scored a tactical victory, but 1,054 of their 2,400 men were either killed or wounded by American marksmen. This battle did not alter the existing stalemate in the siege of Boston; the Americans had hemmed the British in but could not drive them out of the city. Samuel Blachley Webb (1753–1807), a first lieutenant in the Second Connecticut Regiment, was wounded in this battle he so skillfully describes.

*Cambridge June 19th. 1775*

My Dear Brother

The Horrors & Devastations of War now begins to appear with us in Earnest. The Generals of the Late engagement & present maneuvres you will Doubtless hear before this can possibly reach you, however as you may be in some Doubt I shall endeavour to give you some particulars which I hope will not be disagreeable tho' it may be repeating. I know this that last Fryday afternoon Orders were Issued for about 1800 of the province men & 200 of Connecticut men to parade themselves at 6 oClock with one Day's provisions Blanket &c & there receive their Order, (nearly the same Orders in Roxbury Camp also). Near 9 oClock they marched (with Intrenching tools in Carts by their Side) over Winter's Hill in Charlestown & passed the intrenchments the Regulars began when they retreated from Concord & went to Intrenching on Bunckners hill which is nearer the water & [      ] & Shiping. Here they worked most notably & had a very fine fortification which the enemy never knew till Morn. They then began a most heavy fire the Copps. Hill near Dr [Cutlers] Church & from all the Ships that Could play which continued till near night. About one oClock PM we that were at Cambridge heard that the regulars were Landing from their Floating Batterys, & the alarm was sounded & we ordered to March directly down to the Fort at Charlestown. Before our Company could possibly get there the battle had begun in earnest & Cannon & Musket Balls were flying about our Ears like hail & a hotter fire you can have no Idea of. Our men were in fine Spirits. Your Brot. & I Led them & they kept their Order very finely 2 & 2,[1]—My Dear Brother, you'll see by this the Amazing hurry we are in. Capt. Chester is call'd of and begs me to go on with this letter, which I'll endeavor to do, tho if it appears incorrect and uncorrected you must make proper Allowance. After the Alarm on our March down we met many of our worthy friends wounded sweltering in their Blood, carried on the Shoulders by their fellow Soldiers. Judge you what must be our feelings at this shocking Spectacle, the orders were, *press on press on,* our Brothers are suffering and will soon be cut of. We push'd on and came into the field of Battle thro the Cannonadeing of the Ships, Bombs Chain Shott, Ring Shot & Double headed Shot flew as thick as Haile Stones, but thank Heavens, few of our Men suffered by them, but when we mounted the Summit, where the Engagement was, good God how the Balls flew. I freely Acknowledge I never had such a tremor came over Me before. We descended the Hill onto the field of Battle, and began our fire very Briskly. The Regulars feel in great plenty, but to do them Justice they keep a grand front and stood their ground nobly, twice before this time they gave way. But not long before we saw numbers mounting the Walls of our Fort, on which our Men in the Fort were ordered to fire and make a swift Retreat. We covered their Retreat till they come up with Us by a Brisk fire from our small arms. The dead and wounded lay on every side of me; their Groans were pierceing indeed, tho long before this time I believe the fear of Death had quitted almost every Breast. They now had possession of our Fort & four field pieces and by much the Advantage of the Ground, and to tell you the truth, our Reinforcements belonging to this Province very few of them came into the field—but lay sculking the opposite side of the hill. Our orders then came to make the best Retreat we could. We set of almost gone with fatigue and Ran very fast up the Hill, leaving some of our Dead and Wounded on the field. We Retreated over Charlestown Neck, thro the thickest of the Ships fire, here some principle Officers fell by Cannon & Bombs. After we had got out of the ships fire under the Covert of a Hill—near another Intrenchment of ours. We again Rallied and lined every part of the Road and fields—here we were Determined to Die or conquor if they ventured over the Neck, but it grew dark and we saw them pitching Tents. We retired to our Intrenchment & lay on our Arms all Night. Keeping vast Numbers of our Troops out on scouting Parties. They keep up a constant fire from the Ships and floating Batteries all Night, but few of them Reach'd Us. But alas how Dismal was the sight to see the Beautifull & Valuable town of Charlestown all in Flames—and now behold it a heap of Ruin with nothing standing but a heap of Chimneys—which by the by remains an everlasting Monument of British Cruelty and Barbarity in this Battle. Tho we lost it, cannot but do Honor to Us—for we fought with less Numbers and tho they once or twice almost surrounded the Fort we secured their Retreat, but alas in the Fort feel some Brave Fellows. Among the Unhappy Number, was our worthy friend Dr Warren,[2] alas he is no more. He feel in his countrys Cause; and fought with the Bravery of an Ancient Roman. They are in possession of his Body and no doubt will rejoice greatly over it. After they entered our Fort they mangled the wounded in a Most horrid Manner, by runing their Bayonets thro them, and beating their heads to pieces with the Bretchs of their Guns. In this Bloody Engagement we have lost Wilson Rowlanson[3] Roger Fox, Gershom Smith, and Lawrence Sullivan who we suppose fell, (at least thus Prays) into the hands of our Enemy their Souls we hope in the happy Regions of Bliss. Wounded Daniel Derning, Samuel Dilling, Epaphras Stevens, Constant Griswould, none of them mortally, are in fair way, and likely to Recover. To give you the exact Number of the whole of our Kill'd and wounded is Impossible. Opinions are various and no returns yet made to the Counsil of warr—but the best I can find out is about 120 of our Men Kill'd and wounded, perhaps there may be double that number, I cannot say, a few days we shall know exactly.[4] Of the Regulars I doubt not their are many more lost than of ours, the truth of their numbers 'tis not probable we shall know. The Kings troops to the number of 2 or 3,000 are now encamped on the same Hill they were after the Battle of Lexington, have twenty field pieces with them, and lie under the Protection of the Ships. Our grand Fortification is on prospect Hill within a mile and a half of theirs. We have about three thousand Men, & 2.12 Pounders 2 24 pr. & 6.6 pounders. Here we mean to make a stand, should they prove Victorious (which Heaven forbid) and get possession of this Hill we must retire before them & leave Cambridge to the Destruction of those merciless Dogs. But Heaven we trust will appear on our side, and sure I am many thousands of Us must fall before we flee from them. Gage has said that the 19th of June should be made as memorable as the 19th of April is. This is the day and I assure You we are probably on our Guard. . . .

Facsimile, Worthington C. Ford, *Correspondence and Journals of Samuel Blachley Webb* (New York, 1893), I, 63–69. Sometimes spelled Blatchley.

[1] Letter to this point is in the hand of Captain John Chester (1749–1809) of the Second Connecticut Regiment.

[2] Major General Joseph Warren (1741–75) died in the last and successful British assault upon Breed's Hill.

[3] Private Wilson Rowlandson (1733–75) of Connecticut died of wounds on July 1, 1775.

[4] American losses were probably 140 killed, 271 wounded, and 30 captured. See Howard H. Peckham, ed., *The Toll of Independence: Engagements and Battle Casualties of the American Revolution* (Chicago: University of Chicago Press, 1974), p. 4.

# JOSEPH WARD ORDERLY BOOK

## *July 4–12, 1775*

VIVID EVIDENCE of the courage and determination of the growing American forces is provided by the orderly book kept by Major Joseph Ward (1737–1812) as an aide-de-camp to his father, Major General Artemas Ward (1727–1800), commander of the Massachusetts troops. Although he was not formally commissioned as an aide-de-camp until July 20, 1775, Major Ward was already exercising those duties at the headquarters in Cambridge. His orderly book reflects the hope that American liberties could be defended by a concerted effort of all thirteen colonies. Petty rivalry, however, appeared when George Washington (1732–99), appointed commander in chief of the Continental army, arrived in Boston, and General Ward was disturbed at becoming second in command to this general from Virginia. Ward and Washington resented each other and worked together inharmoniously at best. Artemas Ward resigned his post in Boston but continued to command the Eastern Department. Major Joseph Ward served as General Ward's secretary until the latter's replacement by William Heath (1737–1814) as commander of the Eastern Department on September 20, 1776.

4th. The Continental Congress having now taken all the Troops of the several Colonies, which have been raised; or which may here after be raised for the support & defence of the Liberties of America into their pay & Service;[1] they are now the Troops of the United provinces of North America: and it is hoped that all distinctions of Colonies will be laid aside, so that one & the same spirit may animate the whole; & the only contest be who shall render (on this trying occasion) the most essential Service to the great & Common Cause in which we are all engaged. . . .

9th. Col. Gardner[2] is to be buried to-morrow at 3 o Clock P.M. with the military honors due to so brave & gallant an Officer who fought, bled & died in the Cause of his Country and Mankind. His own Regt. except the Company at Malden to attend on this mournful occasion. The places of those Companies in the Lines on Prospect Hill are to be supply'd by Col: Glover's[3] Regt. till the Funeral is over.

10th. No person is to be allow'd to go fishing to fresh Pond, or to approach it on any other occasion, as there may be danger of introducing the small-pox into the Army. . . .

12th. All prisoners taken, Deserters coming in, or persons coming out of Bosten, who can give any Intelligence, any Captures of any kind from the Enemy—are to be immediately reported and bro't to Head Quarters in Cambridge. . . .

Joseph Ward Orderly Book, Massachusetts Historical Society, Boston.

[1] June 14, 1775.

[2] Colonel Thomas Gardner (c.1723–75) of a Massachusetts battalion died on July 3, 1775, of wounds suffered during the Battle of Bunker Hill.

[3] Colonel John Glover (1732–97) of Massachusetts.

# SAMUEL WARD, JR., TO MARY WARD

AFTER THE ENGAGEMENT at Bunker Hill, the British forces and their Loyalist followers remained in Boston. George Washington's army was encamped in the heights surrounding the city. This stalemate, punctuated by skirmishes, was a new kind of test for the army. The boredom and fatigue and the rigors of living in the open field were new enemies to the young Continental soldiers. Captain Samuel Ward, Jr. (1756–1832), of the First Rhode Island Regiment, in a long and personal letter to his sister Polly (Mary) shows the loneliness of the soldier in active service. His joy over receiving news from home and his instructions to keep his garden mirror Ward's sense of isolation from his family. However, the letter also reveals his tenacious determination to continue in the service and the pride he felt in facing fire from the British guns.

**Samuel Ward, Jr.**

*Charleston. Prospect Hill. 17th Augst. 1775*

dear Polly

I acknowledge with unfeigned pleasure the Receipt of your very agreeable & sisterly, & friendly, & Polite & every way cleaver Letter. I had begun to grow uneasy. I know not why unless it was that you had not quite such convenient oppertunities of writing, as I coud have wished You to have had—What is the cause of those little fraternal jealousies that sometimes Alarm the most unsuspicious people in the world—however from the innmost recesses of my soul I was going to say I forgive you. Let me mend the expression & say I am very much obliged to You, the chearfulness with which you sent the things I wrote for, particularly your Almost too kind Mention of my Chest &c. &c. give me the greatest imaginable pleasure, let Fortune frown ever so much upon Me in some respects. Let me be ever so much depressd by Ills as we call them. Your friendship & love will make Me rich, rich indeed. I hear with the greatest sattisfaction that you are all blest with the inestimable Blessings of health, especially that moderate & chearfull health of Mind which shows itself in good sisterhood in being good Neighbours prudent Oeconomists & every way cleaver *good Girls*. I receivd a Line from my dear little chub-faced Dick. I hope my dear Brother that you will immediately put the garden in a good state, hoe up every weed you come across and make it all look very neat & cleaver—dont have it said that your Brother was abroad exposed to the Rains, obliged to sleep on the Ground, Obliged to work upon Forts & Breast-works for the Defence of the Country & that you should not be industrious in raising good sauce & farming it cleaverly in every Respect that You may find Us plenty of Provisions. I Laughed very heartily at your Account of my Valorous behaviour, "he that fights & Runs away" "may live to fight another day" "but he that is in battle slain" "can never live to fight again" however your Brother has been where the Bullets have flew several Times without showing many Marks of fear. I ever had too lofty a disposition to condescend to trouble myself about the reports of those people who give themselves No pains to get proper information. I beg that you would only have a little of my pride, and if ever You want to know how any Man behaves trust not to Common Rumours, enquire of those who are Judges of Merit, of propriety of behaviour, enquire of the honest & candid, I am so strong in my own integrity as not to fear the Censure of such. I dont mean to vaunt of any perfections God knows I am too too Vicious but yet I mean to ever Act as a good Citizen as a lover of my Country, as having a proper respect for the honour of my most venerable Father, and as having a laudable Thirst of Glory. These principles, I hope may be continued to Me by the same God that has hitherto preserved Me from danger, & has given Me a fine state of health.

I am very much obliged to my good friend Clark for his kind Letter it breaths an honest Ardor to serve his Country. I am as much his humble servant as ever. I have been on duty almost ever since Doctor Newman has been here; & am now obliged to write by candle light—he must pardon my silence—I shall write the first oppertunity. Tell him I enlisted in the three towns of hopkinton, Westerly & Charleston 52 Men. Col Babcock 13—Capt Randal 48, Capt. Gardner 21—this Acct to be depended upon, because copied immediately from the size Rolls. I received a Line from Debby shall answer it when I have time perhaps in the morning. Send my guns as she is. I long to see All the dear family. I hope heaven will continually shower down Blessings upon you, family harmony particularly as most worthy the Choirs of the Celestial Regions. My love to Thompson & Greenman & the Neighbours. I write you no news, there is nothing worth relating a few squabbles now & then between the parties is All. I must confess I long to spend a few hours with You, my attention is turnd homewards the more earnestly, the longer I am absent from You, but afirst Me honor—I long to have my [    ] he would make me think less of home. Do have Me a pair of good strong shooes made & Charge them to Me. Give my particular Regards to aunts I should be pleased with a little of aunt Marchants good sense on paper. Dont be timid I will now wish you a good night. May God preserve us to each other. I am your own

SAM WARD JR.

This letter was wrote in the greatest immaginable hurry. Forgive my little impertinencies & you will very much oblige me.

SW

ALS, Ward Papers, Rhode Island Historical Society, Providence.
1 John Randall; Caleb Gardner (1727–1801).

# HENRY BEDINGER JOURNAL

## *August 26–October 25, 1775*

THE AMERICANS' ATTEMPT to remove the British forces from Boston continued for almost one year. A lively account of this period is contained in the journal of Henry Bedinger (1753–1843), who served as a private and sergeant in Captain Hugh Stephenson's (c.1735–76) Rifle Company. Bedinger's unit was part of the newly formed Continental army under General George Washington, who took command at Cambridge on July 2, 1775. Bedinger provides a telling account of the brief and bloody skirmishes at Roxbury and Ploughed Hill that cost over ten lives. He also describes the British burning of Falmouth, Maine, on October 18, 1775. A series of punitive raids on American coastal towns was planned by the British to retaliate for American privateering and the siege of Boston. Fortunately, Boston was spared Falmouth's fate when the British evacuated the city on March 17, 1776. Bedinger was captured on November 16, 1776, and was not exchanged until October 1780.

Saturday Night, 26th. Captain Creasop, Who Came in the Night before, agreed to go and fire on the Centries.[1] About Thirty of our Company, our Captain, Lieut. Scott, and Lieut. Shepherd went along,[2] they all Borrowed Musketts, Loaded them with a Ball and about fifteen Swan Shott. They all Creap Down along a Ditch that passes the Chimneys, and so By the side of the Breastwork. Mr. Scott being that Course before he was Pilot, as he was going Very Softly there Raised out a Centry out of the grass within Twenty Steps of him and fired at him, but missed, he Lay still then but the Regular Run off. In about an hour after there Came about Thirty out to see what it was he fired at, when Capt. Creasop, Capt. Stinson and Scott, all fired on them, and then some of our men fired and all Run, one of our men Lost his Gun by falling into a Hole in the marsh. Next Morning we Saw them Carry Two persons from that place, and Soon Learnt from some Desarters that we kill'd one man & Wounded two more. On the Same Night about four thousand of our men at Cambridge Took possession of Plowed Hill, Near Bunker Hill, and Began to Intrench, and before Sunday morning had made Cover for themselves, but as Soon as the Regulars Discovered them in the morning they Began to Fire and Kept a Continual Fire the whole Day with Bumbs and Balls. Killed an Adjutant Belonging to the Hampshire forces, and a Soldier, also a Volunteer, named [    ] Simpson, had his Legg Shott off with a Canon Ball, and Died the Next Day—he Came from Baxton, Pennsa., a Rifleman.[3]

Aug. 31st. about one Oclock in the Night the Enemy Began a heavy Fire at us, Fired Between 20 & 30 Canon Balls, Killed Two Men of the Provincials, alarmed all the Camps.

Sep'r 1st. 1775. Firing more or Less from Both parties Every Day untill the 11th inst., when one of the Regulars went out from one of the wharfs in a small Conoe to pleasure. The wind and Tide being Very Strong he Could not Get Back, when 1 Serjeant and four men went out In a Whale Boat to assist him, they were all Drove ashore on Dorchester Neck, Captain Stinson and part of the Company Ran Imediately to take them, but tho' pushing off along the Shore Side we were prevented by a Small Creek that Runs through the marsh, when a Number of Provincials Commanded by Lieutenant Sparrow Came Down by way of Dorchester Fort, and Surrounded them, ordering them to Come on Shore Imediately. They having No Arms with them were Obliged to Surrender Prisoners of War—Canons were Frequently Fired, Desarters Came in Great Numbers: one James Finly, a Serjeant in Capt. Price's Compy. of Riflemen, was Tried by a Gen'l Court Martial for Drinking Gauge's Health, Helping a Provincial to a Rifle to Desert with, Expressing himself Against the American Cause, was found Guilty and Sentenced to be Drum'd out of the Camp Sitting on a Cart, with a Rope a Round his Neck. . . .

[*October*] 25th. Just Recd. Inteligence that the Town of falmouth on Casco Bay was burnt Down by some of the king's Ships of War, they Drew up in the Harbour & sent out a Flag of Truce, Informed the people that their Commands was to burn the Town and would Effect it in half an Hour. The Town sent a committee on board to Treat with them, Who with their Influence Got this matter postponed untill 8 oclock the Next day, so that the Inhabitants Got most of their Goods out of the Town. Accordingly about 9 O'Clock the Enemy Began to fire on the Town, and Threw bumbshells and Carcases[4] that Instantly Consumed the whole Town. No person was Kill'd and but one man wounded: under cover of the Smoak the Enemy Landed about 100 men, but were Soon Drove off again by Some minute men Before the Enemy began to fire the people asked why their spite Lay at that Town in particular, They Answered that Every Town within Reach of their Cannon from thence to Georgia should fare the same way. The Same Acc't Gives Inteligence that the Noted Captain Micheal Creasop from Virginia had Died in New York on the     Day of October and the Town was Burnt on the     Day of October.[5]

Danske Dandridge, *Historic Sheperdstown* (Charlottesville, Va., 1910), pp. 108–9.

[1] Captain Michael Cresap (1742–75) of the First Maryland Rifle Company died October 18, 1775.

[2] George Scott (1758–1826); Abraham Shepard.

[3] British forces cannonaded American units commanded by Brigadier General John Sullivan (1740–95).

[4] An iron shell fired from a mortar.

[5] Cresap had also been involved in warfare in the South. A letter of August 1, 1775, to a gentleman in Philadelphia reported Cresap's return from an expedition to Virginia's back country: "I have had the happiness of seeing Captain Michael Cresap marching at the head of a formidable company of upwards of one hundred and thirty men, from the mountains and back-woods, painted like *Indians,* armed with tomahawks and rifles, dressed in hunting-shirts and moccasins, and though some of them had travelled near eight hundred miles, from the banks of the *Ohio,* they seemed to walk light and easy, and not with less spirit than at the first hour of their march. Health and vigour, after what they had undergone, declared them to be intimate with hardship and familiar with danger. Joy and satisfaction were visible in the crowd that met them." (Peter Force, comp., *American Archives . . . ,* Ser. 4 [Washington, D.C., 1840], III, 2.)

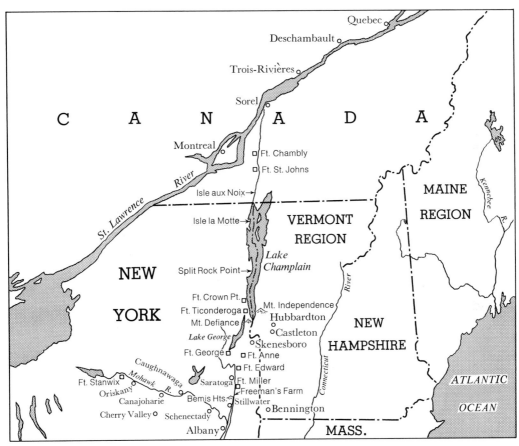

CANADA AND THE NORTHERN CAMPAIGNS

# Benjamin Hinman to Jonathan Trumbull

Fort ticonderoga, an old French fortress on Lake Champlain in northern New York, was captured from the British without American casualties on May 10, 1775, by a Connecticut force led by colonels Ethan Allen (1738–89) and Benedict Arnold (1741–1801). The fort's valuable artillery was then brought to Cambridge, Massachusetts, to hasten the British withdrawal from Boston. Arnold's excessive ambitions were thwarted early when a Massachusetts committee supported Colonel Benjamin Hinman (1720–1810) as commander of the fort. Ambition and particularism served to divide the colonists. As Hinman wrote to Governor Jonathan Trumbull (1710–85), his men in the Fourth Connecticut Regiment did not wish to come under the regulations of the Continental army. The Continental Congress had asked the colony of Connecticut to furnish five battalions or regiments, but by November 1775 enlistees were slow in signing up for service.

The capture of Fort Ticonderoga helped make possible the invasion of Canada. Hinman was in charge of the fort until Major General Philip Schuyler (1733–1804) was placed in command of the northern forts on June 25, 1775.

*Tyconderoga 12th. Octor. 1775*

Honored Sir

Your Favour of the 29th. of Sept I Recd. the 10th. Inst per General Schuyler. Your Honors concern for the Sick gives me some pleasing hopes of the extention of your Paternal care in makeing some provision for their Return Home. At most they have but Six Days provision to Support them on the way. They have not the least help by Waggons or any other way—unless they have money to pay, unless I am Misinformed, the Unhappy Case of the most is Such they have Little if any. The Revd. Mr. Smith through the Goodness of God is so far Recovered that he Set out for home the 4th Instant. As to Mr. Lynchs Account Respecting the Connecticut Forces and my Regiment in perticuler—am Sorrey to say that it is my Opinion if Mr. Lynch was so misinformed it must be the Fruit of an Enimical Disposition towards the Country in General and the Colony of Connecticut perticuler As to my Suffering my men to Depart to there Various homes so as to Reduce them to 100 Men in any Sense whatever must be nothing better than a Great Mistake. On the 7th. of July Including Major Welchs Company, I had at Tyconderoga 479 at Crown point 296 at the Landing 98 at Fort George Captain Mott's 103.[1]—After which Time I have not any Compleat Return. The General Arriving soon after Returns were made from the Respective Posts Directly to the General but not to me. As I trust the General will be kind enough to give your Honor a more perticuler Stating as to the Return Since than I could, I shall only Inform your Honor that from the 7th of July to the Time Mr Lynch was at Ty—I never Suffered one Man to Return home on any pretence whatever, except one Liut. and one Sargeant who was absent a few Days in persuit of 5 Deserters. The General might have Furlowed or Discharged a Small number how many if any I Know not as I have no Account of any. The General has been Careful, not to Furlow or Discharge in any Case where the Good of the Service and humanity Doth not Require it. As to being without Arms I know my Regiment were every Man furnished with Arms and the Greatest part of them one Pound of Powder 3tt. of Ball, all sufficient number flints, the Most of the Arms were Good Some not so good as I could wish tho they were the best that Could be found among the Inhabitants. Bad as they are the General Montgomery[2] thought best to Order the Owners when Discharged or Furlowed to leave them, to Arm such as might Come into the Service with out Arms—which I apprehend may make much Difficulty in Settleing the Accounts Respecting Arms— they being so Dispersed that it is not likely they will ever be in the hands of the Original Owners tho' I have no doubt but the General Will Conduct the matter with all Prudence. As to our all Refusing to be Mustered and come under Continental Regulations—the General gave Out in Orders that we all subscribed the Continental Articals of War—where upon I Did take the freedom to inform the General that I had no Objection to Subscribing my Self but was affraid of the Consequences with respect to the Soldiers, if the Matter was insisted on—as some might Immagine they were not holden except they did Subscribe—others that in Case they should Subscribe they might be held beyond their Expectation when they Ingaged. Knowing the Jealousies of a Soldier in the midst of a Disagreeable Campaign—I was afraid it might tend to the Disadvantage of the Service at the Same time told the General I was Ready to persue his Orders—but took Liberty to tell him my fears, tho I Did not know but they would freely Subscribe. About an Hour after the General was pleased to inform me that he would postpone the Matter till he should hear from Boston, as he thought there would be No Difficulty, and I never heard a word on the Subject since untill I Received your Honrs Letter Respecting our being Mustered. The General Directed me to Order the Commanding Officer of each Company in my Regiment to make an order on their Respective Representatives at home to Deliver their Original Inlistments to such person as should be sent to Receive them, as the General had then and eversince hath Indulged me In unmerited freedom and familiarity. The General gave me Liberty to say that I was not Satisfied as to the Method of procureing the Inlistments where upon there was much Dispute on the Subject but as to any Objection against being Mustred in Case we had been under Circumstances in our Situation—I never had the most Distant thought neither Did one of my Officers Object on any Account, but that of the Inlistments. At the Same time I went to all the Capts of my Regt. then on the Ground and told them that they must make out Muster Roles, found that some Could and others could not do it without sending home. Directly I sent home to Woodbury and brought up the Original Inlistments, then, Informed the General that I was then Ready to Exhibit a Muster Role as I had the Inlistments Come to hand. The General then Told me he believed there would be no Difficulty and as the Campaign was so far Spent &c. he would do nothing about it at present (as General Schuyler Doth not Remember this Circumstance) I believe it was General Montgomery that I was Informed of my being Ready when General Schuyler was at Albany. Am Sorrey for the Misunderstanding hope it may not be to the Disunion of any of the Colonies or the Disadvantages of Connecticut or in any wise Dissarve the Common Cause. I have Con-

16

fidence in the Genls. Friendship, but know he is mistaken a bout my being unwilling to be Mustred on any Account except the Difficulty of procureing the Dates of Inlistments. Capt Buell who will Most likely Do himself the Honor to Deliver this Letter will be able to Inform your Honor further Respecting the Matter of Mustering if you Should think proper to Enquire of him.[3] Should think it Necessary to Send by Capt Buell or Some other way Supply those Officers that want with a Sufficient Sum to Fetch home the Men that Remain with them when ever the Campaign is over as I Imagine Officers and Soldiers are Mostly Destitute. Hope Sir you will Excuse the Badness of this Letter as I have Neither paper pen or penman and 11 OClock at Night. I am Honor'd Sir your Honours Most Obedient Humble Servant

BENJAMIN HINMAN

ALS, Jonathan Trumbull, Sr., Papers, Connecticut Historical Society, Hartford.
[1] Crown Point was captured by Lieutenant Colonel Seth Warner (1743–84) of the Connecticut minutemen on May 11; Captain Edward Mott (c.1735–c.1790) of the Sixth Connecticut Regiment.
[2] Brigadier General Richard Montgomery (1738–75) of the Continental army.
[3] Captain Nathaniel Buell (1734–1808) of the Fourth Connecticut Regiment.

# JAMES VAN RENSSELAER ORDERLY BOOK

MAJOR GENERAL Philip Schuyler's appointment as commander of the northern forts coincided with the planning for the American invasion of Canada. Despite the persistent problems of rank and authority among the Connecticut, New York, and "Vermont" regiments, Brigadier General Richard Montgomery marched northward from Ticonderoga on August 28, 1775, toward the British fortified camp at St. Johns, strategically located twenty miles southeast of Montreal and not far from the Sorel River connecting Lake Champlain and the St. Lawrence River. Schuyler and Montgomery conducted a slow but successful siege from September 5 to November 2, 1775. St. Johns' fall on November 2 opened the way for the capture of Montreal eleven days later. General Montgomery and his 1,200 men could have rested in the warm quarters, enjoyed the food, and made use of the uniforms left in Montreal by the retreating British forces before they moved northward. However, Montgomery's general orders on November 13, as recorded by his aide-de-camp James Van Rensselaer (1747–1827), reveal that many of his conquering troops preferred to return home rather than endure the rigors of a continued winter invasion of Canada. Although he was unable to keep all of his troops in line despite his eloquent supplications, Montgomery was able to continue the campaign to meet Colonel Benedict Arnold's forces, which had marched overland from the Maine coast to Quebec.

*Montreal Novemr 13th. 1775*

The General Embraces this Happy Occasion of Making his Acknowledgements to the Troops for their Patience and perserverance. During the Course of a fatigueing Campaign they have Merrited the Applause of their Grateful Country Men. He is now ready to fulfill the Engagements of the Publick; Passes; together with Boats and Provisions, shall be furnished upon Application from Commanding Officers of Regiments. Yet he Entreats the Troops not to Lay him under the Necessity of Abandoning Canada; of undoing in one day what has been the work of Months; of Restoring to an Enraged and hitherto Disapointed Enemy the Means of Carrying a Cruel war into the very bowels of their Country. Impressed with a Just Sense of the Spirits of the Troops, their Attachment to the Interest of the United Collonies and of their Regard to their own Honour, he flatters himself that none will Leave him at this Critical Juncture but those whose Affairs, or health, Absolutely require their return home. He has Still hopes (*notwithstanding the Advanced* Season of the Year), should he be seconded by the Generous Valour of an Army hitherto so highly favoured by Providence to reduce Quebeck, in Conjunction with the troops which have Penetrated by the Kenebeck River,[1] and thereby Deprive the Ministerial Army of all footing in this Important Province. Those who Again Engage in this Honourable Cause, shall be furnished Compleatly with Every Article of Cloathing requisite for the Rigour of the Climate— Blanket Coat, Coat, Waist Coat, and Breetches, pair of Stockings, Leggens, socks, Shoes, mittins and Cap, at the Continentals Expence. By Order of the General

JAMES VAN RENSSELAER, *Aid de Camp*

James Van Rensselaer Orderly Book, Lloyd W. Smith Collection, Morristown National Historical Park, Morristown, N.J.

[1] An expedition to Quebec commanded by Colonel Benedict Arnold.

# ADONIJAH STRONG TO PHILIP SCHUYLER

ADONIJAH STRONG (1743–1813) was commissary of Benjamin Hinman's Fourth Connecticut Regiment, part of which was garrisoned at Fort George, at the southern end of Lake George in northern New York. Fort George was one of the dilapidated northern fortresses manned principally by Colonel Hinman's ragged and unruly Connecticut regiment. Adonijah Strong reports to Major General Schuyler the theft of military stores—pilfering that was caused by the lack of supplies sent to these far-flung posts.

*Fort George 20th Novr 1775*

Hond. Sr.

Every day in which there is any alteration in the Receiving or forwarding provisions or stores—I Note it & send it to your Honour. Whether they all come safe I cant tell, for I find Oppertunities few to what thay have been. Only add the unfaithfulness of Centinals are such, Nothing in the Stores are safe, any longer than my own Eye is upon them. I have Detected several, both Centinals, & others, but many things I miss, & do not Recover again tho Strict serch, is from time to time made, as on the Night after the 16th Instant, one Barrel full of rum was Stollen, and many Articles, as Rum, Butter, Sugar, Meet &c. both before and since have been stolen and not found. As my Duty Requires I give your honr. this Notice while I am your hons. Obedt. Huml. Sert.

ADONIJAH STRONG *A.D.C.G.*

ALS, Philip Schuyler Papers, New York Public Library, New York City.

# JACOB CHEESMAN TO THOMAS CHEESMAN

JACOB CHEESMAN, a captain in the First New York Regiment of Continentals and an aide-de-camp to General Richard Montgomery, participated in the capture of Fort St. Johns and the fall of Montreal on November 13, 1775. Writing two days before Christmas from the cold encampment before Quebec, Cheesman accurately foresaw the dismal prospect of defeat. Weather, morale, and lack of supplies proved to be as insurmountable as the staunch defenses of the city commanded by General Sir Guy Carleton (1724–1808). A stalemate was broken on December 31, 1775, when General Montgomery and Jacob Cheesman and his company attempted to storm the city. In an attack upon a fortified house, both Montgomery and Cheesman were killed by a lethal volley of cannon and musket fire. Faith in God and a tenacious loyalty to the American cause characterize Cheesman's last letter to his father and are a fitting testament to his ultimate sacrifice.

*Saint Foys before Quebeck, December 23, 1775*

Honored Sir

I am now within one Mile of Quebeck waiting for an opportunity or Rather a Convenient time to enter the City which must be taken by storm. The ground has been covered with snow for several weeks, the weather is very cold and if there does not a convenient opportunity soon offer our Generall will form A Blockade and wait until Spring, and a number of Troops Arive here which I expect will be sent to reignforce us as early as possible our army is dwindled away to almost nothing. Officers as well as men, any Trifling disorder that overtakes them Renders them unfit to Remain Longer with their Company or in the Service of their Country. My Company only Keeps their Officers all in which are in health, for which I thank that God who has hitherto preserved and given us Victory. General Montgomery appointed me to the Command of the Gaspey, a Man of war Brigantine which was taken by a Battery Erected on one Side the River Saint Lawrence. She is now Layed up as there is no passing in the River this season. I cant tell when I shall return home for I cant do like many of my fellow Cityzens after puting my hand to the Plow look Back Expetially now When my Country Calls Loudly for assistance. I hope those who come to Reignforce us will press forward not Shrink like numbers who came about the time I did in the Service both Yonkers and New England men.

My Love to Brothers & Sister My Respects to Messrs. Franklins and Enquir/Friends, and Duty to you and Mama.

Jacob Cheesman

Typescript copy, original manuscript in the possession of the Cheesman family.

# John Lamb to William Goforth

**John Lamb**

Captain John Lamb (1735–1800), who commanded the Independent Company of New York Artillery, participated in the siege of Quebec. In his letter to Captain William Goforth (1731–1807) of the First New York Regiment at Montreal, he describes the delays in the assault on the city caused by the fair weather. Poor weather would help to prevent early detection of an attack on the lower town. Unfortunately, on the night of December 27, when the Americans had planned to attack, the weather unexpectedly cleared after a heavy snowfall. Almost half of the 800 Americans participating in the attack on Quebec were captured, among them Captain Lamb, who lost an eye in the poorly planned American action. Lamb was soon paroled but not formally exchanged until January 1777.

*Du Pree House near Quebec 28th. Decr. 1775*

Dear Sir

I was in hopes a few Hours ago to have had it in my Power to date this Letter, from the Town of Quebec, but have been disappointed; Yesterday Afternoon, the Commanding Officers, of the Respective Corps in this Quarter, receiv'd the Genls. Orders to hold themselves in readiness, at an Hours notice; And about 10 O'Clock at Night we all receiv'd Orders to Rendezvous at certain Places, at 2 O'Clock in the Morning in order to Storm, which was complied with by both Officers and men with the greatest chearfulness and Alacrity, but the Night (constrary to expectation) proving extremely clear, and very Calm, the Genl. thought proper to pospone the Attempt, 'till a more favourable oppertunity, that we may have it in our power to punish those Miscreants, McClean, & Carlton for their Villany;[1] Adieu, I have nothing to add, but my Compliments to Collo. Ritzema,[2] and all Friends, being Dear, Your real Friend, & Huml. Servant

JOHN LAMB

ALS, McDougall Papers, New-York Historical Society, New York City.

[1] Colonel Allan McLean (c.1725–84) of the First Battalion of the Eighty-Fourth Regiment of Foot (Royal Highland Emigrants).

[2] Lieutenant Colonel Rudolphus Ritzema of the First New York Regiment.

# FRANCIS NICHOLS DIARY

## *December 31, 1775–January 1776*

A COLUMN UNDER Colonel Benedict Arnold was no more successful than were General Richard Montgomery and Jacob Cheesman in breaching Quebec's fortified walls. Of the Americans participating in the bold but unsuccessful assault on Quebec, 51 lay dead, 36 were wounded, and 387 were British prisoners of war by New Year's Day. Lieutenant Francis Nichols (1737–1812), of Colonel William Thompson's (1736–81) Pennsylvania Rifle Regiment, was among the captives. Lieutenant Nichols was imprisoned in Quebec's "Seminary," where he was treated well by General Sir Guy Carleton, the governor of Quebec and commander of the British forces in Canada. Nichols' resolve to help a future invading force, however, shows his determination and patriotism. Francis Nichols was exchanged on October 10, 1776, and soon reentered Continental service as a captain in the Ninth Pennsylvania Regiment.

[*December 31, 1775*] The American army made the attack on the City of Quebec. General Montgomery with his army attacked at a place called the Potasse, close by the river St. Lawrence; Col. Arnold and his detachment, composed of the troops that marched with him through the Wilderness, attacked on the opposite side at St. Roque. They marched at five o'clock in the morning and took with them a brass field piece to aid in forcing the barriers, but the snow being deep and the road unbroken, they were forced to leave it behind, after being detained for some time in striving to bring it forward. At half after five the attack began and in a few minutes they were in possession of the first barrier, and captured two pieces of cannon. Here Col. Arnold was wounded through the leg by a musket ball, which prevented his proceeding further. The troops continued to advance and captured the first guard which consisted of thirty men. The main body of the army got broke in striving to bring up the cannon and unfortunately missed the road, their guide being wounded, and the morning being dark, owing to the heavy snow storm, they were forced to countermarch under a heavy fire from the ramparts. Capt. Hendricks having command of the main guard, was in the rear, but he pressed to the front and joined Captains Morgan, Lamb and Lieutenants Steele and Nichols, and attacked the second barrier.[1] Gen. Montgomery being in the advance, had the pickets cut down and passed through. The enemy hearing him encouraging his men, deserted their posts, and threw down their arms, believing that all was over, as Col. Arnold's detachment had possession of the second barrier. A drunken sailor swore he would fire one shot before he would retreat, went to a gun loaded with grape shot, and with a match fired it off, and unfortunately for us killed the brave Montgomery, Capt. Cheesman and Capt. Macpherson his aid de camps.[2] Col. Campbell who usurped the command (for his rank was quartermaster) ordered a retreat.[3] If Col. Campbell had advanced and joined Col. Arnold's troops, he would have met with little opposition, as the citizens had thrown down their arms and we had made numbers of regulars prisoners. When they found that Montgomery's army was retreating, the citizens were prevailed upon to secure fresh arms from the magazine, and as it became light our small number was discovered and they sallied out of the Palace gate after us. Had Col. Campbell advanced, this movement would have been prevented and our success insured. But we held our ground for near four hours under great disadvantages, our guns were getting wet and many of them thus rendered useless. We sustained a heavy fire in our front, right flank and rear. The enemy attempted to turn four guns on us, from a battery within sixty yards of us, when Col. Green ordered a heavy fire on them to prevent it, but from a volley of musketry a ball went through Capt. Hendricks' left breast and he expired in a few minutes; Capt. Lamb received a wound in his left cheek, which he requested Lieut. Nichols to tie up with a black handkerchief he took from his stock. Our rear guard were forced to surrender to the troops which sallied from the Palace gate, and we with the greatest reluctance were forced to lay down our arms, although we had decided to make a stand until night, and if not joined by Gen. Montgomery to retreat. We did not then know of his fall. Lieutenants Cooper and Humphreys fell in the engagement,[4] Capt. Hubbard was wounded in the heel and died shortly after,[5] and Lieut. Steele had two of his fingers shot off. Our detachment numbered between four and five hundred, there were sixty killed and many wounded. We were treated with the greatest humanity; Gen. Carleton allowed us to send for clothing and money. We were confined in the

Seminary, thirty two officers in one room, 31 by 27 feet. Some of the New England officers not having had the small pox, petitioned the General for permission to be inoculated, which he granted and assigned them a separate room; and they were allowed to walk in the entry two at a time for fresh air and exercise. We were shortly after deprived of some privileges, and pens and paper, and were moved about the building to prevent our escaping. Their fears were not ill-grounded, as we were determined should an attack be made on the city to rush out, disarm the guards, set our men at liberty and seize the arms in the magazines, while their troops were on the ramparts.

"Diary of Lieutenant Francis Nichols of Colonel William Thompson's Battalion of Pennsylvania Riflemen, January to September, 1776," *Pennsylvania Magazine of History and Biography* (1896), 20:504–6.

[1] Captain William Hendricks of Thompson's Rifle Battalion was killed in action; Captain Daniel Morgan (1736–1802) of Virginia Riflemen was taken prisoner; Lieutenant Archibald Steele (1741–1832?) of Thompson's Rifle Battalion was wounded and captured.

[2] Captain John Macpherson of Delaware was an aide-de-camp to General Richard Montgomery.

[3] Colonel Donald Campbell of New York.

[4] Lieutenant John Humphries of Daniel Morgan's Virginia Riflemen.

[5] Captain Jonas Hubbard (1739–76) of Massachusetts died January 1, 1776.

# David Wooster to Seth Warner

David Wooster (1710–77) entered Revolutionary service at age sixty-four as a veteran of the Connecticut militia. He assumed command of the American troops in Canada on January 1, 1776, following the death of General Richard Montgomery in the attempted siege of Quebec. In this letter to Colonel Seth Warner (1743–84), the commander of the special Continental regiment of "Green Mountain Boys" that served in Canada during the winter of 1775–76, Major General Wooster's outlook is bleak. He describes the deteriorating position of the Continental forces in the face of unexpected Canadian hostility to their invasion and asks for temporary relief from Warner's unit until regular army forces could be dispatched from the colonies. The small force of 500 to 600 men at Montreal was barely able to maintain control of the city. Reinforcements were not available from any of the northern forts. The Continental Congress finally authorized a relief force on January 19, 1776, after hearing an urgent appeal from Edward Antill (1742–89), who had traveled to Philadelphia from Quebec. Many Americans regarded Canada as a possible "fourteenth colony," but the British army and local hostility insured retreat and surrender for the Continental army after months of bitter cold and numerous hardships.

**David Wooster**
ARTIST: THOMAS HART
PHOTO: THOMAS FEIST, NEW YORK CITY

*Montreal, January 6th, 1776*

Dear Sir,

  With the greatest distress of mind, I now sit down to acquaint you of the event, of an unfortunate attack made upon Quebec, between the hours of 4 and six of the morning of the 31st of December, unfortunate indeed, for in it fell our brave General Montgomery, his aid de camp M'Pherson, Capt. Cheesman, Capt. Hendricks, of the riflemen, and two or three subaltern officers, and between 60 and 100 privates, the number not certainly known, and about 300 officers and soldiers taken prisoners, amongst which are Lieutenant Col. Green, Major Bigalow, Major Meigs, and a number of captains and inferior officers.[1] Col. Arnold was wounded in the leg in the beginning of the action, as was Major Ogden in the shoulder,[2] and brought off to the general hospital; I have not time to give you all the particulars, but thus much will serve to shew you, that in consequence of this defeat, our prospects are rendered very dubious, and unless we can quickly be reinforced, perhaps this may be fatal, not only to us, who are stationed here, but also to the colonies in general, the frontiers especially greatly, very greatly depends upon keeping possession of this country. You know as well as any man, the tempers, dispositions and character of the Canadians, they are not perservering in adversity, they are not to be depended upon, but like the savages, are exceeding fond of chusing the strongest party; add to this our enemies in this country, of whom there are very many, use every method to excite the Canadians against us; the clergy refuse absolution, to all who have shewn themselves our friends, and preach damnation to those who will not take up arms against us, and tell them, that now it is not too late, that we are but a handful of men, &c. I have sent an express to Gen. Schuyler, Gen. Washington, and the Congress, but you know how far they have to go, and that it is very uncertain how long it will be before we can have relief from them: therefore let me beg of you to collect immediately as many men as you can, five, six, or seven hundred, if it can be done, and some how or other get into this country, and stay with us, till we can get relief from the colonies. You are sensible we have provisions of all kinds enough, and the weather in this country is far from being so frightful as many have imagined. You will see that proper officers and soldiers are appointed under you; and both officers and soldiers shall be paid as other continental troops; it will be well for your men to set out as fast as they can be collected, not so much matter whether together or not, but let them set out by 10, 20, 30, 40, or 50, as they can be collected, for it must have a good effect upon the minds of the Canadians to see succours coming in.[3] You will be good enough to send copies of this letter to the people below. I can't but think our friends will make a push, to get into this country. I am confident you will not disappoint my most fervent wish and expectations of seeing you here, with your men in a short time. Now, Sir, is the time to distinguish yourself and obtain the applause of your ever grateful countrymen, of your distressed friends in Canada, and your sincere friend, &c.

DAVID WOOSTER

John Almon, ed., *The Remembrancer, or Impartial Respository of Public Events . . . 1775–1784* (London, 1776), III, 301–2.

[1] Major Timothy Bigelow (d. 1790) of Ward's Massachusetts Regiment; Major Return Jonathan Meigs (1735–1823) of the Second Connecticut Regiment.

[2] Matthias Ogden (1754–1791) of New Jersey served as a brigade major in the Canadian expedition.

[3] Warner was able to send 120 men north by February 1, 1776.

# STEPHEN MOYLAN TO ALEXANDER MCDOUGALL

STEPHEN MOYLAN (1737–1811), a native of Ireland, had settled in Philadelphia in 1768. One week after he became General Washington's secretary and aide-de-camp, Moylan wrote to Colonel Alexander Mc-Dougall (1732–86), who had earlier commanded the First New York Regiment, about suitable accommodations for Washington and his staff in New York City. After General Sir William Howe's evacuation of Boston on March 17, 1776, Washington prepared to move his army to New York City. He sent Major General Charles Lee (1732–82) to supervise construction of fortifications, as he expected a British invasion there. On June 5, the Continental Congress promoted Moylan to colonel and elected him Quartermaster General of the Continental army, succeeding Thomas Mifflin. In his aide-de-camp role he had often been involved with mundane details, but Moylan had made a valuable contribution to the effectiveness of the commander in chief's leadership.

*Cambridge March 14th., 1776*

Sir,

His Excellency being makeing preparations to Leave this, with the Army, it is necessary to Look forward, for the place at New york where he & his Suite are to take up their quarters, talking with the General this day on that Subject, he desired me to address myself to you thereon & to request the favour of your hireing for him a Large house ready furnishd somewhere in or about the Bowry Lane. His family is Large, & he has a number of Horses, you will therefore see the necessity of a Spacious house, & large Stables. I was thinking of Mr. Delancys, which is now unoccupied,[1] but apprehend the old Castle is rather small, of this you must be the best judge, indeed I do not recollect any house where the Situation will be more centrical, as I apprehend the main body of the Army will be encamped somewhere thereabout. A housekeeper who can superintend the Kitchen, a Cook provisions & Liquors of different sorts will be necessary to have Laid in, in short, I believe we shall want everything, & you will have a great deal of trouble which his Excellency hopes will excuse. An honest Sober & diligent man will be wanting as Steward, who will take an inventory of everything in and about the house & who will market & keep account of the House expence. You will agree with him, the terms & his pay. I have the honor to be, Sir, your Most Ob. H: Sert.

STEPHEN MOYLAN *A.D.C.*

ALS, McDougall Papers, New-York Historical Society, New York City.
[1] James De Lancey, who died in 1774, owned a home on the west side of Bowery Lane.

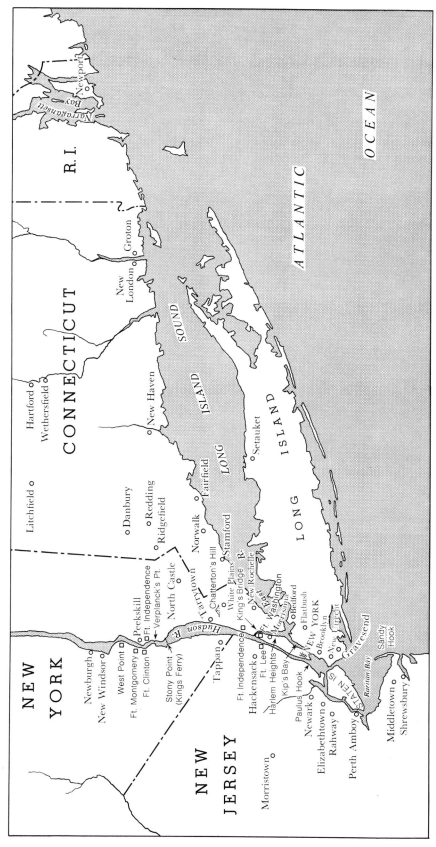

NEW YORK AND CONNECTICUT

# NICHOLAS FISH TO RICHARD VARICK

THE FAILURE of the Quebec expedition compelled the American forces to assume a defensive posture in the Middle Colonies. General George Washington, who authorized the construction of new fortifications in New York City and in the eastern parts of New Jersey to repel the anticipated British invasion, arrived in New York City on April 13, 1775, and took command of the American forces. Nicholas Fish (1758–1833) was a captain in William Malcom's (1745–91) New York Regiment, which was stationed in New York City. Despite fear and uncertainty concerning British tactics and strength, Fish exhibits spirited patriotism and youthful playfulness in his letter to a young friend, Captain Richard Varick (1755–1831). His candid comments display the young patriot's virility and vigor, traits which helped to sustain the men of the American army in their hurried efforts to defend New York City.

*New York May the 16th. 1776*

My dear Varick

Since my last, I have been honoured with an Epistle from you, which lays me under the pleasing obligation of answering it; this Duty I should have performed sooner, had not time and Conveyance been wanting; I am seldom free from Engagement of one kind or other, it is either military, social or of an amourous Nature; my military Employment is extremely agreeable and Duty easy; to command Men whose Hearts are filled with a generous Emulation of excelling each other in the strictest Discipline whose Judgments enable them to discover the Justice of and most righteous Cause, and whose Motive is not mercenary (as with most Soldiers) You may easily suppose can afford no little satisfaction to one who is entrusted with Command over them.

You mention Your Surprize at my Silence; from certain Circumstances, I am strongly of opinion that my last Letter but one never reached You; do not however infer from my not writing to You, that there is any want of Inclination, the contrary of this is true; but it grieves me to think that You should conceive it necessary to caution me so strictly and frequently agt. divulging the Information which Your are kind enough to give me, I am sorry You cannot rely upon my Prudence.

I applyed to Collo. Mc.Dougall agreeable to Your Desire about the Markee,[1] who informed me that the officers were not supplyed with Markees, owing to the scarcity of the Materials of which they are composed. As it is near a Month since the Date of Your favor, I think it best, not to engage one, until I shall hear farther from You, lest You may have furnished Yourself with one frome some other Quarter, if You have not I beg You will inform me thereof in Your next, and I will pay a particular Attention to the providing for You a good one.

My dear Sir, the Place from whence You date the next Letter will determine whether, I shall have the Pleasure of once more seeing You, soon; if from Albany I flatter myself with the pleasing Prospect; if from any other Place it is likely I shall not enjoy that Pleasure which the Presence of my friend would afford me. On friday next our Company will have compleated the Month appointed them by Congress to guard the Records of the Province, which are removed to Bayards farm, immediately upon which, I intend to apply to Mr. Scots for Permission to shut up the Office, as there is not Buisiness enough to make my attendance there necessary, and indulge myself with a ramble through the Country.

You seem to intimate a fear lest if You leave Genl. Schuyler, Your Conduct would be censured; but let me assure You that Your Conduct since with him is too well known, to admit of Censure, therefore lay aside the fear of it and let it not interfere with either Inclinations or Interest.

We have a Report among Us, that the french have opened their Ports to the Colonies, and determined to protect our shipping within a considerable Number of Leagues of their Coasts, it is said a Letter from Saml. Cuvson who resides in one of the french West India Islands to his brother brings this agreeable information. What think You of it? Will it not bring about an European War? I pray to the Lord it may and be the means of securing to us a peacefull Independance upon great Britain. Where are the much talked of Comars. and why do they not arrive? Because it was never intended they should, it was but a mere bug-bear to lull us into inactivity; but if contrary to all human probability they should be sent among Us, immediately upon their arrival secure them, make them Captives, must be Language of every honest American.

I am extremely anxious about the Canadian Expeditian it is iminently important, and 'till lately too little attention has been bestowed thitherward: however if we do but suceed now and take it before a Reinforcement shall arive, I'll bid defiance to the united Powers to that Monster of Great Britain (George the third) and his Coadjutor the Devil to retake it.

Morpheus just now invites me to his Embrace and so irresistably as to compel a Compliance. I am Your most affectionate friend & very humble Servt.

NICHS: FISH

P.S. I live the Life of a Batchelor, no one with me but a Negro, I find from the want of females about House the necessity of them, they are beyond a doubt necessary furniture.

ALS, Fish Papers, William L. Clements Library, Ann Arbor, Mich.
[1] Marquee is a large field tent.

# EDWARD ANTILL TO JOHN SULLIVAN

THE UNSUCCESSFUL ATTACK on Quebec ended the active plans for the conquest of Canada. Nevertheless, American forces remained on the harsh plains of the province until June 1776. Reinforcements for the beleaguered and freezing Continental soldiers under Benedict Arnold did not reach Quebec until April 1776. In early May British forces under General Sir Guy Carleton routed the Americans still encamped near the city. A retreat under Major General John Thomas (1724–76) ended at Fort Chambly. Upon Thomas' death from smallpox on June 2, 1776, General John Sullivan replaced him as commander of the men in the expeditionary force who had not been captured or become sick and died. A defeat at Trois-Rivières on June 7, 1776, completed the dismal military campaign in Canada. Sullivan received a report of the desperate situation of his men from Edward Antill, lieutenant colonel of the Second Canadian Regiment. Sullivan decided then to evacuate the posts at Sorel and Chambly and remove to Crown Point for passage south. Antill's indomitable courage, despite a disastrous year of defeats in the north, is indicative of the American resilience in recovering from such setbacks.

*Chamblee June 13th 1776*

Worthy Sir,

You have doubtless Eer this received a Line from General Arnold, acquainting you with his having Sent me a Tour to Chamblee, this Place, to endeavour to collect a proper Return of the Troops at each Post. I have done my utmost, but have not yet finished, owing to the Scattered Situation of our Men, for [twenty] Miles in Length—as Soon as done, I shall wait upon you. I can in general Terms acquaint you, there are about fifteen hundred at St. Johns, and upwards of twelve here, very few indeed fit for Duty. The loss of Duchamboult, I am clear has lost us the Province[1]—a prudent Retreat, I presume, under our present Situation, is an only Plan if they Should get Possession of our Boats, I am apprehensive I think they may be at Crown Point before us. This, General, is a bold Observation—excuse my Freedom, I have lived ten Years in the [seat] of the Operations, have seen their Manauvers,—depend upon it if they do retard their Operations for Nothing, they are meditating a Plan they will Soon attempt to put in Execution. Secure our Water [    ] on Lake Champlain and, we turn the Tables upon them, & I think we can meet them there upon advantageous Terms. I once more beg you Excuse in a Hurry—Accept my Simple Opinion, if it serves you, I am happy, if not throw them by, yet Still believe me with Respect your most obedient humble Servant

E. ANTILL

ALS, Papers of the Continental Congress, National Archives, Washington, D.C.
[1] Deschambault was abandoned in May by General Thomas.

# PHILIP SCHUYLER TO HORATIO GATES

**Philip Schuyler**
COURTESY OF THE NEW-YORK HISTORICAL SOCIETY

E DWARD ANTILL'S entreaties convinced the American command of the need to retreat south. Brigadier General John Sullivan and the commander of the Northern Department, Major General Philip Schuyler, decided to evacuate posts at Chambly, commanded by General Benedict Arnold, and at Sorel and retreated to Crown Point for passage to Albany. By the middle of June, the tired and sick American forces pushed southward with the aid of boats provided by Schuyler. Philip Schuyler describes the retreat to Major General Horatio Gates (c.1727–1806). By July 1, the American invasion of Canada had ended in defeat.

*Albany June 25th: 1776*

Dear General

About twelve last Night General Arnold arrived here. Our Army has been under the Necessity of leaving the inhabited part of Canada and retreating to Isle au Noix, which has been happily effected without Loss of Men and only nine Batteaus and three pieces of Cannon were left behind.[1] The sick are coming on to Crown point. General Sullivan with the Remainder was at Isle au noix on the 19 and intended to remain there until he received Orders from General Washington or me to retire farther South, altho' I believe he will be obliged to leave it either by his own Army or that of the Enemy. I have recommended a farther Retreat to point au Fere or Isle la-motte, both because it was the unanimous opinion of a Council of War, and the Wish of all the Officers, who General Arnold informs me have addressed him upon the Occasion and because I know it will not be a difficult Matter for the Enemy to occupy both Shores on this Side of him for six Miles and prevent if not a Retreat at least a Supply of provisions.

I wish you to hasten up, with all possible Dispatch that we may advise together on the most eligible Methods to be pursued to prevent an encrease of our Misfortunes in this unlucky Quarter. I have a very confident Hope that our naval Superiority will prevent the Enemy's crossing Lake Champlain and altho' they will exert themselves in building Vessels of Force yet I think we can out build them.

I shall this Day send to Connecticut and the Massachusetts for Ship Carpenters as we cannot be supplied with any from New York. Adieu my dear General and believe me with every friendly and affectionate wish Your most obedient hble Servant

PH: SCHUYLER

Be so good as to take a Bed with me that whilst you remain here we may be as much together as possible.

ALS, Horatio Gates Papers, New-York Historical Society, New York City.

[1] At Isle-aux-Noix the army was wracked by smallpox. Within a few days most of the soldiers encamped there had been stricken.

# SAMUEL SELDEN TO JOSHUA HUNTINGTON

THE IMMINENT ATTACK on New York City in the spring of 1776 compelled General George Washington to request more soldiers for its defense. On June 3, 1776, the Continental Congress agreed to raise 3,500 men from the surrounding colonies. This force, called the Flying Camp, was, however, of no immediate use to the Continental army, which was entirely occupied with the hasty construction of fortifications crucial for the defense of New York City. Washington therefore requested that militia forces from such colonies as New Jersey and Connecticut temporarily fill the gap in manpower. Letters to the Provincial Congress of New Jersey and to Connecticut's governor, Jonathan Trumbull, resulted in an urgent call for men and supplies for New York City. Colonel Samuel Selden (1723–76), of a Connecticut state regiment, was but one of many military leaders who earnestly attempted to muster their forces to help strengthen the American defense of a city that was considered crucial in controlling the Hudson River Valley and maintaining New England's contact with the other colonies. Selden's letter to Captain Joshua Huntington (1751–1820) shows the dire need for prompt action. Selden did not know that the sails of 150 British ships had been sighted off Sandy Hook the previous day. The contest for New York City had been joined. In this campaign Selden would be wounded and captured and would die in Sugar House prison on October 11, 1776.

*Lyme July 6th. 1776*

Sr

Inclos'd you have the express of Genl. Wadsworth to me[1] & the Commands upon him from the head General to forward the Connecticut Regiments designed for Nork department without a moments delay. You are therefore desired, entreated, directed and ordered by all that is desirable and precious to freemen to give all diligence and suffer not a moment delay if it be possible raise equipt and muster your Company.

Rouse the People to see their Danger Stir them up by all that is dear in this life our Wives our Children our property our Liberty is at stake but above all social enjoyments our Religion for which our fore Fathers left their Native Land fled to this wilderness suffered cold, hunger, nakedness, and many of them were tortered and Butchered in the most inhumane manner that they might leave to posterity fredom of Religion and masters of their own Property. I fear some strange intimidation or infatuation has seized the minds of People that they are no more Spirited to venture in the glorious cause we are engaged in; for if we can't defend ourselves at New York I fear all is gone for if they conquer the united strength of the Continent what an easy prey will our little Towns & ports become to them. Pray Sr. loose not a moments time as soon as you have raised 25 Men equipt and muster them and you shall have orders to march immediately. I expected returns long before this Time a moments delay may prove the Ruin of America for ages to come, pursue the Orders of the Genl and conform thereto & let me hear what success you have send me the Number you have enlisted and in what forwardness they are that I may report to the Genl. From Sr. With respect your most humble Servant

SAML. SELDEN

I this Day sent off between 60 & 70 Men from East Haddam.

ALS, William Griswold Lane Collection, Yale University Library, New Haven, Conn.
[1] Brigadier General James Wadsworth (d. 1817) of the Connecticut militia.

# PHINEAS PORTER ORDERLY BOOK

BY THE TIME of the signing of the Declaration of Independence, there were 25,606 Continental soldiers, of whom 18,168 were with General George Washington in New York City and its environs. The Americans there expected a British assault, for the Howe brothers commanded a constantly increasing army on Staten Island as well as a fleet that controlled the numerous waterways around the city. Because of crowded conditions and lack of time to drill his men for battle, Washington enforced discipline by fiat. Washington's constant efforts to enforce military order are reported in the orderly book kept by Major Phineas Porter (1739–1804), who served in Colonel William Douglas' (1742–77) Connecticut State Regiment from June 20, 1776, until his capture by the British three months later during the Continental army's retreat from New York City.

*Head Quarters July the 10 1776*

Parole)
Countersign)

A working Perty of 150 men Properly officered to attend tomorrow morning with their arms Near the Labaratory at 6 oClock to take three Day Provisions. The Commanding officer to come to head Quarters for his orders the Qt Mst Genl to Provide Tents.[1] General Heaths Brigade instead of Repairing to their Iarram Posts tomorrow Morning to hold themselves in Readiness to March as they will Receve their orders from the Brigadier Genl on the Parade at 4 oClock. The Brigadier will attend Head Quarters this Afternoon for the orders. John Butler of Capt Bridghams Compy Colo Baylys Regt.[2] having been tried by a General Court Martial where of Colo Read was President found Gilty of Desertion and Sentenced to Receive 39 Lashes. The General Confirms The Sentence and orders it to be Executed at the Usual Time and Place. The General Doubts not the Persons Who pulled Down and Mutilated the Statue in the Broad way last night were actuated by zeal in the Publick Caus yet it has so much the Appearance of Riot & want of order in the Army that he Disapproves the maners and Directs that in future Such things Shall be avoided by the Soldiers and be Left to be Executed by Proper Authority.[3]

Brigadier for the Day Genl Wadsworth. Field officers for the Piequit Colo Wyllys Lieut Colo Stoutenbourgh[4] & Majr Smith. Brigade Majr Hoops.

*Head Quarters July 11th, 1776*

Parole)
Countersn)

Genl Speners Brigade instead of repairing to their Alarm Posts to hold themselves in Readiness to March tomorrow Morning at 4 oClock.[5] The Brigdr General will attend this Evening at head Quarters for his orders: which he will deliver on the parade tomorrow Morning to the Brigade. As the weather is very warm there will be the Greatest Danger of the Troops groing unhelthy unless the officers and men are very attentive to Clenliness in their Persons and Quarters the officers are Required to visit their men frequently in their Quarters to impress on them the Necessity of frequently changing their Linen cleaning their Rooms and when it Can be avoided not to Cook their victuals in the Rooms where they sleep. If any of the officers Apprehensive of their men being Crowded in their Quarters they are to Represent to The Barrack Master who is to accomodate them in Such a manner as is most Conducive to health and Convenience the Good of the Service the Comfort of The men and the Merit of the officers will be so much Advanced by keeping the Troops as Neet and clean as Possible that the Genl hopes that there will be an Emulation on this head and as a Scruteny will soon be made that who Shall be found Negligent will be Punished and the Deserving rewarded. 40 men Properly officered to Attend Colo Mason and work Under his Directions these men not be Changed as has been the Case but to Continue with him till The Service is compleated. Brigdr for the Day Genl. Hard Field Officer

for the Piquit Colo Baldwin Lieut Colo [    ] Majr Hatfield Brigade Majr for the Day
Henly.[6]

*New York July 12, 1776*

Brigade Orders

   The Blessing and protection of Heaven are att all Times Necessary and Earnestly to be sought After but Especially so in Times of Publick Danger and Distress it is therefore recommended to the officers and Soldiers of this Brigade that they Pay a Steady Reverent & Devout attention on Publick worship and that they be Perticularly Carefull to keep their Cloaths Clean and Neat that Everyone may appear With a becoming Decency on Such oaccasions. . . .

*Phineas Porter's Orderly Book,* Mattatuck Historical Society, Occasional Publications (Waterbury, Conn., 1928), III, 6–8.

[1] Brigadier General Thomas Mifflin (1744–1800).

[2] Probably Colonel John Bailey (1730–1810) of the Twenty-Third Continental Infantry.

[3] In celebration of American independence, a 4,000-pound statue of George III was overturned.

[4] Colonel Samuel Wyllys (d. 1823) of the Twenty-Second Continental Infantry; Lieutenant Colonel Isaac Stoughtenburgh (1739–99) of Malcom's Continental Regiment.

[5] Brigadier General Joseph Spencer (1714–89).

[6] Brigadier General Nathaniel Heard (1730–92) of the New Jersey militia.

# HUGH MERCER TO JOHN DICKINSON

ON JUNE 5, 1776, Colonel Hugh Mercer (1725–77), of Virginia, was promoted to brigadier general and placed in command of the New Jersey defenses and the newly created Flying Camp. For five months General Mercer struggled to use effectively his force of militiamen, state troops, and raw recruits from Maryland, Pennsylvania, New Jersey, and Delaware. The unwillingness of many of them to serve extended terms in Mercer's force is emphasized in Mercer's letter to Colonel John Dickinson (1732–1808), of the first battalion of Pennsylvania Associators. Dickinson, who led his battalion to Eliza-bethtown, New Jersey, in July 1776, was ordered by Mercer to prevent one of his companies from deserting its post and returning to Philadelphia. Dickinson's suggestions and threats, however, did little to keep his soldiers in line. Responsibilities at home and expired enlistments took their toll on the numbers in Mercer's force. Indeed, Colonel Dickinson himself, after losing his seat in the Continental Congress, resigned his commission and returned to his Delaware estate. On November 30, 1776, when 2,000 enlistments expired, Mercer's Flying Camp was disbanded.

*Woodbridge 5th Augt 1776*

Sir,

    The account you gave me of the disposition of the Company of light Infantry in your Battalion, hath appeard; the more I think of it, the more alarming—that no inconsideral steps may be taken. I have had the opinions of the Field officers and others here, on the Affair. They join unanimously in opinion with me that the orders issued last week relative to such of the associators as shou'd presume to desert the Service of their Country at this Critical Time ought to be answered and that at all hazards, the Violation of those orders shall not pass over with Impunity. You will therefor please to signify to the Company above mentioned or to any others of similar disposition that a force sufficient to prevent their march to Philadelphia is ready and will have orders to confine them. This argument is not intended to be used untill every other persuasive motive hath been urged. When every other argument is found not to avail, and the men prepare to desert the Post, you will then call for the Assistance of Col Smallwood too whom I have wrote upon a Subject;[1] I am Sir Your most obed Sert.

HUGH MERCER

ALS, John Dickinson Papers, R. R. Logan Collection, Historical Society of Pennsylvania, Philadelphia.
[1] Colonel William Smallwood (1741–1806) of Maryland.

# Joseph Howell, Jr., to Joseph Howell, Sr.

THE RAPIDLY constructed defenses of New York and New Jersey were tested when British troops under General Sir William Howe landed on Staten Island on July 2, 1776. By August 12, 1776, there were more than 31,000 British soldiers and Hessians stationed within sight of the New Jersey coast and the New York City fortifications. Joseph Howell, Jr. (1750–98), a captain in a Pennsylvania musket battalion, commented on the warlike appearance and the martial spirit of the beleaguered city in this letter to his father. Howell was taken prisoner during the Battle of Long Island on August 27, 1776, and became a long-suffering inmate of the infamous prison ship *Jersey*. His faith in God, his apprehension over his own fate in the imminent battle, and his enduring attachment to his family and his country are all expressed in this letter.

**Joseph Howell, Jr.**
COURTESY OF THE FRICK ART REFERENCE LIBRARY, NEW YORK CITY

*New York, August 14, 1776*

My dear Father

I arrived here last night in perfect Health & Spirits. I was much surprised to see the Fortifications which they have here in every Street almost, and the Wharfs are so strong that I think it is impossible for them enemy to make any Impression without they set fire to the Town which I understand they intend to do by a Deserter who came over last night. He says the Soldiers in general have a great dislike to the service & dread the consequences of attacking us, he likewise mentions that they intend it tomorrow and God the Supreme Being only knows whether I shall ever see those who are near & dear to me again, if it should be the case don't grieve after me as I am satisfied in my own mind that the cause I am engaged in is a righteous one. If this should be the last letter which I hope it will not that thee may Receive from me. It is my will that all I have in this World be equally divided between my four Sisters Eliza Sally Becky & my dear precious little one Sidney & I desire thee in my name & Person to give her & the Rest a kiss for me. The point grows serious therefore may the Almighty the Supreme Being Grant that my Parents my Brothers & Sisters may enjoy Health Peace & Prosperity is the sincere wish and Prayer of a Dutiful Son & Brother

Jos. Howell Jun.

My best love attends my friends in General & to my more particular one Thos. Clarke. If I should be favored with another opportunity I will write more particular but excuse my haste as Mr. Bedford waits for this. Adieus

J.H.

Typescript copy, original manuscript in the possession of Mrs. Elizabeth V. H. Sealy, Scarsdale, N.Y.

# JAMES CHAMBERS TO KITTY CHAMBERS

JAMES CHAMBERS (1743–1805) succeeded Edward Hand (1744–1802) as lieutenant colonel of the First Continental Infantry Regiment on March 7, 1776. He writes to his wife, Katharine, from "Camp at Delamere's Mills," three miles above King's Bridge, the strategic span across Spuyten Duyvil Creek from Manhattan to the Bronx. The battle for New York City was delayed by the desire of General Sir William Howe and Lord Admiral Richard Howe (1726–99) to have their forces recuperate from a long voyage and to gain additional strength from the force returning from the unsuccessful attack on Charleston, South Carolina. The Howe brothers had also spent some time making overtures toward negotiation with General Washington before they became convinced that the Americans were resolute in defending their independence. On August 22, 1776, over 20,000 British and Hessian soldiers crossed to Long Island. The American forces did little, except for random sniping, to retard the advance of the massive invading force. The outnumbered Americans soon came under British bombardment on August 26, 1776. The Battle of Long Island was fought on August 27. James Chambers describes the bravery of the Americans in the face of the indomitable British foe. The battle between 17,000 British and Hessian soldiers and 7,000 Americans ended with 200 Americans dead and 897 captured. Although the remaining Continental forces safely withdrew from Brooklyn Heights across the East River to New York City, the prospects for defending the city seemed bleak.

*September 3, 1776*

My Dear Kitty:

I should have written to you sooner, but the hurry and confusion we have been in for some time past, has hindered me. I will now give you a short account of transactions in this quarter.

On the morning of the 22nd August there were nine thousand British troops on New Utrecht plains. The guard alarmed our small camp, and we assembled at the flagstaff. We marched our forces, about two hundred in number, to New Utrecht to watch the movements of the enemy. When we came on the hill, we discovered a party of them advancing toward us. We prepared to give them a warm reception, when an imprudent fellow fired, and they immediately halted and turned toward Flatbush. The main body also, moved along the great road toward the same place. We proceeded alongside of them in the edge of the woods as far as the turn of the lane, where the cherry-trees were, if you remember. We then found it impracticable for so small a force to attack them on the plain, and sent Captain Hamilton with twenty men, before them to burn all the grain; which he did very cleverly, and killed a great many cattle. It was then thought most proper to return to camp and secure our baggage, which we did, and left it in Fort Brown. Near 12 o'clock the same day we returned down the great road to Flatbush with only our small regiment, and one New England regiment sent to support us, though at a mile's distance. When in sight of Flatbush, we discovered the enemy, but not the main body; on perceiving us, they retreated down the road perhaps a mile. A party of our people commanded by Captain Miller followed them close with a design to decoy a portion of them to follow him, whilst the rest kept in the edge of the woods alongside of Captain M. But they thought better of the matter, and would not come after him though he went within two hundred yards. There they stood for a long time, and then Captain Miller turned off to us and we proceeded along their flank.

Some of our men fired upon and killed several Hessians, as we ascertained two days afterwards. Strong guards were maintained all day on the flanks of the enemy, and our regiment and the Hessian yagers kept up a severe firing, with a loss of but two wounded on our side. We laid a few Hessians low, and made them retreat out of Flatbush. Our people went into the town, and brought the goods out of the burning houses.

The enemy liked to have lost their field-pieces. Captain Steel, of your vicinity, acted bravely.[1] We would certainly have had the cannon had it not been for some foolish person calling retreat. The main body of the foe returned to the town; and when our lads came back, they told of their exploits. This was doubted by some, which enraged our men so much that a few of them ran and brought away several Hessians on their backs. This kind of firing by our riflemen and theirs continued until [ten] o'clock in the morning of the 26th, when our regiment was relieved by a portion of the Flying Camp; and we started for Fort Greene to get refreshment, not having lain down the whole of this time, and almost dead with fatigue. We had just got to the fort, and I had only laid down, when the alarm guns were fired. We were compelled to turn out to the lines, and as soon as it was light saw our men and theirs engaged with field-pieces. At last, the enemy found means to surround our men there upon guard, and then a heavy firing continued for several hours. The main body that surrounded our men marched up within thirty yards of Forts Brown and Greene;[2] but when we fired, they retreated with loss. From all I can learn, we numbered about twenty-five hundred, and the attacking party not less than twenty-five thousand, as they had been landing for days before. Our men behaved as bravely as ever men did; but it is surprising that, with the superiority of numbers, they were not cut to pieces. They behaved gallantly, and there are but five or six hundred missing.

General Lord Stirling fought like a wolf, and is taken prisoner,[3] Colonels Miles and Atlee, Major Bird, Captain Peoples, Lieutenant Watt, and a great number of our other officers also prisoners; Colonel Piper missing.[4] From deserters, we learn that the enemy lost Major-General Grant and two Brigadiers, and many others, and five hundred killed. Our loss is chiefly in prisoners.

It was thought advisable to retreat off Long Island; and on the night of the 30th, it was done with great secrecy. Very few of the officers knew it until they were on the boats, supposing that an attack was intended. A discovery of our intention to the enemy would have been fatal to us. The Pennsylvania troops were done great honor by being chosen the *corps de reserve* to cover the retreat. The regiments of Colonels Hand, Hagan, Shea, and Hazlett were detailed for that purpose. We kept up fires, with outposts stationed, until all the rest were over. We left the lines after it was fair day, and then came off.

Never was a greater feat of generalship shown than in this retreat; to bring off an army of twelve thousand men within sight of a strong enemy, possessed of as strong a fleet as ever floated on our seas, without any loss, and saving all the baggage.

General Washington saw the last over himself.

Printed in Lewis M. Garrard, *Chambersburg in the Colony and in the Revolution: A Sketch* (Philadelphia, 1856), pp. 45–49.

[1] Probably Captain William Steele (1750–1822) of the Pennsylvania Flying Camp.

[2] These were redoubts under the command of General Israel Putnam.

[3] William Alexander (Lord Stirling; 1725–83) was a brigadier general from New Jersey; he was exchanged September 1776.

[4] Lieutenant Colonel James Piper (c.1735–76) of the First Battalion of Miles's Pennsylvania Rifle Regiment died in captivity September 1776.

# DANIEL BRODHEAD TO AN UNKNOWN PERSON

DANIEL BRODHEAD (1736–1809), lieutenant colonel and commandant of the second battalion of Colonel Samuel Miles's Pennsylvania Rifle Regiment, hastily details his activities in the Battle of Long Island on August 27, 1776, for a member of the Pennsylvania legislature. Brodhead describes the courageous stand by his outnumbered Pennsylvania force and provides a critical commentary on the actions of the generals involved in the battle. His comments on the American retreat show the contemporary appreciation of a daring military maneuver. On the night of August 29, over 10,000 men had passed safely across the East River. The Americans lost only three men despite the proximity of many British ships and sentries.

**Daniel Brodhead**

*Camp near Kingsbridge, 5th Sep'r, 1776*

Dear Sir,

I doubt not the Hon'ble the Convention of the State of Penn'a, is anxious to know the state of the Provincial Troops since the Battle on Long Island, and I have now all the information to be expected concerning it for the present, will give them every circumstance that occurs to me. On the 26th of last month, Gen'ls Putnam, Sullivan and others came to our camp which was to the left of all the other posts and proceeded to reconnoitre the enemie's lines to the right, when from the movements of the enemy they might plainly discover they were advancing towards Jamaica, and extending their lines to the left so as to march round us, for our lines to the left, were, for want of Videttes,[1] left open for at least four miles where we constantly scouted by Day, which beside mounting a Guard of one hundred men & an advance party of subaltern and thirty to the left of us, was hard Duty for our Reg't: during the night of the 26th, we were alarmed three Different times and stood to our Arms. As soon as it was light, Col. Miles, from the right of our first Battn., sent me orders to follow him with the second, to the left of our lines;[2] when I had marched about half a mile, I was ordered to the right about to join Col. Willis's regt of New England troops, but by the time I returned to the camp, Major Williams on horseback, overtook me with orders from Col. Miles, to march Obliquely & join him, but could not say where I might find him; I Observed the orders and directed a Subaltern from the front of the Battn (which was marching in Indian file) with a small party to the left of the Battn, and desired Major Patton to send a Subaltern & small party from the rear to the right of the front of the Battalion,[3] which he mistook and took the one-half of the Battn to the right, about two hundred yards, which immediately threw the half the Battn, so far to the rear as to render it very difficult to join without sustaining great loss, for presently after we left our camp we discovered the Enemie's horse & foot to the number of four or five Thousand in our front, and as we could discover nothing of the first Battn, the Enemy being vastly superior to us in Number, I immediately ordered the Battn to gain a Wood to the left and then formed, but seeing a Number of Artillerymen dragging a brass field-piece & Howit through a clear field in order to gain a wood a little to the left of our Front, and knowing the Enemy were also in our rear, I ordered that part of the Battn which was then with me, to proceed to the second wood, & cover the Artillery and make a stand, but the New England Regt aforementioned coming up with us, and running thro' our files broke them, and in the confusion many of our men run with them. I did all in my power to rally the musquietry & Riflemen, but to no purpose, so that when we came to engage the Enemy, I had not fifty men, notwithstanding which, we after about three Rounds, caused the Enemy to retire, and as the Enemy's main body was then nearly between us and the lines, I retreated to the lines, having lost out of the whole Battalion, about one hundred men, officers included, which, as they were much scattered must be chiefly prisoners; during this time four or five Reg'ts, and some of our Riflemen who had joined them, were engaged to the left of us and right of the Lines. I had no sooner got into the Lines than the Enemy advanced up to them and kept up a brisk fire on us, but only one man killed in the

Lines; as soon as we returned the fire with our rifles and musquetry, they retreated, and if we had been provided with a field piece or two, of which we had a sufficient number elsewhere, we might have killed the greater part of their advance party; as soon as the Enemy were beaten from the lines, I was ordered to a point about a mile and a-half to the right, to cover the retreat of the Delaware Battalion and the other Troops that might come over under the constant fire of the Enemie's field pieces and Howits; here I remained 'till almost night before I was relieved, notwithstanding the Generals there had a number of Reg'ts who were not engaged, and had had little or no fatigue. Upon the whole, less Generalship never was shown in any Army since the Art of War was understood, except in the retreat from Long Island, which was well conducted. No troops could behave better than the Southern, for though they seldom engaged less than five to one, they frequently repulsed the Enemy with great Slaughter, and I am confident that the number of killed and wounded on their side, is greater than on ours, notwithstanding we had to fight them front & rear under every disadvantage. I understand that Gen. Sullivan has taken the Liberty to charge our brave and good Col. Miles, with the ill success of the Day, but give me leave to say, that if Gen. Sullivan & the rest of the Gen'ls on Long Island, had been as Vigilant & prudent as him, we might & in all probability would have cut off Clinton's Brigade; our officers & men in general, considering the confusion, behaved as well as men could do—a very few behaved ill, of which, when I am informed, will write you . . . Col. Miles & Col. Piper are prisoners, and I hear are well treated, poor Atly I can hear nothing of.[4] Col. Parry died like a hero. No allowance has as yet been made for the Lieutenant Coll's and Majors Table Expenses, in care of separate commands. I hope we shall be put upon as respectable a footing on that acc't as the Maryland officers are, our present pay being not more than half sufficient to suppoart us according to our Rank in this Tory Country. I am Dear Sir, in great Haste, your most H'ble Serv't.

DANIEL BRODHEAD

P.S. The Great Gen'l Putnam could not, tho' requested, send out one Reg't to cover our retreat.

Printed in Henry P. Johnston, *The Campaign of 1776 around New York and Brooklyn* . . . (Brooklyn, N.Y., 1878), documents section, pp. 63–66.

[1] Vedette is a mounted sentry.
[2] Colonel Samuel Miles (1739–1805) of the Pennsylvania Rifle Regiment.
[3] Major John Patton (1745–1804) of the second battalion of Miles's Pennsylvania Rifle Regiment.
[4] Colonel Samuel John Atlee (1739–86) of the Pennsylvania Musket Battalion.

# GUSTAVUS BROWN WALLACE TO MICHAEL WALLACE

CAPTAIN GUSTAVUS BROWN WALLACE (1751–1802), of Colonel George Weedon's (d. 1793) Third Virginia Regiment, writes to his brother in King George County, Virginia, after rushing northward to join General Washington's outnumbered forces in New York City. Following the recent retreat from Long Island and rampant rumors of an impending evacuation of Manhattan Island, Captain Wallace faced the dismal possibility of imprisonment. He urges his brother to be ready to travel north with clothes and money should he be taken prisoner by the British. His premonitions of further defeat were quickly confirmed.

*Camp on North River 10 miles above New york Septr. 15th 1776*

Dr. Brother

We encamped here the day before yesterday after a very fategueing march our men keep thier health pretty well. I with sorrow inform you that when we crossed Hudsons river and landed in new york we found but 1500 men in the town, which we were taught to believe had no less than 10000 men in it and not above 12 or 13 pieces of cannon. The whole continental army at this time in the Jersyes & New york goverments does not consist of above 23000 men which I heard in Virga. contained 58000 men. General Washington was rejoyced to see us & wishes for the other Virga. troops that are on their march as he is much distressed for troops. Our army are much discouraged at General Lee's not coming from the southward and at their loss on long Island.[1] We lost on that Island 1000 men killed & taken this I can affirm for a truth as I had it from five or six Maryland officers that were in the action & knew how many were engaged & how many were brought off the field. Our affairs here are in great disorder at present. Yesterday there was a Counsil of war betwix our General officers & I believe they have determined to evacuate the city of New york & the Island & make their grand stand at a place called Kings Bridge about 15 miles above new york.[2] If we evacuate the Island of new york we shall loose our Camp & Baggage. Every night we expect an attack and are pretty well prepared for their reception in the small arm way the heavy Cannon are all removed to Kings Bridge & General Washingtons Baggage is now moving from Headquarters to that place.

When I marched from Alexandria Jno. Debutz Isaac Rose & Benga. Green deserted from me. I shoud be glad you woud look for them & confine them in goal in Fredbg.[3] till some troops are marching this way & send them after me with their guard.

If I escape the ravage of war this campaign & the next, you may expect me in Viga. the winter after this. You'l take great care of my cloaths I left in Viga. as I am almost sure of loosing those I have here for the want of a waggon to carry them out of this Island. My Company Waggon & all others are imployed in moving the Country stores out.

I forgot to tell you that there was five compys. of Colo. Smallwoods Battalion Killed & taken on Lond Island. It is reported that the Hessians give no quarter but put every man to the Sword they take.

We have two Battries about two miles from here on the east river & they have two opposite ours have nine & twelve pounders they have 18 & 24 pounders & have been playing on each other for five or six days past. They silenced one of our Battries yesterday evening but it was opened again this morning & they have kept up the heavyest cannonadeing this morning I ever heard.[4] In one of their Battries they have a Mortar from which they throw Booms. The first day they began to throw every one burst in the air and did no damage but since have thrown with some effect. There is fort Washington about a mile from this that is a compleat fort mounting about 20 pieces of Cannon some 18 pounders.

If I shou'd be so unfortunate as to be taken or obliged to quit my baggage and you shoud hear it, push to the northward with all speed with some shirts & as much silver & gold as you can get for the prisoners are much distressed if they have not silver or gold as our paper will not pass with them & I can repay you in Continental money by an order on Colo. Weedon.

My Compliments to the two Jno. Taliafero's Jos. Jones & all friends. I am Dr. Brother Your Affectionate

GUSTAVUS B. WALLACE

Remember me to Harry Vowles & let him know we have all made our fortunes.

ALS, Wallace Family Papers, University of Virginia Library, Charlottesville.

[1] General Charles Lee had been given the command of the defense of Charleston.
[2] A council of war voted on September 12, 1776, to withdraw from the island of Manhattan.
[3] Fredericksburg, Va.
[4] A British attack on the Kip's Bay area began on the day Wallace wrote this letter.

# GEORGE CLINTON TO THE NEW YORK COMMITTEE OF CORRESPONDENCE

AFTER THEIR incessant bombardment of the Americans at Kip's Bay throughout the morning of September 15, 4,000 British and Hessian forces landed on Manhattan Island. Many Continental soldiers avoided potential capture by retreating along the Hudson side of the island to safety on the heights of Manhattan. In this letter to Henry Wisner, Sr., William Allison, and Robert R. Livingston (1746–1813), members of the New York Committee of Correspondence, Brigadier General George Clinton (1739–1812) describes in detail the Battle of Harlem Heights on September 16, 1776. This encounter inflicted heavy casualties on the British and Hessians and helped assuage the commander in chief's distress because of his troops' conduct the day before. Before Clinton was sent to New York City, he had been asked by General Washington to supervise the defense of the Hudson Highlands.

*Kingsbridge 18th Septembr. 1776*

Gentlemen

Since my last many Matters of Importance to the Public and more particularly to this State have taken place; But I have been so Situated as neither to find Leisure or Opportunity of communicating them to Congress. I returned late last Night from the Command of the Piquet or Advance Party in the Front of our Lines and was just setting down to write to the Convention and intended sending an Express when I was favoured with yours of Yesterday.

About the middle of last Week it was determined for many Reasons to evacuate the City of New York, and accordingly Orders were given for removing the Ordinance Military & other Stores from thence which by Sunday morning was nearly effected. On Saturday four of the Enemy's larger Ships by the City up the North River and anchored near Greenage and about as many more up the East River which anchored in Turtle Bay and from the Movements of the Enemy on long Island and the small Islands in the East River we had great reason to apprehend they intended to make a Landing and Attack our Lines somewhere near the City.[1] Our Army for some Days had been moving upwards this way and encamping on the Heights southwest of Coll. Morris's where we intended to form Lines and make our grand Stand.[2] On Sunday morning the Enemy landed a very considerable Body of Troops principally consisting of their light Infantry & Granadiers near Turtle Bay under Cover of a very heavy Cannonade from their Shipping, our Lines were but thinly manned as they were then intended only to secure a Retreat to the Rear of our Army & unfortunately by such Troops as were so little disposed to stand in the way of Grape Shot that the main Body of them almost instantly retreated nay fled without a possibility of rallying them, tho' General Washington himself (who rid to the spot on hearing the Cannonade) with some other General Officers exerted themselves to effect it.

The Enemy in Landing immediately formed a Line across the Island. Most of our People were luckilly North of it and Joined the Army. These few that were in the City crossed the River chiefly to Powles Hook[3] so that our Loss in Men, Artillery or Stores is very inconsiderable. I dont believe it exceeds 100 Men and I fancy most of them from their Conduct staid out of Choice.[4] Before Evening the Enemy landed the main Body of their Army took Possession of the City & marched up the Island & encamped on the Heights extending from Mc Gowns and the Black Horse to the North River.[5]

On Monday morning about ten OClock a party of the Enemy consisting of Highlanders, Hessians, the light Infantry, Grenadiers and English Troops (Number uncertain) attack'd our advanc'd Party commanded by Coll. Knowlton at Martje Davits Fly.[6] They were opposed with spirit and soon made to retreat to a clear Field southwest of that about 200 paces where they lodged themselves behind a Fence covered with Bushes. Our People attacked them in Turn and caused them to retreat a second Time leaving five dead on the Spot, we pursued them to a Buckwheat Field on the Top of a high Hill distant about four hundred paces where they received a considerable Reinforcement with several Field Pieces and there made a Stand. A very brisk Action ensued at this Place which continued about Two Hours. Our People at length worsted them a third Time caused them to fall back into an Orchard from thence across a Hollow and up another Hill not far distant from their own Lines. A large Column of the Enemy's Army being at this time discovered to be in motion and the Ground we then occupied being rather disadvantageous a Retreat likewise without bringing on a general Action (which we did not think prudent to risk) rather insecure our party was therefore ordered in and the Enemy was well contented to hold the last Ground we drove them to.

We lost on this occasion Coll. Knowlton, a brave Officer and sixteen Privates kill'd. Major Leech from Virginia and about Eight or ten subaltern Officers and Privates wounded.[7] The Loss of the Enemy is uncertain. They carried their Dead and wounded off in and soon after the Action but we have good Evidence of their having upwards of 60 kill'd & violent presumption of 100. The Action in the whole lasted abt. 4. Hours.

I Consider our Success in this small affair at this Time almost equal to a Victory. It has animated our Troops gave them new Spirits and erazed every bad Impression, the Retreat from Long Island & ca had left on their minds. They find they are able with inferior Numbers to drive their Enemy and think of nothing now but Conquest.

Since the above affair nothing material has happened. The Enemy keep close to their Lines our advanc'd Parties continue at their former Station. We are daily throwing up Works to prevent the Enemy's advancing. Great Attention is paid to Fort Washington, the Posts opposite to it on the Jersey Shore[8] & the Obstructions in the River, which I have reason to believe is already effectual so as to prevent their Shipping passing. However it is intended still to add to them as it is of the utmost Consequence to keep the Enemy below us. None of Smiths or Remsens Regiment have yet joined me nor do I believe they intend.[9] I have heard that many have gone over on the Island & continued there. I have not been able to get any late Account from thence. We are getting a new Supply of Connecticut Militia in here. If they are not better than the last I wish they would keep them at Home. I hope however they are. They look better. A Regiment or two lately arrived from Virginia. I cant recollect any Thing else worth mentioning. I am with much Respect your most Obedient Servt.

GEO. CLINTON

P.S. I have lately heard & believe Genl Woodhull is not dead as was reported.[10] We shall want Oak Plank for Plat Forms & Square Timber. How can it be procured? I am sure if left to the Q M Genl he will not get it in Time. The Genl. desir'd me to make some Inquiries where it may be had.

ALS, Miscellaneous Manuscripts, New-York Historical Society, New York City.

[1]"Greenage," Greenwich, is now called the Chelsea district. Turtle Bay was located on the East River at present-day 46th and 47th streets.

[2] The home of Loyalist Roger Morris, now known as the Morris-Jumel Mansion, is between 160th and 162d streets in New York City. It is operated by the Daughters of the American Revolution.

[3] Paulus Hook was an artillery fortification.

[4] Fifty Americans were killed and 320 were captured on September 15.

[5] McGown's Farm was below Harlem Heights.

[6] Lieutenant Colonel Thomas Knowlton (1740–76). Martje Davits Fly was near Morningside Heights.

[7] Major Andrew Leitch (c.1750–76) died of wounds received in the Battle of Harlem Heights on October 1, 1776.

[8] Fort Lee.

[9] Colonel Josiah Smith (1723–86); Colonel Henry Remsen (1736–92) of the New York militia.

[10] Brigadier General Nathaniel Woodhull (1722–76), captured during the Battle of Long Island, died of wounds, September 20, 1776.

# JAMES MOORE TO JOHN HANCOCK

ON MARCH 1, 1776, James Moore (1737–77) was commissioned a brigadier general in the Continental army and soon became commander in chief of North Carolina's military forces. During the defense of Charleston against General Sir Henry Clinton's (1730–95) expedition of 1776, General Moore was charged with observing the British fleet in the Cape Fear River. Writing from Wilmington, North Carolina, north of the Cape Fear River, Moore corresponds with President John Hancock (1737–93) of the Continental Congress about detaching two Continental battalions under his command for the reinforcement of General Washington's besieged forces in New York City. Washington, however, evacuated New York before the order was implemented, and on November 29 Moore was ordered to Charleston, where he remained for two months. General Moore died in Wilmington in April 1777 of natural causes. His career, though brief, was sufficient testimony to his devotion to his country's cause.

*Wilmington Septemr. 19th. 1776*

Sir

Yours of the 3d. Inst I had this day the Honour to receive, And shall with all possible dispatch proceed to execute the order of Congress for Marching two Battalions of the Continental Troops to the Reinforcement of the Army at New York.

One intire Battalion, And a considerable part of two others haveing marchd on an Expedition to [Tlarway], will put it out of my power to make up two full Battalions, I flatter myself I shall however be able to march with about eight hundred men, & leave a Sufficient number for the defence of this place.

I hope to begin my march in two days, And be assured Sir nothing in my power shall be wanting, to afford a timely Aid to our Friends engaged in the Glorious Cause of Liberty, than which not any thing will contribute more to my Happiness. I have the Honor to be Sir Your Most Obdt. And Very Hbl. Servt.

JAS. MOORE

ALS, Papers of the Continental Congress, National Archives, Washington, D.C.

# WILLIAM GRAYSON TO WILLIAM HEATH

THE DEFEAT at Long Island made the American defense of New York City temporary at best. However, the lack of military order and discipline in the withdrawal northward to Harlem Heights, despite the efforts of generals Israel Putnam and George Washington, resulted in chaos and defeat when British men-of-war opened fire on American positions on Manhattan Island. William Grayson (1736–90), lieutenant colonel and an aide-de-camp to Washington, issued the following order, in his own name, for the execution of a soldier and the punishment of two officers. Though seemingly harsh, such measures were essential if the Continental army was to remain an effective fighting force.

These men were punished for their lack of courage and for disobeying official commands. It should be remembered, however, that others were also condemned by the British to die for their unswerving allegiance to the new nation. Nathan Hale, a captain in Lieutenant Colonel Thomas Knowlton's regiment, was executed on September 22, 1776, by the British for his espionage activities. Knowlton himself was killed at Harlem Heights on September 16.

*Head Quarters Heights of Harlem Octob. 1st. 1776*

Sir:

His Excy. has desired me to acquaint you that he approves of the Sentence, respecting the condemnation of James McCarmick, as also the sentences on Lieut. Thomas Younkerman of Colo. Hellers Regimt. and of Lieut. Oliver Mildebeyer of Capt. Leonards Company, Col. Lashers regiment;[1] With respect to James McCarmick, it will be necessary for you to appoint the place & time of execution and acquaint his Excy. therewith that he may have an oppertunity of putting it into general orders.

I have it further in command to acquaint you, that whenever any prisoners in your division are charged with capital offenses, that it will be adviseable to send them here for tryal; in other instances you are to proceed as heretofore; His Excy. having some matters to communicate to you, is desirous of seeing you here sometime to day. I am Sir yr. Most Obed. Servt.

WILLM. GRAYSON *ADC*

P.S. His Excy. upon considering farther on the subject of McCarmick, thinks it will be best to order him here for execution, you will therefore be pleased to have this done; You will please to [let] the prisoner know he is certainly to dye & direct that a clergyman may attend him.

W G

ALS, William Heath Papers, Massachusetts Historical Society, Boston.

[1] Colonel Henry Heller (1753–93) of Pennsylvania; First Lieutenant Oliver Mildeberger of the New York militia was cashiered September 1776; Colonel John Lasher (1724–1806) of the New York militia.

# JOHN LASHER TO WILLIAM HEATH

AFTER THE Battle of Harlem Heights, no new British offensive took place immediately. The movement of British troops on the East River in mid-October implied that they intended to encircle the American army. The main American force under General Washington moved into Westchester County to avoid this possibility. Despite the relative isolation of Fort Washington, the Continental Congress and the American generals believed that the river obstructions and the fortifications on the New Jersey shore would be sufficient to thwart a British thrust up the Hudson River. General Nathanael Greene was given full control of the river forts. Colonel John Lasher of the New York militia reports to General William Heath on the lack of men and ammunition at Fort Washington. An attack by the British on October 27 was beaten back by the Americans. Their stubborn defense of this isolated fortress continued until November 16, when Fort Washington fell to the British.

*Camp at Kings Bridge Octor. 26th. 1776*

May it please your Honour

As I was left Commanding Officer at this Post, I examined the Situation of the Fort with regard to Artillery-Men and Ammunition, and finding them very insufficient in case of an Attack properly to defend the same, I thought it would be proper to represent to you the State we are in. We have Six Artillery-Men, about 30 Rounds of Ammunition and the Fort in very bad Order.

It will also be proper to acquaint your Honour that [     ] of the six hundred that were ordered to remain I find by the Returns, there are not above four hundred and many of the Detachments have not ten Rounds a man, and as a Number of the Guards are at a Distance from the Fort, we have not above two hundred Men together, on the Day of Relief, to defend the same. The Enemy has drove off our Guard at Mile-Square and taken possession of the Stores. A large Body of light-Horse & light Infantry appeared on the Heights west of said place to day and we expect to have a Visit from them tomorrow.

I was desired by Coll. Magaw to take up one or both of the Bridges which I did not think prudent in case we should have to retreat,[1] I hope your Honor will give such Orders as you think proper in our Situation. I am your Honor's Most Obedient humble Servt.

JNO LASHER *Colln*

ALS, William Heath Papers, Massachusetts Historical Society, Boston.

[1] Colonel Robert Magaw (1738–90) of the Fifth Pennsylvania Battalion was captured on November 16, 1776, and not exchanged until October 25, 1780.

# TENCH TILGHMAN TO JAMES TILGHMAN

IN JULY 1776 Tench Tilghman (1744–86) was commissioned captain of an independent company that later became part of a Pennsylvania battalion of the Flying Camp. He is best remembered as George Washington's indefatigable and devoted aide-de-camp and military secretary. Captain Tilghman joined Washington on August 8, 1776, as his volunteer secretary. In this letter written almost three months later, he describes for his father, James Tilghman (1716–93), the Battle of White Plains, fought on October 28, 1776. The steadfast resistance of the American forces at Fort Lee and Fort Washington, on either side of the Hudson River, compelled British General Sir William Howe to flank Washington's army by landing near New Rochelle. By October 25, 1776, Howe had reached the vicinity of White Plains, and Washington dispatched his troops to stop the British advance. Howe's British and Hessian troops were able to capture Chatterton's Hill, on the Americans' right flank, but Washington's withdrawal to North Castle prevented destruction of the retreating American army.

*White Plains 31st October 1776*

Hond. Sir

As all Accounts of Actions are much exaggerated before they reach you, I always take the earliest Opportunity of informing you of the Truth and at the same time of letting you know that I am safe and well. On Monday morning we recd. Information that the Enemy were in Motion and in march towards our Lines, all our Men were immediately at their Alarm Posts and about 2000 detached to give the Enemy as much annoyance as possible on their Approach. There were likewise a few Regiments posted upon a Hill on our Right, of which we had not had time to throw up Works, which Hill commanded our Lines which were but slight and temporary ones. About Noon the Enemy appeared full in our Front in vast Numbers, their Light Horse reconnoitered our Lines, and I suppose not chusing to attack them, filed off towards the Hill, on which they began a most furious Cannonade, followed by a heavy Column of Infantry, our Troops made as good a Stand as could be expected and did not quit the Ground, till they came to push with their Bayonets. We lost about 100 killed and wounded. Smallwoods Regiment suffered most, he himself is wounded in the Hand and Hip but not badly.[1] Capt. Brace and Scott killed.[2] From all Accounts of Deserters and prisoners the English Army suffered more than we did, for as their Body was large, the Shot from our Field pieces and Musquets, could scarcely miss doing damage. Six of their Light Horse Men were killed and one of the Horses, a very fine one, taken by one of Miles's Officers and made a present to the General—Content with the possession of the Hill, they sat down about Six hundred yards from us and have never fired a Gun since. We have moved all our Tents and Baggage and Stores before their Faces, and have put them on the Heights just above the plain where they at first were. Every Motion of Genl. Howe since he first landed has evidently been to get in the Rear of this Army, and destroy them by cutting off their Communication for Supplies from the Country. To do this will be extremely difficult if not impracticable, all the Ground he has gained from the Sound Westward, is but about Six Miles and that thro' an open Country where we never thought of attacking them on Account of their great Train of Artillery. They have now just reached the Hills, which are very high and broken, and of Consequence their Motion must be very slow, as we have taken all the Passes. Their heavy Horse from England are all ruined on the passage, we took a Commissary last Night who informs us that 900 horse were embarked, they were on Board 26 weeks, 500 died on the Passage and 400 were landed yesterday reduced to Skeletons. This is a monstrous Disappointment to them—Much has been said of the Clemency of the British Army, at first landing they attempted to restrain the Soldiery, at least from hurting what were deemed Tories, but the Hessians would not be restrained, they made no Distinction and Genl. Howe dare not punish them. The British Troops seeing the Foreigners rioting in plenty and plundering all before them, grew restless and uneasy, and are now indulged in the same Excesses. The people who, tho' informed against as Tories, were protected by Genl. Washington and paid for what they would sell, have come in and informed us that they were stripped of all whenever the Enemy advanced upon them. The Foreigners who have been taken, all agree that a Liberty of plunder without Distinction is what they expect and insist upon. New York was set on fire by a Party of them who robbed a Rum Store and set the Fire agoing in their Liquor.[3] After this, which is strictly true, can they ask the Americans to lay down their Arms, before such a licentious Crew are removed? We are on Horseback or busy from Sun Rise to Sun Set, and all the time I find to write is at Night. I met with an Accident at Harlem Heights which I look upon as irreparable, I mean the loss of my faithful saddle Horse, who died in a few Hours, from every Appearance in high Order and Spirit. I had rode him gently most of the day and never observed him fail, but about two Miles from Head Quarters. I suppose it must have been Bots. I have mounted myself upon a pretty Mare, that will make an excellent Breeder, if I get her home safe. My best love to Grandmother and Sisters and all my Friends, I would write oftener to them and to you, but as I said before I have not time. I am with the greatest affection Yr. most dutiful son

TENCH TILGHMAN

*Memoir of Lieut. Col. Tench Tilghman, Secretary and Aid to Washington* (Albany, 1876), pp. 145–47.

[1] American losses were 25 killed and 125 wounded, while British casualties were over 300 killed and wounded.

[2] Captain Bennett Bracco and Captain John Day Scott, both of the Maryland Regiment.

[3] The New York City fire of September 20–21, 1776, destroyed 493 houses. The British accused the Americans of setting the fire, but rumors to the contrary abounded.

# ISAAC VAN HORNE MEMOIRS

*August 1776–May 1778*

ISAAC VAN HORNE (1754–1834) enlisted on January 8, 1776, as an ensign in Captain John Beatty's company of the Fifth Pennsylvania Battalion. Stationed at Fort Washington in the northern part of Manhattan Island, Van Horne's regiment was called on to cover the American retreat after the Battle of Long Island on August 27, 1776. The steady British advance forced Washington's army to retreat up the Hudson River, cutting off the American garrison at Fort Washington. The garrison, commanded by Colonel Robert Magaw of the Fifth Pennsylvania Battalion, lacked the supplies and fortifications necessary to withstand the attack launched by General Sir William Howe on the morning of November 16, 1776. By afternoon, the British and Hessians had left the weary garrison no recourse but surrender. Fifty-four Americans lay dead, and 2,858 were captured. Among them was Isaac Van Horne, who spent the next two years in prison, first in the Sugar House in New York City and later on Long Island. Van Horne was exchanged in May 1778, and several months later he was commissioned a first lieutenant in Colonel Josiah

**Isaac Van Horne**

Harmar's Sixth Pennsylvania Regiment, rising to captain by the war's end.

At this time the British fleet lay at the Staten Island shore, and the army on the island in full view. The battle of Long Island was fought in August, whilst we were at Fort Washington. The next day after we were ordered to Long Island, and, being fresh troops, covered the retreat over to New York. A few days after I was left dangerously ill of fever in the city. In a few weeks I was so far recovered as to take passage in a vessel to the fort. Sometime after the enemy got possession of New York, Lord Perry came out against us one Sunday morning.[1] The day was spent in skirmishing, with but little loss on either side, and next morning the enemy had made good his retreat to New York. November 16th following, General Howe with the main body of his army, had already taken possession of Kingsbridge above us; another body from New York and the Highlanders having crossed the Bronx, hemmed us completely in, and in the afternoon a surrender of about twenty-two hundred was effected, and we became prisoners of war.

Our capitulation engaged to us our lives, baggage and side arms, but as soon as the enemy took possession of the fort the abuse and plunder commenced; side arms, watches, shoe-buckles, and even the clothes on our backs were wrested from us; very few, if any, of the officers but were stripped of their hats. In the evening we were marched to Haerlem, strictly guarded, and threatened hanging as rebels. From there we were marched to New York, where, after some delay, the officers were quartered in houses deserted by the inhabitants and given their parole of the city; but the soldiers were thrust into Bridwell's sugar houses, &c., where they suffered almost every privation, and soon became diseased and died off so fast as to induce the commanding General to send out the remainder to be exchanged for prisoners we had or might take of them; a great portion of them, however, died on the way home, or after they got home. It must be observed, however, that a great number enlisted with the enemy to save life, while suffering in close confinement and from starvation.

The officers were finally removed to Long Island and billeted on the inhabitants. In the winter of 1777–8 the sound being frozen over and the enemy's lines much circumscribed, they were under apprehension that detachments from the American army might pass over the East River and rescue us; hence, we were shipped on board transports in the Bay of New York, and detained there about six weeks, where we suffered much excessive cold.

In May 1778, about sixty officers of different ranks were exchanged, among which I was one. Soon after I got home I repaired to Valley Forge (headquarters), but the regiment was filled up with officers, and I returned to Bucks, leaving my baggage in camp. The enemy sometime after evacuated Philadelphia, our army broke up in pursuit, and my baggage was lost in the hurry.

Printed in Sidney Methiot Culbertson, *The Ohio Valley Saffords* (Denver, Colo., 1932), pp. 94–95.

[1] General Hugh Percy (1742–1817) of the British army.

# John Lamb to the Continental Congress

## *November 25, 1776*

John Lamb was commissioned captain of the Independent Company of New York Artillery on July 30, 1775. Captured at Quebec on December 31, 1775, Captain Lamb was soon paroled by the British. Although he was named adjutant general and commandant of artillery for the Northern Department on January 9, 1776, the terms of parole precluded Lamb's return to active military service. Nine months later he was still on parole, forbidden by a code of honor to fight until exchanged for some British officer. He petitioned the Continental Congress to complete an exchange with the British so that he might join Washington's army. The Continental Congress ordered his exchange on January 2, 1777, and Lamb received a colonel's commission in the Second Continental Artillery Battalion at that time. Lamb's experience illustrates the earnest desire of many patriots to fight for their country.

To the Honourable Congress of the United States of America.
Gentlemen,

Altho' the Enemy have, contrary to my expectations, liberated me from the dreary Horrours of a Prison, and suffered me to return to my Family and Friends, I am still subject to their power and Controul, liable to be called upon by them to surrender myself a Prisoner whenever they please; and restrained by the sacred Ties of Honor, from drawing my Sword again in defence of my Country, till exchanged for some Officer of theirs. Extremely anxious to be relieved from this truly painful and disagreeable Situation, I waited on General Washington, immediately after my Arrival from Quebec, earnestly soliciting his Interest with your Honours for that Purpose; but as I have not yet heard that such an Event has taken place, owing I imagine to the critical Situation of the two Armies, I take the Liberty to address your Honours on that Subject, humbly requesting, that I may be included in the next Exchange of Prisoners. And as I have unfortunately been prevented by the Fate of War, from taking up Arms again, this Campaign, in support of the Freedom, and Independence of the American States, and being conscious of having done no more than my Duty, in my former Exertions for the public Good, I can have no Claim to your Honours particular Attention: Yet as I have been formerly honoured with your Approbation of my Conduct, and a singular Mark of your Confidence, by an Appointment to the Chief Command of the Artillery in the Northern Department, I flatter myself that I have not been neglected by your Honours in the New Arrangement of the Corps of Artillery. I have the Honour to be, with every Sentiment of Gratitude, Duty, and Respect Gentlemen Your most obedient and very humble Servant

ALS, Lamb Papers, New-York Historical Society, New York City.

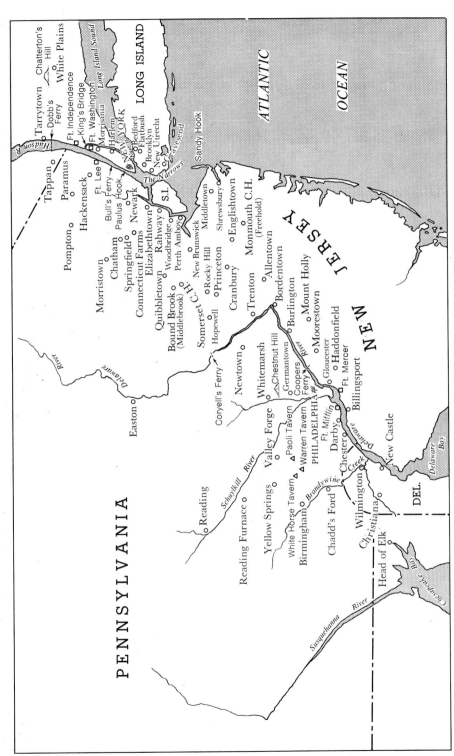

NEW JERSEY AND PENNSYLVANIA

# ROBERT BEALE MEMOIRS

*December 25, 1776–January 3, 1777*

THE SURRENDER of Fort Washington was quickly followed on November 20, 1776, by the fall of Fort Lee. This precipitated the retreat of Washington's army through Hackensack, Newark, New Brunswick, Princeton, and Trenton, crossing the Delaware River to Pennsylvania. This long and humiliating retreat ended when Washington launched a bold offensive on December 25, 1776. After crossing the Delaware River on a bitter cold Christmas night, Washington's troops made a surprise attack on Colonel Johann Rall's Hessians garrisoned at Trenton, New Jersey. In the encounter 106 of the 1,200 Hessians were killed and 918 made prisoners of war. The victorious Continental army dodged Lord Charles Cornwallis' (1738–1805) advancing army on January 2, 1777, and a day later struck quickly and decisively at Princeton, New Jersey. The Americans, suffering 43 casualties, compared to approximately 86 for the British during the fifteen-minute battle, moved on toward their winter quarters at Morristown, New Jersey. The war memoirs of Robert Beale (1759–1843), then an ensign in Colonel Charles Scott's (1733–1813) Fifth Virginia Regiment, include a description of these events. The account, while lacking contempo-

**Robert Beale**
COURTESY OF KATHERINE TYLER ELLETT

rary authenticity, does not unduly suffer from factual distortion. It is a picturesque memoir of the "ten crucial days" of American freedom.

On the twenty-fifth day of December, Christmas Day, I was ordered on a detachment commanded by Captain Wales, to cross the river and show ourselves to the Hessian picket at Trenton. As soon as we had crossed the river, Captain Wales gave me command of twelve men to lead on in advance. I did so, and showed ourselves to the Hessian picket, who fired upon us. We immediately retreated with all speed.

When we reached the river that part of the army immediately under the command of General Washington was coming over. The scouts were composed of men from different regiments and we were ordered to join our respective regiments as they came across. I joined my regiment, the platoons were all commanded, and I became a supernumerary with Captain Fauntleroy.[1] Not one mouthful entered my mouth this day.

It soon became very tempestuous, rain, hail, and snow, but we marched all night and I think somewhere about sunrise, we reached Trenton. The inclemency of the weather had thrown the enemy entirely off their guard. They made but feeble resistance. It was said there were about nine hundred men taken captive. Captain William Washington, afterwards the colonel, led on the advance with Mr. Monroe, the late president, who was only a lieutenant at that time.[2] As soon as the enemy surrendered there was a guard placed over them and they were marched to the river. The balance of our men fell into the utmost confusion, every man shifting for himself. After I had gotten pretty well refreshed with good old Jamaica and excellent beef and biscuits, I asked Captain Fauntleroy and our adjutant, by name, Kelly, to go to the stable and get us a horse apiece. We did so and all mounted, but it was much colder on horseback than on foot, so seeing Colonel Lawson of the Sixth Regiment in the street, asked him what would become of the property taken here.[3] He told us it was for the general good and not individual advantage, upon which I dismounted and set my horse loose.

It was but a few days afterwards that we re-crossed the river and took possession of Trenton. After a few days stay in Trenton our brigade, composed of the Fourth, Fifth and Sixth Virginia Regiments, were ordered to Maiden-head, about half way between Trenton and Princeton. We were then commanded by Colonel Charles Scott, for General Stephens had left us.[4] We lay there three days and nights with nothing but the canopy of Heaven and our blankets to cover us. On the morning of the fourth day, I think the first day of January 1777, we discovered the enemy moving upon us. It was a fine clear day, not a solitary cloud in the atmosphere. We could see the glittering of their guns as they marched in column. We were ordered to retreat before them until we reached the heights of Trenton, there to form and give them battle. There was to our left, a regiment of men, about six hundred, called the German Regiment. Just as the enemy appeared in column this regiment ran away and there was nothing left then but our brigade, not more than two hundred and fifty men, to give them battle. Scott said we must fight them at all events and just as the enemy had displayed their columns and was approaching in order of battle, there rode up one of Washington's aids and directed Scott to bring the men off. A prodigiously clever fellow, by the name of Forsyth, no doubt the father of the present Secretary of State, was major of the brigade.[5] He in a very audible and distinct voice, ordered to the right about face on and off in order. We had not taken more than regular steps until the word "Shift for yourselves, boys, get over the bridge as quick as you can." There was running, followed by a tremendous fire from the British. There were but few lives lost in getting to the bridge. A Mr. Livingston, a very clever young man, who had but a few days before been made an ensign by Colonel Parker, carried the colors.[6] He was shot down in the street with his thigh broken, but the colors were brought off.

This was a most awful crisis. No possible chance of crossing the river; ice as large as houses floating down, and no retreat to the mountains, the British between us and them. Our brigade, consisting of the Fourth, Fifth, and Sixth Virginia Regiments, was ordered to form in column at the bridge and General Washington came and in the presence of us all, told Colonel Scott to defend the bridge to the last extremity. Colonel Scott answered with an oath, "Yes, General, as long as there is a man alive."

The sun was at this time about two hours high and if the British had attacked us that evening the war would have ended—but the finger of providence, not only throughout the war, but particularly at this momentous crisis, confounded the counsels of the enemy, so that they postponed the attack until the next day. Every endeavor was made to convince the enemy we occupied our ground by making an immense number of fires and throwing before first one and then the other to make them believe we were very numerous. But about twelve o'clock, when everything was lulled into the most profound silence, we were ordered to move with all the secrecy and stillness imaginable and by a little after sunrise the next morning we were at Princeton opposed only by about five hundred of the British. The enemy had formed themselves into two different positions about one quarter of a mile apart—the party that was under the immediate command of General Washington, led on by the brave and noble Mercer, marched against one position, the other party of the British were drawn up nearly opposite the College—to them we were opposed—the Fourth, Fifth, and Sixth Virginia Regiments commanded by Colonel Charles Scott to be supported by the Jersey militia. A severe firing of musketry commenced on our left clearly in sight, when we saw our men run. They were rallied and brought to the charge and we saw them run a second time. The Jersey militia had not come up, but Colonel Scott observed— "Boys there are two hundred and fifty Red Coats on yonder hill and about two hundred and fifty of us. We can beat them. Huzza, come on" and down the hill we went, but when we got to the top of the hill there was not one man to be seen. A small Battery stood to our left and the College to the right. 'Twas said, "They are in the Battery," then up to the Battery we went and no one was there. Then they were in the College, but when we passed the College we looked down the hill and saw them running in confusion. We broke directly and every man ran with all speed in pursuit. Lieutenant Eggleston, Ensign Smith and myself out-ran all and came up with a party that had halted and formed near a wood as if to make battle, but seeing us followed by all our men they grounded their arms and surrendered. There were seven officers and thirty men. We marched up to the main street where the other prisoners were collected. They were put immediately under guard and marched off and were directly followed by us, for the British by this time were nearly on our rear—some of a party who had lain for three nights at Maiden-head with but little sleep, marching all night the fourth. We escaped the enemy by taking the road that led to Morristown. There were about two hundred and sixty of the British taken, for I was on their guard until we got to Morristown. In this action at Princeton the gallant Mercer fell—upon the second charge. 'Twas said in the second retreat his horse was killed under him, and he, unable to extricate himself, they pushed forward and unfettered him. The third charge was made by Washington in person, who carried the men to charge bayonet. This was done while we were marching down the hill and the party that we were opposed to, seeing that, ran without firing a gun.

"Revolutionary Experiences of Major Robert Beale," *Northern Neck of Virginia Historical Magazine* (December 1956), 6:500–6.

[1] Captain Henry Fauntleroy of the Fifth Virginia Regiment.
[2] Captain William Augustine Washington (1757–1810) of the Third Virginia Regiment; First Lieutenant James Monroe (1758–1831) of the Third Virginia Regiment.
[3] Lieutenant Colonel Robert Lawson (1748–1805) of the Fourth Virginia Regiment.
[4] Brigadier General Adam Stephen (1722–91) of the Continental army.
[5] Probably Adjutant Robert Forsyth.
[6] Ensign Robert James Livingston; Lieutenant Colonel Josiah Parker (1751–1810) of the Fifth Virginia Regiment.

# John Polhemus Memoirs

## December 26, 1776–January 1777

CAPTAIN JOHN POLHEMUS (1738–1831), of Hopewell, New Jersey, served in the First New Jersey Regiment under colonels Silas Newcomb and Matthias Ogden and was among the 2,400 American troops that crossed the Delaware River on Christmas night 1776. His memoirs, an oral narrative to his grandson, describe the aftermath of Trenton, the Battle of Princeton, and skirmishes between the two armies in the Raritan Valley in January 1777. During the winter encampment at Morristown there were violent clashes between units of both armies.

**John Polhemus**
COURTESY OF
THE HISTORICAL SOCIETY OF PENNSYLVANIA,
PHILADELPHIA

We whipped them terribly & took a thousand Hessians prisoners driving them into the Newtown Jail[1] & yard like a pack of sheep during a severe hail storm. . . . On the 3rd of January 1777 we attacked them at Princeton & drove them to New Brunswick. I was left behind with a rear guard to secure stores and bury the dead, which we did by hauling them in sleds to great holes and heaping them in. I was then relieved by Colonel Chamberlain & his regiment.[2] I had then the opportunity of securing my house and mill at Rocky Hill. Our regement passed on the left side of the Mill stone river where our mill stood, the British passing before us on the other side. One night they lay near the Ten-mile Run & not More than three Miles distant.

In the morning they sent a Company of Dragoons to burn the Mill & cut down the bridge, but as they hove in sight a large company of militia came down the hill, with a field piece and opened on them. They scampered like a drove of oxen luckily for us too, for at that time we had 400 bushels of wheat and large quantities of flour on hand. The Mill belonged to my father-in-law John Hart and myself. He was then a member of the Continental Congress. Going to the mill I found at least 50 of the British which Morgans Rifles had killed, belonging to the 55th British regiment. We buried them and going to the house I found a British Seargent in my bed with a part of his face shot off. Also a number of sick and wounded soldiers. As there was no way by which we could take them with us. I swore every man of them not to take up Arms against the Independence of America, unless exchanged according to the rules of War and left them.

Typescript copy, Leach Collection, Genealogical Society of Pennsylvania, Philadelphia.
[1] Sussex County, N.J.
[2] Possibly Colonel William Chamberlain of the New Jersey militia.

# SAMUEL HOLDEN PARSONS TO THOMAS PARSONS

SAMUEL HOLDEN PARSONS (1737–89) began his long and dedicated Revolutionary War career in April 1775 as a colonel at the Battle of Lexington. After participating in the siege of Boston as commander of the Tenth Continental Infantry, Colonel Parsons accompanied reinforcements sent to New York, where on August 9, 1776, he was promoted to brigadier general. Several months later he wrote this touching letter to his nine-year-old son, Thomas. Parsons' patriotism inspired him to invest much money in Continental securities. Unfortunately it was later greatly reduced by currency depreciation. Throughout the war Parsons held a series of responsible troop commands in the Hudson Highlands and along the Connecticut coast. On October 23, 1780, he was rewarded with a commission as major general.

*December 27th, 1776*

Dear Thomas:

I have sent two Soldiers Home to live at your House. One understands French, the other Painting; you may learn something by them. I wish you to remember your Books, be virtuous & manly in your Behavior, a Comfort to your Mother & Family. Leave off all childish Follies & learn to behave with decency & manly Fortitude. Lay aside that Bashful Conduct. A Modest Behavior, with Resolution & Courage will endear you to all your acquaintances. Falsehood & Lies you must always abhor & detest. Billy will be at home next week. When I shall come Home I can't tell—but remember if I fall in this War, I shall expect you & all my Sons to Arm in defence of the glorious cause of Liberty & lay down your Lives in defence of your Country & to avenge my Death if necessary. Yrs. &c.,

S. H. PARSONS

Printed in *American Monthly Magazine* (January–June 1893), 2:300.

# ADAM HUBLEY, JR., TO AN UNKNOWN PERSON

HESSIANS WERE garrisoned across New Jersey at Bordentown, Burlington, Mount Holly, Princeton, and Trenton in December 1776. On December 27, 1776, Colonel John Cadwalader (1742–86) crossed the Delaware River with 2,000 Continental soldiers and Pennsylvania militiamen. Unable to make a diversionary crossing two days earlier to prevent Hessian Colonel Carl von Donop's (c.1740–77) forces from relieving the besieged Hessian garrison at Trenton, Colonel Cadwalader's brigade easily occupied Burlington on December 27. Three days later they captured Bordentown, six miles south of Trenton, after its Hessian garrison withdrew in panic. On December 31, Brigadier General Thomas Mifflin sent majors Adam Hubley, Jr. (1752–98), and Jonathan Mifflin (1753–1840) from Bordentown with 200 men to harass and capture Loyalists in the area of Middletown Township and Monmouth Courthouse (now Freehold), New Jersey. Major Hubley, of Colonel Joseph Penrose's (1737–1824) Tenth Pennsylvania Regiment, writing to an unidentified Pennsylvania official describes the results of the January 1777 skirmishes in Monmouth County. In nine days the Continental army drove General Sir William Howe's troops from all outposts in New Jersey except Perth Amboy and New Brunswick.

*Bordentown January 4th. 1777*

I am just arrived with Major Mifflin from an expedition in the lower parts of the Jerseys, a place called Monmouth Court House. We arrived there Thursday evening, we were informed of a party of Men consisting of about 200 under the Command of Col. Morris,[1] we there had our party (120 in Number) formed in proper order and intended to attack them in Town, about half an Hour before night Col. Morris it seems got acct. of our Arrival, had his men drawn up and Baggage loaded in order to move off for Middletown about 18 Miles below the Court House, they pushed of from Town and got off about half a Mile within Sight of us, we immediately pushed after them when they made a Halt, we came up about a Qr. of an Hour before Night when we engaged them, they stood us about 8 minutes a very heavy fire was kept up on both sides during that time, the enemy at last gave way and retreated very precipitately—at this time it was quite dark, & we could not see what loss the Enemy sustained—on our side we had none killed—we marched from the field to the Town and lodged there that Night, the next morning we sent a party out to the field we had engaged in, they brought 4 dead Bodies in which we buried. We took during the engagement 23 Prisoners which we brought to this place—we also took from the Enemy 7 Waggon loads of Stores &c. & 12 Horses. I shall set off for Burlington this day to meet Col. Penrose who commands there.

Various will be the Accots. of the Movements of ourselves. This you may depend on is as nearly the State of it as Possible, after our people engaged the Brittish Troops at Trenton—after a severe engagement we retreated from Trenton and took round toward Princetown. This retreat was ordered on purpose, which has proved since to be good Generalship, where our people took between 5 & 600 Prisoners, they had a severe engagement there, and made the English army retreat very precipitately they have taken all there Stores &ca. to a very great amount our Army has now removed from thence to Brunswick where the English have a great store of every thing which before now is in our hands, General How with his main body is now between us, and in all probability must fall in our hands, the Enemy had a vast number Killed at Princetown, our Philadelphia Association behaved like brave soldiers on this Occasion,[2] they fought the enemy for some Considerable time regular in Platoon Fires & repeated them twice. I think I shall have the pleasure of giving you a very good account of our Enemy in a few Days. A Number of our Philada. Association fell on this occasion. I am etca.

ADAM HUBLEY JR.

ALS, Papers of the Continental Congress, National Archives, Washington, D.C.

[1] Colonel John Morris was a New Jersey Loyalist.
[2] Militia units from Philadelphia and vicinity.

# JONATHAN POTTS TO AN UNKNOWN PERSON

DR. JONATHAN POTTS (1745–81) entered Continental service on June 6, 1776, as surgeon for the troops on the Canadian expedition. Writing to a friend, Dr. Potts reports the brutal deaths and injuries of the Battle of Princeton. On January 3, 1777, fewer than 700 American troops under generals Washington, Mercer, and Sullivan attacked Lieutenant Colonel Charles Mawhood's British garrison in and around Princeton, New Jersey. A tragic loss for the patriots' cause was Brigadier General Hugh Mercer, who died on January 12 of mortal wounds and brutal treatment by the British.

62

The brutality of the Hessian and British soldiers in this battle prompted an investigation by the Continental Congress. Dr. Potts became deputy director general of hospitals in the Northern Department in 1777 and deputy director general of the Middle Department in 1778.

*January 5th. 1777*

My Dear Friend

Tho' the Account I send is a Melancholy one (in one respect) yet I have sent an express to give you the best information I can collect. Our Mutual Friend Anthony Morris died here in Three Hours after he recieved his Wounds on Friday Morning,[1] they were three in Number, one on the Chin, one on the Knee and the third and fatal one on the right Temple by a Grape Shot,—brave Man he fought and died Nobly, deserving a much better fate.

General Mercer is dangerously ill indeed, I have scarce any hopes of him, the Villians have stabed him in five different places. The Dead on our side at this place amount to Sixteen, that of the Enemy to Twenty three they have retreated to Brunswick with the greatest precipitation and from Accounts just come from the Hero Washington is not far from them, they have never been so shamefully Drubed and out generaled in every respect. I hourly expect to hear of their whole Army being cut to peices or made prisoners.

It pains me to inform you that the Morning of the Action I was obliged to Fly before the Rascals or fall into their Hands & leave behind me my wounded brethren— would you believe that the unhuman Monsters robed the General as he lay unable to resist on the Bed, even to taking his cravat from his Neck, insulting him all the time. The Number of Prisoners we have taken cannot yet find out, but they are Numerous. I am in haste Your most obedient Humble Servt.

*Sign'd.* JONN. POTTS

Dated at the Field of Action near Princeton Sunday Evening January 5th. 1777

Contemporary copy, Papers of the Continental Congress, National Archives, Washington, D.C.
[1] Ensign Anthony Morris, Jr. (d. 1777), of the Pennsylvania Associators.

# LAMBERT CADWALADER TO PEGGY MEREDITH

THE AMERICAN ARMY'S withdrawal from New York City and precipitous retreat across New Jersey to temporary safety on the Pennsylvania side of the Delaware River were dismal events for the patriots of the new nation. With British forces occupying New York City and New Jersey and threatening Philadelphia, American prospects seemed bleak as winter began. The climate of despair was dispelled by George Washington's attack on the morning of December 26, 1776, at Trenton. More importantly, the engagement was a major psychological victory. Lambert Cadwalader (1742–1823), a colonel in the Fourth Pennsylvania Regiment who had been taken prisoner with the capture of Fort Washington on November 16, 1776, reflects in this letter to Mrs. Peggy Meredith, of Chester County, Pennsylvania, the newly restored, though fragile, confidence in the American side. His description of the anxiety and fear of Mrs. John Nixon, whose husband was a colonel in the Pennsylvania Associators, is a valid portrayal of the ambivalence of the

**Lambert Cadwalader**

worried, yet hopeful, patriots in the winter of 1776–77.

*Philad 7 Jany 1777*

My dear Peggy

I had the Pleasure of yours yesterday Evening without a Date and am glad to hear you are all well. I had a Letter last Night by Phil[1] from Maryland. They are all in good Health at Shrewsbury. Phil has been there twice within these ten Days having paid a Visit to his Brother[2] who is in Kent County. Our little victorious army under G. Washington after having performed that signal Service at Trenton wh you have heard retd. to this Side of the River having rec'd. Intelligence of Johnny's crossing near Bristol[3] the Genl. ret'd again to Trenton & was there joind by Johnny's & Mifflin's Brigades at that place. G. Washington havg recd. Intelligence that the Enemy were marching towards him from Trenton sent off about 700 Men to meet them & endeavors to drive them back but the Enemy proving too numerous our Division retired to Trenton and over the Bridge to the Mill-Hill where the Genl. in the mean Time had posted our Troops. The Enemy took Possession of Trenton and the Genl. keeping up his Fires decamp'd suddenly in the Night & taking his Rout by a back Road got into the Princetown Road & pursued his march towards that place. On his way thither he met with a

Body of British Troops which soon gave Way—he then advanced to Princetown & took a considerable Number of Prisoners. Our loss is Genl. Mercer wounded Col. Hazlet killed[4] & a Capt. of [Marines] with a few Privates. The Genl. then marchd off for Somerset Court House wch is 8 Miles out of the Road to Brunswick in order to join Genl. Heath's army from N England & there is a Report that this has been effected & that our Army is gone forward to Brunsk. Genl. Howe cannot raise a large Force anywhere to make Head against us—so that we expect very great Events in our Town. Our army in the Jersey all together must amount to near 12,000. I forgot to tell you we have taken 5 brass Cannon more in the last affair. I'm in great Hope the Jerseys will be cleared of the Enemy entirely.

I went to see Mrs. Nixon yesterday afternoon and such an object of Distress I scarcely ever beheld—her Fears have made a perfect Conquest over her Reason & she trembles like an aspen Leaf whenever a person enters her House. I think it is one of the greatest Misfortunes that can befall any Person to indulge imaginary Fears & apprehensions & like the [      ] self-Tormentor in Terence he ever [      ] raising up unnecessary Terrors to make oneself miserable & unhappy. Whoever expects to find this World a fairy Tayle of [Pleasure] & Peace of Mind must be really very unknowing in the Science of human Nature and the affairs of human life. Fortitude of Mind must be exer[cised] in order to procure a tolerable share of Happiness & I sincerely pity the Weak[ness] of those who do not so far make Use of their Reason as not to be totally subdued by their Fears & apprehensions. You will hear a thousand Rumors & Reports wh if you give the least Credit to you will be laying up a constant Store of Uneasiness and Disquiet. Depend upon it if anything extraordinary happens I will [      ] be the Messenger-credit no [      ] News of any kind—

L[      ]

ALS, Cadwalader Papers, Historical Society of Pennsylvania, Philadelphia.

[1] Brigadier General Philemon Dickinson (1739–1809) of the New Jersey militia.
[2] John Dickinson.
[3] Colonel John Cadwalader of the Pennsylvania militia and Lambert's brother.
[4] Colonel John Haslet (c.1738–77) of Delaware.

# DAVID WOOSTER TO JONATHAN TRUMBULL

NOT ALL of the American army participated in the victories at Trenton and Princeton. A northern army commanded by General William Heath remained above New York City. The decision was made to probe the British defenses to divert troops from New Jersey. Heath's vacillation in the attack on Fort Independence, near King's Bridge, was a dark cloud on an otherwise brightening military horizon. The siege from January 17–25, 1777, ended in failure. Premonitions of this defeat are evident in this letter of Brigadier General David Wooster of Connecticut, to Governor Jonathan Trumbull. The stress of command and responsibility for failure plagued the Continental officer throughout the war. Ambition and personal rivalries stymied efforts for victory. The patriotic soldier found second guessing impossible to deal with. Wooster paid the ultimate price for his courage when he and Lieutenant Colonel Abraham Gould (1733–77) died during a British raid at Ridgefield and Danbury, Connecticut, on April 27, 1777.

*Saw Pits 9th: Janry: 1777*

Sir

I beg leave to Congratulate your Honour on the Success of the State's Army in the Jerseys, I this moment Recev'd a Letter from Genl. Lincoln at the Peeskills,[1] a Copy of which I enclose and also a Copy of my Letter to him, being inform'd that Genl: Heath was gone into the Jerseys. By the letter your Honr. Will Se that I had form'd an expedition to New York, and by the former you will se that Genl. Heath expects to take the Command here in a few days, and in that Case I must beg leave to return home as it is intirely inconsistant with honour and Justice for me to serve under a man Whose business of life has been on the [Shop]-board and never servd in the Army till this War and thus my Plans formed against New York is intirely Frustrated, and it is not a little Surprizing to me that Genl. Heath should expect the Connecticut Militia to Rendezvous at the Peeskills and leave all the Western Part of Connecticut to the Ravage and Rapine of a worse than savage Enimy, which must have been the Case had it not been prevented by the Small Number of men stationed at this Post. I must acquaint yr. Honr. that the reason why I formd a Design against N. York at this present time, is from the Certain intelligence that I have of the British Troops being almost all ordered into the Jerseys so that they have not more than fifteen hundred men to defend that City, there fore now is the time yea the very time to give them a fatal Stroke, their Ships all haul'd into the Dockes and unrigd so that they cannot be any annoyence to us. But I am sorry to tell your that only about one hundred & fifty of the New Levies are yet arrivd and not one Field officer. Lieut. Col. Canfield is not yet gone home.[2]

I understand that some Gentm. whome I have had to command especially Colo. Cook have theatned and attemptd to prejudise the public & Genl. Assembly against me.[3] If that is the Case reason & justice intitles me to be heard in my own defence. I am, with the Greatest Respect, your honors, most obt. humble Servt.

D. W.

ALS, Jonathan Trumbull, Sr., Papers, Connecticut Historical Society, Hartford.

[1] Brigadier General Benjamin Lincoln (1733–1810).

[2] Lieutenant Colonel Samuel Canfield (1726–99) of the Connecticut militia.

[3] Colonel Joseph Platte Cooke (1729–1816) of Connecticut militia.

# John Cropper, Jr., to Peggy Cropper

THAT THE AMERICAN victories at Trenton and Princeton helped bolster a deteriorating American morale is evident in this letter from Major John Cropper, Jr. (1755–1821), of the Seventh Virginia Regiment, to his wife. Cropper was writing from Philadelphia, which was to be General Sir William Howe's principal objective in 1777. Cropper's regiment stayed in Philadelphia only temporarily and soon joined Washington's army at its winter encampment in Morristown, New Jersey.

*Philada. January 12th 1777*

Dear Peggy,

This Day I am leaving Philadelphia with the Regiment to go to Camp. Last Night we heard the Kings seventh Regiment was intirly taken. To Day we hear that by a Major who comes from Camp that there has been a great Battle in the Jersys & that Howe's Army is half taken Prisoners & kill'd. Soldiers are flocking from every part which I hope will put an End to the War this Winter if our People behave as well as they have. Within three Weeks 2000 Hessians & Englishmen have been brought to this City. Inclosed I send you a Saturdays paper. . . . Write by the first Opportunity direct your Letters to be left at the Conestogoe Waggon in Philada. & I shall get them.[1] I expect to be home in about 3 Months. . . . Our Soldiers are all dress'd in Regimentals at the Expense of the Continent & have rec'd all their Wages. God bless you & my brothers. I am your most Affectionate Husband where ever I goe.

JOHN CROPPER

ALS, Garnet Papers, Virginia Historical Society, Richmond.
[1] Wagons were manufactured from about 1750 in Conestoga Township, Lancaster County, Pa.

# Robert Troup Affidavit

BY ENTERING Revolutionary service, Americans faced the specter of harsh treatment as prisoners of war. Evidence of the severity of British imprisonment is provided in this affidavit sworn by Lieutenant Robert Troup (1756–1832) of Colonel John Lasher's New York militia regiment. Troup, testifying before the Convention of the State of New York concerning the conduct of British officers and troops toward American prisoners of war, stated that he, Second Lieutenant Edward Dunscomb (1754–1814) of his unit, and three other soldiers were captured at the Battle of Long Island on August 27

1776. They suffered threats, filth, misery, and privation during their imprisonment in Brooklyn and New York City. Lieutenant

Troup was exchanged on December 9, 1776, and became an aide-de-camp to Major General Horatio Gates two months later.

*17th Jany. 1777*

Affidavit of Lieut. Robert Troup, made before Gouverneur Morris[1] who was ordered by the Convention of the State of New York, to prepare a narrative of the conduct of British officers and troops towards the American prisoners, etc., and to collect affidavits for that purpose.

Dutchess County, ss:—Robert Troup, Esquire, late lieutenant in Colo. Lasher's battalion of militia, being duly sworn upon the Holy Evangelists of Almighty God, deposeth and saith, that he, this deponent, about three o'clock in the morning of the twenty-seventh day of August last, was made a prisoner of war on Long Island, by a detachment of the British troops; that deponent, together with Lieutenant Dunscombe, Adjutant Hooglandt[2] and two volunteers, were carried immediately to the main body of the British army, and interrogated by the generals of the same; that they were there threatened with being hung for entering into the American service; that from thence they were led to a house near Flat Bush; that several of the British officers came there, by whom they were grossly insulted; that about nine o'clock in the morning they were led in the rear of the army to Bedford; that while there, deponent, with seventeen other officers who had been made prisoners that morning, were confined under the provost guard, in a small soldiers' tent; in which, they were left two nights and near three days; that it rained very hard during the greater part of the time, and the prisoners were obliged by turns to go out of the tent, there not being sufficient room for them to stay within it; that about sixty private soldiers were also kept prisoners at the same place, having also one tent, and only one, to shelter them from the weather; that while deponent was confined at Bedford, he, together with the officers with him, were much abused and treated with the grossest language by almost all the British officers, and in their presence by the British soldiers; that the provost marshall, one Cunningham,[3] brought with him a negro with a halter, telling them the negro had already hung several, and that he imagined he would hang some more, and that the negro and Cunningham also insulted the prisoners shewing them the halter, and in like manner with the British officers and soldiers, calling them rebels, scoundrels, villains, robbers, murderers, and so forth; that from Bedford the deponent and the other prisoners were led to Flat Bush, where they were confined a week in the house of Mr. Lefferts, and kept upon a very short allowance of biscuit and salt pork; that several of the Hessian soldiers while they were confined at Flat Bush, took pity upon their situation and gave them some apples, and at one time some fresh beef, which much relieved them; that from Flat Bush, deponent, with between seventy and eighty officers who were prisoners there, were put on board a small snow lying between Gravesend and the Hook, which had been employed in bringing cattle from England; that they were kept on board the said snow six weeks, and obliged to lay upon the dung and filth of the cattle without any bedding or blankets; that during their stay in the said snow, observing an old main sail which lay on the quarter deck, the prisoners begged the captain to permit them to take it into the hold and lie upon it, which request was refused with much opprobrious language, the captian damning them for a pack of rebels; and telling them the hold was good enough for such scoundrels; that while on board the said snow they were much afflicted with lice and other vermin: that the prisoners applied for soap and fresh water to wash their clothes but were refused; that while they were confined in the said snow they were obliged to drink stinking water which had been brought with them from England, and when they asked for better they were told it was good enough for rebels; that during their stay on board the said snow they were allowed only six ounces of pork and a pint of flour, or the same proportion in biscuit for each man; that they were obliged to wait until all the ship's crew had eaten their breakfast and dinner before they were allowed to dress their victuals; that during their confinement, having procured a little money from their friends, they employed the captain of the transport to go on shore and purchase necessaries for them, which he refused to do without a very large commission, charging them fifteen coppers for a loaf of bread; that from the transport they were brought to the city of New York, and confined in a house near Bridewell, where they were kept upon the same short allowance as they had been on board the transport, with the addition of one ounce of butter per week, and a little rice for each man, procured at the request of Govr. Skeene, as deponent was informed; that when the prisoners were first brought to the said city they were not allowed any fuel, and afterwards only a small quantity of coal, which did not suffice them more than three days out of a week; that during their continuance in New York, the allowance of provisions was dealt out very negligently, and from the scantiness and quality, and the bad state of health they laboured under, he doth verily believe that most of them would have died if they had not been supported by the benevolence of some poor persons and common prostitutes, who took pity of their miserable situation and alleviated it; that the prisoners were continued in confinement at New York until a short time after the taking of Fort Washington, when they were allowed to walk about the town; that deponent understood from several persons that the privates who were prisoners in the city of New-York were uniformly treated with great inhumanity; that they were kept in a starving condition, without fuel or the common necessaries of life; that they were obliged to obey the call of nature in the respective places of their confinement, and from disease and want of care and attention, and by the mere dint of hard usage died daily in great numbers, so that of the prisoners who had been taken on Long island, near one-half have died. And this deponent further saith that while he was as aforesaid confined on board the said transport, Brigadier-Genl. Woodhull was also brought on board in a shocking mangled condition; that deponent asked the General the particulars of his capture, and was told by the said General that he had been taken by a party of light horse under the command of Capt. Oliver Delancey;[4] that he was asked by the said captain if he would surrender; that he answered in the affirmative, provided he would treat him like a gentlemen, which Captn. Delancey assured him he would, whereupon the General delivered his sword, and that immediately after, the said Oliver Delancey, junr. struck him, and others of the said party imitating his example, did cruelly hack and cut him in the manner he then was; that although he was in such a mangled and horrid situation, he had nevertheless been obliged to sleep on the bare floor of the said transport, had not lent him a matrass; that Genl. Woodhull was afterwards carried to the hospital in the church of New Utrecht where he perished, as deponent was on good authority informed, through want of care and necessaries and further this deponent saith not.

ROB. TROUP

*Sworn the 17th Jany. 1777,*
*before me.*
GOUV. MORRIS.

*Journals of the Provincial Congress, Provincial Convention, Committee of Safety and Council of Safety of the State of New-York* (Albany, 1842), II, 410–11.

[1] Gouverneur Morris (1752–1816) was a member of the New York Provincial Congress.
[2] Lieutenant Jeronimus Hoogland of Lasher's Regiment.
[3] William Cunningham (c.1717–91) administered the Provost jail in New York City.
[4] A New York Loyalist.

# EDWARD ANTILL TO JOHN HANCOCK

LIEUTENANT COLONEL EDWARD ANTILL, of the Second Canadian Regiment, complained to John Hancock, president of the Continental Congress, that his regiment was totally unfit for duty, for the men had no clothing or blankets. The supply problems of the Continental army were further increased when the Continental Congress hastily withdrew to Baltimore in December 1776. The Second Canadian Regiment was reorganized in 1777 with the addition of three companies from Maryland and Connecticut to the mostly foreign men who had been recruited one year earlier in Albany, New York. This 460-man regiment had moved to New Jersey from Wilmington, Delaware, by the next spring to rejoin the main Continental army.

*Wilmington Feby. 6th. 1777*

Worthy Sir,
I wrote you Some considerable Time Since enclosing a Return of the Recruiting parties with the Number of men raisd by Each Captain & Requesting the Favor of an Answer to all the particulars therein Mentioned. I am Still so unhapy as not to have had a Single Line from you or anyone by your Order. Upon my Arival here I found the men Naked & many of them Sick for want of blankets & Cloathing, and it became absolutely necessary to furnish them with Some money Towards their pay and Subsistance to keep them Quiet & enable them to procure a few Necessarys having receivd no Directions from you I have taken the Liberty to Draw upon you for two thousand

Dollars which I hope will be honor'd Mr. Hillagus can charge it to our regiment as paid thro my hands to Robert Dill the pay master who will render an Account of the Same,[1] I would be very Glad to hear from you per Post in Answer to my last. The arms at Christian Bridge have been Examined & there are none fit for Service.[2] I am with great Respect your most obedt Hble Servt

EDWD. ANTILL

ALS, Papers of the Continental Congress, National Archives, Washington, D.C.

[1] Michael Hillegas (1729–1804), Treasurer of the United States, 1777–89.
[2] Christiana Bridge, Del.

# CHARLES MYNN THRUSTON TO GEORGE WASHINGTON

THE LONG PERIOD of inactivity during winter encampment usually lasted until the first warm days of May. With the advent of a new season of recruitment and campaigning, the Continental officer corps was replenished and restructured. In this letter to George Washington, Charles Mynn Thruston (1738–1812), of Frederick County, Virginia, thanks the general for his command and outlines the process of selection of his subordinate officers. Ability, not favoritism, was Thruston's criterion for the men selected. Thruston, known as the "Fighting Parson," had lost an arm in a skirmish with British troops on March 8, 1777. This letter is a reminder that George Washington's officers, although sometimes inexperienced in positions of command, exhibited the necessary qualities of leadership and humility.

*Whippeny*[1] *14 March 1777*

Sir

I feel very sensibly for the honour done me in your kind and polite letter of this day, your congratulation affects me, I am obliged and thank you. Give me leave to return it in behalf of yourself and the publick on the speedy recovery from your late indisposition.

Your offer of a Regiment does me great honour, and the genteel manner it is made leaves me without a pretence to refuse it, except such as may arise from a consciousness of my own inability, and the great dificulty there will be, cull'd as the state of Virginia now is, of getting it genteelly officered. Capt. Lewis I think will make an excellent Officer, and am confident with the assistance of his friends in Frederick about Alexandria and Fredericksburgh will readily make up his company. I could wish too that Thornton Washington might be an Officer in the Regiment unless your Excellency has destined him to some other station. If Colo. McDonald will serve, no better Lieut. Colonel could be found.[2] I cannot at present recollect above two or three such Captains as I should be willing to appoint I shall therefore be glad of the advice of yr Excellency and my friend Colo Johnston on this head as I suppose it is high time the business were set a going.[3] I shall add no more as I can neither write nor think but that I am with utmost regard and esteem your Excellencys obliged and most humble Servt.

C. M. Thruston

ALS, George Washington Papers, Library of Congress, Washington, D.C.

[1] Morris County, N.J.

[2] Colonel Angus McDonald (1727–78) of Virginia.

[3] George Johnston (also spelled Johnson) (c.1738–1828), lieutenant colonel and aide-de-camp to George Washington.

# Joseph Spencer to Jonathan Trumbull

Among the problems faced by the leaders of the Continental army were discipline, morale, and the temporary nature of enlistments. The officers' devotion to duty had to be matched by unflinching perseverance of the enlisted men. Major General Joseph Spencer faced a dismal situation at Providence, Rhode Island, in March 1777. In this letter to Governor Jonathan Trumbull of Connecticut, Spencer described the resistance of his men to serving beyond their appointed terms. Officers such as Spencer were responsible for maintaining an essential level of troop effectiveness by setting an example with their own devotion and patriotism.

**Joseph Spencer**

*Providence, March 15, 1777*

Sir

The remaining part of Colo Ely's Regiment under the Command of Colo McClellan and Capt Kingsbury's Co. supposed that the Time of their Engagement terminated yesterday;[1] they have all marched homeward this day. All the Troops from the Massachusetts are also returning Home, their Engagements expired at the same Time (except 327 Officers included) that are engaged untill the first of April, the Time to which Majr Ripley's Command is engaged.[2] Major Ripley's including Officers are (232) there is here now but 559 Troops, except what are of this State. Seeing the Army here would be left so very small, I thought it my Duty to ask the Troops whose Times were out, to tarry a few Days longer untill other Troops might arrive, I accordingly desired the Commanding Officer to publish my Request to them, which was done I believe faithfully. But they all refused to continue here any longer; as they have assigned particular Reasons for their Conduct in that Matter, and the Officers have reported the same to [     ]. I have inclosed a Copy thereof [     ] and Troops that were at Fishers Island when your Honr. wrote last, I am several Ways since informed returned to NewPort on the 11th. instant. There is a Hessian Deserter now at my House that came Yesterday from Rhode Island, he says he was at Fishers Island and that they got there about 30 head of Cattle & some Sheep. He also says there are six Hessian Regimts now at NewPort containing 525 Each and about two Regiments of Britains. I am with great Respect & Esteem Yr. Honrs. most obedt humble Servt

JOS. SPENCER

ALS, Jonathan Trumbull, Sr., Papers, Connecticut Historical Society, Hartford.
[1] Colonel John Ely (1737–1800) and Colonel Samuel McClellan (1730–1807), both of the Connecticut militia.
[2] Major John Ripley (1738–1823) of the Connecticut State Regiment.

# JOHN PAUL SCHOTT TO GEORGE WASHINGTON

THE LONG WINTERS of the American Revolution necessitated additional warm clothing and shelter for the troops. The Continental Congress was unable to provide these supplies consistently, because of its dependence on the support of the states. In this letter to George Washington, John Paul Schott (1744–1829), captain of the Independent Company of Germans, relates his efforts to keep his men clothed and paid. The frustration of officers while attempting to prevent their men from deserting because of lack of pay, the chill of winter, and hunger was responsible for many of the officers' complaints to their generals. The appeal was clear despite Schott's less than articulate style of writing.

*Philadelphia March 24th. 1777*

This is to inform your Excelency that I applyed here for Money Armes and plankits but can't get it without your Excelency is pleas'd to send me a Warrand. I have twenty-five men I am oblig'd to pay £1.1 pr: week for Each man which I think is too much, if I can get plankits I shall put them in the Barraks at Lancaster I have promiss of about twenty men at fort Lanton where I shall go as Soon as I receve your Excelences warrand to draw Money &c.

I am very glad to hear of your Excelences recovery and have the Honor of wishing you Helth. I am your Excelences most Obetiant and most Humble Servant

JOHN PAUL SCHOTT *Captn.*

N.B. Your Excelency will be Pleas'd to Derect the above to the Presetent here as I shall wait for an answer.

ALS, George Washington Papers, Library of Congress, Washington, D.C.

# CHAPTER TWO

# Victory at Saratoga, Defeat in Pennsylvania

*1777–1778*

T HE CAMPAIGN OF 1777 occurred on two separate fronts. Although the British had initially planned an assault in the Hudson Valley to cut New England off from the rest of the United States, General Sir William Howe also decided to attempt to occupy Philadelphia in the summer and fall of that year. General John Burgoyne moved south from Canada in late spring, hoping to join with a force from New York City when he reached Albany.

Opposing Burgoyne was an outmanned group of New York and New England Continental soldiers and militia defending a chain of forts. Aided by Indians and Loyalists, Burgoyne advanced and forced the Americans to abandon hastily their fortified defenses. The brave perseverance of the American officers and men, however, retarded the British advance until the Americans could obtain reinforcements. After the two pitched battles at Saratoga and the relief of Fort Stanwix, Burgoyne's army was surrounded and unable to get reinforcements. The surrender at Saratoga of such a large army was a great boost to the morale of the men in Washington's army. Furthermore, it encouraged the French to aid and support the American effort.

General Sir William Howe's expedition to capture Philadelphia, the nation's capital, was marked by many individual acts of bravery by American soldiers, but poor weather conditions and inexpert command by several officers led to a disorderly retreat of the Continental army. The battles of Brandywine and Germantown were disastrous American losses, with many killed and taken prisoner. By December 1, the British had effectively taken control of the Delaware River after the stubborn American defense of Fort Mercer and Fort Mifflin.

The victory at Saratoga was partial compensation for the train of setbacks in Pennsylvania, but little could provide solace for the long, harsh winter the Continental army had to endure at Valley Forge. The lack of adequate supplies required that goods either be impressed from civilians or that the army skirmish with British foraging parties for the cattle and grain of the region. Lack of clothing and medical supplies hindered the humanitarian efforts of medical men such as Albigence Waldo in caring for the men suffering from disease and frostbite. Dissension and disillusionment prevailed among those who felt that the states and the Continental Congress had either forgotten or forsaken them in their desperate need. Despite these difficulties, George Washington and his officers were able to keep order and, with the aid of Baron von Steuben, to instill discipline.

The withdrawal of the British army from Philadelphia in June 1778 was the first test for the refurbished American army now recovering from the ordeal of Valley Forge. On the battlefield at Monmouth Courthouse the army led by Washington displayed great skill and alacrity in confronting the main force of General Sir Henry Clinton's army in the oppressive heat. Although both armies suffered great losses, the Americans were justly proud of their courage and performance in battle.

The Burgoyne invasion, the campaign around Philadelphia, the winter encampment at Valley Forge, and the Battle of Monmouth were all crises that revealed the Americans' bravery in battle and their capacity to endure prolonged suffering from debilitating hardships.

# Thomas Price to George Washington

The second maryland regiment was formed on December 10, 1776, from remnants of seven Maryland companies, and Colonel Thomas Price (1732–95) received its command. In May 1777 the Second Maryland Regiment had only 147 men. On April 4, 1777, Colonel Price submitted his regimental returns to General Washington from Annapolis, lamenting the shortage of recruits. Price's problem was not unique to his regiment. Unlike their British foe and other European armies in the eighteenth century, the Americans had little regard for regimental depots for the recruitment, training, and equipping of replacements in an orga-

nized manner. The formal recruiting that did exist, as Price's letter to Washington reveals, was inefficient and expensive. The Continental army had many more military units than could possibly have been filled and equipped to be ready for battle with the means available. Nevertheless, the Second Maryland Regiment continued on active duty until the disastrous Battle of Camden on August 16, 1780, when the unit had to be entirely reorganized. Price's letter reveals the hardships of officers who were willing to fight even when they did not have the men necessary to do so.

*Annapolis April 4 1777*

Sir

    I received your Orders dated Morris Town March 12th this day and have Accordingly inclosed you a return of the State of my Regiment and am very Sorry it is not in my Power to send you a much better one. You will I make no doubt be much Surpriz'd when I tell you I have not more than four Commissioned officers belonging to my Regiment which are myself and three Lieutenants, the others Commissioned by the Commissioners (and we have no others Commissioned as yet) have all resigned not less than Six this Day. One of them my Lieut: Colo: and the other five Captains which is Owing to a dispute about Rank between our Regular and flying Camp officers which was not settled untill within this two days. I have repeatedly Ordered the Officers of the Regiment to march their Recruits to this place but have not had that Punctuality paid to them that Ought to have been owing to the Rank of the Officers not being Settled and they Undetermined Whither they would serve or not untill they knew what Rank they would hold. I have             fit for Duty at this Place. Shall March them as soon as I can get Officers which I hope will be in a Very few days 'tho at the same time shall be Oblidged to leave I am afraid the Accounts of Many of those Officers who have resigned & who have received large Sums of Money to goe on with the Recruiting Service. Unless I should receive your further Orders for the Lieut: Colo: who I believe will be appointed this day to March with the first Division and myself to stay behind and forward the recruiting Service. We find a great deal of dif-

78

ficulty in getting Men. However shall at all Events Proceed to Philada: until I shall receive your Orders to the Contrary. I am Your Excellencys most Obedt. Servt.

THO PRICE

# EBENEZER ELMER JOURNAL

DR. EBENEZER ELMER (1752–1843) enlisted as an ensign in the Third New Jersey Regiment and became a surgeon's mate on November 28, 1776. Elmer's journal reveals that disease and sickness were as troublesome as inadequate supplies and miserable winter weather. Perhaps the most serious of the ills discussed by Elmer was smallpox, against which General Washington had his encamped troops and their civilian neighbors in Morris County inoculated. However, hundreds died. Elmer reports one of the numerous skirmishes between British and American foraging parties and pickets in the spring of 1777. The winter encampment was nearly at an end, and parts of General Washington's 8,000-man army were already breaking camp by May 26.

*Die Solis 25th: Maie 1777*

This morning we were alarmed before day by the Pensylvania Troops wh. were moving towards Westfield & leaving the Lines below entirely bare. Abt. 8 oClock I set out for Wfd. to See the Sick but when I came there found they were all moved off to Chatham, & the Troops stores & every thing gone off from here to bownbrok,[1] could not get the least Information, nor did I know what to do as my Chest & two sick were at Mr. Decamp's exposed to the Enemy, nor knew I whether I must follow the Sick or not. PM. Came back found the regulars were out at Samp Town & had plundered Several Inhabitants. Those in this quarter began to pack up for a Start, I concluded as being left to take care of the sick twas my last way to endeaver to get a waggon & Carry my Chest & the sick away after the others but could not accomplish it this evening. The Inhabitants assembled & kept a guard for the Security of the place all night so that tho' I Slept but little yet was not disturbed.

Ebenezer Elmer Journal, New Jersey Historical Society, Newark.
[1] Bound Brook, or Middlebrook, N.J.

# ENOCH POOR TO HORATIO GATES

THE MAJOR BRITISH objective of the 1777 campaign was to isolate the New England states by controlling the Hudson Valley. The southern thrust to the Hudson River of British and Loyalist forces under General John Burgoyne (1722–92) anticipated a linkage with the troops under General Sir William Howe. The British army in Canada was augmented by more than 1,000 Indians commanded by Mohawk Chief Joseph Brant. Burgoyne's force of over 7,000 men reached Lake Champlain on June 20, 1777, for passage south. As early as May, the undermanned fortress at Ticonderoga was anxious about a British assault. Fort Ticonderoga had been strengthened under the direction of Colonel John Trumbull (1750–1831) and Thaddeus Kosciuszko (1746–1817), but despite comparisons of it to Gibraltar, it was imperfectly fortified. Brigadier General Enoch Poor (1736–80) commanded a Continental brigade of almost 1,000 men at Ticonderoga. In this letter he relays a reconnoitering report of the British naval movements on Lake Champlain near the fort to Major General Horatio Gates,

**Enoch Poor**
COURTESY OF THE STATE HOUSE, CONCORD, N. H.
PHOTO: BILL FINNEY, CONCORD, N.H.

commander of the northern forts, headquartered at Albany, New York.

*27 May 1777 Tyconderoga*

Dear Sir

Preparatory to the execution of a Plan to surprize any Posts, which the Enemy might have established on the Lake, I thought proper yesterday to dispatch a Reconnitring Party, with orders to proceed to Split Rock last Night, to spend this Day in observation and return in the Evening, to our established Rendezvous, and make His Report. It has Returned to this Place in the Moment of the embarkation of the Detachment, and informs us that they this Morning landed at Split Rock, about Break of Day, within one hundred and fifty Yards of the Enemies advanced Boat, which the approach of Day discovered, together with two Schooners and Six Gondolas, all within three hundred Yards of them; he observed on the West Shore about Forty Batteauxs, but as their was a thick Fog He cou'd only discover the Form of the Vessels and a Number of Fires. A very heavy Morning Gun was discharged, lower down the Lake, He thinks at Schuylers Island. As this Account induced the strongest suspicions of the

Enemies Approach, I thought it my Duty to forward it to you as speedily as possible, and shall be proud to receive your Commands. You know the strength of the Garrison by the last Genl. Return, If the Post shou'd be invested which I firmly believe I much dread we shall suffer for Provisions. I am Dear Sir Your Most Obdt. & ready huml. Sert.

ENOCH POOR

ALS, Horatio Gates Papers, New-York Historical Society, New York City.

# ARTHUR ST. CLAIR TO HORATIO GATES

ARTHUR ST. CLAIR (1737–1818) had been promoted to major general on February 19, 1777, and returned to the Northern Department as commander of the Continental forces on Lake Champlain. Writing to Major General Horatio Gates, whom he had replaced, St. Clair foresaw clearly the untenability of the American position at Fort Ticonderoga. Burgoyne's large army had reached Crown Point, ten miles above Fort Ticonderoga on Lake Champlain, that same day. With only "Captivity or Death" as his alternatives, St. Clair ordered Fort Ticonderoga abandoned on July 5, 1777. The Continental Congress, General Washington, and the American public were shocked by the retreat. Both St. Clair and General Philip Schuyler, then commander of the Northern Department, suffered immediate discredit but were eventually vindicated by court-martial in 1778.

*Tyconderoga June 27th. 1777*

Dear General

Your Suspicions of the Ennemys Designs have unfortunately proved but too true, considering the Situation of these Posts—had we such a Force as was here last Year I should have accounted it very fortunate that they bent themselves this Way but [    ] find myself able to make but a very feeble Resistance—not above 2000 Men fit for duty and those neither armed nor cloathed as they should be. The Ennemy are at Crown Point and Chimney Point, a large Encampment at both Places, and I make no Doubt but the very first fair Wind we shall have them upon our Hands. My Fate will be determined before this can reach You—but you had been much deceived with regard to the Preparations made here for Defence. Mount Independence has been almost totally neglected whilst they have been fooling away time on works upon this Side that are realy against ourselves, and yet the Mount must be our Dernier Resort for should we abandon it and trust to this Side the Ennemy would most certainly occupy it and then we are done for effectually—to add to our misfortunes we have not above thirty Days meat and for any thing I see very little probability of getting more, which, if the

Militia comes in will be eat up in a very short Time—and the Indians are gone to fall upon Skeensborough and it is said Fort George also.

I am happy that you have escaped these Difficulties tho I am sensible how much more capable you are to seize the Advantages that may present themselves, but of this I am pretty certain I am in a Situation where I have no Prospect of doing much Service to my country and have Captivity or Death before my Eyes—However we will do the best we can, as I determined to sell it as Dear as possible. Adieu—I heartily wish You Health Happiness and Honour and Am Dear General Your Affectionate Humble Servant

AR. ST. CLAIR

ALS, Horatio Gates Papers, New-York Historical Society, New York City.

# ALEXANDER HAMILTON TO ROBERT R. LIVINGSTON

THE MOVEMENT OF Washington's army to Middlebrook, New Jersey, on May 26, 1777, foreshadowed the resumption of active operations between both the British and American main armies and their foraging parties. The British tried on several occasions to lure the American forces into fighting a full-scale battle. Then on June 13, 1777, a British force moved toward Somerset Court House. The next day American units harassed the rear guard of the British force that had been unable to draw the American army away from its encampment in the Watchung Mountains. On June 19, the British avenged the Americans' actions by burning homes along their return route to New Brunswick. On June 22, the major elements of the British army marched to Perth Amboy and were sniped at by American sharpshooters. Lieutenant Colonel Alexander Hamilton (1757–1804), who had become George Washington's aide-de-camp on March 1, describes these events to Robert R. Livingston and defends the army's passive defensive posture. To Hamilton, a "cat and

**Alexander Hamilton**

mouse" game was necessary to preserve the Continental army.

*Head Quarters Camp, at Middle Brook June 28, 1777*

Dear Sir,

Yours of the 25th came to hand last night. Since my last addressed to Mr. Morris, the enemy have been trying a second experiment to tempt us to an engagement, on equal terms of ground. Under the supposition of their intending to evacuate the Jerseys immediately, in order to keep up the idea of a persuit, and to be in a posture to take advantage of any critical moment that might present itself to give them a blow, the chief part of our army, after their retreat from Brunswick, was marched down to Quibbletown, and parties detached thence further towards the enemy. Finding this disposition take place, and expecting that elated by what had passed, we might be willing to venture upon a general engagement, which is Howe's only hope, he came out with his whole army from Amboy early on Thursday morning and made a forced march towards our left, with design, if possible, to cut off some of our detachments, particularly one under Lord Stirling; and propably, if we were not expeditious in regaining the heights, to get there before us, by rapidly entering the passes on our left. Lord Stirlings party was near being surrounded; but after a smart skirmish with the enemy's main body, made their retreat good to Westfield, and ascended the pass of the mountains back of the Scotch plains.[1] The other parties after skirmishing on their flanks came off to join the main body and take possession of the heights. The enemy continued their march towards our left as far as Westfield, and there halted. In the mean time, it was judged prudent to return with the army to the mountains, lest it should be their intention to get into them and force us to fight them on their own terms. They remained at Westfield till the next day, and perceiving their views disappointed have again returned to Amboy, plundering and burning as usual. We had parties hanging about them in their return; but they were so much on their guard no favourable opportunity could be found of giving them any material annoyance. Their loss we cannot ascertain; and our own, in men, is inconsiderable, though we have as yet received no returns of the missing. I have no doubt they have lost more men than we; but unfortunately, I won't say from what cause, they got three field pieces from us, which will give them room for vapouring, and embellish their excursion, in the eyes of those, who make every trifle a matter of importance. It is not unlikely they will soon be out of the Jersies; but where they will go to next is mere matter of conjecture, for as you observe, their conduct is so eccentric, as to leave no certain grounds on which to form a judgment of their intentions.

I know the comments that some people will make on our Fabian conduct.[2] It will be imputed either to cowardice or to weakness: But the more discerning, I trust, will not find it difficult to conceive that it proceeds from the truest policy, and is an argument neither of the one nor the other.

The liberties of America are an infinite stake: We should not play a desperate game for it or put it upon the issue of a single cast of the die. The loss of one general engagement may effectually ruin us, and it would certainly be folly to hazard it, unless our resources for keeping up an army were at an end, and some decisive blow was absolutely necessary; or unless our strength was so great as to give certainty of success.

Neither is the case: America can in all probability maintain its army for years, and our numbers though such as would give a reasonable hope of success are not such as should make us intirely sanguine. A third consideration did it exist might make it expedient to risk such an event—the prospect of very great reinforcements to the enemy; but every appearance contradicts this, and affords all reason to believe, they will get very inconsiderable accessions of strength this campaign. All the European maritime powers, are interested for the defeat of the British arms in America, and will never assist them. A small part of Germany is disposed to make a market of its troops, and even this seems not over-fond of being drained any further. Many springs may be put in motion even to put a stop to this. The King of Prussia may perhaps without much difficulty be engaged to espouse views unfriendly to the Court of Britain, and a nod of his would be sufficient to prevent all future German succours. He as well as most other powers of Europe feels the necessity of Commerce and a large maritime force to be generally respectable. His situation, 'till lately, had been unfavourable to this; but the reduction of Poland and the acquisition of Dantzig in the Baltic, have put it very much in his power to pursue commercial schemes; and may tempt him to be propitious to American independence. Russian assistance is still infinitely more precarious; for besides that it cannot be the true interest of that ambitious empire to put its troops to fate, it is, at present, embroiled with the turks and will want all its men to employ in its own wars. England herself, from the nature of her polity can furnish few soldiers and even these few can ill be spared, to come to America in the present hostile appearance of affairs in Europe. On whatever side it is considered, no great reinforcements are to be expected to the British army in America. It is therefore Howe's business to make the most of his present strength, and as he is not numerous enough to conquer and garrison as he goes, his only hope lies in fighting us and giving a general defeat at one blow.

On our part; we are continually strengthening our political springs in Europe, and may everyday look for more effectual aids than we have yet received. Our own army is continually growing stronger in men arms and discipline. We shall soon have an important addition of Artillery, now in its way to join us. We can maintain our present numbers good at least by inlistments, while the enemy must dwindle away; and at the end of the summer the disparity between us will be infinitely great, and facilitate any exertions that may be made to settle the business with them. Their affairs will be growing worse—our's better: so that delay will ruin them. It will serve to perplex and fret them, and precipitate them into measures, that we can turn to good account. Our business then is to avoid a General engagement and waste the enemy away by constantly goading their sides, in a desultory way.

In the mean time it is painful to leave a part of the inhabitants a prey to their depredations; and it is wounding to the feelings of a soldier, to see an enemy parading before him and daring him to a fight which he is obliged to decline. But a part must be sacrificed to the whole, and passion must give way to reason. You will be sensible that it will not be advisable to publish the sentiments contained in this letter as coming from me; because this will make the enemy more fully acquainted with our views; but it might not be amiss to have them circulated, as those which ought to govern the conduct of the army, in order to prepare the minds of the people for what may happen and take off the disagreeable impression our catition may make. I am Dr. Sir Your most Obed servant

A HAMILTON

ALS, Robert R. Livingston Papers, New-York Historical Society, New York City.
[1] This skirmish on June 26 resulted in 6 British deaths and 30 wounded.
[2] Fabian conduct: avoiding a battle, weakening the enemy by cutting off supplies, and engaging in continual skirmishing.

# JONATHAN POTTS TO SAMUEL POTTS

BY JULY 2, 1777, the British army had reached the walls of Fort Ticonderoga. The British cannon positioned themselves above the fort, while the Americans under General Arthur St. Clair retreated in disorder toward Fort Edward, an outpost on the east bank of the Hudson River. Other American defeats occurred at Hubbardton and Skenesboro on July 7. St. Clair's men reached Fort Edward on July 12, but the American forces could do little more than impede Burgoyne's progress toward Fort Edward. The fort was taken on July 29, 1777. Jonathan Potts, deputy director general of the hospitals in the Northern Department, describes in this letter to his brother, Samuel (d. 1793), the confusion and doubt in the American camp during Burgoyne's relentless march south.

*Albany July 28th. 1777*

Dear Brother

Tho' I sent an express but a few days since yet with knowing how anxious you will be hear our situation have sent Capt. Wittman with this. Since my last we evacuated Fort Edward & returned about 5 miles down the River to a place called Moses's Creek, this was most undoubtidly a prudent step. At this post we are daily getting supplies God only knows whether sufficient or not. Fort George as well as Fort Edward are entirely demolished. Being now in the interior parts of the Country—in the Woods & Heights far from their Shipping we may be quite an equal match. The Damn'd Coffins made are troublesome, not a day but a Scalp or two taken near our very encampment. We have also now & then skirmishing with the scouting parties. We are informed by some Deserters that a few days since the German Troops & British had a fight among themselves at Skeensborough in which the former lost 18 & the latter 80 Men—I am positive great jealousies reign among them. The Enemy have advanced into the Grants. A large Body of Men promising Protection & security to the Inhabitants, some credulous Fools believe them, not taking example from plundered Jersey. They are at

Castletown & Col. Warner is in the Neighborhood with a Body of 3000 Militia[1] as is said to watch their Motions. My Hospital is now here where I have all the Wounded & sick amounting in the whole only to 153. Let me again beg you not to censure rashly our late retreat From Tye—many reasons may be given. Why don't you write by my expresses. Nothing from the westward. Upon the whole I think we shall have warm work in this quarter, but if properly supported make no doubt shall yet come off more than conquerors. Gracious God in whom I put my trust suffer not our Rightious course to perish, because Sinners defend it.

This Moment a letter from Head Quarters informs that the Enemy advanced with 1000 Men to Fort Edward, attacked our Picquet & Kill'd 5 Men & a Young Lady sister to one of my Surgeons, all of whom they scalped & most barbarously butchered.[2] Now for Lex Talionis—by Heavens no Officer or Soldier shall have Mercy from my Hands—God bless & preserve you all—my Love to our Mother & every Relation. I go to Camp immediately with my Surgeons. I am as usual your affect: Brother & Servt.

JONN. POTTS

ALS, Society Collection, Historical Society of Pennsylvania, Philadelphia.

[1] Colonel Seth Warner of the New Hampshire Continental Regiment.

[2] The scalping of Jane McCrea on July 27, 1777, by Indians inflamed the residents of upper New York and the Vermont region. She was the sister of Stephen McCrea, a hospital surgeon.

# EBENEZER STEVENS TO HENRY KNOX

**Ebenezer Stevens**
COURTESY OF THE NEW-YORK HISTORICAL SOCIETY

Brevet Major Ebenezer Stevens (1751–1823) was appointed commander of the Continental artillery in the Northern Department on November 6, 1776, heading the Independent Battalion of Continental Artillery, which consisted of three companies. In this letter to Brigadier General Henry Knox (1750–1806), chief of the Continental army artillery, Stevens describes his role in the retreat from Ticonderoga to Stillwater, New York, a town on the west bank of the Hudson River eleven miles below Saratoga. Major General Philip Schuyler had moved his army there during General Burgoyne's offensive. Schuyler was replaced as commander of the Northern Department on August 4, 1777, by General Horatio Gates, a decision that was tainted by sectional politics and personal friction. Gates reached his command by August 19, 1777.

*Still Water August 7th 1777*

Honored Sir

With heart felt joy I embrace every oppertunity of Wrighting to you, and though for a considerable time I have been deprived that pleasure, by adverse seenes of provedence respecting the situation of the Army in our department, yet coming to a stand I am again in a situation to inform you in some degree of the state and Condition of the Corps which I have the honour to command.

Confined by sickness at the time of the retreat from Tyconderoga I could not take an Active part at that time though I gave the most deliberate Orders the shortness of the Notice of that Measure would admit and am happy to inform you that my Orders where executed in such a manner that had not the enemy pursued in so hasty a manner I should have saved a very Considerable quantity of Stores some small Cannon and the two eight inch howitzers which I had just got compleatly mounted but at skeensborough all fell and I have only now to lament there fall, from that place we retreated to fort Anns where we had a brush which was much to our advantage,[1] from thence to fort Edward, after a short stay to fort Miller, then to Saratoga and lastly to this place were we are bussily employed makg every disposition to get things into a proper course in Order if heedfull to be able to repel any sudden attack. Since my Arrival here Six Officers of the Train have come here from Peeks kill, but as they brought no men with them it was impossible for them to take any Command. I should have been very happy to have had the Gentlemen with me but having my full comple-ment of Officers I thought it would be an Injury to the service to retain them there-fore advised them to join there Regt which they have accordingly done. We are now Collecting Stores from every Quarter as soon as any Considerable quantity arrives I shall be carfull to furnish you with a Return, as I am Conscious to my self that I have invariable made the publick good my moving princeple. I hope and trust that I shall meet with your approbation which being obtained will give a fresh spring to one devoted to the publicks and your honours Service. I am with Great Respect your honours Most Obedient humble Servant

EBENEZER STEVENS

P Script I would beg your honour to send me ten Ammunition Waggons as without them our Ammunition must suffer much in the transportation likewise a large quan-tity of horse harness as we have very little here, and we have a large number of horses United to the Cannon which Ought to be Compleatly fixed as I am sensible you would Chuse they should be.

ALS, B.V. Stevens Papers, New-York Historical Society, New York City.
[1] A skirmish at Fort Ann on July 7, 1777, resulted in several British casualties.

# PETER GANSEVOORT TO BENEDICT ARNOLD

ON JUNE 23, 1777, Lieutenant Colonel Barry St. Leger (1737–89) left Montreal and began a ten-week expedition against American outposts, particularly Fort Stanwix (Schuyler). St. Leger's expeditionary force, consisting of approximately 2,000 Indians, British regulars, Canadian auxiliaries, and Loyalists, was to link with General John Burgoyne's army near Albany, New York. Fort Stanwix, in the Mohawk Valley, con-trolled the principal route through the Iroquois country to Canada. It had been oc-cupied since April 1777 by the Third New York Regiment, commanded by Colonel Peter Gansevoort (1749–1812). St. Leger's forces began a three-week siege of Fort Stan-wix and its 550-man garrison on August 2. A relief force, however, commanded by General Benedict Arnold had been detached from General Philip Schuyler's army at Stillwater, New York, and on August 23 General Arnold received this letter from Gansevoort report-ing the invading army's sudden retreat. Ap-parently, most of the 1,000 Indians in St. Leger's force had deserted. Others left after hearing deliberately exaggerated reports of Arnold's troop strength. General Arnold's strategy of sending a spy to circulate false in-formation had succeeded. Fort Stanwix was relieved on August 23 when Arnold's men arrived.

*Fort Schuyler 22d. Augt. 1777*

Dear Sir

This Morng att 11 oClock I began a hearing Cannonade upon our Enemies Works—which was imediately returned by a Number of Shells & Cannon. About three oClock several Deserters came in who informed me that General St. Ledger with his Army was retreating with the utmost Precipitation. Soon after which I sent out a Party of about sixty Men to enter their Camp who soon returned & confirmed the above Account.

About 7 oClock this Evening Hanjost Schuyler[1] arrived here & informed me that General Arnold with two thousand Men were on their March for this Post in Consequence of which I send you this Information. I am Dear Sir Yours

PETER GANSEVOORT *Colo.*

ALS, Papers of the Continental Congress, National Archives, Washington, D.C.
[1] Spy for Arnold.

# WILLIAM AMIS TO RICHARD CASWELL

WILLIAM AMIS (1756–1824) writes to the governor of North Carolina, Richard Caswell (1729–89), on behalf of his brother, Thomas Amis of Bladen County, North Carolina. As acting commissary of the Third North Carolina Regiment, William Amis had been unable to obtain the necessary stores and supplies even though he mortgaged his own property. This southern regiment remained in the South from its creation in April 1776 until it went north to join the main army in 1777.

*August 22d, 1777*

May it please your Excellency:

The most pressing necessity obliges me to dispatch this message to your Excellency for money. The Troops I'm informed are to march to the Northward in a few days, & it will be absolutely impossible for me to supply them, unless I can draw about £2000. I've already mortgaged my own property for the loan of a few hundred pounds, which is now exhausted.[1] I've been the only acting Commissary and supplied all the Troops here since the departure of our army for the Northward. Your Excellency, seeing my distress, will, I hope, order that one of the Treasurers pay into the hands of the Bearer, John Webb, £2000, and I will be answerable for the same. I could not wait on your Excellency myself, having no person here that I can intrust my business with. I act for, & on behalf of my brother, Thomas Amis of Bladen, who was appointed Commissary to the third Reg't.

I am your Excellency's most obed't. & devoted Humble Serv't.

WILLIAM AMIS

Inclosed is an order on the Treasury

Walter Clark, ed., *The State Records of North Carolina* (Winston, N.C., 1895), XI, 586.

[1] Supporting a family on a depreciating salary and having to leave fields and stores during the war seriously affected the financial well-being of many officers after the American Revolution. For example, Captain Jacob Wright of New York was compelled to appeal to the Society of the Cincinnati for assistance after the war. He wrote them around 1810 explaining:

"I doubt not you will believe me when I say nothing but the most urjant necessity Could Constrane me to make a draught on your generosity.

"I am in very ill health and advised by Phission to Balltown Water, for which I this moment Set out quight moneyless.

"Theirfore take this liberty praying such a Small Sum as your funds on hand and others demands will authorise. Gladly woould I rather give then receive but so a wise providence has ordered it.

"Your goodness I know will lead you to make all due allowances for my Situation and relieve my pain which this occasions." (ALS, Society of Cincinnati, Washington, D.C.)

Another officer, Captain George Handy (1756–1820) of Maryland, wrote to Major Allen McLane (1746–1829) on September 22, 1817, noting, "When the revolutionary war closed I was in Charlestown without a shilling, and when I returned home I had no resources being very poor, and entirely out of business . . . but very unprofitably, being obliged to purchase goods on credit. Consequently I became involved in debt, and a few years after was compelled to sell my certificates at 2/6 in the pound." (ALS, Allen McLane Papers, New-York Historical Society, New York City.) For Wright and Handy, as well as for many others, the price of service in the Continental army was poverty in the years after American independence was won.

# ISRAEL ANGELL TO NICHOLAS COOKE ET AL.

FROM JANUARY 13, 1777, to January 1, 1781, Colonel Israel Angell (1740–1832) commanded the Second Rhode Island Regiment with bravery and distinction. Writing from a camp in the Hudson Highlands, Colonel Angell complains to Governor Nicholas Cooke (1717–82) and the Council of Rhode Island about his regiment's constant lack of clothing, a situation that was undermining the unit's fighting readiness. The Americans were often defeated in part by scarcity of food, shoes, and blankets. This problem remained serious for Colonel Angell's men, for the Second Rhode Island Regiment had to spend the winter of 1777–78 at Valley Forge.

*Camp No 2 August 27—1777*

Gentlemen,

Pure necessity urges me to trouble you this once more in behalf of the Troops under my command; you will easily recollect that I have repeated my Solicitations before you on the Subject of their cloathing as far as was decent.

I did, indeed expect when I came Home to find my men poorly Habitted nor was I disappointed their Dress even exceeded for badness what I had imagined to myself.

Not one half of them can not be termed fit for duty on any immergency; Of those, who of them went with me on a late expedition near to Kings bridge many were bare foot, in consequence of which its probable they won't be fit for duty again for many week 5 of them there deserted to the enemy which I have reason to beleive was principally owing to the non fulfillment of engagements on the part of the State and what may be expected better than this that more will follow their example while they daily experience that publick faith is not to be depended on. In fine the Regiment is scandallous in its appearance in the view of every one—and has because of this incurred from surrounding regiments from the inhabitants of Towns thro which they have lately passed, the disagreeable and provoking Epithets of the Ragged Lousey Naked Regiment. Such treatment, gentlemen, is discouraging dispiriting in its tendency: it does effectually unman the Man and render them almost useless in the Army I am sorry to have occasion to continue my complaint in their behalf but as I look upon it, a matter, not of Empertinence but of Inportance I cannot refrain in justice to them.

I pray gentlemen you would as speedily as possible inform me of the result of your Deliberation on the Matter and let me Know whether they are likely very soon to have relief. If this is not the case I shall look upon myself in Honour Bound to make my Application some where else.

I am gentlemen with all due Respect Your Honours humble Servant

ISRAEL ANGELL *Colo.*

Edward Field, ed., *Diary of Colonel Israel Angell, Commanding the Second Rhode Island Continental Regiment during the American Revolution, 1778–1781* (Providence, R.I., 1899), pp. xii–xiii.

# JAMES GORDON HERON TO JAMES MILLIGAN

THE AMERICAN ARMY embarked on one of its most disastrous expeditions when troops under Major General John Sullivan raided Staten Island in August 1777. Attacks and counterattacks, skirmishes, and kidnapping were frequent occurrences for the inhabitants of the New Jersey towns along the Kills and Newark Bay, opposite Staten Island.

In retaliation for frequent incursions by Loyalists, General Sullivan raided Staten Island on August 22, 1777. This attack resulted in the deaths of 13 men and the capture of 172 officers and 17 soldiers. Captain James Gordon Heron (1749–1809) was sent to New York City after his capture in this engagement. His financial plight is described in this letter to James Milligan (1741–95), a lieutenant in the Seventh Pennsylvania Regiment, stationed at Philadelphia.

*N York Sept. 9th 1777*

Dear Sir

I have had the ill luck to fall into the hands of the enemy on the 22d of augt, in the affair of Statten Island & now prisoner in this place.

I beg of you to use your Interest to get me exchanged if there is a possibility. Pray if either the Col. Butlers are near your place let them know my situation & I am persuaded they will use their best indeavours in my favor.[1] (I mean for my—exchange) if that Should not be effected I pray you, if in your power, send me a little Silver or gold or a Bill will ansr. the same purpose. If you can Comply with my request. you will oblige & I shall as soon as I receive an ans. to this which I beg by the first Opty. send you an order to receive money & notes of mine which now ly in Lancaster to the amt. of £150 if the Regt. lys near plilada. as I'm informed it does. I'll be obliged to you if you will direct Major Taylor to Send my Chest & Chests & Cloaths if an exchange Does not take place. Pray my respects to Miss Milligan. I am Dear Yours most Sincerely.

J HERON

NB pardon me for writing this freely but I hope me present Situation will sufficiently accot. I have 300 dollars in my pocket this moment & Cannot get Sixpence worth for it without exchanging at a gret Disadvantage which I am unwilling to do

JH

ALS, Edward Hand Papers, Historical Society of Pennsylvania, Philadelphia.

[1] Richard Butler (1743–91) and William Butler (1745–89) were lieutenant colonels in the Continental army.

# JOSEPH CLARK DIARY

## *September 10–11, 1777*

WHILE GENERAL JOHN BURGOYNE was marching south from Canada, General Sir William Howe was attempting to conquer and occupy Philadelphia. He sailed from New York City on July 23, 1777, with a large fleet and landed at Head of Elk, in Maryland, with 15,000 men on August 25, 1777. Washington's army marched south to meet the British at Chadd's Ford. The Continental army made a defensive stand at Brandywine Creek, ten miles northwest of Wilmington, Delaware, where Washington hoped to block the steady advance of Howe and his 13,000 British regulars and Hessian mercenaries toward Philadelphia. Because of their more professional army and their superior knowledge of the strategic fords over the creek, the British pushed back the Americans at the Battle of Brandywine on September 11, 1777. Many of the Americans participating in this engagement were not disheartened, however, for they believed they had fought well against the British. Nevertheless, some of the confusion and discouragement of the American retreat is described in the diary kept by Joseph Clark (1751–1813), an adjutant and mustermaster from New Jersey. By the end of the day, American losses were estimated at 700 killed or wounded and 400 captured.

**Joseph Clark**

On the 10th. preparations was making for a Stand, & on the 11th. about 8 oClock in the morning the Alarm Guns fired, & in a very short time the Cannonading began. The Situation of heights on each side of the Creek was nearly alike advantageous for both parties, tho' the situation of the Enemy with their Cannon very much favoured their Design of crossing the Creek. Our Army was drawn up in a line on one side, while the Enemy lay with their main body conceald on the other & indeed the greater part of our line was conceald. We had likewise a party of Light Infantry on the other side of the Creek who had several Scirmishes with the Enemy & we judgd. at the lowest computation kiled 200d. of them & took a Field piece which they were obliged to leave, for want of the horses, & the Enemy being on the advance with a reinforcement. The Cannon continued to play from the different Batteries, tho not very briskly till about ½ after 4 in the afternoon. There were 3 Fording places on the Creek over which we expected the Enemy to pass, the middle one at Brumedgham bottom,[1] where his Excellency was & where on the heights our Batteries were. At this the Cannonading began in the morning. At the upper Ford the Enemy sent a [neat] part of their force about noon, 3 divisions of our Army were sent immediately to oppose them. Viz. Sterlings Sulivans, & Stephen's, but as there were no heights at this Ford, on our side to prevent their landing by Cannon from Batteries, we were oblieged to oppose them after they had crossed; but as their number was larger than was expected they streched their Line beyond ours, & flanked our right wing shortly after the action began. This occasioned the Line to break to prevent being surrounded, tho' the fireing while the action lasted was the warmest I believe that has been in America since the War begun, and as our men on the left of the Line were pretty well stationed, they swept off great numbers of the Enemy before they retreated and from the best accounts I could collect from the Officers in the Action the Enemy must have suffered very much from our people before they broke, tho' indeed Our people suffered pretty much in this action & would have suffered more if Genl. Greene had not been Detached to their assistance[2] by whose timely aid they made a safe retreat of the men, tho' we lost some pieces of Artillery. He however got up too late to form in a proper Line & give our party that was broken time to recover. Notwithstanding this repulse (which was the most severe upon the 3d. Virga. Regt. who thro' mistake was fired upon by our own men. Our whole Body got off with but an inconsiderable loss in men, tho something considerable in Artillery. When the Action began at the upper Ford, the Batteries at the middle Ford opened upon each other with such fury as if the Elements had been in convulsion, the valley was filled with smoke, and now I grew seriously anxious for the Event. For an hour an a half, this horrid sport continued, and about sunset I saw a Collumn of the Enemy advance to one of our Batteries & take it, Under cover of their Cannon. They had crosed at the Ford & were advancing in a large body. What we lost at our Batteries I have not yet heard, As all our Militia were at the lower Ford where no action, & Genl. Green sent to reinforced at the upper Ford, we had not a very large party to oppose the Enemy at the middle Ford. The Body stationed across the valley drew off to the right & formed farther back on an Eminence when an Engagement began with musketry, & the Enemy gave way but as night was spreading its dusky shade thro' the gloomy valley, & our army was something broke it was necessary to leave the field of Action & take care of the Troops, Accordingly after sunset the party at the middle Ford drew off & marched over to Chester, where the whole army by appointmenet met. The sun set when I left the Hill from whence I saw the fate of the day. His Excellency I saw within 200 yards of the Enemy, with but a small party about with him & they drawing off from their station; our Army broke at the right & night coming on adding a gloom to our misfortunes. Amidst the noise of Cannon, the hurry of people, & waggons driving in confusion from the field, I came off with a heart full of Distress. . . .

Joseph Clark Diary, New Jersey Historical Society, Newark.

[1] Birmingham, Pa.

[2] Major General Nathanael Greene (1742–86) of the Continental army.

# ROBERT KIRKWOOD ORDERLY BOOK

CAPTAIN ROBERT KIRKWOOD (1756–91), of the Delaware Regiment, is best remembered for his distinguished service in Nathanael Greene's southern campaign. He also served in other battles, including those of Long Island, Trenton, and Princeton. His orderly book documents the dismal and confused retreat of the American army toward Chester following their defeat at the Battle of Brandywine. The Americans continued their swift retreat toward Germantown, while Howe's army marched without opposition into Philadelphia on September 26, 1777. Kirkwood's orderly book provides a vivid portrait of the aftermath of defeat.

*Head Quarters Sepr 12th 1777*

General Orders

The Commanding Officer of each Brigade is immedietly to Send off as many Officers as he Shall think necessary on the Roads leading to the place of Action Yesterday & on any other Roads where the Straglers may be found & perticularly to Wilmington to pick up all Straglers from the Army and bring them on; in doing this they Should proceed as far towards the Enemy as Shall be convenient to their own Safety, and examine every house, in the main time the troops are to march on in good order through Darby, to the Bridge towards Schuykill & Germain town & there pitch their tents,[1] Genl Greens Division will move last & cover the Baggage Stores. A Gil of Rum or whiskey is to be Served out to each man who has not already that allowance.

Genl Smallwoods light troops will remain at Chester to Collect all the Straglers as they come and tomorrow morning follow the Army, the Directors of the Hospitals will see that all Sick and wounded are Sent to Trentown in doing this Genl Maxwell will give them all necessary assistance,[2] the Genl expects each Regt or Officers commanding Brigades will immedietly make the most exact Returns of their killed wounded & missing.

After Orders

The Officers are without loss of time to See that they are Compleated with amunition, that their arms are in the best order, the inside of them washed clean & well dried, the touch holes pick'd & a good flint in each gun,[3] the Strictest Attention is expected will be paid to this order as the officers must be Sensible that their own honour, the Safety of the Soldiers & Success of the Cause depends absolutely upon a carefull execution of it, the Commanding officers of each Regt is to endeavour to procure Such necessaries as are wanting for his men.

An exact Return of the State of each Regt to be made immedietly.

Major Genl for tomorrow Stevens, Brigadier Conway.[4]

Field officers Coll. Lewes, Major Ball.

*The Journal and Order Book of Capt. Robert Kirkwood* (Wilmington, Del., 1910), pp. 168–69.

[1] Schuylkill River.

[2] Brigadier General William Maxwell (c.1733–96) of New Jersey.

[3] Lack of arms and powder was a serious problem, and their care was an important duty. Captain Gabriel Maupin (1737–1800) of Virginia spent his military career guarding and supervising the powder magazine at Williamsburg. On November 12, 1778, Governor Patrick Henry cited Maupin for his service: "The constant receiving & delivering Arms for repair, sending & receiving them to and from distant Stations & a vast Variety of Matters to be transacted at the principal Magazine, makes his office very laborious & of great Importance. And I certify that I think he discharges his Duty faithfully & diligently, & in Such a Manner as to deserve Approbation." (Box 2, Executive Papers, Virginia State Library, Richmond.)

[4] Adam Stephen; Brigadier General Thomas Conway (1733–c.1800).

# Israel Putnam to Alexander McDougall

In September 1777 there were many American units not involved in the campaign in the north at Saratoga or to the south in the defense of Philadelphia. Many of these Continental army detachments were stationed at Peekskill, Tappan, and other outposts guarding the Hudson River. Generals Israel Putnam and Alexander McDougall, with Connecticut and New York regulars and local militia, had the heavy responsibility of preventing British general Sir Henry Clinton from moving up river to reinforce Burgoyne and at the same time defending lower New York and New Jersey from British incursions. Putnam's letter to McDougall shows the uncertainty regarding the British actions after a raid. Clinton did attack northward at Verplanck's Point in October.

*Peeks Kill Septr 18th 1777*

Dear Sir

I received yours pr Col. Starr Informing that the Enimy had probably left the Jersies;[1] having plundered many horses and Cattle—for which I am very Sorrey. If Gen: Clinton with so Considerable a force was in Jersey, as you Suppose, I think there is great weight in what you Suggest, respecting the danger of their returning in Case you move away. The militia of this State who are ordered to Join you will go home and the detachments who are Coming up from Genl; Parsons will be liable to get Scattered unless they Join you before you march.

By accounts from Genl Washington he retired this Side the Schuykill, but How not pursuing, being busied all friday & Saturday taking Care of the wounded and burying his dead. Genl Washington on the 14th crossed the Schuykill with a reinforcement from the City militia & marched to Chester—Hows advanced Guards being three miles from there. Our loss in killed & wounded doth not exceed One thousand. The Enemy's is Computed as double that number. We lost Seven field pieces.

I think under all Circumstances it will be best for you to tarry untill the detachments Join you & in Case of no Counter Orders from Genl Washington to go on through newark & Elizabeth it being much nearer better Travilling & I think you may pass that way with great Safety, however I believe the point between the Two armies is Settled before this. Genl Gates is within about Eight miles of Burgoine & G Lincoln & Starks near him on his rear. Somthing Important is expected Soon from that Quarter. From your Obedient humble Servant

ISRAEL PUTNAM

ALS, McDougall Papers, New-York Historical Society, New York City.

[1] Colonel Josiah Starr (1740–1813) of the First Connecticut Regiment. On September 12, 1777, British troops under General John Vaughan (d. 1795) attacked toward the Passaic River.

# MORGAN LEWIS TO JOHN BARCLAY

BY THE END OF August 1777, Burgoyne's march to Albany through the forests of New York had been slowed by the stout resistance of local citizens and militia and the military command of General Horatio Gates. Defeats at Bennington, Vermont, on August 16, 1777, and the failure of St. Leger's campaign against Fort Stanwix did not improve the prospects of this British campaign. Burgoyne's army, however, was resupplied and marched southward to confront the militia and Continental units commanded by Gates. American forces led by General Benedict Arnold fortified Bemis Heights in preparation for the assault. On September 19, 1777, the British attack on the heights at Freeman's farm ended in a bloody victory for the British. Over 500 of their men had perished to gain a small tactical advantage. Morgan Lewis (1754–1844), a colonel and deputy quartermaster general of the American army in northern New York, wrote to John Barclay, chairman of the Albany Committee, of the urgent need for supplies to sustain the men resisting Burgoyne's march.

**Morgan Lewis**
COURTESY OF THE SOCIETY OF THE CINCINNATI,
ANDERSON HOUSE, WASHINGTON, D. C.
PHOTO: BRENWASSER, NEW YORK CITY

*Head Qutrs 20th Sept. 1777*

Sir

    We Yesterday had a severe Action with the Enemy about a Mile in Front of our Lines, in which we have every Reason to believe we gained a considerable Advantage over the Enemy. Had Daylight lasted, we should have been able to have given you a more particular Account of our Success. To Day I immagine will, if the Enemy come on, finally determine our Fate. Should the Victory declare on our Side, we shall not have it in our Power to pursue our Enemies for want of Carriages, I must therefore earnestly request you will use every Exertion in your Power, to send us as many as you can possibly procure. Two hundred would not be too Many, could they be had. I am Sr Your Hble Servt.

Morgan Lewis

For God sake do not let us be under the Necessity of Retreating for want of Lead.
M. Lewis

ALS, Lloyd W. Smith Collection, Morristown National Historical Park, Morristown, N.J.

# Henry Brockholst Livingston to Philip Schuyler

Lieutenant colonel Henry Brockholst Livingston (1757–1823) participated in both the fall of Fort Ticonderoga on July 5, 1777, and the first Battle of Saratoga on September 19, 1777, as an aide-de-camp. In this letter to Philip Schuyler, Livingston recounts the latest episode in the long and bitter dispute between generals Horatio Gates and Benedict Arnold that had begun while Schuyler was still in command of the Northern Department. Arnold had been passed over in promotion to major general in February. The personal antagonism of Arnold and Gates over seniority and command responsibilities had repercussions for the American military effort, for Gates did not give Arnold sufficient support to insure a victory at Bemis Heights. Schuyler was Arnold's close friend, and Livingston shared with him an abhorrence of Gates. Livingston exhibits the character of a good officer by remaining in service despite personal antipathy for his commander. The resolution of men like Livingston was rewarded when the Continental army scored a decisive victory over the British on October 7, 1777, at the second Battle of Freeman's Farm. Ten days later, Burgoyne surrendered his army at Saratoga.

*Camp on Behmus' Heights, Sep: 23rd—77*

Dear Sir,

I am this moment honored with your Favor of the 21st. by Major Franks.[1]

Gen; Lincoln arrived here last Evening. Part of his division came in to day—the Remainder are expected to Morrow. I wrote You some time since of his having detached two Parties to Tyonderoger & Mt Independence.[2] Colo: Varick has given you the particulars of their Success. I cannot persuade myself that the Mount will be taken.

I am much distressed at Gen: Arnold's determination to retire from the Army at this important Crisis. His presence was never more necessary. He is the Life & Soul of the Troops—Believe me, Sir, To him & to him alone is due the Honor of our late victory. Whatever Share his Superiors may claim they are entitled to None. He enjoys the Confidence & Affection of Officers & Soldiers. They would, to a Man, follow him to Conquest or Death. His absence will dishearten them to such a degree, as to render them of but little Service. The difference between him & Mr G--- has arisen to too great a height to admit of a Compromise. I have, for some time past observed the great Coolness, & in many instances, even disrespect with which Gen: Arnold has been treated at Head Qrs.. His Proposals have been rejected with marks of Indignity. His own orders have frequently been contravened—and himself set in a ridiculous Light by those of the *Commander in Chief*. His remonstrances, on those occasions, have been termed presumptuous. In short he has pocketed many Insults, for the Sake of his Country, which a Man of less Pride would have resented. The repeated Indignities he received, at length roused his Spirit & determined him again to remonstrate. He waited on Mr G--- in Person last Evening. Matters were altercated in a very high Strain—Both were warm—the latter rather passionate & very Assuming. Towards the End of the debate Mr G--- told Arnold—"He did not know of his being a Major General—He had sent his Resignation to Congress—He had never given him the Command of any division of the Army—Genl Lincoln would be here in a day or two, that then he should have no occasion for him; and would give him a Pass to go to Philadelphia, whenever he chose it." Arnold's Spirit could not brook this Usage. He returned to his Quarters—represented what had passed in a Letter to Mr G--- and requested his Permission to go to Philada.. This Morning, in answer to his Letter, he received a Permit, by way of Letter directed to Mr Hancock. He sent this back & requested one in proper Form, which was complied with. To Morrow he will set out for Albany. The Reason of the present disagreement between two old Cronies is simply this—Arnold is your Friend—I shall attend the General down—Chagrining as it may be for me to leave the Army, at a time when an Opportunity is offering for every young Fellow to distinguish himself, I can no longer submit to the Command of a Man whom I abhor from my very Soul—His Conduct is disgusting to every one, but his Flatterers & Dependants, among whom are some who profess to be your Friends. A Cloud is gathering & may eer long burst on his Head.

Lieut Arden is just returned with eight Tory Prisoners. He made a tour as far as Saratoga—was in your House which he says is much damaged. The Glasses are entirely gone. The Papers ruined & Frame much injured. The Barn & other Out Buildings are safe.

Two Letters were taken from one of the Tories. One from Burgoyne to Brig: Powell, in which he says, we left 200 dead on the Field. He is silent as to his own Loss. He begs that St. Leger may be hastened on. The Indians you have sent us are of great Service. Not a day passes without their taking some Prisoners. Make my best Respects to Mrs. Schuyler & Family. I am Dr Sir &c.

HENRY B LIVINGSTON

ALS, Philip Schuyler Papers, New York Public Library, New York City.

[1] Major David Solebury Franks was aide-de-camp to General Benedict Arnold.

[2] Troops under Colonel John Brown successfully attacked Mount Defiance on Lake Champlain on September 18, 1777, but were unable to surmount the defenses of Mount Independence.

# ELIAS DAYTON NARRATIVE

## *September 11–October 4, 1777*

**Elias Dayton**

AFTER THE CRUSHING defeat at the Battle of Brandywine, the confused American army marched to Germantown, while the victorious British troops occupied Philadelphia. Despite a discouraging series of defeats, Washington planned an attack on the British army garrisoned about five miles north of Philadelphia in Germantown. On October 4, the American and British armies clashed at the Battle of Germantown. The combination of British professionalism and inept American leadership on the field resulted in an American retreat. A valuable eyewitness account of both the engagement at Brandywine and that at Germantown was recorded by Colonel Elias Dayton (1737–1807), whose Third New Jersey Regiment participated in both battles as part of Brigadier General William Maxwell's brigade.

September 11 was faught the battle of Brandewine near Chads Ford & Burmingham Meeting house; the Cannonadeing begun about eight Oclock in the morning at the same time a party of light troops under General Maxwell attacked a party of the Enemy on the opposite side of the river. The action was warm for some time & who should keep the field doubtfull, but upon the Enemy Advancing a Brigade in the rear of those allready engaged, our people gave wey though not untill they had killed a considerable number of Howes men with little loss on their part. About 1 Oclock we received Intelligence of the main body of the Enemy haveing croossed the creek about six miles Above us which was westward in the Country, why this pass was not Attended to is truly astonishing but so it was, & after the Enemy was properly formed on our side, Sullivans Ld. Stirlings & G. Stephens Devisions was ordered to march & attack them. Accordingly they all marched immedietly & between 3 & 4 Oclock in the afternoon formed the largest part of the three Divisions upon a hill near B. meetinghouse, The Enemy very soon Advan. to Attack, I beleive before G.S.D. was formed as they changed their ground on which they first draw up, a number of them was marching past my Regiment when the fire first began, consequently I belive never fired a gun, in half an hour at furtherst the whole of our men gave wey. The Enemy pursued briskly by which means A number of our wounded as allso some well men fell into their hands in the whole about 400 and six or eight peices of brass Cannon six pounders. The pursuit continued untill after sun set when the Night aproching allso a check they got from a part of G. Greenes Devision caused the Enemy to give over the pursuit. We had continued marching and countermarching from the 11th. of Septr to the 4th. of October except a small scirmizing on Sept. about the 18, near the white Horse Tavern on the Lancester road between the Advanced parties of boath Armies, we were drawn up in order of battle expecting every Moment to engage the whole of the Enemies Army after remaining about 2 hours in order of battle and it beginning to rain very hard we were ordered to march of the ground which we did about 12 Oclock Midday. The storm incressed & we marched the whole Night through the heavyest storm allmost that Ever was known. All our Cartridges was wet and I much feared the ruen of the whole Army would have been the consequence, & indeed it must have been the case had G. Howe Advanced upon us in this situation but fortunately for us he never mooved towerds us, but continued his rout by easey marches towards the fords where he intended to pass the Schulkill. Our first halt was at or near a place called the yellow Springs. Here our stay was very short as we had not any Amunission. We mooved off to Reading Furnace[1] A very strong part of the Country by nature, where I believe no Army would think of pursueing, from Reading we marchd and countermarched about the Country untill Octbr. 2d. when we encamped at worcestor twenty miles from Philidelphia. The Eavening of the third we marched off with the whole Army with design to Attack the Enemy who lay near German Town about fifteen miles distant from us, unfortainately for us the Night proved very dark which so retarded our march that we did not reach the Enemys Advanced post untill sunrise, whereas our design was to Attack them at first dawn of day,—at sunrise the fire began. Their advanced party soon gave wey, our people pursued them closely to the main Body which they immediatly attacked likewise & they soon gave wey & were pursued from field to field with great loss on their side. We suffered considerable in Advancing by a party of the Enemy had thrown into a large stone House sp. to belong to Benjm. Chew,[2] at this place fell Capt. McMyer & Ensign Hurley of Col. Ogdens Regiment, Capt. Conwey, Capt. Morrison, & Capt. Baldwin & Lt. Robinson wounded of the same Regiment, together with about 20 men; of my Regmt. Lt. Clark & Ensign Bloomfield wounded[3] & 18 men killed & wounded, my horse was shot under me at same place within about 3 yds, of the Corner of the House. About this time came on perhaps the thickest fog known in the memory of man which together with the smoke brought on allmost Midnight darkness it was not possible at one time (I beleive for the space of near half an hour) to distinguish friend from foe five yards distance, this obliged all our parties to give over the pursuit as they were in danger of fireing upon their friends & probably did several time before the fire ceased. At this instant the Enemy rallyed their scatered forces and advanced upon us when we retreated in our turn, allthough with very little loss. I beleive Every man we had eighther killed or wounded meet his fate full in front as he was advancing. We lost one Brigadier General who was shot in the thy with a cannon Ball of which wound He died three days afterwards, our good Major Weatherspoon was shot dead by a common shot in the head as we were advancing through the Streets of German Town. . . .[4]

AD, Elias Dayton Papers, New Jersey Historical Society, Newark.

[1] Not to be confused with Reading, Pa.

[2] Benjamin Chew (1722–1810), jurist who became a Loyalist.

[3] Captain Andrew McMires (c.1745–77); Ensign Martin Hurley; Captain John Conway (1742–1802); First Lieutenant Isaac Morrison; Captain Daniel Baldwin; and First Lieutenant Robert Robertson, all of the First New Jersey Regiment; and First Lieutenant William Clark and Ensign Jarvis Bloomfield, both of the Second New Jersey Regiment.

[4] Brigade Major James Witherspoon.

# JOSEPH BLACKWELL TO WILLIAM EDMONDS

FOG AND CONFUSION helped create the conditions for the bloody American defeat at Germantown. Joseph Blackwell (1755–1823), a second lieutenant in the Third Virginia Regiment, vividly recalled that violent encounter in this letter to his brother-in-law, Colonel William Edmonds (1734–1816). Blackwell's courage is demonstrated by his casual mention of the wound he received. American losses in the Battle of Germantown were estimated at 652 killed or wounded and 438 captured.

**Joseph Blackwell**

*Camp 36 Miles from Philia., October 10, 17[77]*

Dr: Sir,

I take this oppertunity to let you know that I am well, hoping this will find you and family the same. On the forth Instant between break of day and sun rise our army attacked the enemy at a place calld chesnut hill we beat the enemy back about three miles to a place So. German Town we was then force to retreat. The enemy had such fine cover behind the houses that we must Suffered grately in beating them out. When we were advancing we saw a great many of the Enemy that lay dead on the field. Our lost was as near as I can find out was about five Hundred kild and Wounded very few of our Wounded fell in the enemys hand. From the best information we can get the enemy lost is much grater then ours we have very good authority that the enemy lost was upwards of five hundred kild dead and about three times the Number wounded. The enemy lost four Brigaders Generals kild.[1] We lost Brigader Genral Nash Majr. Toles Colo Mathes.[2] I dont no of any other field Officers we lost. Capt. John Eustace got kild[3] I dont know of any other Officers of your acquaintances that was kild. Three men of Capt. Tho Blackwell Compa. got Slitely wounded.[4] Got my Breeches cut Just by the knees with a bullet. I have not seen Nether of the Captain Blackwells this two weekes. Capt. Wm. Blackwell[5] went the country sick I under stand he is geting well. Capt. Tho Blackwell is at a fort on the Dillaware I am inform'd. I think it Needlas to mention any thing about the battle at Brandy wine as I amagine you have had a full act. of it. Nothing More at present but give my love to Sister family & all other asking friends. Am Sir Your very Hbl. Servt.

Jos. Blackwell

NB I expect every day when we shall have the third Battle with the enemy and then I am in hops I shall be able to give you a better act. of the times.

JB

ALS, in the possession of Edmunds Family, Lynchburg, Va.

[1] This total included General Agnew.

[2] Brigadier General Francis Nash (1720–77) was killed during the battle, and Colonel George Mathews (1739–1812) of the Virginia Line was captured. He was exchanged on December 5, 1781.

[3] Captain John Eustace of the First Virginia Regiment.

[4] Captain Thomas Blackwell (1752–1831) of the Tenth Virginia Regiment.

[5] Captain William Blackwell of the Eleventh Virginia Regiment.

# James Morris Memoirs

## *October 3, 1777–June 1778*

The sufferings of the troops during the winter encampment at Valley Forge were equalled by the hardships imposed on the soldiers captured by the British at the battles of Brandywine and Germantown. A memoir by James Morris (1752–1820), a first lieutenant in the Fifth Connecticut State Regiment, was written years after the events. Despite the intervening years, Morris was able to recapture the despair of his incarceration in a Philadelphia prison. The cold and starvation he recalls were common complaints of all of the victims of the hazards of war. Morris fared better than those who never left the Philadelphia prison alive. He was not exchanged, however, until January 3, 1781.

. . . on the Evening of the 3d. of October 1777. The army had orders to march about 6 O clock on said Evening, the army under the immediate command of General Washington began their March for Germantown, I left my baggage & my Bible which my father bought for me when I was six years old, in my trunk. I march with only my military Suit. and my impliments of War, without any change of dress or even a blanket. We marched that Evening and reached Germantown by break of day the morning of the 4th. a distance of about twenty miles. The memorable battle of Germantown then commenced, our Army was apparently successful in driving the Enemy from their encampment, and victory in the out-Setting seemed to march on our standards. But the success of the day by the misconduct of General Stephens, turned against us.[1] Many fell in battle, and about 500 of our men were made prisoners of War, who surrendered at discretion. I being in the first company, at the head of one collomn that began the attack upon the Enemy, consequently I was in the rear in the retreat. Our men then undisciplined were scattered. I had marched with a few men nearly ten miles before I was captured, continually harassed by the British Dragoons, and the light Infantry. I finally surrender'd to Save life with the few men, then under my command, & marched back to Germantown under a guard. Samuel Stannard my waiter a strong athletic man, carried my blanket and provisions, with a canteen of Whiskey. He had made his escape, and was not taken. Of course I was left without refreshment from break of day in the morning thro' the whole day. Thus I was driven back to Germantown after performing a march of about forty miles from the Evening before at 6. O clock. I reached Germantown a prisoner of War about Sunset fatigued and much exhausted. I was the last officer taken with about twenty men. The rest that had been taken early in the day, were conveyd to Philadelphia. The Evening of the 4th. of October was very Cool. I was put under a quarter Guard with the few men with me, in an open field around a Small fire. No provision was made for the Prisoners, the men with me had a little food in their knapsacks, but I had none. A little after Sundown, I was Shivering with the cold and I asked the Sergeant of the Guard if I might see the Commander of the Regiment. He informed me that he quartered in such a house, about 20 rods distant. The Sergeant who was manly and sympathetick waited on me to the house and informed the Commander that there was an American Officer a prisoner at the door who wanted to See him. The Colo. Said he would See him after he had done supper. Accordingly I sat down in the Stoop before the door and after sitting about fifteen minutes the Colo. came out and sat down in the Stoop with me. He asked me many questions respecting my motives for going into the War and rising up in rebellion against my lawful Sovieign and answered him pleasantly and as evasively as I could consistently with decency. He asked me what I wanted. I told him I was in a suffering condition, I had no blanket or any covering to Shield me from the cold. I wished for Liberty to sleep in the house, and that I Stood in need of some refreshment. The Col. ordered his Servants to get me some victuals and Said I might go into the room where they were. I went into the room, the Servants very politely Spread a table, Set on some good old Spirits and a broiled Chicken, well cooked, with excellent bread and other food of the best kind. The servants Sat off in the room and waited on me in the best manner. This was really the Sweetest meal of Victuals that I ever ate! When I had done supper I asked the Sergeant who had conducted me there, what the Colo. Said respecting my lodging in the house. The Sergeant replyd. that the Colo. told him that I was not on parole, and that he was not authorized to grant a parole of honour, and that I must go out and be with the guard. I then asked the Sergeant if I could be furnished with a blanket for that night. The Soldiers who were waiters to the Colo., immediately brought me a large and clean rose Blanket and said it should be for my use that night. I accordingly went out into the field and lay down among the Soldiers who were prisoners, wrapped myself in the blanket, kept my hat on my head and Slept Sweetly thro the night. Before I lay down the Sergeant informed me that he observed I had a Watch in my pocket and that I had silver knee-buckles if I would give them to his care he would return them to me in the morning, as the soldiers of the Guard would probably rob me of them whem I was asleep. I accordingly committed them to his Safe keeping, who very honourably returnd them to me, the next morning. It being the 5th. of Octr. The prisoners this day had their allowance of provisions dealt out to them for the day. These were Cooked by the Soldiers who were prisoners, and I partook with them in one common Mess. Nearly the Setting of the sun of the 5th. The Prisoners were ordered to be escorted by a guard to Philadelphia, the distance about six miles. I thus marched on, and arrived at the new Jail in Philadelphia about eight O clock in the Evening. I was locked into a cold Room destitute of every thing but cold Stone Walls and bare floors—no kind of a Seat to sit on—all total darkness, no water to drink or a morsel to eat; destitute a blanket to cover me, I grouped about my Solitary cell, and in moving about I found that there were two or three persons lying on the floor asleep. I said nothing to them, nor they to me. I Stood on my feet and leaned my back against the wall, and Sometimes moved about the room, and then to change my position I Sat on the floor, but no Sleep nor Slumber; parched with thirst and no one on whom I could call for a drop of Water. In Short, it was a long, dismal, dreary and most Gloomy night that I ever beheld. I reflected on the miseries of the damned in that eternal, friendless prison of despair, but still hope hoverd around my Soul, that I Should see another morning. Morning finally arrived, and at a late hour, we were furnished with some very hard Sea bread and Salted pork, and I was able to obtain Some Water to drink. Being alltogether Moneyless I could purchase nothing for my comfort. I pretty soon Sold my Watch for half its Value, and with the money I recd. for it I was able to procure some food pleasant to my taste. I wholly gave up my allowance of provisions to the poor Soldiers. At this time and in this Jail were confined 700 prisoners of War. A few Small rooms were Sequestered for the Officers. Each room must contain sixteen men, we fully covered the whole floor when we lay down to Sleep, and the poor Soldiers were shut into rooms of the Same magnetude with double the number. The poor Soldiers were soon Seized with the Jailfever, as it was Called, and it Swept off in the course of three months 400 men, who were all buried in one continued Grave without Coffins. The length of a Man was the width of the grave, lying three deep one upon another. I thus lived in Jail from the 5th. of Octr. 1777, till the month of May, 1778. Our number daily decreasing by the King of Terrors. Such a Scene of mortality I never witnessed before. Death was so frequent that it ceased to terrify. It ceased to warn; it ceased to alarm Survivors. I was confined there with officers from the Southern States. The card table and the Bottle were there Companions, and the Common saying was "let us do this to kill time". O! what a Lesson of instruction! When the longest life is but a dream, a Shadow & a Vapour, yet its precious moments were a burden. I made a Contract with a good family in Philadelphia to furnish me with two meals per day for two dollars per week. I thus lived during my Continuance in Jail, and by means of this good family I obtained the priviledge and use of the public Library in the city. My time was devoted to reading. The noise of the card table the common routine of employment, day after day ceased to disturb me because it had become so familiar. I read and wrote, leaning up the wide recess of the window, to my advantage and improvement. Time passed pleasantly with me while I daily conversed with myself. I endeavored to prevent my minds becoming Sour by the severities of misfortune. Early in the Spring I began to loose my usual alertness and activity, and by the beginning of May I had become so debilitated, that I was admitted on parole in the city, on the 16th. day.

I there continued with the kind family which had befriended me thro the winter till Sometime in the month of June, when the British Army left the City of Philadelphia. I was put on board with the other prisoners of War, and Sailed down the River Delaware and went to New York. We were 12 days on our passage.

James Morris Memoirs, Town Clerk's Office, Morris, Conn.
[1] General Adam Stephen was found drinking during the battle.

# WILLIAM BROWN WALLACE TO MICHAEL WALLACE

SECOND LIEUTENANT William Brown Wallace (1757–1833), of Colonel William Grayson's Additional Continental Regiment, rejoices to his brother Michael at Burgoyne's surrender and the end of General Sir Henry Clinton's expedition to the Hudson Highlands on October 22. Rumors circulated at Washington's headquarters that the British were rapidly evacuating nearby Philadelphia. These hopes were, however, premature, for General Sir William Howe and the British army continued to occupy that city for nine more months. The Philadelphia campaign, which had appeared near its end in late October, kept the Continental army in the field until December 11, 1777. Fortunately, the youthful enthusiasm of officers such as Wallace helped sustain the battered army in the long winter ahead.

**William Brown Wallace**
COURTESY OF THE SOCIETY OF THE CINCINNATI, ANDERSON HOUSE, WASHINGTON, D.C.

*Head Quarters Oct: 23d 1777*

Dr Brother
I wrote you some time ago Concerning the defeat of our Northern tyrant Borgoyne which is fact & we have taken 5000 prisoners with him all his Artillery

Baggage Millitary stores &c too tedious to mention. The day before yesterday 4000 of Hows Army retreat'd over Schuylkill with most of their Baggage & it is now Currantly beleived about this place that they are Evacuating Philadelphia with the greatest precipitation. We heare from the Northard that our Brave Genl: Gates has cut of Clintons retreat & is in a fair way of defeating him also. Today 2 of the Enemys Ships of war was set on fire in the Delaware by our Galleys & were totally distory'd so that the friends to Liberty may now with propriety rejoyce.[1] Gust Jas & Tom are well.[2] I am Dr brother yrs &c

WM B WALLACE

ALS, Wallace Family Papers, University of Virginia Library, Charlottesville.
[1] American cannonading from Fort Mifflin in the Delaware River.
[2] All were brothers who served in Virginia regiments.

# SAMUEL WARD, JR., TO GEORGE WASHINGTON

WASHINGTON had been unable to prevent the capture and subsequent occupation of Philadelphia, but he continued to have confidence in the capabilities of the defense system of the forts along the lower Delaware River. An important link in this defensive chain was Fort Mercer, at Red Bank in Gloucester County, New Jersey, which was garrisoned by 400 men from Colonel Christopher Greene's (1737–81) First Rhode Island Regiment and Colonel Israel Angell's Second Rhode Island Regiment. On October 21, 1777, General Sir William Howe dispatched 2,000 Hessian soldiers and artillerymen under Colonel Carl von Donop to capture Fort Mercer. Major Samuel Ward, Jr., of the First Rhode Island Regiment, reports the successful American defense of the fort to General Washington, headquartered less than fifteen miles from Philadelphia. Ward's letter is included in a broadside that the Continental Congress had printed to bolster American morale. British losses in this bloody encounter outnumbered American casualties by ten to one.

*Red-Bank, 23d October, 1777*

Sir,

By the desire of Col. Green, I congratulate your Excellency, on the success of the troops under his command, yesterday. On the 21st instant, four battalions of Germans, amounting to 1200 men, commanded by the Baron Donop, Col. Commandant, landed at Cooper's ferry, and marched the same evening to Haddonfield. At 3 o'clock yesterday morning, they marched for this place; when the guard at Timber-Creek Bridge were informed of their approach, they took up that bridge, and the enemy filed off to the left, and crossed at a bridge, four miles above. Their advanced parties were discovered within a quarter of a mile of the fort, at 12 o'clock, at half after four o'clock P. M. they sent a flag to summon the fort, who was told, that it should never be surrendered. At three quarters after four they began a brisk canonade, and soon after advanced in two columns, to the attack. They passed the abattis, gained the ditch, and some few got over the picquets, but the fire was so heavy that they were soon drove out again, with considerable loss, and retreated precipitately, towards Haddonfield.

The enemy's loss amounts to 1 Lieutenant Col. 3 Captains, 4 Lieutenants, and near 70 killed, and the Baron Donop, his Brigade Major, a Captain, Lieutenant, and upwards of 70 non-commissioned officers and privates, wounded and taken prisoners.[1] We are also informed that several waggons are taken. He also enjoins me to tell your Excellency, that both officers and private men behaved with the greatest bravery. The action lasted 40 minutes, Col. Green's regiment has two serjeants, 1 fife, and 4 privates killed, 1 serjeant, and 3 privates wounded, and one Captain, (who was reconnoitring) taken prisoner. Col. Angel has one Captain killed, 3 serjeants, 3 rank and file, and 1 Ensign, 1 serjeant, and 15 rank and file wounded, 2 of Capt. Duplessis company were slightly wounded; too many handsome things cannot be said of the Chevalier, who as well as his officers shewed a truly heroic bravery.[2] There has been already brought into the fort near 300 muskets, a considerable number of swords, cartridge boxes, &c. There has been a smart firing between ours and the enemy's fleet this morning; several fire-ships have been sent down the river. I am with the greatest respect, Your Excellency's most obedient humble servant,

SAM. WARD

Contained in broadside, *Intelligence from Red Bank* (Lancaster, Pa., 1777).

[1] Von Donop was one of the 153 Hessians to die from volleys from American guns fired at close range.

[2] Captain Thomas-Antoine Chevalier de Mauduit du Plessis was a French officer and was in the Continental artillery.

# WILLIAM RAYMOND LEE TO WILLIAM HEATH

ALTHOUGH THE WINTER encampments at Valley Forge and Morristown are notorious for the wretched conditions that prevailed, soldiers also endured miserable winters in countless other locations less well-known. Evidence of some of the suffering of soldiers in Cambridge, Massachusetts, is provided by Colonel William Raymond Lee (1745–1824) in his letter to Major General William Heath, then commanding the Eastern Department from headquarters in Boston. Colonel Lee, who commanded one of the sixteen Additional Continental Regiments from January 1, 1777, complained that his field officers had no wood to keep warm and implies that they might be forced to set fire to buildings in Cambridge for heat.

*Cambridge Novr. 14, 1777*

Sir

Mr. Abel Pierce Forman of the Smiths has apply'd for help out of the Regiments of Militia have examin'd Brooks's Find Two Soldiers who are willing to go into the Works provided thay can be allow'd the customary wages that the other Workmen have at the Same business. Shall wait your directions thereon.

The Officers are exceeding uneasy with respect to their Quarters, as the Cold Weather approaches fast, & but very little Wood renders their Situation very disagreeable.

Should be glad to have the Answer to the Questions Tomorrow, as they are Sanguine to know.

This morning Road Round the lines & found the Field Officers, & Some Others walking by their Barracks to keep themselves from Perishing with Cold not one Stick of Wood to put into the Fire, & if some other Method cannot be found to supply them they must either perish or burn all the Publick buildings. I am with Respect Sir your Most Obd. H Servt.

WILL R. LEE

ALS, William Heath Papers, Massachusetts Historical Society, Boston.

# JOHN HEARD TO GEORGE WASHINGTON

THE AMERICANS' stubborn defense of Fort Mercer resulted in General Sir William Howe's determination to reduce the Delaware River forts with the superior British firepower on land and water. On November 10, 1777, warships and shore batteries began cannonading the island redoubt Fort Mifflin, and by November 15 the remaining American defenders had retreated to Fort Mercer. John Heard (1754–1826), a first lieutenant in the Fourth Continental Dragoons, reports the movement of 5,000 men under Lord Cornwallis to the river in preparation to attack Fort Mercer. The Americans abandoned the fort on November 21, 1777. Heard's letter demonstrates the Continental soldier's skill in collecting intelligence that helped prevent the capture of a large number of the defenders of the river forts.

*Frankford 18th. Novembr 1777*

Sir

I am just now creditably inform'd by Mr. Peter ⟨Cooper⟩, direct from the City, that last Night at 11 oclock, a large Body of the Enemy under the command of Cornwallis, march'd to the Neck. Their intentions are to cross over the River below the

Fort. Mr. Cooper further adds, that this detachment has so much weaken'd them, that, they have not now, in the City, Men sufficient to Man their Lines. I have recieved various Accts: of this, which, tho, in themselves they do not all agree, yet all in this, that a large Number has actually gone off.

Mr. ⟨Cooper⟩ received this piece of Intelligence from a Sergeant, who supposing him & two or three who were with him, to be well affected to the Royal Army, had communicated this to him. As Capt. Craig is now absent & I now command, I have thought proper to send this.[1] I have the honor to be your Excellencys mo. huml. Servt.

JOHN HEARD

ALS, George Washington Papers, Library of Congress, Washington, D.C.

[1]Captain Charles Craig (d. 1782) was wounded at Brandywine on September 11, 1777, and did not serve again.

# JACOB PIATT ORDERLY BOOK

## *November 30, 1777*

INADEQUATE QUARTERS, shortage of supplies and stores, and the inactivity during a long and dismal winter encampment were a potential source of disciplinary problems for the officers and men of the Continental army. The orderly book kept by Jacob Piatt (1747–1834), a lieutenant in Colonel Matthias Ogden's First New Jersey Regiment, provides insight into the interest shown not only by officers but also by the Continental Congress in emphasizing the need for religious values. A congressional resolve of November 25, 1777, quoted in Piatt's orderly book, stresses the appropriateness of prayer for divine assistance in the bitter struggle for liberty.

**Jacob Piatt**
PHOTO: PHOTO STUDIOS LTD., LONDON

For as much as it is the Indespensible duty of all men to adore the superinting providence of Almighty God, to acknnoledge with gratitude their Obligations to him for benefits reciv'd and implore such farther blessings as they stand in need of And, it having pleas'd him in his Abundant Mercy, Not only to Continue to us the Innumerable bounties of his Common Providence, but also to smile upon us in the Prosecution of a Just and Necessary war for the Defence of Our Rights and Liberties, it is therefore farther Recommended by Congress that Thursday the 18th day of Decemr. next to be set apart for Solemn Thanksgiving & praise, That at one Time & with one Voice the good people may Express the Greatfull feelings of their hearts and Consecrate themselves to service of their Divine Benefactor, and that together with their Sincere Acknowledgments & Offrings, they may Join the Confession of their Sins and Supplications for such further Blessings as they stand in need of.

Jacob Piatt Orderly Book, New Jersey Historical Society, Newark.

# Henry Beekman Livingston to Robert R. Livingston

THE CONDITIONS endured in winter encampment were as much true tests of patriotism as was the heat of battle. Already a veteran of campaigns in Canada, Henry Beekman Livingston (1750–1831), a colonel in the Fourth New York Regiment, found the winter of 1777–78 at Valley Forge to be an exacting trial of his endurance and courage. His letter to his brother, Robert R. Livingston, is an accurate summary of the urgent and serious problems of inadequate clothing, erratic supply by the states, and the high prices paid to merchants who sold their wares reluctantly.

*Valley Forge, 24th: Decr: 1777*

Dear Robert

I just now was so Happy as to receive Your Letter of at Head Quarters together with one from Caty which was very entertaining as it was wrote with an easy elegance peculiar to herself.[1] I think her Correspondence a valuable one and wish my Situation and Manner of Life would permit me to give her more of my Attention I hope She will not attribute my not writing oftner to neglect as my Daily Avocations and disagreable Manner of Life is the true Cause. Ib: Power, has not been near me which slight I am much Vexed at as I wished for an Opportunity of writing home. I have so much to write of more Importance that I can say but Little of our Situation here. Let it suffice for the present to tell You we have retreated to within Six miles of Brandy wine on the West Side of School Kill with our Front towards Philadelphia and are now Building Huts for our winter Quarters without Nails or Tools so that I suppose we may possibly render ourselves very Comfortable by the Time winter is Over. Our Troops are in General Almost Naked & very often in a Starveing Condition through

the Mismanagement of our Commissaries who are Treading in the Paths of our Quar-
terMasters and Forrage Masters who have already Starved our Horses Burgoins Army
was not worse [provided] with Forrage when in their Greatest Distress. The Enemy are
rolling in the Fat of the Land having played the Soldier Sufficiently to secure them the
Best of Quarters. All my men except 18 are unfit for duty for want of Shoes Stockings
and Shirts. Breeches and Coats Hatts they Can do without tho its disagreeable. And to
add to this miserable Tale we are becoming exceedingly Lousey I am not myself ex-
empted from this Misfortune the few Shirts I had with me are Quite worn out what I
Shall do for a New Stock I am at a Loss to determine. Jack left four and some other
Articles of Cloathing with a Mrs: Clift at Fish Kills the Rest were sent with my Chest
from Albany. You would Oblige me if You would write to Mr: Derick Schuyler to
know what Sloop they were put On Board of as he had the Direction of that Matter all
my Stock of summer Cloathing was in it which makes it a Great Loss. Please to let John
know that the Box of Clarret I agreed with him for would be very wellcome at this
Time as Liquor of no kind is to be had here nor Sugar nor Tea nor Vegetables of any
Kind. A Deputation of Quakers have Applied to General Washington to go to Philadelphia Markets as they Could not subsist themselves in this Part of the Country. The
State of Connecticut have lately furnished their Troops with very Good Cloathing at
the Old Prises. It were to be wished that our State instead of turning Merchants would
Immitate so Laudable an Example the Prises Charged by Mr: Henry to the Soldiers is
about 5 times as much as what Congress say they will furnish us for They have in a
Late Resolve requested the Different States to furnish their Troops with the Necessary
Articles of Cloathing And have determined that the Overpluss Shall be a Continental
expence. I wish You would make this known if it is not already I wish the State Sutler[2]
was sent on not with Liquors but other necessaries such as Tea Sugar Coffee Choco-
late as we can scarcely Live without them having for some time past been without Vegetables of any Kind. Poor Jack has been necessitated to make up his Blanket into a
Vest and Breeches if I did not fear starveing with Cold I Should be tempted to do the
Same. I Should be with You this winter but General Washington has determined that
no Furloughs be granted to Field Officers. What the Numbers are Its impossible for
me to tell You I Should think about 15000 Man the Enemy about 7000. I am much
Obliged to You for Your Recommendations but fear they will have no Effect untill
Spring when I am determined to Resign if it Can be done with Honour. Mr: [     ] I
hope is not Ignorant of my Intentions as I shall then expect to go upon my Farm. I
Should have settled with the State of N.Y. for the Cloathing of My Regt: But the Pay
Master is exceedingly ill at present of the jaundise at N: Haven. Please to make this
known. I must Confess I was much disappointed in the Letter I received from Arnold
Transmitted by Mama. I wish You had not encumbered Yourself with my Horse But
Given him to the Butcher to keep at 40/ or 50/ a Month Both my Mares are exceed-
ingly Emaciated. I fear I shall lose them by Spring. Wm: Livingston is just Arrived in
Camp having made his Escape from a Guard Ship where he was placed after having
been Confined for three weeks with 13 others in a Dungeon 14 feet Square a Major
Stewart Came with him. They had no Ligt but through a Grate through which their
Raw Porke was put Daily Mrs: Morterine at her Earnest Request Obtained leave to see

him only once. A French Frigate of 28 Guns lately arrived at Portsmouth with 18.9 Inch Mortars Bond Shot Small Arms and other Stores this may be depended on as fact. She has Orders to make prize of all English Merchantmen & Brot in with her two Prizes. I hope You wont Find My Letter is Tediously Long. Remember my Love to Polly etc. etc. I Am Your Affte: Brother

HENRY B. LIVINGSTON

ALS, Robert R. Livingston Papers, New-York Historical Society, New York City.
[1] Catharine Livingston (1752–1819) was Henry's sister.
[2] Sutler: one who sold provisions to the army.

# ALBIGENCE WALDO DIARY

## December 14–29, 1777

THE ENCAMPMENT at Valley Forge lasted over six months. During this long period of inactivity, 2,500 of George Washington's army died of hunger, exposure, and sickness. The harsh conditions of that winter are vividly recalled in the diary of Albigence Waldo (1750–94), a surgeon in the First Connecticut Regiment. Inadequate shelter, chronic illness, wretched food, emotional torment, and deteriorating morale were all elements in Waldo's story. Illness forced Waldo to leave the service in 1779.

December 14.—Prisoners & Deserters are continually coming in. The Army which has been surprisingly healthy hitherto, now begins to grow sickly from the continued fatigues they have suffered this Campaign. Yet they still show a spirit of Alacrity & Contentment not to be expected from so young Troops. I am Sick—discontented—and out of humour. Poor food—hard lodging—Cold Weather—fatigue—Nasty Cloaths—nasty Cookery—Vomit half my time—smoak'd out of my senses—the Devil's in't—I can't Endure it—Why are we sent here to starve and Freeze—What sweet Felicities have I left at home; A charming Wife—pretty Children—Good Beds—good food—good Cookery—all agreeable—all harmonious. Here all confusion—smoke & Cold—hunger & filthyness—A pox on my bad luck. There comes a bowl of beef soup—full of burnt leaves and dirt, sickish enough to make a Hector spue—away with it Boys—I'll live like the Chameleon upon Air. Poh! Poh! crys Patience within me—you talk like a fool. Your being sick Covers your mind with a Melanchollic Gloom, which makes everything about you appear gloomy. See the poor Soldier, when in health—with what cheerfulness he meets his foes and encounters every hardship—if barefoot, he labours thro' the Mud & Cold with a Song in his mouth extolling War & Washington—if his food be bad, he eats it notwithstanding with seeming content—blesses God for a good Stomach and Whistles it into digestion. But harkee Patience, a moment—There comes a Soldier, his bare feet are seen thro' his worn out Shoes, his legs nearly naked from the tatter'd remains of an only pair of stockings, his Breeches not sufficient to cover his nakedness, his Shirt hanging in Strings, his hair dishevell'd, his face meagre; his whole appearance pictures a person forsaken & discouraged. He comes, and crys with an air of wretchedness & despair, I am Sick, my feet lame, my legs are sore, my body cover'd with this tormenting Itch—my Cloaths are worn out, my Constitution is broken, my former Activity is exhausted by fatigue, hunger & Cold, I fail fast I shall soon be no more! and all the reward I shall get will be—"Poor Will is dead." People who live at home in Luxury and Ease, quietly possessing their habitations, Enjoying their Wives & families in peace, have but a very faint Idea of the unpleasing sensations, and continual Anxiety the Man endures who is in a Camp, and is the husband and parent of an agreeable family. These same People are willing we should suffer everything for their Benefit & advantage, and yet are the first to Condemn us for not doing more!!

December 15.—Quiet. Eat Pessimmens, found myself better for their Lenient Opperation. Went to a house, poor & small, but good food within—eat too much from being so long Abstemious, thro' want of palatables. Mankind are never truly thankfull for the Benefits of life, until they have experienc'd the want of them. The Man who has seen misery knows best how to enjoy good. He who is always at ease & has enough of the Blessings of common life is an Impotent Judge of the feelings of the unfortunate. . . .

December 16.—Cold Rainy Day, Baggage ordered over the Gulph of our Division, which were to march at Ten, but the baggage was order'd back and for the first time since we have been here the Tents were pitch'd, to keep the men more comfortable. Good morning Brother Soldier (says one to another) how are you? All wet I thank'e, hope you are so (says the other). The Enemy have been at Chestnut Hill Opposite to us near our last encampment the other side Schuylkill, made some Ravages, kill'd two of our Horsemen, taken some prisoners. We have done the like by them. . . .

December 18.—Universal Thanksgiving—a Roasted pig at Night. God be thanked for my health which I have pretty well recovered. How much better should I feel, were I assured my family were in health. But the same good Being who graciously preserves me, is able to preserve them & bring me to the ardently wish'd for enjoyment of them again.

Rank & Precedence make a good deal of disturbance & confusion in the American Army. The Army are poorly supplied with Provision, occasioned it is said by the Neglect of the Commissary of Purchases. Much talk among Officers about discharges. Money has become of too little consequence. The Congress have not made their Commissions valuable Enough. Heaven avert the bad consequences of these things!!. . . .

December 29. . . . All Hell couldn't prevail against us, If Heaven continues no more than its former blessings—and if we keep up the Credit of our Money which has now become of the last consequence. If its Credit sinks but a few degrees more, we shall then repent when 'tis too late—& cry out for help when no one will appear to deliver. We who are in Camp, and depend on our Money entirely to procure the comforts of life—feel the Importance of this matter—He who is hording it up in his Chest, thinks little more of it than how he shall procure more. . . .

Printed in *Pennsylvania Magazine of History and Biography* (1897), 21:299–323.

# JOSEPH CLARK DIARY

## *January 10–19, 1778*

JOSEPH CLARK was among the many Continental soldiers forced to endure the cold winter of 1777–78 at Valley Forge. Supplies were short despite foraging expeditions in the countryside; transport wagons had not been properly allocated and team and artillery horses died. Mutiny and mass desertions were feared by Washington and his staff, but patriotism surmounted even the miserable conditions suffered by the encamped army. The diary kept by Clark while at Valley Forge is a vivid reflection of those hard times. The only encouraging aspect of the long ordeal was the news of the French alliance with the new nation and the announcement of the appointment of Nathanael Greene to be quartermaster general. Grumbling and discontent could not be curtailed among the enlisted men. Washington lost one quarter of his 10,000 soldiers there. The American spirit, however, endured.

About the 10th: of Jany: 78 A quantity of Blanketts Stockings & Shoes a'rived at Camp from Virga. & was distributed among the Virginia Troops. Almost daily reports prevailed in Camp of a war between England & France for my own part I coud not tell whether to look upon it as a matter of reallity or amusement. About this time also a general dissatisfaction prevailed in the Army with Congress, especially amongst the Virginians, who now appeared to have lost much of that public Spirit & heroic resolution which at first rouzed them up to vigorous exertions. Tis true the Virginia Troops at this time was very naked for Clothing, as was indeed the Army in general, espcially for Shoes. However I could not see the propriety of blaming Congress for all our deficiencies, could they have seen into futurities, they might perhaps have prevented. About the 15th: of Jany. we had our Hutts nearly compleated & the men in comfortable Quarters. Monday Jany. 19th. A party of about 200 of the Enemys Lt. Horse attacked an advanced party of our Horse 8 or 10 in number before they were dressed in the morning; but by the bravery of Capt. Lee & his little party they were prevented entering the house & driven off with the loss of 2 killed & 4 wounded.[1] Capt. Lee's Lieut. was slightly wounded. Same day some of our small Scoutts were attacked by parties of their Horse but came off without loss. The Cry against Congress still continued as high in Camp as ever, men of no less rank than Colonel's spoke of them with the greatest contempt & detestation, indeed every body of men who were entrusted with supplies for the Army shared largly in the profusion of Curses & Ill will of the Camp. I plainly saw there those whom the Cry of Liberty had called into the Field could now, (when the same Cause ceased to be a novelty) be held in it by no other tie than that of Interest.

Joseph Clark Diary, New Jersey Historical Society, Newark.
[1] Captain Henry ("Light Horse Harry") Lee (1756–1818), of the First Regiment of Light Dragoons, received thanks from the Continental Congress for his defense of the Spread Eagle Tavern near Valley Forge.

# Anne Louis de Tousard to Horatio Gates

Silas Deane (1737–89), a member of the Continental Congress, had looked to Europe to find officers interested in Continental commissions. One officer who distinguished himself in Continental service was Anne Louis de Tousard (1749–1817), a Frenchman who fought at the battles of Brandywine and Germantown. He served first with General Philippe Charles Jean Baptiste Trouson du Coudray (1738–77), who had arrived in America in May 1777 with eighteen officers and ten sergeants. In this letter de Tousard requests permission to serve in the Northern Department under commanding general Horatio Gates. Later, de Tousard was breveted lieutenant colonel by the Continental Congress and was voted a life pension for his gallantry at the Battle of Newport, Rhode Island, on August 29, 1778.

**Anne Louis de Tousard**

*Boston the January 13th. 1778*

General
When you left philadelphia to take the Command of the Northern department, I asked of general Ducoudray his permission to repair your army; but having ordered me, in the mean time, to survey and draw the plan of the country between wilmington

and philadelphia, he deprived me of the honour of attending you in the most glorious Campaign, that was ever heard of in America.

Our general having been unfortunately drowned,[1] and the Congress having refused to employ us agreeably to our treaty with his ambassador in france, and according to our commission which we received from the King of france for this expedition, all the officers of artillery are ready to embark by the first opportunity.

Having received from the french minister of War a Congé of two years to spend in America,[2] I think I cannot make better use of the second year of it, and more profitably for my own business, than in asking your agreement for repair your army.

I do ask neither appointment, nor rank, and I will think myself happy, if at the end of the next campaign, which shall be certainly as glorious to you as the last, I may carry along the testimony of your esteem; you may depend that I shall do every thing necessary to deserve it.

May be you would not remember my name. I was introduced to you by the late Gal. Ducoudray in Philadelphia, and I shew'd you a plan of drawing to which you was kind enough to give your approbation.

I Will expect your orders and in Whatever parts of my service you call me, my assiduity in performing your orders shall proofe you how much I am, General, Your most humble and obedient servant

DE TOUSARD *artillery offer.*

ALS, Horatio Gates Papers, New-York Historical Society, New York City.
[1] On September 15, 1777.
[2] *Congé:* leave of absence.

# JOHN McDOWELL TO ANTHONY WAYNE

JOHN MCDOWELL (1748–1814) was a captain in the Seventh Pennsylvania Battalion. In this letter to Brigadier General Anthony Wayne (1745–96), stationed at Fort Ticonderoga, McDowell informs him of his desire to transfer to medical duty because of the lack of medical personnel in the American army. McDowell served his country in that capacity until November 3, 1783.

*Liberty Village, February 1, 1778*

Dear Genl.

As Surgeons are extreamly scarce in our Army; and the Regiments, many of them suffering for want of them—And as the Regiments, from their Smallness, have no Necessity for so many Officers as they now contain: I have determin'd with Your Permission, to go into the Medical lines, as Surgeon to the 6th Pennsylva. Regt. I hope as I am not quiting the Service of my Country; but only leaving one Office to serve in another, which in my Opinion, with Respect to the present State of the Army, is more necessary; Your Honor will please to accept of this as a Resignation of my Captaincy in the 7th Pennsylva. Regt. I am, my Dear Genl. Your Honor's most Obedient And very hble. Servant

JOHN MCDOWELL

ALS, William Irvine Papers, Historical Society of Pennsylvania, Philadelphia.

# FRANCIS MURRAY TO GEORGE WASHINGTON

THE 1777–78 winter encampment had shortages and privations in every quarter. An inefficient quartermaster corps left the men with little food or clothing and magnified their suffering and discontent. General Washington desperately ordered foraging expeditions to seize privately owned goods for the army's use to provide some relief. Major Francis Murray (1731–1816), of the Third Pennsylvania Regiment, took part in one foraging expedition to Newtown, in Bucks County, Pennsylvania, twenty-two miles northeast of British-occupied Philadelphia. Major Murray was concerned with compensation for the cloth seized from the Bucks County civilians, as this letter reveals. Not long after writing this letter, Murray was taken prisoner and was not exchanged until December 25, 1780. He never returned to military service, but his partially successful efforts to obtain cloth while serving at Valley Forge were important in preventing some of the men from freezing to death.

*Newtown Feb. 13th. 1778*

Sir:

    Col. Stewart about Ten Days since Seized a Quantity of Cloth by approbation of your Excellency at Mr. Thomas Jenks Fulling Mill, belonging to divers Inhabitants of this County.[1] At that Time and Since there has been near 1000 yds. brought and Lodged at my House, where it now remains and nearly the Same Quantity remaing at said Mill to be finished off, and then to be brought here. A few days ago I received a letter from Col. Stewart, informing me that He had your permission to take the White Cloth for his Regiment, and in consequence thereof, I have employed the Taylors of his Regimt. together with several others Who I expect will finish the Same in A Short time. As Col. Stewart has given no directions Concerning the other Cloths, I think it necessary to inform your Excellency that there is between 7 and 800 yds of good Cloths of different Colours remaining at my House; which the owners are Dayly applying to me for, and insinuates that I detain them of my own authority only.

Having no particular orders how to act Respecting said Cloths, Would be glad to have your Excellencys Directions Concerning the Same. I would observe that these People to whom the Cloths belong are in General Wealthy, or in easy Circumstances, and there is Reason to Suspect there is many of them aganst the present measures.

However there are several of them frindly to the present Cause. And there are several poor People that the Want of their Cloths will prove very distressing to them and theire Families. Would beg leave to recommend that the Cloths taken be Valued and paid for as soon as possible, as some people Suspects they never will.

It is Suprising what numbers of people pass to Philadelphia from this and other places Daily, And am informed they Carry on Marketing little inferior to former times. There being no Guards on the Road between here and the City: the Militia being about Four Miles back from the Cross Roads. It is not in my power to do any thing in Respect of Guaring the Roads, having only one Subalteron and 18 Privates, Siven of which are Stationed to Guard the Fulling Mill While the Cloths are finishing off. Sir I have the Honour to be with Respect your Excellency, Most obedient

FRANCIS MURRAY *Major*

ALS, George Washington Papers, Library of Congress, Washington, D.C.
[1] Colonel Charles Stewart (1729–1800) was a commissary of issues.

# WILLIAM RUSSELL TO THE CONTINENTAL CONGRESS

## *March 13, 1778*

ON DECEMBER 19, 1776, William Russell (1735–93) became colonel of the Thirteenth Virginia Regiment. During the 1777–78 winter encampment at Valley Forge, Colonel Russell commanded one of the six Continental regiments under Brigadier General John Peter Gabriel Muhlenberg (1746–1807). Only 22 of Russell's 169 men were reported present and fit for duty at Valley Forge in the March 1778 regimental returns. With a sense of urgency, Colonel Russell wrote to the Continental Congress of his regiment's depleted ranks. In addition, many members of his regiment were stationed on the western Pennsylvania frontier. Hundreds of miles from the main units of the Continental army, the soldiers in the west had the added problems of loneliness and fear for the safety of their families. To assure military preparedness on the frontier and to alleviate the mental suffering of his troops, Russell recommends the immediate reunion of the separated portions of his regiment, then stationed at Valley Forge and across the Allegheny Mountains at Fort Pitt. Colonel Russell's letter reveals that he felt great compassion for the personal sufferings of his men and possessed as well military acumen. Colonel Russell continued in service until No-vember 3, 1783, when he was breveted briga-dier general.

Honorable Gentlemen,

The Officers of that part of the 13th. Virginia Regiment that is now here, have desired me to state their present situation to you, and to request your serious attention to a matter not only of consequence to themselves but to the country at large. The present situation of our Frontiers, where most of the Regiment were raised, is precari-ous and alarming: under perpetual apprehensions from the neighbouring savages, the inhabitants are obliged to crowd into forts, or withdraw themselves altogether from their settlements. Ruin and distress inevitably follow, and the most diligent and active exertions of the heads of families are necessary to preserve them. In such circum-stances the Officers conceive there is every reason to induce your honorable board to direct their march to that part of the country, where private as well as public interest are so strongly united to stimulate the most vigorous exertions against their own and their countrys enemies. But there are other arguments still stronger that might be urged. It seems agreed on all hands, and it wood be absurd to suppose otherwise, that the force now at Fort Pitt is absolutely necessary, and indeed insufficient for the defence of that important barrier.[1] Part of the Regiment is left there; and the greater part torne from their distressed families, were ordered to join the Army, notwith-standing the assurances they had received that they shoud be stationed there.

The consequence followed which all might forsee, that they grew exceedingly un-easy on account of their connexions, distressed their officers with petitions, which, altho reasonable they could not grant, and at length finding all applications useless and flattering themselves with that forgiveness which they afterwards met, by joining that part of the Regiment at Fort Pitt they deserted largely and out of three hundred men I marched down in July, by the last return there were only seventeen men present fit for duty. It was natural to expect that when a large part of the Regiment was left over the mountains, that the remainder both officers and soldiers wood be anxious to join them. Whoever has been in service will know how exceedingly dis-agreeable is the division of Regiments into detached bodies.

Officers lose a relish for the Service when their command dwindles into a handful of men, and it becomes utterly impossible to instruct them in military movements, or the discipline of a regular Army. What makes it still more disagreeable is, that not only the Regiment, but every company in it is divided, except one and that is over the mountains.

Thus it is impossible to prevent desertions from this part of the Regiment to that. Colo. Gibson has the direction of that,[2] and Major Campbell, nine Captains and my selfe have the command of the handfull here. But Colo. Gibson has long been entitled to a regiment, and must soon join it, and then the disposal of the officers and the regi-ment will be still more absurd, as there will be no field Officer with the main body at Fort Pitt, and all the field Officers and a very great superabundance of the others to the part down with the Army. In short, I would beg leave to represent to your Honors, that there is no place where the 13th: Virginia Regiment can be stationed with so much advantage as on the other side the Allegany. If they stay there, the regiment will be full and the men contented, as long as public and private interests coincide together. If they are sent down the country, their apprehensions for their families will occasion desertions and at any rate frequent applications for furloughs. But if they are divided, the part stationed here will be forever undone, as their interests are entirely against their stay, and the tie resulting from the union of men in Companies and Companies in a regiment becomes dissolved, and it will be impossible to keep them with any kind of content in the service.

I conceive these matters will be worthy your careful attention, as men are more wanting then Arms. If we do not shew attention to their reasonable desires, but sacrifice them to present occasions without looking forward to future contingencies, we may soon lament our unhappy inattention, and perhaps be exposed to the triumps of our enemies. I would therefore beg leave to conclude with the two following requests, either that the small part of the regiment now so unhappily situated here, be immediately ordered to the neighborhood of Fort Pitt, or if that most desirable request cannot be obtained, that then the whole regiment be drawn together and no longer continued in their present disagreeable detached situation. I have the honor to be, Gentlemen, with the greatest respect, your Most Obed. Servt.

W RUSSELL *Colo. 13th. Va. Regiment*

ALS, Papers of the Continental Congress, National Archives, Washington, D.C.

[1] Pittsburgh, Pa.

[2] Probably Lieutenant Colonel John Gibson (d. 1822) of the Thirteenth Virginia Regiment.

# ROBERT TROUP TO HORATIO GATES

INTERNECINE QUARRELS over power, rank, and privilege plagued the Continental army throughout the American Revolution. Perhaps the most serious power contest General Washington faced was the "Conway Cabal." Although the precise nature of the cabal is still unknown, New Englanders in the Continental Congress and the Board of War under Major General Horatio Gates hoped to replace or eclipse the power of George Washington. Lieutenant Colonel Robert Troup, an aide-de-camp to Gates, suggested to Gates in this letter that Baron de Kalb was unqualified to command a new Canadian expedition. The promotion of Johann, Baron de Kalb (1721–80) on November 6, 1777, to major general over Thomas Conway exacerbated the already troubled situation. Baron de Kalb was resented by many for being a foreign adventurer rather than an officer dedicated to the cause of American liberty. Gates and Conway continued in the army service after the affair, and Baron de Kalb became the Marquis de Lafayette's (1757–1834) second in command for the abortive invasion of Canada. Washington, of course, survived the "Conway Cabal" and continued as the commander in chief of the Continental army, but bickering and factions remained a debilitating problem for the officer corps.

*Albany, March, 26th. 1778*

Dear General,

Two Days ago your Letter, of the 14th. Instant, was delivered to me, by Capt. Kennedy, and I beg you will accept my sincere Thanks for the Friendship it contains.

As I am interested in your Welfare, I cannot express the Joy I feel at your happy Delivery from the Vengeance of General Wilkinson.[1] A Duel! How alarming the thought! To be wounded, crippled, and perhaps killed! "That's the Rub."

You may say what you will, but I swear, by the Great Toe Nail of Sir Thomas A. Becket, that you are a fortunate Man. Yes, You are a fortunate Man. To depreciate the Value of a new coined Brigadier General, without receiving a Challenge, Kick, or Cuff, is to me as miraculous as the Convention of Saratoga. But leaving this doughty Heroe, to be tortured on the Rack of his own Conscience, let me speak to you on Matters of public Concern.

The Marquis, being fond of Power, is much chagrined with the thought of joining the Southern Army. Tho he has seen the late Resolve of Congress, he will remain here, till it is sanctified with the approbation of the Head-Quarters. His Delay, in some Measure, fetters the Alertness of General Conway, who wishes to avoid a Dispute, that may only terminate in malicious Invective. Inclosed are the Letters which have passed between them on the Subject.

In Compliance with your Request I have called for the different Returns in this Department: I now send you that of Fort Schuyler: the others will be ready by the Beginning of next Week. I shall then go to Fish-Kill, & endeavour to transmit you an account of Affairs in that Quarter. I use the word "transmit," because I must stay some Time in Jersey, for the Reason I assigned in my last. I am determined, however, to return to York Town, when Circumstances will permit, and regret that I am longer to be separated from a Family, which has ever loaded me with unmerited Favors.

I went with General Conway, this afternoon, to view the Laboratory, and Park of artillery. The Regularity, conspicuous in both, drew my Admiration; and I believe Major Stephens is one of the few Officers, in our Army, who does not consider Method as altogether idle & superfluous.[2] The Adjutant of his Corps is charged with a particular Report to you, which, among other things, will serve to shew you his Zeal to forward the Service.

Kosiuszko left this, for West-Point, on Monday.[3] When I cease to love this young Man, I must cease to love those Qualities which form the brightest, & completest of Characters.

If you are desirous of beguiling a tedious Hour—if you long to hear all the pleasing Variety of laughing—give the Bearer, Dr. Treat, a general Invitation to breakfast, dine, and sup with you. He is a lineal Descendant of *Democritus,* who has ever been justly esteemed the Father of Jollity.

I wish to have my Respects presented to the Family, and beg leave to subscribe Myself, Dear General, Your much obliged, and Very humble Servant

ROBT. TROUP

ALS, Horatio Gates Papers, New-York Historical Society, New York City.

[1] James Wilkinson (1758–1825) resigned as deputy adjutant general of the Northern Department and as a brigadier general on March 6, 1778. He was secretary to the Board of War until his resignation on March 31, 1778. He did have words with Gates, who had been his friend, and a duel was threatened, but both resolved their differences.

[2] Major Ebenezer Stevens.

[3] Colonel-Engineer Thaddeus Kosciuszko. In 1778 Kosciuszko had planned the fortification of West Point. That important fortress was converted into a military academy based, in part, on the recommendation of Timothy Pickering. On April 22, 1783, Timothy Pickering, colonel and quartermaster general, wrote a long series of recommendations about West Point's future in an American defense system. He strongly advised that the fortress be designated as headquarters for the training of American officers. In 1802 the academy enrolled its first class.

# SHEPARD KOLLOCK TO JOHN LAMB

LIEUTENANT SHEPARD KOLLOCK (1750–1839), of the Second Battalion of Continental Artillery, asks his commanding officer, Colonel John Lamb, to discharge him, for he believed that an end to the war was near. He alludes to the British peace commission headed by Frederick Howard, Fifth Earl of Carlisle, which failed because of strong resistance from the Continental Congress and the army. Lack of promotion was another of his reasons for requesting a discharge. Late in May 1778 General Washington learned that the British in Philadelphia were to be evacuated to New York City across New Jersey. Kollock could not, therefore, be discharged until January 3, 1779. Within a year after his discharge, he began publication of the *New-Jersey Journal* at Chatham to inform and inspire the state's soldiers and patriots.

*New Windsor May 15, 1778*

Sir,

As there is now a Prospect of a Termination of the War, and its more than probable there will be no Campaign this Year, beg I may be indulged to resign my Commission, my domestic Affairs requiring my personal Attendance. I have very cogent Reasons for making this Request; Reasons which, in my Oppinion, would justify the most abrupt Resignation; but as I entered the Service from a patriotic Principle, was not willing to discourage the Same, therefore passed over, with impunity, several very ungenerous Promotions. I would not wish to wound your Ears with a Repitition of

Grievances, which, I believe, are repugnant to your Sentiments, and did not originate from you, however I can't help observing that I look upon it as an unprecedented hardship of four Supernumerary Captain Lieutenants being appointed to your Regiment; also my Commission dated in Febuary, though appointed in December, Second Lieutenants and Serjeants appointed to Captain Lieutenants, and, to my knowledge, not from Acts of Merit. These are Grievances of such a Glaring Nature, I find it difficult to digest them. I look upon the present Commission I hold as tantamount to my Abilities, but when I take a Survey of some above me, have the Vanity to think I could fill the important Post of Captain Lieutenant with equal Applause, therefore beg, if I am not Capable of Promotion in my Turn, I may be discharged from the Service. I am, Sir, Your's with Respect,

SHEPARD KOLLOCK

ALS, John Lamb Papers, New-York Historical Society, New York City.

# CHARLES BULKELEY MEMOIR

## 1778

PRISONS WERE SOMBER places for the Continental soldier and sailor. Many preferred the hazards of attempting escape to the known and unrelenting conditions of life in confinement. Captain-Lieutenant Nathaniel Nazro (1754–c.1782) of Massachusetts, captured aboard the privateer *Hannibal*, attempted escape from the Mill Prison in England in 1781. First Lieutenant William Capers (1758–1812), of South Carolina, was able to flee from British-occupied Charleston in 1781. Probably the most exciting escape story is that of Lieutenant Charles Bulkeley (1753–1848), who was captured twice and was able to gain his freedom both times. On March 9, 1778, he was captured off Barbados while serving aboard the U.S.S. *Alfred*, commanded by Captain Elisha Hinman (1732–1805). His journal describes his confinement, his dramatic escape, and his flight to safety in France. The unswerving determination to return to service and the free nation they fought for characterized such adventurous men.

We sailed for England & arrived at Portsmouth, were landed at Gosport & examined & confined in Fortune Prison about one mile from Gosport.[1] We were confined in the upper part of the Prison, with the Liberty of the yard in the day time & at night Lamps were placed all around the prison to prevent escapes. In consequence of complaints recd, a Presbyterian Priest by the name of Wren was permitted to come into the prison Weekley & to supply many of the wants that the prisoners stood in need of. We now made arrangements to make our escape—we cut through the floor into the black hole & then through another floor for the purpose of digging out, the Black Hole being the place that the prisoners were confined in on account of any offences they may have committed. Before breaking out we agreed in case we got sepperated to meet at a certain place in London. We dug in a Slanting direction so that there might be dirt overhead sufficient that it might not cave in. The tools we had to work with were an old chisel & a broken fencing foil, we made small bags to put the dirt in, we found great difficulty in secreting the dirt at first, we put some in our chest, the fireplace below being stoped up, we took some bricks out of the chimney in the upper loft & took the bags & lowered them down to the bottom & with a triping line empteed them so that they might not be any noise heard from the falling of the dirt, we were over 3 weeks in digging out. We made a lottery for the purpose of having regular turns in going out, for the prevention of confusion & noise, the guard being very near to the hole dug for our escape. Before going out we put a pair of Trowses, Shirt & stocking, over our other cloths & covered our heads & hats, & after getting out we took them off & threw them away. The hole was so small that Capt Harrison of a States Brig of Virginia, after trying to get out was wedged in, we were obligd to pull him back by the legs. After our escape we went to Gosport for the purpose of crossing to Portsmouth. Three of us got a Post chaise (Mr Richards having seperated from us by accident).[2] We had to go by the prison just at day light & before any alarm was given, & arrived at London in the afternoon being 75 Miles & here we all again met & staid a few days & visited St. Pauls Church & the Tower & were well worth seeing. Capt Welch & Lt Hamilton went to Holland[3] & Lt Richards & myself, went to Deal 75 miles from London & got a passage in an open Smugglers Boat & crossed the channel for france in the night & landed at Calais.

Charles Bulkeley Journal, New London Historical Society, Shaw Mansion, New London, Conn.
[1] Falkland Prison.
[2] Lieutenant Peter Richards of the *Alfred*.
[3] Captain John Welch and Lieutenant William Hambleton of marines assigned to the *Alfred*.

# JOHN HEARD TO GEORGE WASHINGTON

## *June 25, 1778*

THE LONG MONTHS at Valley Forge did include some moments of hope for the suffering soldiers. The alliance with France had brought with it the promise of new manpower and naval support. In addition,

General Sir William Howe, who was replaced by General Sir Henry Clinton in March 1778, never attacked the army while in winter encampment. Clinton recognized the possibility of entrapment in Philadelphia between

French ships and the American army and thus made plans to evacuate. Clinton began the evacuation on June 8, and his slow march across New Jersey invited attack. General Washington broke camp on June 19 and was near Clinton's rear guard by June 24.

At Valley Forge on February 8, 1778, John Heard had been made a captain in Colonel Stephen Moylan's Fourth Regiment of Continental Light Dragoons. Although this cavalry unit dwindled to thirty poorly equipped men during the next four months, it was essential in monitoring the march of the British army across New Jersey. Captain Heard's mounted troop maneuvered ahead of the advancing enemy, enabling him to give Washington valuable intelligence of the movement of Clinton's army in New Jersey from Allentown to Monmouth Courthouse.

Sir

The Enimy Advance gard is encampt about A Mile & three Quarters from Allentown on the Cranberry Road this you may Depend on. I am a going over to the Monmouth Road to see Weather they are Advanced on that Road as soon as I return I will Despatch a Horse man immediately to Inform you. I am yr. Humbl. St.

JOHN HEARD *Lt.*

ALS, George Washington Papers, Library of Congress, Washington, D.C.

# FRANCIS NICHOLS TO GEORGE WASHINGTON

## *June 26, 1778*

BY JUNE 26, 1778, an American attack on the British army moving across New Jersey was imminent. Major Francis Nichols, of Colonel Richard Butler's Ninth Pennsylvania Regiment, was one of the many valiant officers who risked their lives to gain valuable intelligence of Clinton's movements for Washington. Two British deserters informed Major Nichols that Clinton's army, then en route from Philadelphia to New York City, was bound for Monmouth Courthouse.

*Friday 10 Oclock A:M*

May it Please your Excellency

I have the Pleasure to inform you that the front of the Enimy moved of this morning at foure oclock. At Half after Seven I procured a guide and went under cover into thire incampment and found all the army moved But the Rear Guard. On our Return we fell in with two British Soldiers Neare thire incampment (who say they are Disarters) they inform us that, the Enemy moved as above mentioned and is to Halt at Monmouth Courthouse. This I send you by Express the Disarters I send you under Guard probly they may give you some information which may be of Importance.

    We are Just going to fall in the Rear of the army to procure further inteligence. I have the Honour to Be your Excellencys Most Humble Servant.

FRANCS. NICHOLS *Major*

ALS, George Washington Papers, Library of Congress, Washington, D.C.

# JOSEPH CLARK DIARY

## *June 28, 1778*

BY JUNE 27, 1778, Washington's army was encamped between Cranbury and Englishtown, New Jersey. Major General Charles Lee was given command of the advance troops that were to engage the British forces the next day at Monmouth Courthouse. Lee's dilatory behavior in establishing contact with the enemy on the morning of June 28 enabled the strung-out British regiments to regroup. Lee's actions are described in Joseph Clark's diary. Only the courage of the officers and men under Lee and the firm leadership of General Washington saved the battle from being a bloody rout for the Americans. The Battle of Monmouth ended as a tactical draw, but the Americans were convinced they had been victorious by forcing the British from the field of battle. Lee was court-martialed for his actions from July 4 to August 12, 1778.

    Sunday June 28th: The 2 Armies had drawn near to each other, when in a Council of war it was thot. proper to attack them accordingly the proper dispositions were made and parties of Militia & regular Troops were detached to provoke them to the attack. After some trifelling Scirmages in the early part of the day, the Enemy were drawing off below Monmouth, when Genl. Lee with his Command, advanced upon them and began the Cannonade, the Enemy immediately turned & prepared for the Attack, Genl. Lee finding his ground not so advantageous, withdrew gradually to lead them on, tho' tis said he at length withdrew so far, & so fast as to be highly culpable. However having secured proper heights a resolute stand was made, & prodigious execution done with the Cannon. A large flanking party was sent down upon the left of the Enemys Line who did great Execution, small parties of Musketry were stationed at different places on the Enemys Right, who were also very serviceable. The Cannonade began about 10 oClock, & continued till late in the Afternoon, when the Enemy gave way & retreated some distance; then halted, and it was expected would come on again to the attack, in the mean time, our Men having pursued them some distance were drawn up & posted in such manner as to recieve them to the best advantage. But the day being so excessively warm, & the Enemy so handsomely drubbed already, they did not attempt to meet us again. His excellency commanded in person, & the Officers & Men in general who were in action, behaved with the greatest Spirit. There were upwards of 250 of the Enemy buried in the Field and about 40 of our people. The number of wounded & prisoners on either side I have not been able to collect. About 12 oClock at night the Enemy went off with the greatest precipitation and our Troops next day came up to English Town.

Joseph Clark Diary, New Jersey Historical Society, Newark.

# James McHenry Journal

THE BATTLE OF MONMOUTH, one of the few battles in which both major armies stood their ground and fought, has been vividly described in several contemporary accounts. One of the best perspectives on that sultry day is that of James McHenry (1752–1816), a surgeon who had been taken prisoner in November 1776 and had been only recently exchanged in March 1778. McHenry was appointed Washington's secretary and was consequently intimately involved in the dynamics of battlefield leadership. His detailed narrative of the long march to overtake the British and the subsequent battle comes from his unique vantage point as Washington's secretary.

**James McHenry**
PHOTO: PETER A. JULEY, NEW YORK CITY

*Valley Forge 18 June 1778*

Early this Morning by intelligence from M Lane[1] Sir Henry Clinton & the British Army evacuated Philada. & took post on the Jersey side.

Everything being arranged for our March, and a division under General Lee proceeded towards the Delaware in the Evening. . . . [June 21, 1778] A Rapid Mornings March—excessive hot. Some of the Soldiers die suddenly. Reach Coryls Ferry—Encamp on the Pennsylvania side. The General crosses with the spare baggage and artillery. Head Quarters at one Holcombs in the Jersey. Here are some charming Girls—but one of the Drums of the Guard more a favorite than Hamilton. Division of Lee & Wayne 4 Miles in advance of Coryls. General Arnold advises that the Enemies advanced Guard commd. by General Leslie consists of 2000—Main Body 5000—rear Guard 2000 under Knyphausen—Their shipping below Rudy Island. . . . 28th. The Baron Steuben & Col Laurens reconnoitre.[2] Find the encampment up, & their rear formed at the Court House. They appear ready to March. Genl. Lee informed of this by Col. Laurens.

Gen. Lee moves his Men to the attack. The Enemy advanced two Regiments by files into the woods near the Court House. These being reported to Genl. Lee as heavey Columns he immediatly ordered a halt & Varnums Brigade to repass a Bridge which they had just crossed. The Enemy were now more closely reconnoitred & Gen Lee ordered the Troops to advance—But our advance Troops had got into disorder—were much exhausted by marching & countermarching— the moment lost for attacking the Enemy. They had now formed their order of Battle & came on briskly to the Charge with the Cavalry in Front.

Our few Horse were charged by all theirs, & were obliged to give way 'till supported by the infantry.

Livingston & Col. Stewart were ordered to turn their left—where the Enemy charged their front. These Regiments were then ordered to fall back & form in the Village—from thence they retired to Rus-House and the rest of the detachment through the Woods. General Lee again ordered a retreat having a fine defile unguarded.

In this juncture Genl. Washington meets the detachment, having recd. no notice of the order to retreat. He was much surprised, chagrind and disapointed; and instantly perceiving there was no time to be lost—for the Enemy were in full view & full March to improve the advantage they had gained over Lees detachment—He directed some of the disordered Troops to form, 'till the Main Body cou'd take a position of support.

The moment was critical, and the safety of the whole army depends upon a firm opposition.

Colonels Stewart & Ramsay's Troops were nearest the General.[3] He encouraged the Men—He took the officers by the Hand—He told them how much depended on a moments resistance, He said he was satisfied every thing would be attempted. Col. Ramsay & Col. Stewart gave him assurances of their exertions, & in that instant the whole was involved in the smoke of Battle.

As these two Regiments were to sustain the assault of the whole British line, it is not to be supposed they coud make a long opposition. They were obliged to give way—& retreated into the woods—but not before they had given our Main Body time to form & take an advantageous ground.

Two Regiments of Varnums Brigade, under L. Col. Olney recd. the next Shock of the Enemy, who keep advancing.[4] The British Cavalry dashed upon them with great impetuosity—but cou'd not stand a cool & well directed Fire from our Troops. This opposition did Olney great Honor.

We had now every thing disposed for a general action—our center was covered by a Morass—the left commanded an extent of open Ground on the Flank which made it difficult for the Enemy to turn in rear—and the right was covered by a ravine & close wood.

Lord Stirling commanded our left-Wing & General Greene the Right. Olney was at length obliged to give way—but he did it with great dignity. Livingston who acted on his right, was very powerfull in his Fire, & did much execution. Lord Stirling planted a Battery of Cannon on the right of his Wing, & made a detachment of Infantry under Col. Scilly & Col. Parker of the 1st. Virga. Regiment which penetrated the woods & fell vigorously on the Enemys right flank.[5] This obliged the Enemy to give way.

After this small repulse they appeared in motion towards our left.

General Wayne keeps them at Bay in front, having occupied a Barn & orchard, which he defended with Bravery.[6] At this instant when they pressed upon Wayne on all sides, Genl. Greene took possession of a Piece of Ground on their left with a Brigade under the immediate command of Genl Woodford.[7]

It was now the fate of our Army was to be decided. The firing was supported with equal vigor—and neither party seemed inclined to give way—all was dubious—when General Greene opened a Battery of Cannon which [    ] the Enemy. This, & General Waynes fire at length forced them to retire with considerable loss—& gave us the ground upon which they had faught, & all thier wounded & killed.

Night set in and we failing in our attempt to turn the Enemys flank—composed ourselves to sleep behind the line of Battle under a large Tree.

"Journal of a March a Battle and a Waterfall By Major James McHenry Secretary to His Excellency General Washington," Emmet Collection, New York Public Library, New York City.

[1] Captain Allen McLane.

[2] Colonel John Laurens (c.1756–82); Friedrich Wilhelm, Baron von Steuben (1730–94).

[3] Lieutenant Colonel Nathaniel Ramsay (d. 1817) of Maryland.

[4] Lieutenant Colonel Jeremiah Olney.

[5] Joseph Cilley (see Joseph Cilley to Thomas Bartlett, July 22, 1778); Colonel Richard Parker (d. 1780).

[6] Brigadier General Anthony Wayne.

[7] Brigadier General William Woodford (1734–80).

# ARCHILAUS LEWIS ORDERLY BOOK

A VIVID ACCOUNT of the aftermath of the Battle of Monmouth on June 28, 1778, is contained in the orderly book kept by Archilaus Lewis (1753–1834) as adjutant for Colonel Joseph Vose's (1739–1816) First Massachusetts Regiment. Lewis had been commissioned a lieutenant in this newly formed regiment on January 1, 1777. During the battle 37 American soldiers died of sunstroke. Over 250 British and German soldiers were buried. The battle ended in a stalemate with casualties of approximately 350 for each side, but Americans viewed it as their victory and celebrated the event along with the second anniversary of American independence on July 4.

*Head Quarters Freehould, Monmouth Countay June 29th. 1778* . . . The Commander in Chief Congratulates the armey on the Victoray obtaind over the armes of his Britannake Majistey yeasterday & thanks most Sincearly the gallant officers and who Distinguishd themselves upon this occation—and Such others as by there Good order & Coolness Gave the happiest presages of what might have be Expected had they Come to Action. Genl. Dickerson[1] & the Militia of this State are also thankd for ther noble Spirit which they Shewn in opposing the Enemy on there march from Phelidilphier and for the ade which they have given by [    ] and Impeading there motions so as to Allow the Continetulle troops time to come up with them. A party Consisting of 200 men to parade Immedatly to bury the Dead Slaine of Boath Armies. Genl. Woodfords Brigade is to Cover this party. The offcrs of the american Armey are to be Buried with Militeray Honnours due to men who have nobly fought and Dyed in the Cause of Liberty & there Country. Doctr. Cockring will Derect what is to be done with the wounded & Sick.[2] He is to apply to the Qt.M.Gen. and Adgt. Genl. for Necessry Assistance. The Severall Detachments except those under Colo. Morgan are to join there Respective Brigades Immedaly and the Line to be formd Agreable to the orders of the 22d Inst. The armey is to march from the Left the [    ] Line in front the Cavelray in the Rear, the march to begin at 5 oClock this after noon.

Hd Qrs. English town June 30th 1778 . . . The men are to Wash them Silves this after noon and appear as Deacent as posiable—7 o Clock this Evening is appointed that we may publickly Unite in thanksgiving to the Supreme Disposer of Human Events, for the Victoray which was obtain on Sunday over the flower of the British Armey. . . .

After order July 3rd . . . To morrow the Anniversary of the Declaration of Independancy will be Celebrated by fireing thirteen Cannon and fudejoy of the whole Line the armey by formd. on the Brunswick Side of the River at 5 oClock in the after noon. The ground appointed by the Qr Mr. Genl. The Soldres are to Adorn there hatts with Green Baughs and to make the best appearance posiable. The Dispersion will be given to morrow in orders. Duble Allowance of Rum will be Servd out.

Archilaus Lewis Orderly Book, Maine Historical Society, Portland.

[1] Major General Philemon Dickinson.

[2] Dr. John Cochran (1730–1807).

# JOSEPH CILLEY TO THOMAS BARTLETT

**Joseph Cilley**
COURTESY OF THE STATE HOUSE, CONCORD, N.H.
PHOTO: BILL FINNEY, CONCORD, N.H.

JOSEPH CILLEY (1734–99), a colonel in the First New Hampshire Regiment, vividly recalled the brutality of the day-long Battle of Monmouth fought in temperatures approaching 100 degrees. He and many of his fellow officers proved their patriotism in the din of battle on that sultry day.

*Camp 4 miles above White Plains, N.Y., July 22, 1778*

Dear Sir:

Your favor of the 10th of July came safe to hand, by Major Titcomb; am much obliged to you for its contents. I left Valley Forge the 18th of June, with the right wing of the army, under the command of General Lee, in pursuit of the enemy, who left Philadelphia the 10th. The whole of our army pursued, with His Excellency, General Washington. Crossed the Delaware at a ferry called Corell's,[1] where it was thought best to send out several parties to harass the enemy's rear. General Scott was sent first,[2] with 1600 men picked from the whole army, in order to watch the enemy's motion. I was ordered on this party, soon after it was thought best to give the enemy battle. General Lee was sent on this errand. He called in General Scott—in short, he had 5,000 Continental troops, besides a number of militia. On the 28th of June he was ordered to attack the enemy with his party, and that General Washington with the whole army would support him. We were at a small town called Englishtown, about 4 miles from Monmouth Court House, where the enemy lay. We begun our march before sunrise, proceeded toward the field of battle; came to the plain; the enemy gave way; seemed to be in great confusion, without making any opposition, except some scattering musketry and a few field pieces playing on both sides at long shot, when, to my great surprise, I saw the right wing of our party giving way in great confusion. There was a morass in our rear; I thought whether it was not intended to cross that, in order to take better ground. There was a wood in the rear of the party I was with. We were ordered to cross and form in that wood, where we lay some time. The enemy observing this, halted, came to the right about, and pursued us about two miles, when General Washington came up, ordered our party to make a stand to check the enemy, whilst the army could form, which was done immediately. The severest cannonading ensued as ever was in America. Our men behaved with great fortitude. The cannonading lasted between two and three hours. I was in the front line of our army, in the left wing. His excellency ordered me to take the battalion that I then commanded, consisting of 350 rank and file, detailed from Poor's, Glover's, Patterson's, Larnard's and Varnum's brigades, with Lieutenant Colonel Dearborn and Major Thair, (who were with me) to go and see what I could do with the enemy's right wing, which was formed in an orchard in our front.[3] Marched on toward them until I came within about forty rods, when I ordered my battalion to form the line of battle, which was done. The enemy began a scattering fire. I ordered my men to advance, which they did in good order. When the enemy saw that we were determined to push close on them, they gave way and took post in a scout of wood and gave me a very heavy fire, under the cover of several pieces of artillery. I advanced within a few rods, give them a heavy fire, which put them in confusion. They run off. I killed a number on the field. Took between twenty and thirty prisoners. Should have pursued further, but the extreme heat of the weather was such that several of my men died with the heat. We took possession of the field. Found left on the field about three hundred of the enemy's dead, with several officers. Amongst them was Colonel Moneton, who commanded the first battalion of Grenadiers.[4] They retreated that night about eleven o'clock in great confusion. Left at the Court House five wounded officers and about forty soldiers. We should have pursued, but our army were so overcome with the heat that the General thought not advisable to pursue. Desertions still continue from the enemy at the least confusion. Their army is weakened two thousand five hundred since they left Philadelphia. I think Clinton is brought himself into a fine hobble. He has now a strong French fleet in his front and General Washington in his rear. I think we shall Burgoyne him in a few weeks, which God grant may be the case. Doubtless the particulars of the strength of the French fleet will come to your hand long before this, or I would give some account of them. This may suffice. They are able to flog all the British sheep in America.

My love to your wife and mother. I am, Sir, with respect, Your friend and humble servant.

J. CILLEY

N.B. General Lee's behavior is now on trial for his conduct.[5] How it will turn is uncertain. It is my opinion that if he had behaved well we should have destroyed the major part of Clinton's army.

Sir: Hurry Mr. Odihorne about my collar.

ALS, Society of the Cincinnati, Exeter, N.H.
[1] Coryell's Ferry.
[2] Brigadier General Charles Scott.

[3] Enoch Poor, John Glover, John Paterson (1744–1808), Ebenezer Learned (1728–1801), and James Varnum (1748–89), brigadier generals in the Continental army; Lieutenant Colonel Henry Dearborn (1751–1829) of the Nineteenth New Hampshire Regiment; and Major Simeon Thayer (1737–1800) of Rhode Island.

[4] Colonel Henry Moncton (1740–78) died while commanding the Second Battalion of Grenadiers.

[5] Lee was found guilty of disobedience, misbehavior, and disrespect.

# Thomas Clark to James Hogg

AFTER THE stalemated Battle of Monmouth on June 28, 1778, the British army undertook no extensive field operations in the northern states. Colonel Thomas Clark (d. 1792), whose First North Carolina Regiment had fought at Monmouth, writes to James Hogg of Hillsboro, North Carolina, from White Plains, New York, where Washington's army was encamped. Colonel Clark, who would later be wounded and captured, expresses his faith that American independence has been firmly established and alludes to the expected movement of portions of General Sir Henry Clinton's army from New York to Florida and the West Indies. The retreat from Monmouth and the depletion of Clinton's army by these troop movements spelled a loss of prestige for the British and a resurgence of American confidence in the patriot cause. However, years of fighting would remain.

*Camp White Plains, Sept. 6th, 1778*

Dear Sir:

A few days ago I received a letter from your Brother dated New York August 19th 78. He complain that the hot weather has brought back a little of his old complaint, but is very anxious to return to Carolina, and hopes that time will be given to consider the New Constitution and Laws before any oath is tendered him. He is also very desirous to have a meeting with me.

I have always had a great friendship for your Brother and never considered him as an enemy to this Country, I would be glad to have a meeting wt. him could it be done with any Convenience. Burgwin, Cruder, McCullock, and several other gentlemen from Carolina are at New York and I believe intend to make up the matter with their Country if they Can, a great change Mr. Hogg. The wisdom of Congress and the Conduct of Gen. Washington have waded through innumerable difficulties, but what can not a Country do when its liberties are at stake. Our independence is now I think firmly established by which Britain has lost her right hand. We have a fine army well disciplined, well armed and accoutered; what can they not do in this situation when they have performed wonders without any one of them. We charge them with Bayonets and with smaller numbers drove them before us, this is a fact. It is supposed they are about to leave New York. They are like the wandering Israelites equally cursed by their maker; this Campaign I think will deprive them of any foot hold in America. Please make my Compliments to Mrs. Hogg and family and all friends. I am Dr. Sir, your obedt. humble Servt.

TH. CLARK

P.S. Your Brother at present has a small touch of the Gout, should he come out this way I will do all in my power to procure him a safe pass to No. Carolina.

Walter Clark, ed., *The State Records of North Carolina* (1896), XIII, 478.

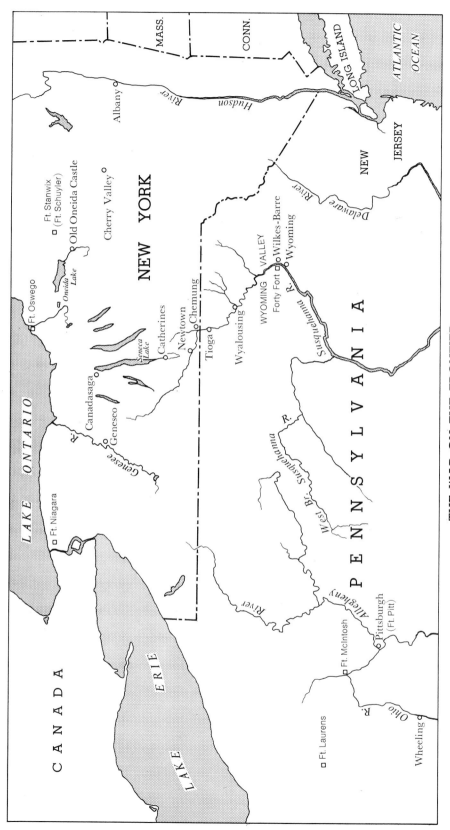

THE WAR ON THE FRONTIER

# CHAPTER THREE

# The War in the North:
# Indians, Battles and Skirmishes,
# Mutiny, and Conspiracy

## 1778–1781

THE BATTLE OF MONMOUTH was the last major battle in the North between the armies of Washington and Clinton. The north became a region of battles and skirmishes fought with smaller forces. The Continental army made several thrusts and feints on the periphery of occupied New York City. Operating from the hills surrounding the city, the American army distinguished itself in such engagements as Stony Point, New York, and Paulus Hook, New Jersey. The British incursion into New Jersey in June 1780 confirmed that the British were unable to provoke a major engagement and were equally unable to attack Washington's base at Morristown.

Indian massacres of settlers and soldiers on the frontiers of New York and Pennsylvania in 1778 induced the Continental Congress to authorize a punitive expedition led by Major General John Sullivan against the Six Nations. Despite disciplinary problems and the rough terrain, the expedition suc-

ceeded in defeating the Indians, burning villages, and destroying crops. The frontiers, however, continued to be dangerous for the Continental soldier throughout the remainder of the war.

The chronic problems of inadequate supply and depreciation of pay diminished the effectiveness of the army and helped to undermine morale. Symbols of this decline in dedication to the American cause were Benedict Arnold's treason in 1780 and the mutinies of the Pennsylvania and New Jersey lines in 1781. By the winter of 1781 in the north, it was clear that long service had wearied the Continental officer and soldier. However, their actions in battle against Indians, Loyalists, and British regulars on the coasts and frontiers, the energy expended in crucial efforts to suppress discontent and mutiny, and the constant concern for the conditions that created these problems indicated the caliber of the Continental soldiers' courage and patriotism.

# Anne Louis de Tousard to Henry Laurens

R̲ELATIONS WITH THE Indians in New York and Pennsylvania were a major factor in military operations on the northern frontier after 1777. The Six Nations (the Mohawks, Onandagas, Cayugas, Senecas, Oneidas, and Tuscaroras) initially pledged neutrality in a conference at Albany in 1775. However, all but the Oneidas and the Tuscaroras fell under the influence of Sir John Johnson (1742–1830), Major John Butler (1728–96), and the Mohawk chief Joseph Brant (1742–1807). The relative neutrality of the Oneidas can be credited in part to the French volunteer Anne Louis de Tousard (1749–1817), who made a valuable contribution to American freedom by soliciting military support from the Oneidas in the troubled area around Fort Stanwix. De Tousard's letter to Henry Laurens (1724–92), president of the Continental Congress, describes the successful negotiations with the Oneida chiefs, or sachems, in March and April 1778. The Oneida warriors sent to George Washington served as guides in the Sullivan expedition of 1779. De Tousard further proved his dedication to the American cause when he lost an arm in the Battle of Newport on August 31, 1778.

*Head Quarters 23th. May 1778*

Sir,

Having received orders of the General Marquis de la Fayette to go with Lt Col. Gouvion to help him in Building the fort of the Oneidas,[1] and in Engaging their Warriors to Join the Army of His Excellency General Washington, I went to their Castle, and after a month of deliberations, I receive their promise to send a party of Indians to Join the army.

I write here the Copy of the letter of Mr. S. Kirkland, their minister which will acquaint you with the good dispositions I have found the Indians in for the United States of America.

"At the request of some of the Oneida Chiefs—you will please to Inform His Excellency General Washington and the Marquess de la fayette that the present State of affairs among the Indians in this Department forbid their Sending a large party to the Grand Army. Should matters take a favourable turn in a Convention of the six nations now setting at Onondaga—His Excellency may expect a Considerable number of their best warriors to repair to his Camp.

Among the party now going are several of Ability & Influence in their nation—particularly Thomas Hongost—Angur—Jacob Reed & Daniel a Son of one of their best men &c. Your

Sam. Kirkland Minsry.[2]

To Mr. De *Tousard* 24th. April 1778"

The Day before we went from fort Schuyller, the Whole nation of Oneida was meet to receive the presents which the honourable Congress had favoured them with, for their Constant affection to the United States of America. The Chiefs addressed them the Speech of which I send you the traduction.

"An Adress of the Oneida Sachems to a Party of young Warriors bound to General Washington Conducted by Mr De Tousard.

Nephews, Warriors open your Ears you are now parting with your Uncles the sachems. 'Tis Common on Such occasion to Speak a few words. Young Warriors often neads advice. You are undertaking a long march. You will be exposed to fatigues and many temptations, and many will be your observers—not only americans, but Some chiefs warriors from our father The french King.

Keep in mind that warriors sustain an Important Character. They Can do much good or Commit Great Enormities. They are to do Good by removing out of the Way such evils as threaten the peace of the Country. Here they may display the hero, but private revenge is to be Carefully avoid'd. To abuse and plunder a helpless (and it may be an innocent family) is beneath the Character of a Warrior.

Nephews Keep in mind, you are bound to the Grand army of america, and will be Introduced to General Washington the Chief Warrior, and to a great officer of our father the french King the Marquess de la fayette at whose particular application you go. Any misconduct in you, if only a little, will be of Extensive Influence. The reproach not Easily whiped away. Therefore observe a line of Conduct proper for Warriors. Let there be always a good agrement betwixt you. Be always of one mind. Have one object in view & don't let every one think himself a head warrior or that he use all Those freedoms which are Indulged at home—but Let one and all yeld Implicit obedience to Mr De Tousard who will conduct you in the march and fight with you.

Beware of strong Liquor the Common beguiler of Indians. Nephews If you observe good order, Sobriety and play the man, your deportment in this Case will resound through the american army, be noticed by General Washington the Chief Warriors and finally reach the Ears of our father the french King. And we Sachems shall then rejoice to hear from you.

Ojistall alias Grass hopper
Speaker in behalf of the Sachems

To the above the warriors reply'd—Return'd Thanks for their Good advice—promasing Implici'd obedience to Mr De Tousard Their Conductor—that Good agreement should subsist betwixt them and Clos'd with appointed exhortation to the Sachems to Maintain one Uniform line of Conduct in their deliberations, pursue them with resolution and not restrain the Warriors. fort Schuyler april 24, 1778 Intrepret'd by Saml. Kirkland [     ]"

I went away from fort Schuyller the 29th of april last and I have repair'd to his Excellency the 15th of the present. I have done all my power to Keep the whole party sober and to hinder them from abusing the people in the Country. And I hope that you shall have no Complaints against them.

I Could have given you, Sir, an account of my Behaviour sooner, had not I been commanded to march with the fifty Indians and ten french men. I have had the occasion to acquaint the british light horses with the hollow of the Indians, and their hability in firing; but I have lost three french men on the spot, one of 'em was barbarously murdered, his tongue, nose and ears cutdoff, four were made prisoners, and myself owe my liberty, perhaps much more to two Indians, and two french men who stood constantly by me, and kill'd two Light horse at whose fire my horse had throwd me down, and who were close by me. I cannot tell the exact number of the Light horses killed, but my people fired pretty smart though running away, and I have seen my self five or six killed.

I pray you, sir to believe that I have done all my power, though not Commissioned as officer by the honourable Congress, to prove to the United States of america, how ready I am to serve them with all my activity and understanding. I am with the utmost respect Sir your most obedient and humble Servant

DE TOUSARD

ALS, Papers of the Continental Congress, National Archives, Washington, D.C.

[1] Lieutenant Colonel Jean Baptiste Gouvion (1747–92).

[2] Samuel Kirkland (1741–1808) was a Congregational missionary to the Oneidas who played a vital role in obtaining the neutrality of the Oneidas.

# ZEBULON BUTLER TO HORATIO GATES

IN THE SUMMER of 1778 Major John Butler commanded a British Ranger Regiment that had been recently recruited along the New York-Canadian border. He advanced from Fort Niagara with as many as 1,100 Tories and Indians planning a savage raid on the settlers in Westmoreland Township, in the Wyoming Valley of eastern Pennsylvania. Most of these settlers had moved from Connecticut to this area, which was claimed by both Pennsylvania and Connecticut. Upon receiving news of the enemy's approach, Colonel Zebulon Butler (1731–95), of the Second Connecticut Regiment, called out the militia and accepted command of the settlement's defenses. On July 3, Colonel Butler wrote in vain for help to Major General Horatio Gates. Butler believed that the militiamen and settlers could defend their settlements until American military relief arrived. However, Major John Butler's forces routed the local militiamen near Forty Fort that day, killing as many as 227 soldiers at the Battle of Wyoming. Colonel Zebulon Butler and his wife escaped on horseback to Wilkes-Barre. Many others were less fortunate, however. A widespread massacre of patriotic settlers followed the battle. The Wyoming Valley settlement around Westmoreland Township was largely destroyed.

*Westmoreland 3d: July AD1778*

Hond: Sr:

We are now beset by a Number of Indiands & Tories under the Command of Mr. Butler, their Numbers are uncertain, but supposed to be about six or seven hundred they have now penetrated into the heart of this Settlement, killing & scalping all they come across, that make any resistance, they seem determined if possible to destroy this Settlement. I can only ask the Advice & Assistance of the Honorable Board of War.[1] I think we can keep the fort if we shall be obliged to retreat into it for six or eight Weeks; tho I am determined that, that shall be the last resourse. We expect an Ingagement with the main Body of the Enemy this Afternoon, or Tomorrow Morning, what the event will be is uncertain, tho I hope for the best. Can only desire if the Board think proper there may be some forces, that are handy detached as soon as possable to reinforce the Militia, who are Spirited to the last degree, & seem anxious for an ingagement. The Bearer hereof can inform the Board any particulars that shall be required. Am Your Honor's most Obedient humble Servant

ZEBN. BUTLER *Lt. Colo Comdr.*

ALS, Papers of the Continental Congress, National Archives, Washington, D.C.
[1] Gates was no longer president of the Board of War.

# JEREMIAH VAN RENSSELAER TO MATTHEW VISSCHER

JEREMIAH VAN RENSSELAER (1740–1810) served as paymaster of the Third New York Regiment under Colonel Peter Gansevoort. In this letter he conveys the latest military intelligence of Indian and Tory movements to his friend Matthew Visscher (1751–93) of Albany County, New York. In 1778 the combined menace of Indians and Tories, as shown by the Wyoming massacre, required that strong military action be taken on the northern frontier. Van Rensselaer's unit was involved in this important American defense effort on the northern frontier, for the Third New York Regiment had been stationed at Fort Stanwix since April 1777.

*Fort Schuyler 6 July 1778*

Dr Scribe

Abt. 3 hours Ago Lieut Staats Returned from Oswegatje,[1] out 14 days, with 6 Onida Indians, and a Serjeant formerly our drum Major. Their Inteligence is that in 7 days, from this place they Came in the River St. Lawrence A Considerable Way Above their Intended port. They there Seen on an Island A Considerable Number of Men & Boats at the Banks. They proceeded down to Oswegatje & When Within Abt. 400 yeards three of the Indian venterd to go into the fort Which was only A piquet, and after being there Some Litle time they Returned 2 person's on horseback at that time was Going out for A Ride to pass our Ambuscade. The Aforesaid Serjeant taken the Oppertunity deserted from the Lt: and Gave them the Alarm and Deserted to the Enemy. Was at the Return of the Indians met by them on horseback driving John Like to the fort. Upon the Alarm being given they were obliged to make the best of their way of there being a Large Number of Indians then that at that place. Returned from Bucks Island to Escort their Women to that place. By the Inteligence the Indians have obtained there is A Number of Troops. With the Indians Intended to Invest this place. Which Account Corrisponds with the Inteligence Received from the Tuccorora Indians, a few days Ago, that they were Making up St. Lawrence with a Large Quantity of Provision, & Military were Lodged at Catoraque, and so forth.[2] Little Mc: is Gone to Oswego with 20 Men & 4 Indians we Expect his Return in 3 days, provided he does not take a Scotch prise. Which I hope and Belive not he has none but true Americans With him and these I dare Say Good, Musick I belive we will have at this place in 8 or 10 days. To which the 3 Bato: are in hope & Confidendt that the American foes Will Again dance the Shamefull hornepipe.

I Communicate you this to you as being the only person Who will Corrispond an Absent frind, your's being the only Letter I have Received at this post from my frinds and am much Indebted to you for the Same tho Old When it Came to hand. Be pleased to Communicate the News to Mr. Rensselars personally in A Carefull manner. I am Dr Scribe Your humbl Servt.

Jer VRensselaer

ALS, bound in John W. Francis, *Old New York Reminiscences* (New York, 1865), vol. xiii, item 129.

[1] Second Lieutenant Gerrit Staats (1722–c.1781) of the Third New York Regiment. Oswegatje: Ogdensburg, N.Y.

[2] Cataraqui (Fort Frontenac) is on the Canadian side of Lake Ontario.

# John Paul Schott to Edward Hand

On september 6, 1776, John Paul Schott, a native of Prussia, was commissioned captain of the Independent Pennsylvania Company. His unit first became part of Major Nicholas Dietrich, Baron de Ottendorf's Independent Company and later joined the legion commanded by Lieutenant Colonel Charles Armand-Tuffin, Marquis de la Rouerie. In March 1779 Captain Schott's 55-man company was posted in the Minisink area of Orange County, New York. Schott warns Major General Edward Hand that the patriots of the Minisink area would be in grave danger without the presence of Continental troops. Schott's company was, however, reassigned to the Wyoming Valley of Pennsylvania, where it participated in General John Sullivan's expedition against the Iroquois. The Minisink patriots were the victims of a savage attack by Mohawk chief Joseph Brant on July 22, 1779, in which many civilians and 44 militiamen lost their lives. Schott's faulty English grammar is a reminder that it was not only native-born Americans who were willing to risk their lives for American liberty.

*Dewitt's fort March 14th 1779*

I receiv'd your Kinde favour yesterday. Have tould Captn Dewitts your desier.[1] He is very Sorrow he did not know of the Genls. comming up to Major Dekers[2] or els he wou'd with plesure have waited on the Genl. in regard to this post if the General will bee pleasd to consiter that the Safty of the Poeple all on this Site and over the mounthins depents on this Gaurd and if these troops was takin away as it is right on the road the all Say must fly from their Hous's. I wonder that Captn. Cutaback can ask any troops which are here with anything at all he likewise has but two fire plas' in his House and fill'd up with Men Women and Childerin. He says he wand'd but five or six man which is impossible to detach men by fives and six as it can't bee expected that they can bee on Gaurd every day tho the General can do as he pleas's but I think that this place requires troops more than any place on pienpack.

The General will be so kinte as to desier Major Dunn to send me some paper this is the last sheed I had, the serjt was detaned by Coll. Cortland arrivd this menuit.[3] I wou'd bee much oblig'd to the Gen'l to order the Commesary to Essure Gaurd and fadange rum for my Men as I am about finishing the fort and you will much oblige Sir your most obetiend and Most Humble Servant

JOHN P. SCHOTT *Captn*

ALS, Edward Hand Papers, Historical Society of Pennsylvania, Philadelphia.

[1] Captain Thomas DeWitt of the Third New York Regiment.
[2] Probably Major Johannes Decker (1735–1804).
[3] Colonel Philip Van Cortlandt (1749–1831) of the Second New York Regiment.

# JAMES GILES TO HIS MOTHER

THE MISERABLE CONDITIONS of Valley Forge were only some of the horrors encountered by the Continental soldiers in subsequent winter encampments. From December 11, 1778, to June 3, 1779, most of Washington's army encamped at Middlebrook, New Jersey. The prolonged period of isolation from home and family created a great sense of anxiety and loneliness, even when the soldiers' physical needs were being met. James Giles (1759–1825), a young lieutenant in the Continental artillery, spent much of that winter at New Brunswick, New Jersey. In this touching letter to his mother, he relates his experiences in the service, including the subtle changes in his youthful optimistic outlook, his boredom, his enduring faith in his country, and the love of his family.

*New Brunswick, March 20, 1779*

My Dearest Mama

A favourable opportunity offering, am not disposed to let it pass, therefore sit down to devote some of my lieusure time in writing you.

In the first place, must beg leave to introduce to you, Colonel Buford, the Bearer of this, an acquaintance of mine, shou'd be very happy you'd look upon him as such;[1]

When I look back, my D. Mama, and see how time passes away, I'm lost in Wonder and Astonishment; but a few Days since I entered my twentieth year, and it's now going on three years since I left Home. The Enemy, at that time were advancing with gigantic strides, and endeavouring to wrest from us, every thing valuable, every thing we hold dear in this life; the Prospect was gloomy; it was then a time when the situation of Affairs called aloud for every virtuous son, nobly to step forth and vindicate the course of his injured country, roused at the Call, I left Home for the first time, determining to lend an assisting hand as far as my abilities would admit. The Seperation was painfull, but I then vainly thought, it wou'd be but for a time short after, Papa was taken Prisoner and carried to New York; you soon followed, and I was left alone; My inclination always led me to be in the service. The opportunity was favourable—I embraced it. I then entered upon the great Theatre of the World, young and inexperienced, and exposed to all the Vices and Follies of an army: The numberless Difficulties I had then to encounter with, made me tremble for the Consequences; it was then my Dr. Mama, I most wanted your wonted advice and support, but you were gone. Friendless in a manner, I threw myself upon the Divine Protection humbly imploring the great Governor of the Universe, to look down with an Eye of Pity and Compassion upon me, and that he wou'd be my Guide and Director, through all the Tryals and Difficulties of Life; With a firm relyance on his gracious Protection, I stept forward, to discharge the Duties of my Station, since which, the Hardships I've endured in common with my fellow Soldiers, are trifling, when put in Competition with the great object, we are contending for.

I have been here for some time past and have it in my Power to stay till the first of May; I wou'd wish to go home, but there are many obstacles which will prevent, such as the Want of a Horse in particular, there being none to be had any where about this place, by the Country being kept in constant alarm; By going to the Park I shall there have it in my Power to attend on W. Colles, our Preceptor, with whom all the officers are daily studying the Mathematicks but then there is such a Scene of Dissipation there, that it wou'd require all the fortitude, I'm master of, to withstand it. By staying here, I can pass the time away very agreeably, there being many polite families here, with whom I have the honour of being acquainted with, my liesure hours, I can devote to reading. Now, whether the trifling advantages I might reap by being at the Park are to be put in Competition with my future Character in Life; I say my future Character, for there's no knowing what Impression the many Temptations, I'd there be exposed to, wou'd make on me; for my opinion is that it will in a great Measure depend upon my present Behaviour and the Principles I at this time of Life adopt. I believe I need not hesitate long about the Choice, nevertheless my D. Mama, I wou'd wish to pay the utmost Defference to your Advice, and for that purpose, sincerely wish you'd take the Pen in hand and write me by Colonel Buford, your Sentiments thereon; as it's most probable, our seperation will continue as long as the War lasts, let me beg of you, my Dear Mama, to embrace every opportunity in writing me; to hear from the family at all times, wou'd add much to my happiness you are so circumstanced, that either you or Papa can always devote some liesure time for that Purpose, and by throwing in some friendly hints with respect to my conduct in the Army, wou'd make them still more acceptable; In the mean time I shall not be wanting to offer up my ardent Prayers to Heaven, humbly beseeching the Supreme Disposer of all Events, to dispell the gloomy Clouds that now o'erspreads us, and is ready every moment to burst upon us; and to grant that the happy day may soon arrive, when we can once more return to our own Homes, in the Arms of Peace, Liberty and Happiness; that he wou'd in a particular manner shower down innumerable Blessings upon you my honoured Parents, that he wou'd be pleased to be your Guide and Director, through all the Changes and Vicissitudes of Life, and that when it is his blessed Will, that you leave this frail, fleeting Life, he may receive you into the Mansions of Celestial Bliss.

JAMES GILES

P.S. Please make my tenderest Regards to Uncle and Aunt Helme, and all enquiring friends, the Dommine in particular—tell Uncle Arthur, if he has any Inclination to visit Burlington, I shou'd be glad, he'd come through this Place in a Chair and take me along—he will find an old Acquaintance here, a Captn. Crowel, who once sailed as Second Mate, with him,[2] Uncle Arthur being Chief Mate—he's on Parole, a Prisoner of ours—direct to me as Lieut. Artillery—adieu.

J.G.

ALS, Sophia Roorbach Papers, Duyckinck Collection, New York Public Library, New York City.
[1] Colonel Abraham Buford (1749–1833) of the Eleventh Virginia Regiment.
[2] Captain Thomas Crowell (b. 1724) of Middletown and Perth Amboy, N.J.

# AARON AORSON TO PHILIP SCHUYLER

THE EVENTS OF the first six months of 1779 provided a severe trial of endurance for the young American republic. The extensive northern frontier furnished many opportunities for raids by regular British troops and their Loyalist and Indian supporters. These conditions led to Sullivan's punitive expedition against the Six Nations. During this bleak period, Captain Aaron Aorson (1741–90) was garrisoned with the rest of the Third New York Regiment at Fort George, on the southern tip of Lake George in northern New York. Americans had held this fortress since the British abandoned it

following their humiliating surrender at Saratoga. Aorson's letter to Major General Philip Schuyler describes the constant fear of border raids and the persistent lack of supplies. Schuyler had resigned his commission as major general on April 19, 1779, but remained on the Board of Commissioners for Indian Affairs, in which capacity he attempted to reduce the ravages of border warfare waged by the Six Nations. Anxiety, boredom, and depressing rumors were all part of the difficult experience of being a soldier posted in the north.

*March 23rd 1779*

Sir

Agreeable to your instructions I sent a scout to Ticonderoga the 19th which returned the 22nd but made no discoveries of an Enemy, they were informed by a scotchman who lives at Mount Independence, that there had not been any of the Enemy there since last Fall, and that there nearest station was the Isle Aux Naux. The scout was prevented from going to Crown point by the great depth of the snow and the want of snow shews.

I believe the Indians you sent him will be of little service. I requested one or two of them to go with the scout to Ticonderoga, but they refused; saying they were afraid of being taken by the Mohawk Indians who were constantly about that place.

We are in great want of stores of all Kinds at this Post. There is not a single Barrel of Flour and but a very few Barrels of salt Beef at present in the Commisary store. Intrenching Tools also are wanting.

It will be impossible to set Pickets round the stone Barracks (which might be done in a much shorter Time than to frame the Pickets) as plenty of stone is near and have it Abbitu'd, but should be glad of your approbation as soon as possible. I am sir Your most Obedient and very huml. servant

AARON AORSON

N.B.

Coll. Schuyler has wrote to the Quarter Master Genl. for Intrenching Tools, which I whould be very glad to have forwarded immediately.[1]

ALS, Philip Schuyler Papers, New York Public Library, New York City.
[1] Probably Colonel Stephen J. Schuyler (1736–1808) of the New York militia.

# ZEBULON BUTLER TO THE PRESIDENT OF THE BOARD OF WAR

INDIAN WARFARE flared again on the New York-Pennsylvania frontier on November 10, 1778, when Indians and Loyalists led by Walter Butler and Joseph Brant attacked Cherry Valley, New York. Such atrocities as the massacre of 32 women and children aroused the Continental Congress to act. On February 25, 1779, it authorized George Washington to punish the frontier Indians. Horatio Gates declined the command of a punitive expedition, and the authority was given to General John Sullivan. The conditions on the frontier were reported by Zebulon Butler in this letter to the president of the Board of War. Butler's courageous defense of the scattered settlements on the frontier territory around Forty Fort helped to check the spread of the warfare and impede the Indian and Loyalist violence until the arrival of Sullivan's force.

*Garrison Wyoming, March 23d. 1779*

Honord. Sir

The Intent of this is to Inform the Board of Warr with thee Cituation of this Post The Inclosd. Returns the Number of men Quantity of Provision &c will Survisor that part. On the 21st. Inst. there Appear'd A Large Boddy of Enemy Advancing on the west Side Susquent.[1] where we had A Block house Previous to their Being Discoverd: To Night they had taken an Old man Who was out on his Private Business. The Enemy Advanced on the Flatts in Open field and Scattered in pursuit of Cattle Horses &c. I sent an Officer and Twenty five over if possible to prevent them taking them Away. Our Men at first Obligd. them to Retreat off from the Flatts till they Came to or Near A Wood where our Men Discoverd. two Large Boddys Supposed to be Above two Hundred our Men Retreated fiering the Enemy Advance fiering But our Men got Back well the Enemy Immediately in Larger Boddies pursued, Collecting Cattle and Horses our Men Continued pursuing and fiering on them And Notwithstanding the Activity and Bravery of our men, the Number of the Enemy were So Superior to our Men the Enemy Carried off Sixty Head of horn Cattle twenty Horses Burnt five Partley full of Grain and Hay, A Number of Dwelling Houses and Killed A Number of Hoggs and Sheep and Left them Lying on the Ground. The Scurmishing held from three of the Clock till Sun Down, and we had No Man killed, taken or Wounded Except the old man first Mentioned, tho Number of our men had Bullets through their Clothes and Hatts and Some their Ramrods Shot out of their Hands. While I'm writing this A Large Boddy were Discoverd. Advancing for this Side towards the Fort. They Surrounded the fort on all Sides and Began to Collect all the Cattle and Horses that were any Distance from the fort, We fiered Cannon at them from the Fort and took A Small peice out and Advanc'd And fiered at them, with A Number of Men drove them Back to A Wood where their Number Appeared Large. We Rescued Some Cattle and Horses But they took off fifty one Head of Horn Cattle and ten Horses, Burnt three Barnes and three Houses. In the Affair of this day we had two men wounded hope Not Dangerous none taken or Killed. We Could not Desern Tories from Indians, but Some talked Plain English and bid us Give up Damd: Rebels &c or they Would kill us—but they went off this Night. After the Congress has this Acct. I hope they Will think it Necessary to Reinforce this post with two or three Hundred Men.

But must Submitt to the Wisdom of Congress and only Say I have the Honour to be Your Honours Most Obt. Servt.

ZEBN. BUTLER

N.B. With this I Send Another to his Excellency Genll. Washington with A full Acct. of the Late Affair and Returns of our Men Provision &c.

26th. March 1779 It Has been Such an Extreem Heavy Snow it has not been in my Power to Send off the Express. This Day we Discoverd. Smoaks of Buildings Burning About four Miles below on the River Where we have A Guard kept in A Block-house to Guard A Mill. 27th. March Two men from the Mill Guard informs A Party Appeared in Sight of their Block House Burnt three Barnes With Grain Hay and flax and two Houses with Some Provision. No Indians been Discoverd. this day Yet. 28th. Nothing Since Yeasterday Exepting it Appears the Enemy are not yet Gone as we Discover Large Smokes Back on the Mountains this day. I'm your Most Obt. Humble Servt.

ZEBN. BUTLER

As I have had no Money Sent to this Post this Some Months Should be glad that Exact may be Supplyed with Exchange Money if he Should Want.

ZEBN. BUTLER

ALS, Papers of the Continental Congress, National Archives, Washington, D.C.
[1] Susquehanna River.

# DANIEL BRODHEAD TO JOSEPH REED

INDIAN ATTACKS had plagued Americans on the western frontier from the time they first began to settle in Indian territory. Colonel Daniel Brodhead commanded both the Eighth Pennsylvania Regiment and the western operations of the Continental army from headquarters at Fort Pitt (Pittsburgh). His letter to President Joseph Reed (1741–85) of the executive council of Pennsylvania details the conditions faced by his scattered regiment on the frontier. Between August 11 and September 14, 1779, Colonel Brodhead commanded an expedition up the Allegheny Valley from Pittsburgh. This mission, directed at the villages of the Mingoe and Seneca Indians, had been organized in conjunction with Sullivan's expedition against the Iroquois and diverted the Indians who would otherwise have massed against Sullivan. Brodhead received a commendation from the Continental Congress on October 27, 1779, for his valiant military achievements.

*Head Quarters Pittsburgh April 15th, 1779*

Dear Sir,

Your very obligding Letter of the 21st. January I have not the Honor to receive untill the 5th. Instant.

I hope you are by this time well acquainted with the late Military Operations in this department. His Excellency the Commander-in-chief has now honored me with the Command of it and my whole attention shall not be wanting to strike terror in our Enemy and secure the Settlements in this Fertile Country.

I trust my Letters to certain Gentlemen in high office have had a happy affect in promoting an attention to An early Campaign. Had my Predecessor taken the necessary steps we might now have been ready, to check the Coitiffs, who keep the Inhabitants in one continual alarm; which I foresaw must inevitably be the consequence of ill timed measures and an inattention to the necessary supplies for the Troops to enable us to make an early movement into the Enemies Country this Spring.

I shall yet loose a number of good Officers on account of the Arrangement. The jealousy arises on account of so many Captains, inferior to some of mine, being detached from the 13th. P. to my regt. Captn. Dawson is a good duty officer but a very improper one for the Service here & Captain Carnahan is by no means equal to Captain John Finley;[1] I wish Captains Stokely & Finley could be put into their places in my Regt. because they are both good officers & Gentlemen on whom I can depend in the Wilderness as well as the Champain.[2]

Your generous concern for the sufferings of the army in general is well known to the officers of our & other States and I wish to thank you in a particular manner for the regard you are pleased to express for our Regt. in particular. In my last letter which I sent by express I have endeavoured to advise you of the circumstances of the Army & Country on this side the Alleghany Hills and I will at present endeavour to give you a full account of circumstances or at least so much as may be necessary to lead you into a general idea of our situation.

You will readily conceive that the command of a Department left in great confusion will naturally involve one in much trouble to extricate it and put things into a regular train for the necessary operations of a Campaign And I wish this may apologize for any omissions that I may be subject to writing this Letter.

The Indians at present are daily committing Murders in Westmoreland to such a degree that it is apprehended they have formed a camp on some of the Waste lands of the Inhabitants, but I suppose Col. Lockory must have informed you of this,[3] and I have ordered ranging parties to cover them & drive out the Indians; and to intercept such as may hereafter approach, this plan appears to me from a considerable share of experience to be the most eligible. Untill I am furnished with a supply of Provisions (for at present we have not over three days meat to subsist the troops of this Garrison) to enable me to attack some of their Towns. From every consideration I am persuaded the Delawares may be engaged to fight against the six Nations—though more numerous, than themselves provided they are well supported by us & we have the means, that in Indian Goods Trinkets & black Wampum to pay them for their Services. I am much oblidged for the kind Notice you have bee pleased to take of my Son & sincerely wish he may merit your esteem.

I am informed that several Companies are raising for the defence of the frontiers of Westmoreland &c. for the term of nine Months. This I apprehend will prevent me from raising recruits during the War. However I hope they will be subject to the Orders of the Commanding officer in this Department and that I shall be at liberty to recruit such of them as are willing to engage during the War towards the expiration of that Term.

As we shall seldom have any opportunity if any during this Campaign, to apply for supplies granted by the State I wish those now to be sent may be as ample as circumstances will permit.

Speeches are gone out to several of the Western Indian Nations and I am encouraged to believe that most of them will be quiet this Summer, if not Friendly.

It is to be wished that Congress will order an extra Number of Shoes & Linnans for this department. I assure you Soldiers are continually on their feet in this Service & require double the Number of Shoes worn by the same Number in the grand Army.

My regiment is at present much scattered above one hundred under Major Vernon are posted at Fort Laurens[4] twenty five at Wheeling & the like number at Hallidays Cave some employed as Artificers some as Boatmen Waggoners &c. The Garrison at Fort McIntosh is of my Regt. & some of them are here. There is such a prodigious delinquency in the staff department and that their Men are mostly supplied from the line.

The Mingoes are the principal disturbers of our Settlements and I beleive the route that will be taken this Campaign will affectually cover them.

I should be greatly oblidged for the News Papers by every opportunity other reading that you may judge necessary to keep me in a State of Civility will be very acceptable for in this Country a man is almost in danger of growing wild.

Should any thing interesting hereafter happen in this department you may depend on knowing it from me by the first conveyance. With the most perfect regard & esteam I have, the Honor to be your Excellency's most obedt. & Hble. Sarvt.

Daniel Brodhead
*Colo. commandg. Westn. Department*

ALS, Joseph Reed Papers, New-York Historical Society, New York City.

[1] Captain Samuel Dawson (d. 1779), Captain James Carnaghan, and Captain John Finley, all of the Eighth Pennsylvania Regiment.

[2] Captain Nehemiah Stokeley (d. 1811) of the Eighth Pennsylvania Regiment.

[3] Lieutenant Colonel Archibald Lochrey (1733–81) of the Pennsylvania militia.

[4] Major Frederick Vernon of the Eighth Pennsylvania Regiment.

# Jonathan Forman to George Washington

Continental soldiers often were forced to contend with the anguish and frustration of being unrewarded by adequate support and compensation for their loyal efforts. Captain Jonathan Forman (1755–1809), of the First New Jersey Regiment, expressed his bitterness at the failure of New Jersey's legislature to show concern for the personal hardships endured by the Continental officers. His regiment was among those units that had been stationed at Elizabeth-town in the winter of 1778–79 to protect the state's vulnerable coastline from attack by the British and Loyalists in New York City. De-spite the continued lack of adequate compensation for vital activities, Jonathan Forman served the cause of liberty until November 13, 1783.

*Elizth. town, May 8, 1779*

Sir

General Maxwell has communicated to us the substance of a letter from your Excellency of yesterday. It has made us very unhappy that any act of ours should give your Excellency pain; but we trust when you are made acquainted with the circumstances that induced us to take those measures, that so far from censuring us, you will approve our conduct. The reasons that we have not heretofore made your Excellency acquainted with our peculiar hard circumstances were, that it would be giving you uneasiness, without answering any valuable end, for we are truly sensible of the incessant pains your Excellency has taken for the benefit of the Army. You are pleased to say, that you cannot but consider the late step of the Officers hasty and imprudent, that it was not hasty we will readily prove, and whether imprudent, future events in some measure must determine, tho' dire necessity, within, admitted no alternitive. It will be proper to inform your Excellency that the Officers of the Jersey Brigade have repeatedly, and at almost every session of the Assembly since January 1777, Memorialized them upon the Necessities of the Troops, and the reasonableness of their making them some compensation for their services, that the Members of the Legislature (individually) always assured the Gentlemen who waited on them with the memorials, that something very Generous should be done for the Troops; but we have the misfortune to inform your Excellency that not a single resolve was ever entered in their Minutes in our favor, untill within two weeks. So long ago as last winter we informed the Council of our determination to leave the service unless we were properly provided for, and from them we again received assurances that provision should be made for us. At the begining of the present session a Representation was sent to them signed by every Officer of the Brigade (a Copy of which we have inclosed) and so far were they from complying with the reasonable requisitions contained in it, that *they have referred it to Congress.* Thus are we circumstanced; we have lost all *confidence* in our Legislature, Reason and Experience forbid that we should have any. Few of us have private fortunes, many have families who already are suffering every thing that can be received from an *ungratefull Country,* are we then to submit to all the inconveniences, fatigue and Danger of a Camp life, while our Wives and our Children are perishing for want of common necessaries at home, and that without the most distant prospect of reward, (for our pay is now only *Nominal*). We are sensible that your Excellency cannot wish nor desire it from us. We are sorry that you should imagine we meant to disobey Orders, it was and still is our determination to march with our Regiment and do the duty of Officers until the Legislature should have a reasonable time to appoint others, but no longer. We beg leave to assure your Excellency, that we have the highest sense of your Ability and Virtues, that executing your orders has ever given us pleasure, that we love the service, and we love our Country; but when that Country gets so lost to virtue and justice as to forget to support its servants, it then becomes their duty to retire from the service.

We are your Excellencys, Obedient, huml. Servants

*In behalf of the Officers*
*of the first Regiment,*
JONA. FORMAN *1st. Capt.* [*1st*] *Regt.*

ALS, George Washington Papers, Library of Congress, Washington, D.C.

# DANIEL PUTNAM TO JEREMIAH WADSWORTH

MAJOR DANIEL PUTNAM (1757–1831) began service in the Continental army as an officer in the Twentieth Continental Regiment and in May 1776 became an aide-de-camp to Major General Israel Putnam, his father, whom he served until the latter's retirement in December 1779. In the winter of 1778–79 General Putnam commanded the troops of the Connecticut line that were quartered around Redding, Connecticut. Writing to Commissary General Jeremiah Wadsworth (1743–1804), Major Putnam reports the gathering of Continental units in Easton, Pennsylvania, for General John Sullivan's expedition and provides details of one of the many coastal raids by contingents of British regulars and Tories to punish Connecticut for attacks on British shipping in Long Island Sound.

*Camp Reading May 10th: 1779*

Dear Sir,

The Wolf Skins which you sent on will be finished today, but the Calf Skin will not be Compleated this three or four Days. As it is probable we shall leave this place in a few days, I wish to have your directions, whither I shall send them forward to Hartford, or whither I shall leave them with Capt. Starr at Danbury.

One Regiment of Poors Brigade has marched for *Eastown* in Pennsylvania,[1] and the Remainder of the Brigade are to follow in a short time. 'Tis said their destination is for Detroit—where they are to be joined by a part or the whole of Clintons Brigade of York Troops.[2] How far these Conjectures may prove true, I cannot pretend to determine. But they all I think clearly indicate a Northern Expedition of Importance. I wish that our ill fortune in that Quarter may not continue.

Since our Guards have been called off from the Sea Coast of this state, the Enemy have exhibited some Specimens of Enterprize a little unusual for them. A few nights since a party landed at Capt. Sellicks, who was absent, and by that means escaped being Captur'd. But his Clerk two others, and Doctor Bushnell fell into their hands.[3] The last mention'd Gentleman was there in the prosecution of his unremitted efforts to destroy the Enemy's shipping. As he is unknown to most people, it is possible he may not be discover'd by his real name, or Character, and may be consider'd a less acquisition than he really is.

The Day after this affair, a party of about 50 Landed at Sellecks Farms, and carried off each man a sheep, before the Militia could be collected to oppose them. These incursions will doubtless be frequent & troublesome this Summer, tho not decisive & important. My best Compliments to your family, and believe me Your affectionate friend & humble servant

D. PUTNAM

Our good friend Silliman, I suppose you know was taken off a little time since.[4]

ALS, Jeremiah Wadsworth Papers, Connecticut Historical Society, Hartford.

[1] Brigadier General Enoch Poor.

[2] Brigadier General James Clinton (1736–1812).

[3] Probably David Bushnell (1740–1826), who invented a submarine and was a captain lieutenant in the Corps of Sappers and Miners.

[4] Brigadier General Gold Selleck Silliman (1732–90) of the Connecticut militia. He was captured by Loyalists on May 1, 1777.

# ABNER MARTIN DUNN TO ALLEN MCLANE

LOYALISTS AND INDIANS were a constant threat to the Continental army in frontier areas. Lieutenant Abner Martin Dunn (1755–95) writes to his captain, Allen McLane, of a mounted troop from Delaware, about new barbarities committed by the Tories and Indians in the Wyoming Valley. Lieutenant Dunn, who was garrisoned at Fort Penn in that section of eastern Pennsylvania, also reports the deaths of Captain Joseph Davis and six others, all brutally murdered by Indians in April 1779. Ten months after the savage massacre of patriot militiamen, regulars, and civilians at Cherry Valley, the carnage on the frontier continued.

*Fort Penn May 12th. /79*

Dr. Sir

I take the Fowlowing Method of Letting you no how affairs are situated with me and the Company. Ever since I rec'd your letter which is about 2 Weaks I have been waiting for an Oppertunity to inform you of our Affairs but none has as yet arrived. I have at length Concluded to send the berrer Sergeant Ferrot to you with the Following Account.

The 22d of April the Regt under the Command of Major Prowell Marched from this Place for Wyoming[1] & within 9 Miles of the Garrisson they Mett with the Unhappy Accident in loosing Capt Davis & Mr. Jones[2] & 5 Men of the Regt: which were Misfortunetly Masecreed by the savages. News which I am sure will Grate the Ears of every well wisher. I myself was left with the Baggage at the above Mentioned Place & coud not Posablely Proceed on to the Regt: as yet But Expect to set out to Morrow. I this Moment Recd. an Account that Regt is Marched from Wyominge down the sisquehannah as far as sun berry. I shall overtake it as soon as Posable & March to head Quarters as soon as the Exegences of Affairs will Permitt me. I Conclude Subscebing myself Sincere Friend & Most

A M DUNN

I am almost dead with the Melenchy. Thoughts of my Frds: Davis & Jones

ALS, Allen McLane Papers, New-York Historical Society, New York City.
[1] Major Joseph Prowell (1753–1805) of the Eleventh Pennsylvania Regiment.
[2] Second Lieutenant William Jones of McLane's Partisan Company.

# OLIVER SPENCER TO EDWARD HAND

THE SULLIVAN EXPEDITION was a two-pronged attack on the Indians of the Pennsylvania and New York frontier. Three brigades under General Sullivan were to join forces at Easton, Pennsylvania, to form one element of the attack. The second element, commanded by Brigadier General James Clinton, proceeded from Canajoharie, New York, down the Susquehanna 'River with plans to join Sullivan's force at Tioga, Pennsylvania. Sullivan's passage north took longer than anticipated, and he did not reach Easton until May 7, 1779. Inadequate supplies and the rough terrain severely tested the patriotism of the soldiers participating in this expedition. Oliver Spencer (1736–1811), a colonel in the New Jersey Continental Brigade, describes his men as "Ragged as beggars" in this communication to Brigadier General Edward Hand.

*Locust Hill, June 4, 1779*

Dr General

Your favour of the 2d came Safe to hand am Glad to hear of the Safe arrival of Col Smith and his party at Wyoming. Hope to have the pleasure of Seeing you in a few days, but we have got a very Rough Country to make smoo[th] for by Col Smiths Description of it we have yet the worst part of the road to make, however, we shall make it pretty good, if it takes us a little more time. I'm Sorry you have deprived us of a good number of men Just got Acquainted with making the roads, which will Occasion our being Longer Detained on the roads, however all for the best, We will work our way through as soon as possible. I am Dr Sir with Esteem your Most Obedt Servt

OLIVER SPENCER

P.S. Please to present my Compliments to all the Gentlemen of my Acquaintance.

Our men are as Ragged as beggars and Im afraid we Shall be So long detained on the roads that we Shall loose our chance for our part of the Cloathing which I'm informed is Sent onto Wyoming for us. We have now Malcolms Regiment Join with mine which Consists of near 300 in the Whole, & therefore Shall have Occation of more Cloathing. I'm etc.

ALS, Emmet Collection, New York Public Library, New York City.

# GOOSE VAN SCHAICK TO JAMES CLINTON

COLONEL GOOSE VAN SCHAICK (1736–89), of the First New York Regiment, was congratulated by the Continental Congress for his leadership in the April 1779 campaign against the Onondaga Indians that had culminated with the destruction of Onondaga Castle (now Onondaga, New York) on April 21, 1779. Throughout Sullivan's expedition against the Six Iroquois Nations, which followed the Onondaga campaign, Colonel Van Schaick's regiment was garrisoned at Fort Stanwix (Fort Schuyler), where Brigadier General James Clinton had begun to collect supplies for the thrust into the Indian country. Van Schaick reports to Clinton the strength of the hostile Indians as compared to the undermanned garrison at Fort Stanwix and comments on the shortage of ammunition. Van Schaick later assumed command at Albany while General Clinton participated in Sullivan's expedition.

*Fort Schuyler June 5th. 1779*

Sir

Yesterday about two OClock as a covering party was going out with three Waggons, they were attacked and partly surrounded within a quarter of a mile of the Fort. They made a small resistance but were soon overpowered by number. The enemys force were supposed to be near one hundred, White men and Indians, and that from this Garrison twenty five. I had three men killed, three Wounded and nine missing. A strong party was immediately dispatched after the enemy but to no purpose. This day the Indians at two different times made their appearance out of the Skirt of the Woods by a small party and immediately returned. These Manouvres I suppose were made to draw us out. As I did not know the strength of the enemy, and that of my own being barely sufficient for the Defense of this Garrison in case of an Assault I declined sending after them.

I have wrote to the Commanding Officer at Fort Harkimer and would by all means advise that the Boats destined for this Garrison be strongly guarded from Fort Harkimer.[1]

The ammunition is not yet arrived, I have at the Request of the Oneidas sent an Officer and thirty men to their Fort.

Mr Dean this moment returned from Oneida, by him I am informed that the enemy are Collecting in the Seneca's Country, and have been Joined by a Considerable Party from Niagara & by another from the Southward I suppose to be from the back part of Ulster County, that provisions is transporting for them from Niagara. I am your Obedt. Servt.

G V SCHAICK

ALS, Miscellaneous Manuscripts, New-York Historical Society, New York City.

[1] More than 200 boats were used in Clinton's expedition.

# ANDREW HUNTER DIARY

THE SULLIVAN EXPEDITION demanded stern discipline to enable the soldiers to march and fight in rugged terrain with order and alertness. Andrew Hunter (1750–1823), chaplain of the Third New Jersey Regiment from June 1777, kept a journal of the expedition. His entry for July 1, 1779, includes a description of the stern measures necessary to maintain order. The treatment of one of the prisoners mentioned, however, shows that discipline accompanied by a sense of humanity was the hallmark of the Continental officer.

*Thursday July 1st.* [1779]. In the morning visited the criminals & this being the day of execution I pressed the Substance of religion upon them. Dined at Col. Ogden's with a large company.[1] About 3 O'Clock the criminals attended by Dr. Rogers,[2] Dr. Kirkland and myself began to move towards the place of execution. The troops were taken out in order, and all the inhabitants attended, to see the awful spectacle. At the gallows after we had given the necessary advice to the unhappy creatures about to leave the world Dr. Rogers addressed the spectators in a pathetic manner & Dr. Kirkland made a prayer. The elder of the prisoners, Roseberry, was then executed, while the other, Miller, sat in the cart expecting his dreadful doom; but the clemency of the General had interposed between him and justice, and the officer of the day began to read a paper which proved to be a pardon. He appeared to more affected with his pardon than with a prospect of his dissolution. He shewed many signs of penitence and prayed that his family might have the forgiveness of their country. Wrote to Mrs. Hunter by Col. Brearley.[3]

Andrew Hunter Diary, Princeton University Library, Princeton, N.J.

[1] Colonel Matthias Ogden.
[2] William Rogers (1751–1824), a Pennsylvania chaplain.
[3] Colonel David Brearley (1745–90) of the First New Jersey Regiment.

# WILLIAM SHEPARD AND JOSEPH VOSE TO JOHN GLOVER

ARREARS IN MILITARY PAY bedeviled the Continental army and undermined morale. Depreciation of Continental currency made the purchase of necessary supplies difficult and the pay almost worthless. Colonel Joseph Vose, of the First Massachusetts Regiment, and Colonel William Shepard (1737–1817), of the Fourth Massachusetts Regiment, jointly warned Brigadier General John Glover, commander of the Continental troops in Providence, Rhode Island, of "Great uneasiness" because of the troops' unpaid wages for 1777 and the inequities among different regiments. Vose and Shepard display the loyalty and support of officers for the just complaints of their men.

*Providence 7th: July 1779*

Sir,

Great uneasiness & Complaints has taken place among the Non Commission'd Officers & Soldiers of the Regts. under our Command in your Brigade on Accot. of the parts of back Rations not being paid them for the Year 1777 while the Colonels Bigelow & Wigglesworth's Regts. in the same Brigade have been paid up.[1]

We therefore pray you Honor for, & in behalf of the above Non Commission'd Officers & Soldiers, that you would please to give Orders that they may be paid.[2] We are Sir, Your most Obedt. Servts.

WM. SHAPERD *Colo.*
JOSEPH VOSE *Colo.*

ALS, Horatio Gates Papers, New-York Historical Society, New York City.

[1] Colonel Timothy Bigelow (d. 1790) of the Fifteenth Massachusetts Regiment and Colonel Edward Wigglesworth (1741–1826) of the Thirteenth Massachusetts Regiment.

[2] Officers in some states were repaid with land that had been seized from Loyalists. With this in mind, Captain Lemuel Clift (1755–1821) appealed to the Council of Safety of Connecticut on March 7, 1781: "That your memorialist having since the commencement of the present War, been engaged in the service of his Country, and now serving in the Connt. Line of the Continental Army, and that he has a Family destitute of a place of Residence; which renders your Memorialist's situation peculiarely distressing and that he is earnestly desirous of continuing his services to his Country, in support of its Liberties & Independance—Which his present circumstances appears to forbid: to remedy his destresses Your Memorialist, begs to leave to observe that there is a small dwelling house & tract of land, lying in the Township of Plainfield; which by law is Confiscated to the Publick; and as an Appropriation of those Estates are made for the payment of the ballances which may be found due to the Officers, and Soldiers, of the Connt. Line for the Year 1780: He humbly prays your Honor that they would authorize & Empower your Memorialist to receive Said tract of land, and Dwelling House, as far as it may extend to the Balance which may be found due to your Memorialist for the Year 1780." (ALS, Connecticut State Library, Hartford.)

# WILLIAM BURNET TO WILLIAM HEATH

IN JULY 1779, the British, angered by at-tacks on their shipping in Long Island Sound, launched punitive raids against the Connecticut coast by land and sea. Raids led by General William Tryon (1729–88) with 2,600 men on New Haven, Fairfield, and Norwalk from July 5 to 11, 1779, made that coast a battle zone. Dr. William Burnet (1730–91), who had been appointed physician and surgeon general of the Eastern Department on April 11, 1777, informs Major General William Heath that the British had departed Long Island Sound. Heath had recently become commander of Continental troops east of the Hudson River. Dr. Burnet explains the delay in getting medical and hospital supplies to Heath's forces. Burnet provided much help for the injured and sick of the Continental army and remained in service until the end of the war.

**William Burnet**

*Danbury July 17 1779*

My dear General

My Horse was so very dull & stumbled with me so much, that it was not in my Power to reach Danbury the Night before last. However I got here before Breakfast in the Morning, very weary indeed, & had the Satisfaction to find Dr. Holmes was just gone to your Assistance with the necessary Opperation. As soon as possible, I got ready a Waggen & Horses, & a strong Reinforcement of Medical & Hospital Stores, determined to join you again with the greatest Speed, but in the Afternoon I heard, that the Enemy had left the Sound, & you was returning with the Division, which was soon confirmed by the discharged Militia. Notwithstanding, if I had had a Horse that I could ride without Danger of my Life, I should have come to you Yesterday, tho' I hear my Son is very sick at Generl. Greene's.[1] Upon Dr. Turnor's promising to visit you in a Day or two, & furnish the Surgeons with what the Hospital can afford,[2] I have concluded to set off, for Fish Kill this Morning. If I reach it tomorrow Night safe, I shall be well off. Dr. Turnor will be ready at any Time, to assist you with all the Strength of the Hospital if needed, tho' I see no Danger of your wanting it, unless it be Medicines & Stores. If you continue in these Posts, I will endeavour to come down to you soon, but it does not appear likely to me, that you will. The Enemy I think will now bend their Course toward Jersey, & compleat the Destruction of that poor State, as there is nothing to prevent them, & they have a particular Antipathy against it. It gives me great Pleasure to hear that Generl. Wayne has Taken Stoney Point.[3] I hope we shall soon regain the Possession of Kings Ferry. Please present my best Compliments to all the Gentlemen. I am Dear General with much Esteem your most obedt.

WM. BURNET

ALS, William Heath Papers, Massachusetts Historical Society, Boston.

[1] Nathanael Greene.

[2] Surgeon General Philip Turner (d. 1815) of the Eastern Department.

[3] Brigadier General Anthony Wayne, with 1,200 men, captured the fort at Stony Point, New York, on July 16, 1779, and took over 400 prisoners.

# SILAS TALBOT TO HORATIO GATES

**Silas Talbot**
ARTIST: RALPH EARLE

THE AMERICAN NAVAL effort in the American Revolution was often weak and unorganized. Their French allies challenged British naval supremacy in 1778, but Count d'Estaing's (1729–94) fleet was defeated in a series of engagements with the British. The Continental navy remained small and continued to rely heavily on independent privateers. On November 14, 1778, Silas Talbot (1751–1813) of Rhode Island was commissioned lieutenant colonel for his bravery when commanding the ship *Hawke*. Under his leadership, the men of the *Hawke* had seized the armed schooner *Pigot* and its crew of forty-five in Narragansett Bay on October 29, 1778. Talbot was later wounded in an action at sea in the spring of 1779. In this letter to Major General Horatio Gates, Talbot describes another of his brave raids on British shipping. This intrepid sea captain served until the end of the war.

*On Bord the Continental Sloop Argo*
*New London Harbor the 7th August 1779*

Sir

Saild from Providence River last Sunday the first Int on a Cruze at Sea agreeable to your Honnours Command. The Wensday following I Retook the Schooner Count

d. Stang Prise to the King-gorge.[1] She Mounts four Carrige Guns. On friday I fell in with the King Gorge Stanton Hazerd Capt. and after She fierd three Broad Sides (which I took No notis of being determind to Run her bord and deside the Matter at once) She Struck to us. This Menover of Mine which they See we ware determind to Bord them throd them into Such a Pannick that they Becom an Eiasy Conquest for I Never fierd but two Guns before they asked for Quarters. I have Brought in 30 Prisoner and Retook [18] Eighteen of our Prisoners Made by Capt. Hawgerd. I shall Put to Sea agane as Sun as I can Land the Prisoners which will be in twelve howers. I trust & believe the taking of the King gorge (as well as retaking of Count d.Stang) will be Matter of grate joy to the State of Rhode Island & Conneticut as She has anoyed our Vessulls & had [Exseadingly] for the Eighteen Month & Capt Hawgerd is a Person who we Longed to Cetch for Som time. I am dear Genl your most obedt and most humble Sert.

SILAS TALBOT

ALS, Horatio Gates Papers, New-York Historical Society, New York City.
[1] Probably H.M.S. *George*.

# JOHN ROSS ORDERLY BOOK

GENERAL JOHN SULLIVAN's troops advancing against the Six Iroquois Nations had reached Wyoming, Pennsylvania, by June 23, 1779. The forces reached Tioga, Pennsylvania, on August 11, after a one-week stay in the Wyoming Valley. The orderly book kept by Major John Ross (1752–96), of the Second New Jersey Regiment, reveals the disciplinary problems encountered during the campaign. Among the most serious was the soldiers' habitual contempt shown toward the friendly Tuscarora, Oneida, and Stockbridge Indians, who had volunteered their aid to the Continental forces during this campaign. Other problems resulted from the rigors of the long, tedious expedition, which gave rise to personal disputes and friction. On August 22, 1779, the forces of generals Clinton and Sullivan finally united at Tioga to begin the Indian campaign.

*Head Quarters June 16th. 1779*

The revally to Beat to morrow morning half after two OClock at which time the Troops will turn out load their Baggage an' fix for marching.

At three the Genl. will beat upon which the Tents will be struct and loaded the Waggons prepar'd and everything put in Order for Marching. At 4 Oclock presisely the Assembly will Beat when the Troops will parade and march into the Street before Head Quars. Arranged to march after the Following Order 150 men from Genl. Maxwells Brigade as and Advanced Guard and Commd. by a field Offr. then 2 three pounders. Next Maxwells Brigade, Then Col. Proctors Artillery[1] Then Genl: Poors Brigade, then the Baggage of Maxwells, next the Baggage of Proctors then that of Poors Brigade, then that of the Comr. in Chief, fowlowed by the stores of the Army Than the pack Horses the Rear Guard of 110 Men from Poors Brigade Commanded by a field Offr. The discharge of a Cannon will Notify the Troops when the March is to begin.

No Flank Guards will be necessary the first day all waiters Except those belonging to the Genl. & Field offrs: to Carry Arms and march in thier respective Companies a faithful Noncommissioned Offr. & as many Careful Sentinals as there are Baggage Waggons Belonging to the Regiment will while on the March Compose the A Baggage Guard. The Brigade Qr: Mrs: to Attend Col. Sherriff Qr: Mr: Genl: Who will daily go forward off the Army, in order to fix upon a place & mark out the Ground for Incampment. The Adjutant to make out a Return of the Names of the Men that are not able to march; To the Adjutt. Genl: this Evening, that they may be left for a Guard for the Stores As the Army march on. Subns: who are not Able to march are Also to Return their Names. The Offrs: to have Every thing in perfit Readiness this that Nothing but the Concerns of the March may Employ their Attention in the Morning. Colo. Hooper will order all the soap at this place to be forwarded with the Commissiaries Stores.[2] All Prisoners belonging to the Army as well as the Torrys to be sent to the Main Guard this Evening and Marchd. on in the Morning. The Genl: being Inform'd that some of the Soldiers have been so Imprudent as to speak Contemptously and Ridicule the Indians who have Come to join Us, He desires that such Imprudent Persons would reflect upon the Cruelty of such Conduct, Nothing can be more ungenerous than to Redicule those who have come Voluntarily to Venture their Lives in our Aid, besides this it would be, the highest Peice of Imprudence to give Umbrage to a people who are about to lend us the Most Generous Assistence. All the Warriors of the Oneidas Tuscaroras and Stock Bridge Indians are About to Join Us which will be an Amazing Addition to the Strength of our Army as well as of being the Means of furnishing Guides who are perfectly Acquainted with the Country. The person therefor who after this Notice gives the Least Discouragement to those people must in Malice to his Country far Exceed the Most Inveterate Tory and must Expect to be treated Accordingly. . . .

*Head Quarters Tioga August 12th: 1779*

Brigadier Poor Field Offr. Spencer

At a Genl. Court Martial where of Col. Shreeve was president held at Wyalousing the 7 Inst. Capt. Vananglier Commisy. to Genl. Hands Brigde.[3] was tried for Unjustly and Cruely beating Serjt. Arbley of the German Battn. found Guilty of the Charges and Sentencd. to be reprimanded in Genl. Orders the Commander in Chief Approves the Sentence of the Court and Cannot help Observing from the Whole Tennor of the Evidences vended in Court it Appears that Capt. Vananglier was not only Guilty of an Abuse of Power but Manifested a Malavolent temper Scarcely to be Equalled though the Genl. will never Countenance Soldiers in Disrespectful Behaviour to Offrs: and will entertain a poor Oppinion of an Offr. who Suffers himself to be insulted without

Immediately Chastening the Soldier who may attempt it, Yet he Can never Suffer Officers to beat and abuse their Fellow Soldiers Wantonly; Blows should never be Given but except when they are Necessary to the Preservation of Order and Dicipleing and [    ] Unaccountable Unaccompanied with these Marks of Malavolence and Cruelty which, were Apparent in the whole of Capt. Van Anglers Behaviour, which renders his Conduct still more Criminal was that he was a Non Commissioned Offr: whom he made the Object of his Inhumanity and had it been a private Soldier the Treatment Could not Admit of the Least Justification. Capt. Vanaglier is Released from his arrest and Cautiond against Similar Conduct for the future.

A Board of Field Officers whereof Col. Courtland was prest. Appointed to Settle the Rank of Lieuts. Swartz & Cramer of the German Battn. having Reported that Lieut. Cramer ought to Receive the Rank he now holds, The Commander in Chief Directs that he hold the Rank he Now possesses.

Comming: Offrs: of Regts: and Corps are Directed to have a thorough Examination of the Arms and Amuntition of their Respective Corps and see that everything be in perfect Readiness for Action. The Army will hold themselves in perfect Readiness to march at the Shortest Notice as they will soon be Call'd upon to move against a Savage and Barbarous Enemy to Our fellow Citizens has Rendered them proper Objects of our Resentment the Genl: Assures them it is Impossible to be Opposed with equal numbers Nor Can he think if ever their Numbers were equal they Could not withstand the Bravery and Discipline of the Troops he has the Honor to Commd: It ought to be Remembered that Nevertheless they are a Secret Rapid and Destructive Enemy seeking every advantage and availing themselves on every Defeat on our part Tho, they can Never withstand the Shock of a Brave and Resolute Troops Yet should we be so Innatentive to our own Safty as to give way before them they become the most Dangerous and Distructive Enemy that Can possibly be Conceived of they follow the Unhappy fugitives with all the Cruel an Never relenting hate of prevailing Cowards are not satisfied with Slaughter till they have totally destroyd. their Opponent. It therefor becomes every Soldier and Officer to Determine Never to fly before them but either Conquer or perish which will ever Insure Success. The Genl: does not mention those things under the least apprehension of either the offrs: or Soldiers failing in any part of their Duty but that every one may go into Action with the same Spirit and Determination. Should this happily be the Case Nothing but an Uncommon frown of Providence can prevent us from obtaining that Success which will Insure peace and Security to Our Fronteirs and afford Lasting Honor to our Concerns.

John Ross Orderly Book, Charles Munn Collection, Fordham University, Bronx, N.Y.

[1] Colonel Thomas Proctor.

[2] Deputy Quartermaster General Robert L. Hooper (1730–97).

[3] Colonel Israel Shreve (1739–99) of the Second New Jersey Regiment; Captain John Van Anglen (d. 1812) of the First New Jersey Regiment.

# Adam Hubley, Jr., Journal

Lieutenant colonel adam hubley, Jr., commanded the Eleventh Pennsylvania Regiment from May 13, 1779, to January 17, 1781. His most noteworthy battle experiences were as a member of Sullivan's expedition. Sullivan's advance force moved from Tioga about twelve miles to the Indian village of Chemung, New York, with the hope of capturing its inhabitants, who were primarily farmers. On August 13, 1779, a column that included Hubley's regiment, under the command of Brigadier General Edward Hand, was to attack the village. The Indians of Chemung, however, had been warned of the impending American raid and had abandoned their village. The frustrated Continental soldiers could only burn the Iroquois settlement. Hand's brigade was also involved that day in a skirmish with the Indians led by the Mohawk chief Joseph Brant and the Loyalist Rowland Montour. The advance column then returned to Tioga to rejoin Sullivan's 4,000-man expeditionary force.

*August 13th, 1779.* Eight o'clock, P. M., the army having marched last evening in the following order, viz: Light corps, under command of Gen. Hand, led the van, then followed Gens. Poor and Maxwell's brigades, which formed the main body, and corps de reserve, the whole under the immediate command of Maj. Gen. Sullivan. The night being excessively dark, and the want of proper guides, impeded our march, besides which we had several considerable defiles to march through, that we could not possibly reach Chemung till after daylight. The morning being foggy favoured our enterprise. Our pilot, on our arrival, from some disagreeable emotions he felt, could not find the town. We discovered a few huts, which we surrounded, but found them vacated; after about one hour's march we came upon the main town. The following disposition for surprising the same was ordered to take place, viz.: Two regiments, one from the light corps, and one from main body, were ordered to cross the river and prevent the enemy from making their escape that way, should they still hold the town. The remainder of the light corps, viz., two independent companies, and my regiment, under command of Hand, were to make the attack on the town. Gen. Poor was immediately to move up and support the light corps. We moved in this order accordingly, but the savages having probably discovered our scouting party the preceding day, defeated our enterprise by evacuating the village previous to our coming, carrying off with them nearly all their furniture and stock, and leaving an empty village only, which fell an easy conquest about 5 o'clock, A. M. The situation of this village was beautiful; it contained fifty or sixty houses, built of logs and frames, and situate on the banks of Tioga branch, and on a most fertile, beautiful, and extensive plain, the lands chiefly calculated for meadows, and the soil rich.

The army continued for some small space in the town. Gen. Hand, in the meantime, advanced my light infantry company, under Capt. Bush,[1] about one mile beyond the village, on a path which leads to a small Indian habitation, called Newtown. On Capt. Bush's arrival there he discovered fires burning, an Indian dog, which lay asleep, a number of deer skins, some blankets, &c.; he immediately gave information of his discoveries, in consequence of which the remainder part of the light corps, viz.: the two independent companies, and my regiment, under Gen. Hand's command, were ordered to move some miles up the path, and endeavor, if possible, to make some discoveries. We accordingly proceeded on in the following order, viz.: Captain Walker, with twenty-four men, composed the van, the eleventh regiment, under my command, after which the two independent companies, the whole covered on the left by Tioga branch, and on the right by Capt. Bush's infantry company of forty men. In this order we moved somewhat better than a mile beyond this place. The first fires were discovered, when our van was fired upon by a party of savages, who lay concealed on a high hill immediately upon our right, and which Capt. Bush had not yet made. We immediately formed a front with my regiment, pushed up the hill with a degree of intrepidity seldom to be met with, and, under a very severe fire from the savages. Capt. Bush, in the meantime, endeavored to gain the enemy's rear. They, seeing the determined resolution of our troops, retreated; and, according to custom, previous to our dislodging them, carried off their wounded and dead, by which means they deprived us from coming to the knowledge of their wounded and dead. The ground on the opposite side of the mountain or ridge, on which the action commenced, being composed of swamp or low ground, covered with underwood, &c favored their retreat, and prevented our pursuing them, by which means they got off.

Our loss on this occasion, which totally (excepting two) fell on my regiment, was as follows, viz.: two captains, one adjutant, one guide, and eight privates wounded, and one sergeant, one drummer, and four privates killed. Officers' names: Captain Walker, (slight wound,) Captain Carberry, and Adj. Huston, (I fear mortal.)[2]

After gaining the summit of the hill, and dislodging the enemy, we marched by the right of companies in eight columns, and continued along the same line until the arrival of General Sullivan. We then halted for some little time, and then returned to the village, which was instantly laid in ashes, and a party detached to cross the river to destroy the corn, beans, &c., of which there were several very extensive fields, and those articles in the greatest perfection. Whilst the troops were engaged in this business, Gens. Poor and Maxwell's brigades were fired upon, lost one man, killed, and several wounded. The whole business being completed, we returned to the ruins of the village, halted some little time, and received orders to return to Tioga Plain, at which place we arrived at 8 o'clock, considerably fatigued. Lest the savages should discover our loss, after leaving the place, I had the dead bodies of my regiment carried along, fixed on horses, and brought to this place for interment. The expedition from the first to last continued twenty-four hours, of which time my regiment was employed, without the least intermission, twenty-three hours; the whole of our march not less than forty miles.

*Saturday, August 14th.* This morning 10 o'clock, A. M., had the bodies of those brave veterans, who so nobly distinguished themselves, and bravely fell in the action of yesterday, interred with military honours, (firing excepted.) Parson Rogers delivered a small discourse on the occasion.

Was employed greater part of the day in writing to my friends at Lancaster and Philadelphia, which were forwarded the same evening.

*Journals of the Military Expedition of Major General John Sullivan Against the Six Nations of Indians in 1779 With Records of Centennial Celebrations* (Auburn, N.Y., 1887), pp. 151–52.

[1] Captain George Boss (Bush) of the Eleventh Pennsylvania Regiment.

[2] Captain Andrew Walker; Captain Henry Carberry (d. 1822); and Second Lieutenant-Adjutant William Huston, all of the Eleventh Pennsylvania Regiment.

# SAMUEL BLACHLEY WEBB TO HORATIO GATES

COLONEL SAMUEL BLACHLEY WEBB, commander of an Additional Continental Regiment, was captured by the British on board the *Schuyler* on December 10, 1777, during an unsuccessful American expedition to Setauket, Long Island. At home in Wethersfield, Connecticut, during a parole of almost three years, Colonel Webb writes to Major General Horatio Gates at Boston. Webb conveys the news of the war in the West Indies. French forces under Count d'Estaing had captured the islands of St. Vincent on June 16 and Grenada on July 4, 1779. Admiral John Byron's (1723–86) British fleet pursued and engaged the French at the Battle of Grenada on July 6. Both sides claimed victory, but the French had successfully defended Grenada and had greatly damaged the British fleet. Colonel Webb endured sixteen more months of enforced inactivity, for he was not formally exchanged until December 1780. Webb then served until the war's end, rising to brevet brigadier general.

*Wethersfield in Connecticut 13th. Augt 1779*

Dear Sir,

When I was last with you I promised to have sent you a piece in Manuscript wrote with freedom respecting Congress, and another a representation to Congress about Mr Lee signed by W. H. Drayton and Wm. Paca,[1]—the first of these since I saw you has been published in the News papers—the other I now enclose,[2]—it should have been done long before this but that I have been on a Journey to the Westward from which I have just returned. I hope it will sufficiently alarm the freeman of our Country, and be a means of their choosing, in future Men of more virtue and integrity than some of the present members, 'tis time they should be sifted. I am pleased with a prospect of having my freedom anounced me in a few days and hope I may not be disappointed, when I shall have the pleasure of seeing you. Our news from the West Indies is pleasing. I have seen the Capitulation of St. Vincents, and the Philadelphia paper gives an acct. of the Grenades being taken by Count De Estang—that Admiral Byron came up to rescue it from him, Genl. Grant landed with 2,500 Men and made three unsuccessfull attacks on the French Troops.[3] Count De Estang sent five Frigates to block up the English Transports—then went out with his fleet and met Byron, a long & Bloody engagement ensued; the English fleet at the close of the day ran five Mile to Leeward and 'twas reported had lost five capital Ships. This intelligence comes by a Capt. Robinson in 18 days from Martini'ce and is credited. The prevailing opinion is De Estang rides triumphant in the West Indies. I confess I am led to believe it, if so the English must loose all their valuable possessions in those Seas. Another account from Philadelphia says the King of Prussia has sent his Ambassador to the Court of Great Britain to act as Mediator between that court, France & America,[4] the truth of these matters you must soon be possessed of—if true I think we may soon set ourselves down in peace which must be the wish of every good Man. With Compliments to the fair you honor with your Company & Gentlemen of your family I am Sir, Your Most Obedt & Very Huml. Servt

SAML. B. WEBB

ALS, Horatio Gates Papers, New-York Historical Society, New York City.

[1] William Henry Drayton (1742–79), member of the Continental Congress from South Carolina, 1778–79; and William Paca (1740–99), member of the Continental Congress from Maryland, 1774–79.

[2] Webb alludes to the Silas Deane-Arthur Lee controversy in which Lee's criticism of Deane's diplomatic activities resulted in Deane's recall to America in 1778. Members of the Continental Congress took sides in the controversy.

[3] Major General James Grant (1720–1806) of the British army.

[4] Frederick II, king of Prussia, 1740–86.

# ISRAEL ANGELL, JEREMIAH OLNEY, AND SIMEON THAYER TO HORATIO GATES

THE MORALE and discipline of the Continental soldiers were continual problems for their officers. Personal disputes among the enlisted men, grumbling over pay and rations, and reluctance to obey orders added to the tension within the Continental army. Many officers of the Continental line were forced to exert a special brand of firmness and strong leadership to keep their troops together. Three Rhode Island officers, Colonel Israel Angell, Lieutenant Colonel Jeremiah Olney, and Major Simeon Thayer describe their disciplinary problems to their commander, Major General Horatio Gates. Their remarks indicate the staunch resolution to duty that was a hallmark of the patriot.

*Camp Barbers Height,[1] August 20, 1779*

Respected Genl.

Permitt us to acquaint you, we are Inform'd applications have been made by Some Inhabitants as well as the Relations of Geo. Millernon (who is now under Sentence of

Death) with a view of obtaining the Genls. pardon, & Should it by any possible means be effected, we have but too much Reason to Fear the Consequences! as in vain have we Seen pardon twice already extended to the Regmt. in former Instances of mutiny! & Sorry we are to Say that Instead of having the desir'd effect, it has been productive (and on less occation) of a Still more Dangerous & extensive mutiny than either the preceeding ones! 'Tis with painfull Reluctance we are Constrain'd to Say that Should the prisoner pass with Impunity we have every Reason to expect ere long (and on Some trifeling occation) another mutiny Fraught with more dangerous Consequences than the last, as the banefull Spirit of Sedition Still Survives in the Regmt. for which two Soldiers have been lately punish'd who had the audacity to Revive the Subject of the last mutiny, & Several others we believe have been equally guilty in this particular, but we cannot produce Sufficient evidence to Justify punishment, and Such we know full well to be the Spirit for mutiny & Sedition too long already Cherrished by nearly every Non Commisd. officer & private in the Regmt.! That Sure we are this Dangerous & growing Spirit of Sedition will never be Eradicated but by Sevear & timely Examples, Such as discipline & the Strictest Justice will Support.

To use the inflicting punishments of any kind upon offenders is always painfull, but Since the good of the Service & Support of discipline so Essentially depends upon it, we are frequently Reduc'd to the Disagreeable Necessity of Seeing it put into execution! And when we know the dangerous Spirit of Sedition Still prevails in the Regmt., we Should be Criminally guilty did we not advise you therewith, that you might the more Effectually gard against & prevent by Some prudent means, the Spirit of mutiny from Spreading Its banefull head in Future. We are, Sr., with all possible Respect, Your most Obedt. Servts.

Israel Angell *Colo.*
Jere. Olney *Lt. Colo.*
Simeon Thayer *Majr.*

ALS, Horatio Gates Papers, New-York Historical Society, New York City.
[1] Barber's Height is a hill overlooking Narragansett Bay, R.I.

# WILLIAM ALEXANDER TO JOHN JAY

INSPIRED BY General Anthony Wayne's capture of Stony Point, New York, on July 16, 1779, the Continental command planned a similar action against the British garrison at Paulus Hook, a peninsula protruding into the Hudson River (now Jersey City, New Jersey). In the early hours of August 19 a force of 400 Virginia and Maryland Continentals led by Major Commandant Henry, "Light Horse Harry," Lee, of the Light Dragoons, braved 500 yards of salt marsh to reach the outlying British defenses at Paulus Hook. Their surprise attack under cover of darkness resulted in the deaths of 50 of the British regulars, Hessians, and Loyalists and the capture of 158 others. Major General William Alexander (Lord Stirling) relates the details of Lee's bold raid in this note to John Jay (1745–1829), president of the Continental Congress. Lee's men had been detached from Alexander's command at Paramus, New Jersey, on August 18 for the raid on Paulus Hook. On September 24, 1779, Alexander received congressional thanks for his support of this engagement.

**William Alexander**

*Paramis August 20, 1779*

I moved from the camp at Ramopegh to Hackensack New Bridge, that evening I sent off Major Lee who had taken great pains to gain a knowledge of the enemy's situation, with about 400 men, in order to surprize the garrison at Powles Hook, which they effected before daylight the next morning, and brought off 160 prisoners which I have sent on to Philadelphia. The killed and wounded left behind is uncertain, as it was necessary for the troops to come off before the day appeared. They are all returned safe to camp, with the loss of not more than four or five, after a march of upward of eighty miles in less than three days. Further particulars you will no doubt receive through his Excellency Gen. Washington—This I write on my way to camp at Romopogh.

*Memorial of the Centennial Celebration of the Battle of Paulus Hook, August 19, 1879* . . . (Jersey City, N.J., 1879), p. 62.

# Adam Hubley, Jr., Journal

## *August 29, 1779*

On August 26, 1779, the combined forces led by General John Sullivan left Tioga to continue their bloody assaults on the Indians and the Loyalists and to destroy their villages and encampments. Sullivan's expedition had engaged only in skirmishes since it began in Easton, Pennsylvania, months before. The Continental soldiers finally met the enemy's full force in battle near Newtown, six miles southeast of present-day Elmira, New York, on August 29. The British opposition at the Battle of Newtown included 250 Rangers commanded by Major John Butler and his son, Walter, 15 members of the Eighth Regiment of Foot, and 800 Loyalists and Indians led by Joseph Brant and Captain John McDonnell. Lieutenant Colonel Adam Hubley, Jr.'s, journal provides a valuable description of the ensuing combat.

*Sunday, August 29th.* This morning at 9 o'clock the army moved in the same order of the 26; the riflemen were well scattered in front of the light corps, who moved with the greatest precision and caution. On our arrival near the ridge on which the action of the 13th commenced with light corps, our van discovered several Indians in front, one of whom gave them a fire, and then fled. We continued our march for about one mile; the rifle corps entered a low marshy ground which seemed well calculated for forming ambuscades; they advanced with great precaution, when several more Indians were discovered who fired and retreated. Major Parr,[1] from those circumstances, judged it rather dangerous to proceed any further without taking every caution to reconnoitre almost every foot of ground, and ordered one of his men to mount a tree and see if he could make any discoveries; after being some time on the tree he discovered the movements of several Indians, (which were rendered conspicuous by the quantity of paint they had on them,) as they were laying behind an extensive breastwork, which extended at least half a mile, and most artfully covered with green boughs and trees, having their right flank secured by the river, and their left by a mountain. It was situated on a rising ground—about one hundred yards in front of a difficult stream of water, bounded by the marshy ground already mentioned on our side, and on the other, between it and the breastworks, by an open and clear field. Major Parr immediately gave intelligence to General Hand of his discoveries, who immediately advanced the light corps within about three hundred yards of the enemy's works, and formed in line of battle; the rifle corps, under cover, advanced, and lay under the bank of the creek within one hundred yards of the lines. Gen. Sullivan, having previous notice, arrived with the main army, and ordered the following disposition to take place: The rifle and light corps to continue their position; the left flanking division, under command of Colonel Ogden, to take post on the left flank of the light corps, and General Maxwell's brigade, some distance in the rear, as a corps de reserve, and Colonel Proctor's artillery in front of the centre of the light corps, and immediately opposite the breast-work. A heavy fire ensued between the rifle corps and the enemy, but little damage was done on either side. In the meantime, Generals Poor and Clinton's brigades, with the right flanking division, were ordered to march and gain, if possible, the enemy's flank and rear, whilst the rifle and light corps amused them in front. Col. Proctor had orders to be in readiness with his artillery and attack the lines, first allowing a sufficient space of time to Generals Poor, &c., to gain their intended stations. About 3 o'clock, P. M., the artillery began their attack on the enemy's works; the rifle and light corps in the meantime prepared to advance and charge; but the enemy, finding their situation rather precarious, and our troops determined, left and retreated from their works with the greatest precipitation, leaving behind them a number of blankets, gun covers, and kettles, with corn boiling over the fire. Generals Poor, &c., on account of several difficulties which they had to surmount, could not effect their designs, and the enemy probably having intelligence of their approach, posted a number of troops on the top of a mountain, over which they had to advance. On their arrival near the summit of the same, the enemy gave them a fire, and wounded several officers and soldiers. General Poor pushed on and gave them a fire, as they retreated, and killed five of the savages. In the course of the day we took nine scalps, (all savages,) and two prisoners, who were separately examined, and gave the following corresponding account: that the enemy were seven hundred men strong, viz., five hundred savages, and two hundred Tories, with about twenty British troops, commanded by a Seneca chief, the two Butlers, Brandt, and M'Donald.[2]

The infantry pushed on towards Newtown the main army halted and encamped near the place of action, near which were several extensive fields of corn and other vegetables. About six o'clock, P.M., the infantry returned and encamped near the main army.

The prisoners further informed us that the whole of their party had subsisted on corn only for this fortnight past, and that they had no other provisions with them; and that their next place of rendezvous would be at Catharines town, an Indian village about twenty-five miles from this place.

*Journals of the Military Expedition of Major General John Sullivan Against the Six Nations of Indians in 1779 With Records of Centennial Celebrations* (Auburn, N.Y., 1887), pp. 155–56.

[1] Major James Parr.
[2] Four Americans died in the battle.

# ANDREW HUNTER DIARY

ANDREW HUNTER was an observer as well as a participant in the Battle of Newtown. His journal records the brief but bitter encounter. Both Major John Butler and Chief Joseph Brant were captured in the fray. The clash at Newtown was the only major encounter in Sullivan's long campaign to end frontier violence.

*Saturday 28 Augt. 1779.* On account of our late arrival last night we did not move till 3 o'Clock P.M. and arrived at Chemung about 6 o'Clock. On this days march we crossed the Caiuga branch to the west side and after marching about two miles we recrossed it. The Stream was not more than middle deep; but so rapid that many of our men and horses were swept down and would have been drowned had it not been for the timely assistance of those who were stronger. I myself dragged one and carried another across. At Chemung there are fine flats on both sides of the river. This day Genl. Sullivan ordered the troops to live upon corn and beans to lengthen out our provision assuring us that we should not be credited by that day's rations. Our distance about 4 miles and our course N.W.

*Sunday Augt. 29.* Marched from Chemung about 11 o'Clock. After marching about three miles our advanced party was fired on by a few Indians. The Army was halted and reconnoitring parties sent out who discovered that the enemy had thrown up extensive works of wood and bushes on the farther side of a small creek and swamp, the right of which extended almost to the confluence of this creek with the Caiuga branch. The General after giving the necessary orders to every department detached Genl. Poor's brigade to turn their right flank and at the same time began a canonade in their front with two pieces of artillery which soon occasioned them to leave their works with great disorder. Genl. Poor however fell in with them on their way to take post on a high hill to the left of their lines, and had a severe scatering engagement and caused them to retreat in great confusion. We had during the whole action only three men killed and about 30 wounded. We took 11 scalps and two prisoners both Tories. The engagement began about 2 o'Clock and continued 'till 5 in the afternoon after which we marched on about 2 miles and encamped at a small town, on the ground where the enemy had lain about 8 days we found large quantities of corn growing on the flats on both sides of the river, which we effectually destroyed. We took a great deal of plunder at different places and secreted in different ways. It appeared upon the examination of the prisoners that the famous Butler and Brant were both of the party and that their number was 220 whites called Butler's rangers and 400 Indians. I attended the amputation of an officer's leg the same night which was a scene more distressing than that in the day.

Andrew Hunter Diary, Princeton University Library, Princeton, N.J.

# "An Authentic Account" of John Sullivan

## September 1779

The expedition against the Six Nations was fully described by chaplains and colonels, but few letters of the generals in command have survived. The following narrative of the campaign and the climactic Battle of Newtown was written by an aide for Major General John Sullivan to be sent eastward to an anxious nation. Sullivan's personal observations vividly portray the violent battle between the Continentals and the Tories and Indians.

The Two Bodies Under General Sullivan and General Clinton formed a junction at Tioga and Marched from thence into the Indian Country on the 26 of last Month. They arrived the 28 at a Settlement called New Town on the Cayuga branch, at Which place the Savages had Assembled their Whole force with a Number of Whites under the Command of the Two Butlers Brant and one McDonald and Were Very advantageously posted and intrenched having endeavoured to Conceal their works With Oak Bows planted between the entervals of the pine Trees with Which the Country was Covered. Our advanced Parties having Discovered them Gave Notice to the main Body Whereupon General Hand with the Light Troops Took post in the Woods infront and began Skirmishing. The Indians Sallied Out Several Times and Retired to draw him on to their Works but to no effect. In the mean Time the main body Came up and General Poor Who Commanded was Ordered to Turn the enemies Left which he effected after some opposition and Dispossessed them of a high eminence that commanded the Rest of their encampment. A flight instantly ensued with Great Terror and Precipitation the enemy left. Eleven Warriors and One female dead on the Spot with a Great Number of Packs blankets Arms Camp equipage and Trinkets. They were persued three Miles—the whole of which way was Tracked with blood a few prisoners were Taken who Reported that the enemies main Strength had been Collected at that place Consisting besides the Whites of the warriors of Seven Nations that it had been Resolved to make three principal Stands there and that they had waited Eight days for this purpose. They also Reported that a Great Number of Wounded had been Sent of on horse back and in Canoes When the Messenger Came away our Troops were employed in desolating the Settlement Which was One of the Largest and Richest in the Indian Country and Considered by the Savages as their chief Magazine. The number of Villages already Destroyed Amounted to fourteen Some of them Capital Ones. Our Loss in the Action was three killed and a proportion wounded. From the extent of their encampment the enemy must have been numerous. Our Troops to a man beheaved with Distinguished Gallantry Which it is only to be Lemented was exerted against So worthless an enemy. . . .

Contemporary Manuscript, Miscellaneous Manuscripts, New-York Historical Society, New York City.

# Tjerck Beekman Journal

Second lieutenant Tjerck Beekman (1754–91) served under Colonel Philip Van Cortlandt in the Second New York Regiment. His journal records his participation in the Sullivan expedition against the Six Nations. He describes the routine of marching and the destruction of the Indians' crops and shelter after the Battle of Newtown. On August 31, 1779, three villages were burned by the Americans. Beekman details the relentless march north that continued the burning of the chief settlements of the Seneca Indians. After reaching Geneseo, New York, the Sullivan expedition turned back toward Wyoming and Easton. The expedition was criticized for its tactics, but it did temporarily disrupt the Indians' frontier ravages on behalf of the British government.

*Thursday august 26th.* The Army marched Leaving 150 men as A Garrison to the four block Houses Which Were built upon a Narrow neck of Land between the Susquehannah and the Tioga Branch. The Rest of the Army Proceeded forward a few miles, incamped early in the Day upon account of A Very Bad Defile Which They Had to Pass. A very high mountain came Down to the River. The Artillery and Pack Horses Hands Brigade Poors Brigade & Maxwells Brigade Crossed the Defile in the Night. Incamped on the Lower Parts of Chemung Flatt—G Clintons Brigade Remained on this Side With the Cattle.

*Friday august 27th.* At Day Brake Struck tents Loaded our Baggage and marched. Soon after overtook the Rest of the Army at 10 A.M. The Whole Marched agreably to the Order of march Established 24 May last. Marched about 4 miles Incampd on Chemung Flatt.

*Saturday aug 28 1779.* At 9 A.M. struck Tents Loaded the Pack Horses and marched at 10 for Chemung Passing a Very Bad Defile. Arrived at Chemung about Sun Down. Incampt.

*Sunday aug 29th 1779.* Clear morning the General Beat at 9 A.M. At 10 the Army marched for Newton through this march a Number of Short Hills Defiles & Morasses. At 12 arrived Within one mile of the town Where We found the Enemy Had Erected A Small Work from the mountain to the River. Soon after Small Parties of our Rifle Men began to skirmish With the Enemy. In the meantime G Clintons & Poors Brigades Were Sent off to the Right to Gain the Enemys Rear so as to intercept their Retreat marching through a Very thick Swamp and crossing a very High hill. At ½ Past three the Artillery began a Cannonade upon Their Works Which Continued for about 9 minutes When they left them in the utmost Confusion. Retreated over the top of a very High Hill Which We forced from them by the Point of the Bayonet Leaving 12 of their Dead on the field. We took one Prisoner a White Man informd that Butler & Brant Were their Commanders that they Had about 600 White men and about 300 Indians With them. We had about 30 men Killed & Wounded in this Engagement. The Enemy carried a number of their Wounded in cannoes up the River.

*Monday august 30th.* A Large Party was ordered out to Destroy the Cornfields

Which Consisted of About two hundred acres of Good Corn besides a Vast Quantity of beans Pumkins &c. Newton Consisted of about Dozen Houses. This Day the General Proposed to the Troops of putting them on half Allowance of Beef & flour for such a time as they could Procure Plenty of Vegetables. At the Same time assured them that they should be Paid for the Remainder in cash at the Market Price. When the Question was Put it was answered throughout the Whole Line by three Cheers.

*Tuesday 31st august.* At 11 A.M. Struck tents and began the march Destroyed Several Small Huts on the Bank of the River. Incamped at Dark on a Large Pine Plain. Marched about 10 miles. This Day Crossed the Cayuga River.

*Wednesday September 1st 1779.* At 10 A.M. struck tents and began our march, Marching about 2 miles, came to A Large Swamp and Very Bad Defile which Detained the Rear of Army till 10 at Night before they Passed Leaving all the Cattle and the Best Part of the Pack Horses in the Swamp. The Horses Several of them died and Great Wastage in the flour. Hands brigade With the infantry Got in Chatharines town. G Clintons Obliged to Put up in the Swamp.

*Thursday 2 Septr 1779.* At 6 A.M. G clintons Brigade Collected the Cattle and Pack horses. Loaded them and began their march for Chatherines Town wheir the front of the army had Arrived the Day before. The enemy had evacuated the town before they got in in Great confusion Leaving behind them an Old Squaw who informed the Genl. of a Council being Held there a few Days before, that the Indians Were Very much frightened, that some of them Had Proposed to Sue for Peace but Butler told them that they might be Sure We Would Give them No Quarters that they Would make Another Stand and if they found they failed Would Retire to niagara Where there Wifes and Children Should be Supplied With Provisions, from Newton to Catherines town is 18 miles.

*Friday 3 September 1779.* At 9 am struck Tents at 10 began our march. Marched about 3 miles. Came to the Head of the Seneca Lake Which is 39 miles in Length about 4 miles Wide lays near North & South. The Army marched upon the East Side of the Lake. The Land along the Lake extraordinary Good. Timbered With white oak. In this Days March Crossed Several Creeks Emptying themselves in the Lake. Marched this Day 11 miles ½.

*Saturday Sept. 4 1779.* At 10 a.m. Struck Tents and began our marching Parrelel to the Lake in Sight of it all the time Crossing a number of Beautiful fine Runs of Water. In this Days march Destroyed a few Scattering Houses along the Lake. Incampt on a Nole With a fine Run of Water in our Rear. Marched this Day 11 miles.

*Sunday September 5.* At 10 a. m. struck tents and began the march ½ after for Appleton Where We arrived 3 P M. This Place by all appeareances is Pretty Ancient Consisting of a number of Good Houses Great Quantity of Corn and a number of Apple Trees, Peach trees & marched this Day about 6 miles. Very Good Land.

*Monday sept 6 1779.* Last night Lost a number of Cattle & Horses. Parties sent out to Look them up. The parties arrived at 3 P. M. Brought in a number of cattle at 4 P. M. The Army marched in the distance of about 3 miles Crossed 3 Considerable Defiles Encamped in the Woods near the Lake. An Express arrived this Day from Tioga. Informed us of the Capture of the Garrison of Paulus Hook by Major Lee.

*Tuesday sept 7 1779.* At 9 am began our march for canandesago. Passing a few

Defiles at 2 P. M. the infantry crossed the outlet of the Seneca Lake. The Rest of the army Crossed soon after. Marched about 1 mile along the Head of the Lake, turned off to the Right for the town Where we arrived at 9 P M. This town is the Great Castle of the Seneca Nation—There we found a White Male Child of about 3 years Old Almost Starved to Death. By appearance this Place Consists of about 60 Houses, Pretty Large in General and Well built: a number of large Apple Trees and Peach and seems to Have been long settled. Found an Anvil and Number of Black Smiths tools which had been left by traders Likewise a Plough in the field.

    *Wednesday septr. 8 1779.* The Troops remained at Kannadasago to wash. Parties Detached down the Lake to Destroy some corn fields and a small Town at 4 P.M.

James R. Gibson, Jr., ed., "Journal of Lieutenant Tjerck Beekman, 1779, of the Military Expedition of Major General John Sullivan Against the Six Nations of Indians," *Magazine of American History* (August 1888), 20:134–36.

# Aquila Giles and Peregrine Fitzhugh to John André

**Peregrine Fitzhugh**

ON SEPTEMBER 28, 1778, a British force commanded by General Charles Grey (1729–1807) surprised some 100 sleeping members of Lieutenant Colonel George Baylor's Third Continental Light Dragoons at Old Tappan, New York. Sixteen were slain and over 50 captured, including Lieutenant Peregrine Fitzhugh (1759–1810). From a prison in the village of Flatbush on Long Island, Fitzhugh and Major Aquila Giles (1758–1822) request parole from Major John André (1751–80), then serving as General Sir Henry Clinton's deputy adjutant general. Their request went unanswered, for Fitzhugh was not exchanged until October 25, 1780, and Giles was not released until November 10, 1780.

*Flat Bush November 30th: 1779*

Sir,

    Permit us to trouble you, once more on the subject of a Parole.[1] As the reasons for which we were detained, after having His Excellency the Commander in Chiefs permission before, have now subsided, we flatter ourselves, he will now grant us that privilidge. The request being made by you insures us success. We do not address Sir Henry, not wishing to take up his time. Colo. Gordon informed us that as soon as Governor Hamilton was released that we had but to address you, and our request wou'd be complied with. Shou'd you think proper to do us the favor, it will be ever acknowledged. We have the Honor to be with great regard Sir Your most Obedient and most Humble servants

AA GILES
PEROGND: FITZHUGH

ALS, Sir Henry Clinton Papers, William L. Clements Library, Ann Arbor, Mich.

[1] Many other prisoners suffered through long periods of confinement. Captain Nathan Goodale (1743–93) of the Fifth Massachusetts Regiment was captured at King's Bridge on August 30, 1778. In a letter of August 19, 1779, of General William Heath to Jeremiah Powell he was described as "a Brave and Good officer a Partizan beloved and respected in the army and would render the Public particular Service were he exchanged." (ALS, Massachusetts Historical Society, Boston.) Goodale was finally exchanged October 9, 1780, and served until the end of the war.

# PETER COLT TO ROYAL FLINT

THE CONTINENTAL ARMY survived despite persistent shortages of money and supplies. The hardships that these continuing problems engendered are discussed in this letter from Peter Colt (1744–1824) to Royal Flint (1754–90). Both men were from Connecticut. Colt served as deputy commissary general of purchases in the Eastern Department from August 9, 1777, to July 4, 1782. Flint served as assistant commissary of purchases from May 27, 1778, to February 1780. Faced with the prospect of cold and hungry soldiers, Colt noted the futility of requesting supplies from Jeremiah Wadsworth, commissary general of purchases for the Continental army from April 9, 1778, to January 1, 1780. The sarcasm in Colt's letter was justified by the many bewildering and vexatious problems in attempting to obtain adequate supplies for the army.

*Decr. 21 1779*

Dear Sir

Your Favr. of the 9th Inst. came to hand yesterday with the Inclosed Resolution of Congress have made out a Return of Persons who act under my direction in this Department—shall request their continuance in Service untill I know my successor in office. I am surprized at the virtue of the soldiery that their Officers should have influence and to keep them together when they were well fed & cloathed tho their pay was nothing, was not passing belief. I dread the Consequences of Cold nakedness & Hunger! As to forming the Magazines I have no choice. Colo. Champion has directed all his People to, wholly, stop delivering Cattle to be bareled without Cash,[1] he can't furnish what is wanted fresh, & has even signified that the Troop at wt Point & its dependances must be fed solely on Salted Meat. This is a terable Stroke for our not half-formed Magazines. I am also wholly destitute of Cash. I am thereby rendered unable to remedy this evil. When Col. Wadsworth left this [     ] Camp I expected another Comy. General; but not the One you mention as his Successor. Upon what Terms does he come in? Some New System I conclude is abroach by the Returns ordered to be made. Pray what part are you to act in this shifting of Scenes? When are we to expect to see Colo. Wadsworth & yourself this way? I conclude the old Game is playing over again—viz, Stoping payment to the *old Servants,* that the *New* may have Cash in hand to begin their administration with. This has been playd on me more than Once, & I again expect to feel the ill Effects of it. Necessity will make a Patriot of me & shall sacrifise my care, health & small Patrimony in my Countrys Cause, whether I chuse it or otherways.

We have a report that Congress have Resolved to remove from Phila. either to Virginia, Albany, or Hartford. For my own case, I wish it may be to the Latter.

The Inclosed Return you will send with others to the Board of War, & believe me to be Sincerely your obd Servt.

PETER COLT

I have wrote so many tedious Money Letters to Colo. Wadsworth. He will excuse my not multiplying them, there would be no variety.

ALS, Jeremiah Wadsworth Papers, Connecticut Historical Society, Hartford.
[1] Captain Henry Champion (1723–97) of the Third Connecticut Regiment.

# JAMES FAIRLIE TO CHARLES TILLINGHAST

GEORGE WASHINGTON's army spent the winter of 1779–80 at Jockey Hollow in Morristown, New Jersey. This winter was considered by contemporaries to be the coldest in memory. James Fairlie (1757–1830), a major and aide-de-camp to General Baron Friedrich Wilhelm von Steuben, vividly describes camp conditions to his friend Charles Tillinghast (1748–95). Loneliness and longing for news from Fish Kill, New York, were hard to bear. Worse by far was the privation of having nothing but deplorable food, sometimes only dog meat. Fairlie, writing from his icy hut near Morristown, describes times of near starvation.

**James Fairlie**

*Coll. Catlands Quarters¹ near Morristown, January 12, 1780*

My Dear Charles

Every person that I have seen from Fishkill for this two months past, I have inquired, whether they have any Letters from my friend Charles to me, but No No were there answers continually. What is the Reason? Say you Son of a Gun? I'll tell you what I would have you make amends by writing me (as a Certain Capt. says) a darn long Sensible Letter.

Oh! my dear Charles we have been almost starved, we had not a mouth full of meat but two pound, and a half, from the first to the Eighth Inst. but thank God! we have now plenty and a prospect of a Continuance of it. During our hungry time, I Eat several meals of Dogg, and it Rellish'd very well.

I have a word for your New Dictionary, made use of a by Certain Mr. Shoote Burvillion for Oblivion.

Give my Compliments to [      ], Tyson and all our male friends, like wise to Sally J——— & all our female ones. Remember me to Mr. Schancks family and Coll Hughes by all means. Your

JA FAIRLIE

ALS, Lamb Papers, New-York Historical Society, New York City.
¹Colonel Philip Van Cortlandt.

# RICHARD CLOUGH ANDERSON AND NATHANIEL WEBB ORDERLY BOOKS

## *1778–1780*

T HE WINTERS OF 1778–79 and 1779–80 were the somber echo of earlier encampments in the cold huts of the north. Middlebrook and Jockey Hollow were dismally familiar to the staunch patriot who had served in each of these campaigns and was then subjected to the arduous conditions of the winter camp. In the harsh environment of camp life, the order and discipline that were taught through formations and maneuvers were more than mere routine exercise. They trained the soldier for instant obedience under fire and dutiful response to commands. The inspections and formations kept both officer and soldier fit for combat. The training program designed by Major General and Inspector General Baron von Steuben introduced a system of uniformity in drilling troops and created a more direct relationship between the officer and his men. The lessons learned at Valley Forge in the spring of 1778 were retained and used on the frozen fields of Middlebrook and Morristown. The orderly book of Richard Clough Anderson (1750–1826), a major in the First Virginia Regiment, details the instructions and directions involved. The orderly book of

**Richard Clough Anderson**
COURTESY OF THE SOCIETY OF THE CINCINNATI,
ANDERSON HOUSE, WASHINGTON, D.C.

Captain Nathaniel Webb (1737–1814) also contains examples of von Steuben's orders.

. . . And march as close as possible every Officer leading his platoon towards the point of vew; in proportion as the platoons have advanced at a proper distances for forming; the Commanding Officer of the Battalion commands, halt *front! dress!* Observing to give the word *halt!* when the two thirds of the platoons have passed the left, of the proceeding one because in the march by files notwithstanding all the care possible a platoon generaly loses its distance; at the last word of command *dress!* every officer dresses his platoon by the first and point of vew; and then takes his post again on the right of his platoon in the front rank; &c. for all the rest. When the column has been formed by wheeling by platoons to the left, it is displayed by the right, in the same manner *Vice Versa;* except that the officers remain on the right of their platoons after the commands halt; front; and dress.

The Brigade Inspectors and other officers, will carefully attend during this week in order that we may be able to pass to greater things next week.

Directions for Inspectors of Brigades to establish the authority of the non Commissioned officers to make them attentive as well as to cure the men of bad habits and false motions when under Arms, it is directed that they carefully watch the Conduct of the men and are to point out such as do not remain steady under Arms or move a miss; if they themselves are negligent and unobservent of their men, they are rigidly punished as the only means of preventing such disorder; a few awkward careless will always disfigure the uniformity of movements and lesen the credit of the Battalion.

The Brigade Inspectors will therefore chose some good Officer out of each Battalion to exercise the new recruits, the Men coming from Hospitals as well as the awkward and careless, this Officer will employ one or two of the most expert Serjeants, under him and train the men either in front or rear of the Battalion, he will also instruct the N.C. Officers who must be exercised apart. They must be taught to march Straight forward towards a given point of vew; which may be the better effected by placing them ten or twelve paces apart in a line and making them March in that manner, they are to be taught their facings and will then be formed in close order, in one rank and practized in wheeling and Dressing, they will next march by platoons; preserve Their exact distance and dress with the platoons before them. They are to command in turn with a Bold loud Voice an Article of the greatest importance, to which the officers will pray the strictest attention.

Richard Clough Anderson Orderly Book, Virginia State Library, Richmond.

Major General Baron De Steuben's Instructions for Manoevering the Troops.

At 8 oClock in the Morning the Inspectors of Brigades will Assemble The Major 1 Capt. 1 Sub. from each Company of their Respective Brigades & acquaint them of the following Regulations, Then take 20 Men without Arms & proceed to performance of the following Elementary Evolutions

1st. The Position of the Soldier is to be Carefully attended to, he must stand Straight & firm upon his Legs, without Affectation, his Shoulders square to the front & keep back his Head upright, both Arms hanging down by his Side without Constraint, these 20 Men are to be formed in one Rank & in such a Manner as that the whole Line is connected by a slight Junction of their Elbows, they must dress by the Right & left their Eyes cast to the Right without advancing the Head.

2dly. The Soldiers placed in the Ranks & dressed as has been directed, are to march to the front at the Word of command, *To the front, March.* The Soldiers raise their left feet at once, look to the right & advance forward, with a free easy & natural Step, regulated by the Officer of that Wing, without bending their Knees too much or projecting their Breasts—always closing to the side their Eyes are fixed upon & when crowded on that Wing, enclining or gaining Ground to the opposite Side.

3dly. As it is of the greatest importance to have an equal & uniform Step throughout the whole Army, the Inspectors are to attend particularly to the Soldiers keeping a due & regular Time to their Step & to the Officers not making any Alteration in it.

4thly. There will be only two Steps used for the Manoevers, viz, the Slow, & the quick Step, but the Soldiers must be thoroughly acquainted with the former, before he is taught the latter. . . .

Nathaniel Webb Orderly Book, Lloyd W. Smith Collection, Morristown National Historical Park, Morristown, N.J.

# EBENEZER STANTON TO THOMAS GOLDSTONE SMITH

DESPITE IMPROVEMENTS in the quarters and the commissary corps made since Washington's army had last encamped at Morristown, New Jersey, from January 6 to May 28, 1777, the ordeals of the exceptionally cold winter of 1779–80 imperiled Washington's 10,000 to 12,000 men. The army desperately needed food and clothing during these severe months. This critical poverty of the army and its inability to provide properly for its men discouraged the reenlistment of veteran Continental soldiers and the recruitment of new men. This bleak situation is discussed by Ebenezer Stanton, paymaster of Colonel Henry Sherburne's Additional Continental Regiment, in this letter to his cousin Thomas Goldstone Smith.

*Camp Near Morris Town Feby. 10, 1780*

Dear Tommy

Haveing A Favoaurable Oppertunity to Acquaint you that I Enjoy A good State of health Readily imbrace the same and at the Same time to Enquire after yours. I would inform you that our main Army Lies About three miles to the Southard of morris Town where they are Comfortably Hutted and in good health but verry Poorly Clad in general. They have been Rather scanted for Provisions but have it more Plenty at Present. I might Say a Great Deal more of the Sufferings of the Army in this Department this winter but thank it Verry Unnecessary as I am Persuaded all things will Come Right in the End. I Lay in A tent till the 21st of Jany. which you may Judge was

Not verry Agreeable when the Snow & Rain had A Free Course in to it. I Cannot inform you of Any Capital movements of the British Army Except Six thousand under the Command of General Clinton hath Embarckt.[1] From New york supposd to bee bound to Georgia but have No intiligence of their Arrival yet. We have Upwards of Fifteen thousand men Inlisted For the war and am in hopes their will bee A Number Mor Reingage whos times Expire Soon. It is Rather Dull Recruiting at Present as the Depretiation of the money hath been So Rapid and Still Continues So to bee that it make the Soldiers Rather Dull to Engage as the money Can bee but Little Service to [    ] but [    ] hopes the Army will bee kept together till we have gain'd the Point we hav been so long Contending For. If the Army could bee Supported I have Not the Least Reason to think that A Man would wish to Leave it till Peace and harmony was Restord to A bleeding but Unconquered and Still to bee Unconquered Country. For my Own Part if we was Paid According to Agreement I Could wish I had two Lives to Loos in Defence of So Glorious A Caus Sooner than bee Over Come. I was Free born and if I Can Suport my Selfe I will Stand or Fall in Defence of my Country.

I am in hopes that we shall have No need to Call on the Gentlemen in the Country for Assistance the Ensuing Campaign but that they may remain at home Peaceably and take all the Comfort and happiness they Can wish for. Their is So few of you that the Fair Sex will be Left Alone and Nobody to Defend them if you and [    ] more should be [     ][2] in Case of an attack at the Garrison of Long Point.

My Most Sincere regard, to your Dady & Mama Love to your Brothers & Sister & to all your Friends & Mine the Ladies at the Point have my Compliments enclosd. in this. Must End with Subscribing my Selfe your Most Affectionate Friend & Couzen

E STANTON

NB: Give my Compliments to Mr. J. Crary.

ALS, Lloyd W. Smith Collection, Morristown National Historical Park, Morristown, N.J.
[1] General Sir Henry Clinton's army sailed from New York on December 26, 1779.
[2] Three words illegible.

# Aquila Giles to Eliza Shipton

MAJOR AQUILA GILES served as an aide-de-camp to Major General Arthur St. Clair before being imprisoned by the British. He was confined to the house of Colonel William Axtell, commander of the sixty-man Nassau Blues, from May to December 1779. There he met and fell in love with Eliza Shipton, the Loyalist colonel's niece. They were wed almost seven months after this letter was written. Major Giles served until the end of the American Revolution.

**Aquila Giles**
ARTIST: GILBERT STUART
COURTESY OF WADSWORTH ATHENEUM,
HARTFORD, CONN.

*Philada. March 31st. /80*

There being no danger of this getting into improper hands, I cou'd not omit asking how my dear E——— is. I should have wrote you from Amboy, letting you know what length of time I was to be absent, but was apprehensive it might fall into your Uncle's hands. Colo. G. offered to be the Bearer of any commands to the Island. I arriv'd yesterday, went to the assembly last night & tomorrow Morning set out for my Father's—& on the 12th. of next month (my Parole then expiring) I shall be in N York. I hope this will find you on the Island. Rember me to Cousin Nancy, & believe me to be with every sentiment of affection Sincerely & truly yours

AA. GILES

ALS, Giles Papers, New-York Historical Society, New York City.

# MICHAEL JACKSON TO WILLIAM HEATH

COLONEL MICHAEL JACKSON (1734–1801) commanded the Eighth Massachusetts Regiment from its formation on November 1, 1776, until it was disbanded on June 12, 1783. In the following letter, he complains to General William Heath, commander of the Continental troops on the Hudson Highlands, about his inability to maintain a fighting force because of arrears in pay and a shortage of supplies. Colonel Jackson's regiment was posted at West Point, the strategic fortress overlooking the Hudson River, which Washington had called the "Key to America." The future commander at this post was Benedict Arnold, the Continental army general who was already conspiring to surrender West Point to the British. This letter illustrates the great morale problems caused by legitimate grievances, personal friction, and frustrated ambitions.

**Michael Jackson**

*West Point April 13, 1780*

Dear Genl.

Yesterday I Recd your Favor Dated the 15 of march. After I had Rote to you I Recd a letter from his Excelency General Washington that he had Recd them and that he had Forwarded them to the board of war: am Gratly obliged to you for the Cair you have Taken for me.

As to the Clamors of a Favorite Colo. you are not insancable whom I mean and whether they have Reason for it I leve the world to judge. It Doth not Concern me.

You tel me I must act the Philosopher as well as the Soldier. I must have more of them Qualifications than any man born before me to keep my Temper if our State presist in what they have begun. The Cloud Blackens a univarsal murmer Prevails the officers Due not Complains one half so much on their own aCount as they Do for the poor Soldiers who have Fought and Bled for their Country. Will the Court [    ] of bountys I wold ask this plain Question if the money had not altred any whether at the Close of the war the Court Expect the Soldry wold pay the bountys back again.

Why Do not the Court Call appon those officers and Soldiers who ware at Stony Point to know what money they Recived that it may be Derected from their pay. Thay have not Recived thir prise money for Tacking Burgoine. I hope thay will not stop it until thay Know what it amounts too: wich in the End will inabel them to pay of the Grand Penobscot Expidition.[1] I do not mean to Reflect on that afair but on thir Conduct Since wich is obvious to the world thay have Dun Rong.

If the pay of the army is Good why is thir not more in the Field why so many officers Resining.

Capt. Varnum & Capt: Bancroft of my Regt have Resined within this three Days past with a Grate Number of other Good officers[2] and what is it for its for no other Reason but this thay are not well Delt by. I have not heard of one Soldier inlisting for a month past: & you may Depend appon it. No more will inlist without better incuridgement 96 men of my Regt will leve me this month whos Times are out. Almost all my old Soldiers have left me. I have about 80 on Furlough and if 60 Returns I Shall Think my Self well of. Dear Sr. I Deu not mean to paint Things worse then thay are and appon my word & Honor I have not Sence and larning anuf to paint it in its proper Colours. Thir is not so Good Provshion for the Soldiers as I Think might be. Will not the army have to pay a Conductor for bringing on our Stores when he is a Trading for him self are wee not to pay an issuing Commesy. 90 pound pr month with Extry Expence though he is now at home and his Two assistances at 60 pounds Each. I Culd wish the State Commesy. might be Colled appon to Know whay thay have Delivered to Each Ration for Six month past. If my memory Serve me wright wee have not Recived 3 pound of Sugar and half that Quantity of Coffe I belive for 8 months past. I have Entred too large a Field for me & must Close by Subscribing my Self your most Humbl. Sert.

M JACKSON

ALS, William Heath Papers, Massachusetts Historical Society, Boston.

[1] An attack on the British fort at Castine, Maine, by troops sent by the state of Massachusetts resulted in the loss of men and ships. The ships of the Massachusetts expedition were set on fire August 14, 1779. This raid cost seven million dollars.

[2] Captain James Varnum (1747–1832) of the Eighth Massachusetts Regiment resigned on October 6, 1780; and Captain James Bancroft (1739–1831), of the same regiment, resigned May 12, 1780.

# John Steele to William Steele, Jr.

The long, hard winter of 1779–80 ended abruptly with a British attack in June 1780. A mutiny in the Connecticut units on May 25, 1780, suggested that the prolonged period of inactivity had had an adverse psychological effect on the troops. General Sir Henry Clinton hoped that a thrust into New Jersey toward Morristown would result in the desertion of many men in Washington's army. British forces under General Wilhelm von Knyphausen landed at Elizabethtown Point on June 7. New Jersey militia and Continental army contingents slowed the British advance toward Springfield. In many battles the casualties among the troops were equaled in distress by property destruction and deaths and injuries among the civilian population. The Battle of Connecticut Farms, New Jersey, on June 7, 1780, ended with the destruction of the entire town, accompanied by prolonged violence against the inhabitants in the area. John Steele (1758–1827), a captain in the First Pennsylvania Regiment, was an eyewitness to the atrocities committed by von Knyphausen's Hessian and British troops at Connecticut Farms. In this letter to his brother, William Steele, Jr., John Steele is indignant at the brutal murder of Mrs. Hannah Caldwell, Parson James Caldwell's wife. After the sacking of this small hamlet, the 5,000 British soldiers withdrew to Elizabethtown.

*Head Quarters Morris Town, June 14, 1780*

Dear Will:

I have omited several opportunities of writing with a daily expectation of seeing you, and my brother Jake, which I now cease to hope for, as we have taken the field for several days in consequence of a sudden, and unexpected excursions of the Enemy, from Staten Island into Jersey, who have, (as usual,) committed the most cruel and wanton depredations by burning, and destroying the houses and property of many peacable and defenceless inhabitants; but the most striking instance of their barbarity was in taking the life of a most amicable lady, wife to Parson Caldwell of Springfield,[1] who left nine small children, the youngest eight months old which sat on its Mama's lap a witness to the cruel murder, though insensible of its loss; did not their barbarity end there, for after several skirmishes (in which it is thought we killed at least 150 and a proportionable number wounded, together with several officers, one of which was General Sirling)[2] they retired to Elizabeth Town Point, where they remained fortifying and possessing themselves of parts of the town; and 'tis said that two nights ago they made an indiscriminate sacrifise of all the females in the place; a cruel slaughter indeed! Yesterday a captain from the British army deserted to us, the cause to me unknown, but he is beyond doubt a damned rascal but it all conspires to make glorious the once dreaded (though now ignominious) armies of Britain.

I am at present enjoying myself incomparably well in the family of Mrs. Washington, whose guard I have had the honor to command since the absence of the General and the rest of the family, which is now six or seven days. I am happy in the importance of my charge, as well as the presence of the most amiable woman upon Earth, whose character should I attempt to describe I could not do justice to, but will only say that I think it unexceptionable; the first and second nights after I came it was expected that a body of the Enemy's horse would pay us a visit, but I was well prepared to receive them for I had not only a good detachment of well disciplined troops under my command, but four members of Congress who were volunteers with their musquets, bayonets and ammunition. I assure you they have disposed of a greater share of spirits than you have ever seen in that body or perhaps ever will see as long as they exist. I leave you to judge whether there is not considerable merit due their commander. I only wish I had a company of them to command for a campaign; and if you would not see an alteration in the constitution of our army against the next, I would suffer to lose my ears and never command a Congressman again. The rations they have consumed considerably overbalance all their service done as volunteers, for they have dined with us every day almost and drank as much wine as they would earn in six months.

Make my best love to my dear sister Betsy, parents, brothers and sisters, as well as to all my good neighbors, but in a most particular manner to some body I cant write to for fear of miscarriage. I am your affectionate Brother

JACK STEELE

ALS, in the possession of Mrs. Charles Robinson Smith, New York City.
[1] Hannah Ogden Caldwell married the Reverend James Caldwell (1734–81) in 1763.
[2] General Thomas Stirling of the Forty-Second Regiment of Foot.

# NATHAN BEERS DIARY

## June 22–24, 1780

ON JUNE 23, 1780, General Sir Henry Clinton, who had just returned from a southern campaign, ordered von Knyphausen, posted at Elizabethtown, to attack again westward in the Springfield area. He was opposed at the bridges before the town by Continental units led by General Nathanael Greene and the local militia. The diary kept by Nathan Beers (1753–1849), paymaster of the Connecticut regiment commanded by Colonel Charles Webb (1724–c.1780), describes the brief but intense encounter. The Americans were able to check von Knyphausen's advance, but the British soldiers' cruelty to the citizens and wanton destruction of homes made the victory a cheerless one for the Continental soldiers.

*22 Thursday.* Tea with Mrs. Richards. Evening Orders to be in readiness for a sudden movement.

*23 Fryday.* Alarm Guns (signall of the Enemys advance) fired at 6 OClock. Jacksons & our Battalion marched immediately to Springfield. Line formed half mile West of Springfield Meeting House. Consisting of 1 Jersey Jacksons & our Battalion with 2 Pieces of Artillery under Capt Johnston. Angells Regimt (& One Piece of Artillery under Capt Thompson) posted One Mile in front with Orders to defend the pass at the Bridge.[1] At ten OClock the Enemys advance made their appearance on the heights 1½ Miles East of Springfield Meeting house. Here they formed & detached a part of their force on the Vauxhall road with a view to gain the Heights on our left (called Newwark Mountain. Here they met with a Sufficent Check from the Party under Major Lee. At Eleven OClock the Enemy made their advance in front on the Springfield road with a very heavy Column. The Opposition they mett with from Angels Regt though Spirited did not prevent their getting possession of the Town, where after remaining 4 hours & destroyed upwards of 20 Buildings withe the Meeting House they retired. Loss of the Rhode Island Regt in killd wounded & missing 41.

*24 Saturday.* At the interment of Capt Thompson who fell yesterday (both his Leggs shot off with a Cannon Shot).[2]

Nathan Beers Diary, Beers Family Papers, Yale University Library, New Haven, Conn.

[1] Colonel Israel Angell; Captain-Lieutenant Thomas Thompson of the Second Continental Artillery.
[2] Fifteen Americans died in the battle.

# WILLIAM IRVINE TO ANN IRVINE

THE SECOND THRUST by von Knyphausen toward Springfield was not anticipated by Washington, who had already left Morristown and moved north. William Irvine (1741–1804), a brigadier general who had served in the Continental army since 1776 and had been inactive for almost two years on parole, led Pennsylvania units advancing toward the Hudson Highlands. Irvine's troops hastily returned to New Jersey but did not arrive until after the engagement at Springfield and the resulting devastation. Irvine described the destruction to his wife, Ann, who waited anxiously for him at home in Carlisle, Pennsylvania. Von Knyphausen returned to Staten Island, leaving behind a wide swath of destruction.

**William Irvine**
COURTESY OF THE NEW-YORK HISTORICAL SOCIETY

*Camp five miles from Morristown*
*June 24, 1780*

My Dearest love

You will think I have nothing to do but write letters, as I have wrote you every two or three days for some time—the last by young Mr. Slough. Our main body left short hills three days ago. Yesterday morning the Enemy advanced to Spring field a Village of about 40 houses eight miles from Elizabethtown—which place they have burned to the ground—together with a fine Church & other publick buildings. When the news reached us we were near Mr Lotts on the rout to Pumpton. We put about and marched towards them—with all possible expedition, but by the time we reached this place The BARBARIANS, had returned to Elizabethtown point. This morning we have not heard what is become of them. I am in hopes they have retreated to Staten Island. On their March to Springfield—two Brigades of Continental Troops—Lees Corps of Horse[1] & the Militia fought them inch by inch for the whole eight miles. It is thought they must have lost many. We have lost a few—cant say exactly how many as no returns are yet come to hand. Brother Andw. was in the action.[2] I presume he is safe or I should have heard. I believe all will be quiet again for some time. I am my dearest love yours most affectionately.

Wm: Irvine

my penn is miserable
& f. in haste

ALS, William Irvine Papers, Historical Society of Pennsylvania, Philadelphia.
[1] Major-Commandant Henry Lee.
[2] Captain Andrew Irvine (d. 1789) of the Seventh Pennsylvania Regiment.

# SAMUEL COGSWELL TO HIS FATHER

THE PROBLEMS of inadequate supply and depreciation of pay were onerous but not insurmountable. In this letter to his father, Lieutenant Samuel Cogswell (1754–90) remarked that the many vexations of army service were often accepted by those patriots who had faith in their government. In this regard, his description of the camp at Preakness (now Wayne), New Jersey, is an accurate view of the chronic problems and inherent patriotism of the Continental soldier and his officers.

*Camp Prackness, N. Jersey, July 15, 1780*

Dear and Honored Sir,

You will undoubtedly be glad to know that your son has safely arrived at camp, and with health sufficient to do the duty of a Soldier. I left New Haven the day after my father did, and at evening reached Stamford. As I passed through Fairfield and Norwalk (the first time I have seen them since their distruction) I was almost persuaded to vow eternal enmity to the name of Britons. My better feelings were aroused by reflecting on the baseness of human Nature, and compassionating the situation of the unhappy sufferers. I tarried at Stamford six days. From Stamford I came to West Point, at which place I tarried long enough to take a view of all the principal fortifications there. My knowledge of fortifications is very trifling, but I could, however, make up my judgment, partly from my own observation, but more from the remarks of others who have both ability and opportunity to become perfectly acquainted with the natural as well as artificial strength of the Post. Every hill on each side of the River upon which forts are erected appeared formidable by Nature, but the amazing strong works which are raised on every convenient place make them terrible to the view, and much more so if approached in a hostile manner. From many considerations it is believed that the Post is only defended by a small force, although it should be attacked by a very large one. From West Point I travelled in company with General Arnold to this Place. The most of the Army I found destitute of Tents, and encamped in a Wood with no other security from the inclemency of the weather than the boughs of Trees, or now and then a Bark Hut. The evening after my arrival in Camp, a rain began, which continued almost two days, the most of which time I was wet to my skin, as were all that were with me. This served as an hardening, but it gave me a cold, the effects of which I am not perfectly rid of yet.

But we have now the happiness to be covered with Tents of the best kind, which, with the prospect I have of regaining my health, makes me very contented. I find all the gentlemen, and indeed all the Lords of the Regiment to which I belong, very destitute of every convenience. I thought the place of their encampment very suitable to their appearance, and I still think they ought not to have left the woods till they had been clothed anew from head to foot. Besides being very ragged and very dirty (which by the way they were unable to prevent for want of a change of clothes), they were supplied with but half allowance of Meat, Bread, or Rum. Whilst I pity the poor fellows for the neglect with which they were treated, my admiration was drawn forth at a view of the patience with which they bore it.

Not a single complaint have I heard made by a Soldier since I joined the army. Every one seems willing to wait for a compensation till his country can grant it to him without injuring herself, which happy time we expect is near at hand. The arrival of the French Fleet at Newport, of which I doubt you have full information, very greatly exhilarates our Spirits, and gives us glorious prospect of soon retaliating for the loss of Charlestown. We expect speedily to have the pleasure of joining the troops of our glorious Ally at the White Plains, the consequence of which must be nothing short of a complete Clintonade. The only regret I feel on the occasion, is this, "that America should be so lost to her own glory as well as interest, and at a time, too, when she abounds in the best Soldiers, as to suffer a foreign force to enter her territories, and fight her battles." It carries with it a disgrace which she will never be able to wipe out. This is at present my opinion, which I am sensible is worth very little, and which I may probably have reason to alter in a very short time. I wish I may. Should an attempt be made upon New York, the danger will be great, and Death will be very busy, for the besieged will doubtless defend themselves with the most obstinate bravery. Then, Sir, I know you will shudder for your Son. But at the same time you wish for his safety, I hope you will as ardently wish that his conduct may be such as may do honor to himself and to his friends, so that if it should be the will of Heaven that he shall be found among those who shall nobly fall in the defense, and for the support of so glorious a cause as that in which we are engaged, you may have reason to say, "I thank thee, Heaven, my Boy has done his duty!" But it is time for me to put an end to this very long letter. However, you will consider, Sir, that your patience will not be exercised in this way very often.

The Bearer is a Soldier of the Regiment, whose time is out.

Ephraim O. Jameson, *The Cogswells in America* (Boston, 1884), p. 241.

# CHARLES TURNBULL TO WILLIAM IRVINE

CAPTAIN CHARLES TURNBULL (1753–95), of Colonel Thomas Proctor's Fourth Battalion of Continental Artillery, presents an ammunition return to Brigadier General William Irvine, commander of the Second Brigade of General Anthony Wayne's Pennsylvania line. Both Turnbull and Irvine had recently participated in the unsuccessful attack on a stockaded blockhouse at Bull's Ferry (now Hoboken), New Jersey, on July 20 and 21, 1780. The blockhouse had been held by 70 Loyalists under the command of Thomas Ward. After an artillery bombardment failed to destroy the walls, Wayne's force rushed the stockade. This hasty decision to storm the fort resulted in 64 casualties. Captain Turnbull explains that the artillery units were unable to damage seriously the Tory blockhouse. Although the attack was unsuccessful, the Americans at Bull's Ferry fought with extraordinary courage throughout the engagement.

*July 24, 80.*

Dear General

The inclosed is a Return of Ammunition which I want and with your leave will draw it from the park of Artillery this Morning.

I am unhappy it was not in my power on 21 Insnt to make a breach in the Block house, I am in hopes you are Convinced Sr: that nothing was wanting, in my Officer (Capt. Lt. Douglass)[1] and Men in that Respect, as you may be Assured it wou'd have given me the greatest pleasure to Reduce such a Nest of—

I am of Oppinion (with Permission) Sir with two twelve pounders and One Howitzer we might with great ease take that place but our Metal was too light to Penetrate the Works, and Ammunition expended.

In my return of the Wounded Yesterday to you In a hurry Ommited mentioned the loss of my horses. I had one killed and two Wounded which was done in our retreat. I have the Honour to be Sir Your most Obt. & Huml. Sert.

CHAS. TURNBULL

ALS, William Irvine Papers, Historical Society of Pennsylvania, Philadelphia.
[1] Captain-Lieutenant Thomas Douglass of the Fourth Battalion of Continental Artillery.

# John Graham to Goose Van Schaick

Major John Graham (1756–1832) served in the First New York Regiment under Colonel Goose Van Schaick for seven years until the war's end. Garrisoned at Fort Stanwix (Fort Schuyler) in Iroquois country, Major Graham reports a skirmish with hostile forces to his commanding officer. Sullivan's expedition had failed to end border warfare in northern New York. In the spring of 1780, marauding Mohawks, with some support from British regulars and Loyalists, initiated a series of raids against Oneida settlements. The Oneidas, who had joined Sullivan's expeditionary forces, fled to the security of the lower Mohawk Valley. Loyalist Mohawk chief Joseph Brant, commanding approximately 500 Loyalists and Indians, was once again responsible for these frontier raids. His attack on the American post at Fort Stanwix (Fort Schuyler) and the vengeful destruction of Oneida livestock occurred after Sir John Johnson's destruction of Caughnawaga on May 22 and before Brant's sacking of Canajoharie on August 1 and 2. Major Graham reports that the outnumbered American garrison at Fort Stanwix took its Oneida allies into the fort for their mutual protection.

*Fort Schuyler July 27th. 1780*

Dr. Sir,

Yesterday about six OClock in the afternoon a body of about eight hundred of the Enemy including two hundred whites encamped a little below the Indian field. I sent some of the Oneidas amongst them who inform that they saw several British Officers one a German who wore a Star at his breast. Joseph Brant was with them. This morning about sunrise they paraded a little below the Old Fort—in full View. We immediately saluted them with the Artillery & drove them back after which they fell to killing the Horses & Cattle belonging to the Oneida Indians that were not put up & firing at the Fort till Nine O'Clock. Our Artillery behaved exceeding and I believe killed some of them. They are now returned to their Camp for how long I can't tell.

Sionondo & Peter are with them and have got their families the rest of the Oneidas are with us in the Fort & seem determined to oppose them. Previous to this I had sent Capt. Hicks, with sixty Men, & fifty Oneida Warriors to Guard up the Boats from Fort Herkermer.[1]

The situation of the Garrison oblidged me to take this step as I was informed by Express that Capt. Van Renselaer could not proceed for want of a Guard.[2] I recd. information of the Enemies approach yesterday in good time to inform Capt. Hicks who has fortifyed himself at Old Fort Schuyler agreeable to my orders. The Gasshopper is of opinion that the Enemy are coming to Beseige the Fort & this party is come to cut off our communication. You know the situation of the Garrison & the condition we must be in should the Boats miscarry. I have ordered Capt. Hicks to continue Fortifying his little Fort till he is relieved from below. Our little handfull of men behaved with the greatest spirit and chearfullness & are determined to defend the Fort while they can get a horse or Dog to eat, what pity such brave Troops should be used in such a Scandalous manner. I remain in haste yours

JNO. GRAHAM

ALS, George Washington Papers, Library of Congress, Washington, D.C. Enclosed in Van Schaick to Washington, July 29, 1780.
[1] Captain Benjamin Hicks (d. 1833?) of the First New York Regiment.
[2] Captain Nicholas Van Rensselaer (d. 1848) of the First New York Regiment.

# JOHN ELY TO JEREMIAH WADSWORTH

THE PRISONER OF WAR faced degradation, despair, starvation, and death. Officers were often accorded more humane treatment; they were frequently placed in housing away from the front and were exchanged for British prisoners of equal rank. John Ely, a colonel in the Connecticut militia who had been taken captive during an expedition to Long Island in December 1777, describes the life of the prisoner. In this letter to Jeremiah Wadsworth, he shows that his emotions have ranged from "Pain & Anxiety" to boredom and loneliness. Prolonged confinement and suffering often tried the patriotism of Americans during the Revolutionary War. Ely was finally exchanged on December 5, 1780.

*Flatt Bush, September 21, 1780*

Sir

I Receivd your favour Dated in May last which gave us a Flattering Prospect of some Assistance in the Pecuniary way from the State. As we have not heard a Syllable since conclude it has like all other our aplications sufferd Abortion. Yet we are fully assurred that your Efforts & good wishes has not been wanting.

If I had a Spiritt of Devination Perhaps I could Tell the reason of an Exchanges not Takeing Place etc. etc. Is it Impossible or am I Doomd to this State of Indolence & Exile. That Through the Channel of the State an Exchange by Discimelar Ranks being applyd that I should be Liberated. Be asurd that I Dont like to Spend an other winter here.

The Officers on this Island are Exceeding Sickly this fall at least two thirds are Sick and convalessent. Notwithstanding which 3 Runs away when one Dies. But you may be assurd Sir that from the State of our Finances the Sickness of our Officers many of which are unable to Furnish themselves wh. the Common Necessarys of life much more any thing comfortable in Sickness that it has Given me Great Pain & Anxiety. I can Only add that I have been happy in affording them all the Phisical Relief that my Invention or the art of Substitution can afford. My Compliments to all Friend & Beleive me to be with Every Sentiment of Esteem & Regard your friend and Very, Humbl. Servt

JOHN ELY

ALS, Jeremiah Wadsworth Papers, Connecticut Historical Society, Hartford.

# JOHN JAMESON TO GEORGE WASHINGTON

ON SEPTEMBER 23, 1780, three volunteer militiamen challenged a lone horseman on the road leading to Tarrytown, New York. The rider claimed he was John Anderson, but upon investigation he was found to be Major John André, an aide-de-camp to General Sir Henry Clinton. Major André was taken in custody to North Castle, where Lieutenant Colonel John Jameson (1751–1810) of the Second Regiment of Continental Light Dragoons commanded American troops. The prisoner possessed secret military papers concerning West Point, its garrison, and its fortifications, which Colonel Jameson enclosed in the following letter to General Washington. The commander in chief soon realized that André's traitorous informant was Major General Benedict Arnold. Arnold had offered his services to the British as early as May 1779, motivated more by money than by a desire to betray America. He had assumed command of West Point on August 3, 1780. Arnold escaped to a British ship in the Hudson River, and André was hanged on October 2 for espionage. Washington was forced by Arnold's treason to take immediate measures to prevent a British capture of West Point, the principal Continental fortification

**John Jameson**
COURTESY OF THE MASONIC HALL,
CULPEPER, VA.

in the Hudson Highlands. Arnold's betrayal has become more famous than John Jameson's quick and effective apprehension of Arnold's British cohort, Major André.

*North Castle Septr. 23d. 1780*

Sir

Inclosed you'll receive a parcel of Papers taken from a certain John Anderson who has a pass signed by General Arnold as may be seen. The Papers were found under the feet of his Stockings he offered the Men that took him one hundred Guineas and as many goods as they wou'd Please to ask. I have sent the Prisoner to General Arnold he is very desirous of the Papers and every thing being sent with him But as I think they are of a very dangerous tendency thought it more proper your Excellency should see them. No Troops have embarked as yet that I can learn the Shipping lies ready and much talk in York about an embarkation.

From every account that I can hear they mean an Attack on the Troops at this place and I must beg leave to assure you that it is out of my power to keep the Troops so compact as I could wish or to move so often as I really think necessary from the scarcity of Provision & Forage & the difficulty of procuring [     ] necessaries also that about one half of the Men are without Blankets or Cooking Utensils for which reason I am obliged to quarter them at houses. Col. Wells's Men have Tents and most of their Baggage which are rather difficult to move about. I am with regard & Esteem Your Excellenceys most Obedt. Servant

JOHN JAMESON

ALS, Courtesy of the Hawkes Papers Committee, Union College, Schenectady, N.Y.

# WILLIAM BEAUMONT, JR., TO SAMUEL DAGGETT

TO THE LOYAL PATRIOT, Arnold's conspiracy was a shocking event. The traitor's plans are fully narrated in this letter of Lieutenant William Beaumont, Jr. (1753–1807), of the Connecticut Continental line, to Samuel Daggett. In describing the betrayal, Beaumont's emotions range from outrage at the deed to great sadness that a man of Arnold's bravery and spirit would surrender his love of country for wartime pecuniary ambitions. This loyal lieutenant exhibits a consistency of devotion to his country that the celebrated general could not achieve.

*Camp Tappan, September 27, 1780*

Hond. Sir

From the acquaintance which I have had with you I shall take the liberty to write believing you to be a man zealous for the good of your country and cannot behold but with Indignation those wretches who for any Considerations would betray it. What a mixture of passions must agitate the breast of every true patriot when they think of the different appearances under which the once brave but now infamous treacherous Arnold has shewn himself.

Be! astonishd! o friends of american freedom. Could it have been thot that Arnold who two years ago exerted himself so much for the reduction of Burgoyne and the British army could be so lost to duty honor and Patriotism as to perpetrate the Horrid Crime of delivering in to the hands of the Enemy the forts Garrisons and Stores at west point and yet as strange as it appears it is true that he had agreed for the sake of a little money to put them in possession of it but providence has disconcerted this Deep laid dark and treasonable plot In a way that plainly shews the hand of heaven in the discovery.

The providential train of circumstances attending this discovery are enough to Convince the most Stupid sceptic of an overruling providence that has to this time preservd the liberties of america and brought to light this daring Conspiracy. The particulars of the discovery are thus, three or four Militia soldiers near Tarry town Met a man Dressd. like a Country man and it being rare to see any travelers in that part of the country so near the enemies lines. They mistrusted he must be some spy they stopd him and charged him with it he denied the charges but guilt the companion of Villains shewd itself on his Countenance and they were not groundless when he found they would not let him go he offerd them a hundred guineas his horse and Gold watch which they took upon them conditions but told him he must go to General Washington (who was at fish Kill on his way to Camp from Hartford) and thus instead of taking him to General Arnold Who Commanded the post at west point and was thirteen miles nearer Providence so ordered it that they took him to his excellency. When he arrived there Colo. Hamilton one of Genl. Washington's Aid, Knew him to be Mr. Andre Adjutant General to the british army.

By his writing, the general found that General Arnold was confederate with him. He had before Sent his horses down to Gener. Arnolds Quarters. Expecting to stay with him that night he went immediately on board of his barge and made all the haste he could down to Robinsons by water but before he could possibly arrive there Arnold heard that Mr. Andre was taken and went off immediately on board of a British flagg that lay in the river and made all the sail he could to pass Kings ferry before General Washington could send to stop him which he Effected. General Washington at his arrival at Robinsons house Immediately Dispached Colo Hamilton to Kings ferry to stop the flagg there but it had passd before he could reach the ferry. Thus this Famous! Infamous! Arnold has Escapd Justice but Im sure his Conscience will not let him in heavn.

Mr. Andre has been throug all our encampments and had the maps of our forts and strength of the army and Garrisons. This is as near the particulars of this Complicated Affair as I am able to get and I have had considerable advantages to know you will perhaps hear of the affair before this reaches you but there will be so many Reports it will be dificult to get the truth of it. I am Sir your very Humble servt.

W Beaumont Jr.

This Affair hapened last Monday the 25th of Sept. 1780

W B

ALS, Miscellaneous Manuscripts, New-York Historical Society, New York City.

# JAMES REED TO MESHECH WEARE

THE AMERICAN REVOLUTION brought personal loss and suffering to countless patriots who had taken up arms in defense of liberty. James Reed (1724–1807) had been an innkeeper and landowner in Fitzwilliam, New Hampshire, when the conflict began. He fought at Bunker Hill and served at Fort Ticonderoga, commanding in turn the Third New Hampshire Regiment and the Second Continental Regiment. At Crown Point, New York, in the summer of 1776, he lost his sight when he contracted smallpox. He was appointed a brigadier general on August 9, 1776, but his health forced him to resign a month later. Reed's daughter wrote in 1780 to Meshech Weare (1713–86), president of the New Hampshire Council, seeking support for her blind father's petitions to the Continental Congress for financial relief because of his disability.

**James Reed**
COURTESY OF THE STATE HOUSE, CONCORD, N. H.
PHOTO: BILL FINNEY, CONCORD, N.H.

*Keene october 6th. 1780*

To the Honobl. Judg Wair President of the State of New Hampshire: Honoured Sir, Althoug I am under malencoly Surcumstances on the Account of Total Blindness which Renders me intiarley helpless Beg Leve to a dress my self to your Honour in the Following maner that is I thinke my self Very hapey that I had the Honour to heir the Voice of your Honour the States aturney with the Rest of the Honobl. Corte yeastarday in the County of Cheshire. Honered Sir, as I have many things I have a Grate Desior to communecate to your honour & the Rest of the Honobl. Corte Still Feairing I Should be too teedeous I would confine Myself & Be as concise as Posebale & only Say att the Conclusion of the former War the feuteuges of which I had gon throu, I moved a Numerous family into an uncontteseted Town within this State thair Prosued to Cultevite By open Road, for the Benifite of sd. State untill this unhapy War. In the year Seventy five was called from my Settlement for the Servise of my Cuntrey had the Honour to comand a Ridgment from this State for which Honour I would not be unmindfull tho' Sence I have had the Honour to Receve a Comition from the thirteen united Stats with the Ranke of Brigadeair Genll: for which I hope I have a Gratefull Sence altho Entiarly Deprived of Being Searviceable in The active Part & find myself under nessety of Praying the assisteance of those in whose Power Sir, to helpe me. I Desiar to Return with Gratiude thankes for favors all Redy Recvid & att the same time Beg to informe how the Surcomstances Lies att this time alltho I Pettitioned to the Contenentall Congress in the year Seventy Eight & have had no Return alltho I have Recvd. the Nomenal Sums of my Establish Pay for Sum of the Time Sence the Date of my Condition I have not Recived any alowance as Depreation att any Time Nor Neither have I Recived Aney Subsistance Money from the Continent for moor thes two years Last Posted Excepien one Ration of Salte Provision for my self Nor no Waggers for moor then twelve month Last Posted & Sir what Ever I have formely Recvd. of Either Hathe Been att Grate Expence to me Sir mutch moor mite be Said But I Shall Conclude with Sainge that I hope of Laying my Case moor open to the State aturney But Sir Would Beg the favour of your Honour if you Should think my Pretentions to be Jist that I may have my afaires Setteled without Sutche Grate Expence to me. I have the Honour to be Sir your most obedient Humbell Sarvt: Elizt Hinds Reed

JAMES REED B: G

LS, Meshech Weare Papers, Massachusetts Historical Society, Boston.

# BENJAMIN TALLMADGE TO JEREMIAH WADSWORTH

BENJAMIN TALLMADGE (1754–1835) was commissioned a major in Colonel Elisha Sheldon's Second Regiment of Continental Light Dragoons on April 7, 1777, but directed most of his efforts to managing George Washington's network of spies. On October 15, 1780, Major Tallmadge writes about military news from the West Point area to his friend Jeremiah Wadsworth, who had resigned the position of commissary general of the Continental army on January 1, 1780. Long-standing problems of supply and Indian depredations continued to plague the many Continental units posted in the Hudson Highlands. Nevertheless, on November 23, 1780, Major Tallmadge led eighty of his dismounted troopers from Fairfield, Connecticut, in a successful raid against Fort St. George on Long Island. George Washington and the Continental Congress commended Tallmadge for his bravery in that foray.

**Benjamin Tallmadge**
COURTESY OF THE LITCHFIELD HISTORICAL SOCIETY, LITCHFIELD, CONN.

*Pines Bridge Octo. 15th. 1780*

Dear Sir

For want of News I send You enclosed a late Resolution of the Legislature of the State of N. York. It looks like a Step which will be productive of good to the Army and the Public. I am aware that it looks rather too much like countenancing military Government, but You must go and do likewise or I fear we shall have *starving* upon *starving* till we are too poor to fight. The Garrison at West Point is again at short Allowance, and our Detachment at no allowance at all.

We have two Dragoons of our Regt. (both Natives of the Country) under sentence of Death. One for Deserting to the Enemy—the other for attempting to desert, stealing my horse, and attempting to take him along. I expect one or both of them will be sent down to this Post for Execution, as an example. Compliments to your Lady, family & inquiring friends. I am, Dear Jerry, with great Sincerity, Your most Obedt. friend & Servt.

BENJA. TALLMADGE

P.S. We are just informed that forts Anne & *George* are taken by the Enemy, & fort Stanwix besieged.[1] A Part of the York Troops are under marching orders.

B.T.

ALS, Lloyd W. Smith Collection, Morristown National Historical Park, Morristown, N.J.

[1] Major Christopher Carleton, leading British regulars, Loyalists, and Indians, captured Fort Anne and Fort George on October 10–11, 1780.

# Daniel Lyman to John G. Wanton

THE NORTHERN and southern armies were often either buoyed by victories or dismayed by defeats that occurred in other theaters of the war. The bloody defeat of the American army at Camden, South Carolina, was not interpreted as a major setback by the northern troops, according to this letter of Major Daniel Lyman (1756–1830), aide-de-camp to General William Heath, to his brother-in-law. Lyman also relates other news and provides an account of a foraging expedition. The letter was intercepted by the British. It may have helped prove that Americans were undaunted by a defeat when ultimate victory was still possible.

*West Point Novr. 24th. 1780*

My Dear Brother

In complyance with your requests my promise, and from a desire of testifying my gratitude for your civility & friendship, which I could as soon wish to forget, as not to deserve, I am induced to present you with a *Detail* of the Military Movements in this Department, and every other occurrence, which my immagination may suggest as interesting to a person of Leisure, Retirement, & Observation.

This Campaigne, from a variety of causes, which human penetration could neither foresee, nor prevent, after an expence, which illy suited the feeble state of our finances, and only flattered our hopes with decisive operations, has stole away, without furnishing materials for either Censure or Applause.

The operations of the Enemy have been little more successful. The action at Camden, between Generals Gates & Cornwallis, can be considered as nothing more, than a promiscuous carnage, and the respite from slaughter only furnished a stimulus for more vigorous exertions. Unable to improve their advantages, and bouyed up by a success, which in its operation, proved merely ideal, they have been checked in the very commencement of their rapid progress, by a handfull of determined Freemen; their Detachments destroyed, & their hopes blasted. This event tho apparently small in its beginning, has been productive of most happy consequences. The Militia convinced, that there is nothing invulnerable in the *garb* of a Briton; that their own safety, and happiness, under the smiles of Heaven, depend on their bravery & enterprize, and that they have nothing to hope from the Cruelty, Perfidy, & insatiable avarice of their Enemies, have at length determined to act with spirit, & free their Country from an invasion. Our last authentic accounts from the Southward, mention the retreat of Cornwallis from Charlotte 40 miles towards Charlestown—our Light Parties hanging on his Flank & Rear, and the Main Army under Generals Smallwood and Gist on their march to attack him. By an intercepted letter, from Genl Leslie, who commanded the Detachment which landed up Cheasopeak, to Cornwallis, we learn, that he had dispatched several Expresses but had not received a line from him since his arrival: and further adds, that from an Enterprize of ours, their affairs were totally deranged in that Quarter. These, and a variety of other events evince, that the Tables are turned, and that our affairs in that Department begin to wear a more favorable aspect.

The extreme scarcity of hay & grain at this place, & the supplies which may be procured from below have induced the General to order a grand Forrage to be made as low down as Maroneck, within six miles of Kingsbridge. Its vicinity to the enemies Lines, where they have their main Force, & the situation of the ground, which forms a Penensula, bounded on the East by the sound, & on the West by Hudsons River, made every precaution necessary to carry the Plan into execution; with safety to the Troops and advantage to the Public. The covering Party consists of 1500 regular Troops, including Sheldons regiment of Cavalry and three regiments of Militia, commanded by the brave General *Stark*.[1] They marched from this the 21st. inst., arrived at Maroneck the 23d. at 2 oClock P.M. The Teams to the number of between 2 & 300 arrived soon after the Party, & were on their return loaded with forrage early this morning. It is expected they will drive off a great number of Live Stock. General Stark has orders to remain on the ground to coopperate with a Detachment from the main Army, in an enterprize which will be attempted tomorrow morning at 4 oClock. I wait for the particulars. May the event be happy. Novr. 27th. The badness of the night prevented the intended Enterprize. The Forragers have returned with large Quantities of grain & hay. The Main Army will take up Winter Quarters in the vicinity of this place. General Washingtons Head Quarters will be at New Windsor 8 miles above this.

I received a letter from Providence dated the 9th. inst. requesting me to send for my black horse or give orders what should be done with him. I think there must have been some mistake. I have sent another Express after him. I hope he is with you however write me by the next Post.

The General has not appointed another Aid. I hope it will be Cogswell. Shall use my influence to effect it. Give my love to Mamma my Brother Sister Little George &c. Yours in sacred Friendship

DANL LYMAN

ALS, Sir Henry Clinton Papers, William L. Clements Library, Ann Arbor, Mich.
[1] Brigadier General John Stark (1728–1822).

# ENOS REEVES LETTERBOOK

LIEUTENANT ENOS REEVES (1753–1807) of Colonel Richard Humpton's Tenth Pennsylvania Regiment, vividly describes the beginning of the mutiny of the Pennsylvania troops on January 1, 1781, while encamped for the winter at Mount Kemble, Morris County, New Jersey. The mutiny was encouraged by unredressed grievances of arrears in pay, shortage of supplies, miserable quarters, and the terms of enlistment. Parts of ten infantry regiments and the artillery regiment of Major General Anthony Wayne were involved in the mutiny. The men and their sergeants contended that their enlistments had expired and that they were wrongly rebuffed in their efforts to be discharged. On the night of New Year's Day, fired by an issue of rum, they disobeyed their officers and prepared to leave camp. The mutineers intended to present their demands to the Continental Congress in Philadelphia.

**Enos Reeves**
COURTESY OF THE MINNEAPOLIS INSTITUTE OF
ARTS, MINNEAPOLIS, MINN.

*January 2 1781*

Yesterday being the last time we (the officers of the regiment), expected to be together, as the arrangement was to take place this day, we had an elegant Regimental Dinner and entertainment, at which all the Field and other officers were present, with a few from the German Regiment, who had arrived with the men of their regiment that belong to the Penna. Line. We spent the day very pleasantly and the evening 'till about ten o'clock as cheerfully as we could wish, when we were disturbed by the huzzas of the soldiers upon the Right Division, answered by those on the Left. I went on the Parade and found numbers in small groups whispering and busily running up and down the Line. In a short time a gun was fired upon the Right and answered by one on the right of the Second Brigade, and a skyrocket thrown from the center of the first, which was accompanied by a general huzza throughtout the Line, and the soldiers running out with their arms, accoutrements and knapsacks. I immediately found it was a mutiny, and that the guns and skyrocket were the signals. The officers in general exerted themselves to keep the men quiet, and keep them from turning out. We each applied himself to his own company, endeavored to keep them in their huts and lay by their arms, which they would do while we were present, but the moment we left one hut to go to another, they would be out again. Their excuse was they thought it was an alarm and the enemy coming on.

Next they began to move in crowds to the Parade, going up to the Right, which was the place appointed for their rendezvous. Lieut. White of our regiment in endeavoring to stop one of these crowds, was shot through the thigh, and Capt. Samuel Tolbert in opposing another party was shot through the body, of which he is very ill.[1] They continued huzzaing and fireing in riotous manner, so that it soon became dangerous for an officer to oppose them by force. We then left them to go their own way.

Hearing a confused noise to the Right, between the line of Huts and Mrs. Wicks, curiosity led me that way, and it being dark in the orchard I mixed among the crowd and found they had broken open the magazine and were preparing to take off the cannon.

*Mount Kemble. January 2 1781*

In taking possession of the cannon they forced the sentinel from his post, and placed one of their own men. One of the mutineers coming officiously up to force him away (thinking him to be one of our sentinels) received a ball through the head and died instantly.

A dispute arose among the mutineers about firing the alarms with the cannon, and continued for a considerable time—one party aledging that it would arouse the timid soldiery, the other objected because it would alarm the inhabitants. For a while I expected the dispute would be decided by the bayonet, but the gunner in the meantime slip'd up to the piece and put a match to it, which ended the affair. Every discharge of the cannon was accompanied by a confused huzza and a general discharge of musketry.

About this time Gen. Wayne and several field officers (mounted) arrived. Gen. Wayne and Col. Richard Butler spoke to them for a considerable time, but it had no effect—their answer was, they had been wronged and were determined to see themselves righted. He replied that he would right them as far as in his power. They rejoined, it was out of his power, their business was not with the officers, but with Congress and the Governor and Council of the State; 'twas they had wronged and they must right. With that, several platoons fired over the General's head. The General called out, "if you mean to kill me, shoot me at once, here's my breast," opening his coat. They replied that it was not their intention to hurt or disturb an officer of the Line, (two or three individuals excepted); that they had nothing against their officers, and they would oppose any person that would attempt anything of the kind.

A part of the Fourth Regiment was paraded and led on by Capt. Campbell, to recapture the cannon;[2] they were ordered to charge and rush on—they charged but would not advance, then dispersed and left the officer alone. Soon after a soldier from the mob made a charge upon Lieut. Col. William Butler, who was obliged to retreat between the huts to save his life. He went around another to head him, met Capt. Bettin who was coming down the alley,[3] who seeing a man coming towards him on a charge, charged his Espontoon to oppose him,[4] when the fellow fired his piece and shot the Captain through the body and he died two hours later.

[1] Lieutenant Francis White of the Tenth Pennsylvania Regiment; Captain Samuel Tolbert of the Second Pennsylvania Regiment.

[2] Captain Thomas Campbell of the Fourth Pennsylvania Regiment.

[3] Captain Adam Bettin of the Fourth Pennsylvania Regiment was killed in the mutiny.

[4] Spontoon: a short pike carried by infantry officers.

# SAMUEL HOLDEN PARSONS TO THOMAS MUMFORD

MAJOR GENERAL Samuel Holden Parsons commanded the Connecticut division at winter encampment near West Point. He reports to his friend Thomas Mumford of Groton, Connecticut, on the mutiny of the Pennsylvania line on January 1, 1781. The mutineers had proceeded in formation to Princeton, where on January 3 efforts to negotiate failed temporarily. Parsons, noting that their grievances were common among the Continental troops and were in fact justifiable, feared that the mutiny would spread to his own soldiers. His men did not mutiny, and on January 22, 1781, Lieutenant Colonel William Hull (1753–1825) of Parsons' Connecticut division led a successful raid on Lieutenant Colonel James De Lancey's Loyalist battalion at Morrisania, New York. Parsons was commended by the Continental Congress for his troops' behavior during that raid.

*Camp Highlands 6th Jany '81*

To attempt to conceal what will soon become public to our Friends & Enemies will serve no good purpose but the Knowledge of the Disease is one Step to a Cure. Know then that the whole Pensylvania Line have mutinied and seisd. their Artillery Ammunition Baggage &c. and still remain in Armes and bending their March towards Philadelphia, in attempting to quell this Defection several Officers lost their Lives. Want of pay, Clothing & Provisions are the Ostensible Grounds of this Defection: No Money having been receivd since the first of April last, very little Clothing & many Times no Provision, these are Complaints in common among the Troops & very justly made. I wish to see a Remedy soon. The Militia of Two Counties in Jersy are out to quell this Mutiny, the Consequences God only knows. There present appears no Disposition among the Soldiers at this post to follow their Example, but I fear unless some Measures are speedily taken to furnish pay & supply Provisions (especially Bread) we shall not long enjoy the Happiness of which results from the better Conduct, Patience & Perseverance of our Troops than those of our Neighbours: in Short few Men could be found voluntarily to endure every Misfortune arising from Want of Money, Cloths & Provisions. We have Nothing else worth your Attention in this Quarter, the Officers find their Hands & Hearts full to keep the Troops patient, I have built me a Hutt & live among them as one Means of quieting them and the Exertions of every Officer in his Station is necessary to guard against the Evils to be feard from a total Derangment of our public Affairs. I assure you we live a Life of great anxiety & Carefullness. I should always be happy in receiving a Line from you but have not had that pleasure this Winter. I am with Respects to your Family, yr Friend & hl Servt.

SAM H. PARSONS

ALS, Miscellaneous Manuscripts, New-York Historical Society, New York City.

# ARTHUR ST. CLAIR TO JOSEPH REED

THE PENNSYLVANIA LINE mutineers showed an earnest desire to avoid bloodshed and deal peaceably with the Continental Congress as they moved toward Philadelphia. The period of negotiations continued to be, however, a difficult time for the Continental army officers. Fears that the British would intervene and profit from the discontent of the rebellious soldiers were confirmed by the presence of two spies from General Sir Henry Clinton in the mutineers' camp. General Arthur St. Clair, who had been rebuffed in his efforts to deal with the rebels, wrote to Joseph Reed, president of the executive council of Pennsylvania, who was negotiating with the disgruntled and disobedient men. He expressed his anxiety over this serious and widespread breach of discipline. Fortunately, St. Clair's fears, which accounted for his order to place artillery on the Delaware River to prevent the troops from marching southward, were lessened when the recalcitrant soldiers spurned Clinton's spies and agreed to a peaceful settlement. This infamous event was resolved, in part, by the respect of the disgruntled men for the integrity of their officers.

*Morris Town Janry. 7th. 1781*

Sir

Mr. Donaldson would inform you of the ill Success of the Embassy The Marquis & myself were sent upon, and the short Notice we received to leave Prince Town. We thought it prudent to take the Mutineers at their Words as there was no Prospect of our being of any Service, and it was not improbable they might think it, upon second Consideration, adviseable to detain Us: & we have heard that they have since made Genl. Wayne Colonels Butler & Stewart Prisoners & admit no Person to see them but thro the Committee.[1] They were impatient to see Your Excellency or some of the Council of Pennsylvania, but their Demands are so Extravagant, and they got on so smoothly hitherto that I have no hopes of any thing but Force reducing them to Reason.

The Ennemy have made no Movement yet in Consequence of this Affair and it may be that they are so much weakened by their late Detachments as not to be able to spare a sufficient Body, but I am persuaded that if they were in Jersey great Numbers would desert to them, as it is certain that british Emmissarys have set this Matter a going, and many of them have confessed to Us that it was proposed to them to lead them all there. This however they nobly refused.

The General is not yet arrived, and some Appearances of similar disposition in the Jersey Troops induced Colonell Barber who commands them[2] to move them to Chatham so that we are here in a very awkward Situation and have this Moment heard that they have sent some Person to bring off the remaining few—perhaps a hundred and all the Stores, and we have not a Soul to prevent it—the Militia being all out already. This may not be true, but if it is attempted it must be prevented at all Hazards. I have the Honour to be Sir your most obedient Servant

AR. ST. CLAIR

ALS, Lloyd W. Smith Collection, Morristown National Historical Park, Morristown, N.J.
[1] Colonel Walter Stewart of the Second Pennsylvania Regiment.
[2] Lieutenant Colonel Francis Barber (1750–83) of the Third New Jersey Regiment.

# WILLIAM SHUTE TO ELIAS DAYTON

WILLIAM SHUTE (1760–1841) was commissioned ensign and paymaster of the Second New Jersey Regiment on June 17, 1780. He wrote to Colonel Elias Dayton one week after Dayton had assumed command of Shute's regiment which was encamped near Pompton, New Jersey. Ensign Shute writes from the camp that had served as winter quarters for three New Jersey Continental regiments since the previous November. Shute discusses the relative scarcity of essential supplies for the New Jersey soldiers.

The New Jersey line, encouraged by the treatment of the rioting troops from Pennsylvania, mutinied on January 20, 1781. Instead of negotiating, George Washington ordered Major General Robert Howe's (1732–85) North Carolina units to capture the mutineers. Two leaders were executed. This swift action ended the mutiny, but the endemic problems of supply shortages and inadequate pay remained. Neither of the two mutinies of 1781 were aided by the officers, nor were they aimed at them. Officers like Shute, who continued in service until November 3, 1783, were called upon to keep order and at the same time to show concern for the plight of their men.

*Jersey Camp Jany 8th: 1781*

Dr Colo:,

Yours of the 31st. Ultimo came to hand this evening by Major Hollinshead.[1]

My not acknowledging the Receipt of the Continental Mare before this, must be imputed to forgetfullness; she has arriv'd and I flatter myself will answer every present purpose.

Am very sorry the Beef answer'd not your expectation, if it had, it would not of answer'd mine, but I assure you, it was the best in my possession.

From the Fifty head since receiv'd, I little expect one (*only*) may be taken that will answer your purpose, he must be slaughter'd tomorrow as I have nothing for him to subsist on, two Quarters of which shall be laid aside for your use.

Should be happy in complying with your requisition with respect to Candles, but I have not one on hand, neither have I receiv'd any since arriving in Jersey last; the first I procure shall be at your service. On Receipt of this if no opportunity should offer to forward the flour to Elizth. please to take the weight, and make use of it. I am sir with respect, your hbl servt.

WILLIAM SHUTE

ALS, Ely Collection, New Jersey Historical Society, Newark.

[1] Major John Hollingshead (1748–98) of the Second New Jersey Regiment.

# ABRAHAM GEORGE CLAYPOOLE ET AL. TO WILLIAM IRVINE

CAPTAIN ABRAHAM GEORGE CLAY-POOLE(1756–1827), of the Third Pennsylvania Regiment, joins with other officers in protesting to Brigadier General William Irvine. The mutiny of the Pennsylvania line had led to some concessions to the men. The officers had resisted the mutineers, even though they admitted the justice of their protests over pay, supplies, and terms of enlistment. The officers of the Pennsylvania regiments did not mutiny but were forced to petition because of their own personal difficulties of lack of pay and confusion of clothing contracts in Philadelphia. The tone of the petition is both urgent and respectful of their superiors. The camaraderie and group loyalty of the officer corps often prevented mass dissension and desertion.

**Abraham George Claypoole**

*Philadelphia February 6 1781*

The Captains who were appointed to represent the Necessities of the Officers to General St. Clair finding a Construction put upon that Representation, injurious to their Characters as Officers & which they did not mean to convey, think themselves obliged to explain it.

After pointing out the numberless Difficulties they were reduced to for want of Pay & informing him they had made Contracts for Cloathing in the City, which they were bound in honour to fulfill before they left it (of the Necessity of which Contracts the Public has been informd in an Address, from the President of        January) they requested the Order for their leaving Town should be postpon'd untill these Difficulties were removed—for this Purpose also requested the General to make an Application to the President & Council; & added that they were desired to assure him, if they were not furnish'd with a Sum not less than £50 each previous to the Order for marching to their respective Places of Rendezvouse many of them (if not all) would necessarily be oblig'd to retire as Citizens. This as nearly as can be recollected is the Substance of their Representation. It was intended to shew the unavoidable Consequence of a Non-Compliance with their just & reasonable Request, & not as an Alternative by way of Threat. This is evincible from the delicate Mode of verbal Application, which they conceived more proper at this Juncture than a written Remonstrance.

JOHN DAVIS *Capt 1 P R*
JOS McCLELLAN *Capt 2 P R*
A. G. CLAYPOOLE, *Capt 3. P R*
WM. HENDERSON *Capt. 4 P Regt.*[1]
WM LEAR *Capt. 5th. PRegt.*
GEO: BUSH *Captn. 6th PRegt.*

ALS, William Irvine Papers, Historical Society of Pennsylvania, Philadelphia.

[1] Captain John Davis (1753–1827); Captain Joseph McClellan (1747–1834); and Captain William Henderson (1756–1811).

# John Cochran to Thomas Bond, Jr.

On January 17, 1781, Dr. John Cochran became the Continental army's fourth surgeon general and the first doctor with the title "Director General of Hospitals of the United States." Cochran had already served in the medical department during Dr. William Shippen's (1736–1808) arrest and court-martial for speculation in needed medical supplies. Dr. Cochran inherited numerous problems from his predecessors. In this letter to Thomas Bond, Jr. (1712–84), purveyor of the Hospital Department, Cochran emphasizes the persistent shortage of medical supplies undermining the care of patients and increasing the mortality rate among hospitalized soldiers. Arrears in pay threatened to deplete the ranks of the medical corps by provoking resignations. Through his appeals, Cochran was able to improve some of the problems of the hospitals. This dedicated man served until the close of the war.

**John Cochran**

*New Windsor March 25th. 1781*

Dear Sir

I was favour'd with yours of the 20th. Ult. about 15 days ago on my way to Albany which accounts for my not answering you untill now as I only return'd last night.

I am sorry to inform you that I found that Hospital entirely destitute of all kinds of stores, except a little vinegar which was good for nothing—and frequently without Bread or Beef for many days—so that the Doctor under those circumstances was oblig'd, to permit such of the patients, as could walk into town, to beg provisions among the inhabitants.

The stores from Danbury are arriv'd at Fishkill, I am informed, so that I propose a small supply to be sent there from that Quarter provided those you mention to be on the way, arrive in time for the people who are to be inoculated.

On my return I found a letter from Mr. John De La Mater informing me that he had an offer from you of continuing in service, as your Clerk and pay Master to the Hospital Department the latter of which he concieves will give him full employ; you are the best judge of this matter, therefore will act accordingly. He wishes to have his pay fix'd, and to have his appointment, and that his chief place of residence should be at Danbury, the propriety of the latter I am at a loss about. From long acquaintance with him, I believe him to be a verry honest man, and verry capable of a business. I shall write and inform him that the matter rests with you, and that I have wrote you on the subject. I much approve of Dr. Wilson's going to Virginia, and if Junifer accompinies him he will have an excellent assistant, and if join'd by the two Mates Dr. Treat informs me he has order'd there.[1] I hope they will be sufficient for that service.

I have already mention'd the gentleman you recommended, to the medical committee, to fill the vacancies of Hospital Physicians & Surgeons, in the strongest terms, except Dr. Cowell, with whom I am little acquainted, either as to his medical abilities or his industry.[2] These being ascertain'd, he claims his promotion of course from long service, and I shall recommed him with pleasure. But I think it is probable Congress will introduce some of the derang'd seniors; this however proper, will discourage the Mates, who are a verry usefull part of the Department, and on whom much dependance must be placed.

As it will be impoper for me to leave Head Quarters untill Latimer comes up, whom I expect shortly, or Craik arrives,[3] you cannot expect me in Philadelphia. I think you had better make out an estimate for the ensuing campaign, with the assistance of Dr. Treat and present it to the Medical Committee, you and he are better judges of the requisites for the hospitals, than I can be, from the nature of the different services we have been employ'd in for some years. (I pity our distres'd condition on the score of money, and unless a sufficiency can be procur'd at the opening of the campaign, we are undone.) Forster being dead, it is probable I shall be able to procure the stores at Windsor Conecticut, as soon as money can be furnish'd to the assistant Purveyor to attend to that duty. I am Dr. Sir your most Obedt. & humble servant

JOHN COCHRAN D. M. H.

Contemporary Copy, New York Academy of Medicine, New York City.

[1] Goodwin Wilson, hospital physician and surgeon of Pennsylvania; Daniel Jenifer (1727–95), hospital physician and surgeon of Maryland; and Malachi Treat, chief hospital physician of New York.

[2] John Cowell (1760–89) of New Jersey.

[3] Henry Latimer (1752–1819), hospital physician and surgeon of Delaware; James Craik (1730–1814), chief physician and surgeon of the army.

# MORGAN LEWIS TO JEREMIAH WADSWORTH AND MR. CARTER

MORGAN LEWIS (1754–1844) was named colonel and deputy quarter-master general of the Northern Department on September 12, 1776, and served in that capacity until the end of the American Revolution. Lewis' letter to Mr. Carter and Colonel Jeremiah Wadsworth laments the unfortunate cycle of overdrawn supply accounts and agitated creditors that plagued the Continental army.

[*September 26, 1781*]

Gentlemen

The Embarrasments Mr. Parker and myself have experienced from your Removal to the Southward,[1] being thereby prevented from receiving of you those Supplies of Cash which we otherwise should have done, have induced us to transmit a rough scetch of our Accot. Currt. on which we earnestly request you, to send us the Ballance; that we may be enabled to discharge our Debts on Accot. of Flower for which our Creditors are very Clamorous.

You will observe in stating the Accot. I have debited you with the whole Sum of 94500 Livres equal to 12000 hard Denars which we are in Advance on Accot. of Forrage. I have done this because I conceive, as it was understood between us that the Advances for Forrage were to be made by you in Bills, we ought not, nor do I believe you would wish us to experience any Disadvantage from our Goods being left on Hand by an unexpected Movement of the Army. We are of opinion we ought to have a Credit for whatever Ballance may be due to you on the Bill and Forrage Accot. until we can convert our Goods on Hand into Cash.

The Flower delivered to the Eastward I have mislaid the Memorandum of, but think, as nearly as I can recollect, it was 1300 Bbbs. which I have rated at 200[   ] each. Should there be a Mistake in the Quantity, you doubtless have it in your Power to rectify it.

Mr. Parker the Day before Yesterday was here and shewed me a State of his Private Accot. with you on which he owed a Ballance of 18000 Livres nearly including the Sum of 12900 Livres recd. of Mr. Wadsworth at Albany, which were brought into private Accot. as he informed me, at the Request of Colo: Wadsworth. In said Accot. he has debited you with only 2 thirds of Goods sent by Watson.

The Quantity of Forrage we have delivered you Amounts to 3146 Bushels of different Species. The Quantity on Hand to 2739. These Quantities are exclusive of some other small ones, an Accot. of which has not yet come to Hand.

We have 500 Bbbs. of Cuyler's Flower turned upon our Hands which is a heavy stroke upon us.

Our Reports here of your Operations are many and various. We are led to believe you have destroyed both the British Fleet and Army. May your Successes be as briliant as they are reported to be, and may you return crowned with Laurels, in which Case, our Enemies may be induced to sue for the Olive. I am Genn. Your most Obet. Servt. In Behalf of Parker and Lewis

MOR: LEWIS

ALS, Society of the Cincinnati, Washington, D.C.

[1] Wadsworth had become commissary to the troops of Jean Baptiste, Comte de Rochambeau (1725–1807).

# ALEXANDER McDOUGALL TO WILLIAM HEATH

**B**OTH SOLDIERS and civilians were physically and emotionally drained by the six years of war. The soldiers of the northern army were continually tormented by supply problems during the long winters. In this emotional letter, General Alexander McDougall, who had served in the Continental army since June 1775, describes the ever-present inadequacy of rations and quarters for his men. Despite the successes of the Continental army on the southern front, another cold and lonely winter was in store for the men in the forts surrounding British-occupied New York City. McDougall's anger with the miserable conditions facing his men is clearly expressed in this letter.

*West Point, 20th. November 1781*

Sir

The Sufferings of this Garrison for want of Bread is intolerable, under the unavoidable pressing Fatigue, it is obliged to perform. In this State of scanty Supply, I am induc'd to believe, the Posts *above* are better, if not fully supplied; notwithstanding the proper and equitable mode of Distribution, of the Commissary, who has the general Direction of the Issues. Since the Fatigue became so general *here;* (as it has been for six or eight weeks) no nonCommissioned, or Rank or file, in, or out of the works, has drawn more than *one Ration:* As *all* are employed, who can be got on fatigue, *all* on that Duty, should have the same support & Subsistance. The Artificers of every Discription, have no more,—but I suspect this is not the *Case* throughout the Department.

In the beginning of the Campaign, the Commander in Chief, in order to forward the Boats, then building, was obliged to yield to the Request of some of the distress'd boat builders, to draw a considerable Quantity of Provisions, more than one and a half Ration, which I suspect is still continued, as well as this quantity to each Artificer, and Boatman. Those in the public Service in any Capacity, *not at this post,* have many Advantages over this Garrison, in the Article of Subsistance, or Exchange of Provision. The former can readily *exchange* Beef for Flour, or Vegetables: and the poor Soldier or Artificer here, is *limited*—It is with Difficulty that he can either exchange, *beg* or *steal.* Confident of the Equity and Humanity of your Heart, I flatter myself, that any Proposition will be chearfully received by you, which will have the least Tendency to relieve the pressing and indiffensible Calls of Nature, and to put *all* the Troops under your Orders, as *nearly* as possible in the same Capacity of Subsisting. Under this persuasion I beg leave to propose for your Consideration that an Estimate be made on Returns, of *all* the Rations issued in the Department; and that Artificers, or men on *hard* fatigue, may draw the same Rations—that those Artificers, or Boatmen, who are posted in the well settled part of the Country, have the Difference; or the Excess of what they draw; *more* than a Soldier, issued in Beef, pork, or Fish, or Flour, when this is the plentest in the Magazines—And as Circumstances shall arise, the *whole* in one Species; because the *Position* of this Garrison is such, that it is as difficult to exchange flour for Beef, as Beef for flour; but the former can exchange those Articles, readily with the Country—or in our Distress for bread, that none draw *for a Ration,* more than a *single one;* and that according to this *Ration,* the Provision be issued, till we are *better* supplied—And to prevent their having a *full* Supply above, when we are starving below, that an officer from this Post, be sent to *each* of the Stores above, who will have a *Sympathy for this Garrison,* whose Business it shall be, to inspect the Issues, to see that they always correspond, with the general Disposition, you may please to make. . . . This Garrison have been without Bread five, and an Half days in October, and eight days in this month: and that all the flour, which was at this post, on the 18th Instant, *works included,* was two Barrels of good, & twelve of bad flour. . . .

I have sent this by a trusty Serjeant, as the contents of it are important. I, therefore, beg; you would please to order him a Receipt for it. I have the Honor to be Sir Your humble Servant,

ALEXR. McDOUGALL *M: General*

P.S. The Troops have been without flour since the 18th, they are served for to day; but there is none for to morrow, which falls to our proportion.

I certify the foregoing to be Copy of the original.

ALEXR. McDOUGALL *M General*

Contemporary copy, Lloyd W. Smith Collection, Morristown National Historical Park, Morristown, N.J.

# Nehemiah Emerson, Jr., to Nehemiah Emerson, Sr.

Captain Nehemiah Emerson, Jr. (1749–1832), writes home to his father about family matters and his lack of adequate clothing. Emerson and other members of the Tenth Massachusetts Regiment were quartered in the barracks near West Point, protecting the Hudson Highlands. Although there were no further major battles there, a substantial contingent of the Continental army remained in the area to offset British strength in New York City. Emerson's respect for his father and his loneliness while on duty are expressed in this letter home.

**Nehemiah Emerson, Jr.**

*N Hampshier Huts Decbr. 31st 1781*

Honerd Sir

After my Duty to you I have the Happiness to inform you that I am well. I hope this will find you and all frinds injoying the same Blessing.

My Duty to my Mother my Love to my Brothers and Sisters.

Sir Please to Not forgit my Regards to my grand mother and aunt Salley simonds uncel West & aunt West and all frinds.

Sir if you have an opertunity Please to Make my Compliments to Mr: Shaw & Mrs Shaw if Mother has got some shirts I should Be glad if She will Send me a Coppell if Brother Samuel has got me a pair of Briches I should Be glad of they Could Be Sent on By Lt. Raymond for fear that I Shall Not able to git a furlow in the Spring.[1]

I have wrote a Large Number of Letters & have Not had one from home this Some Months if it shou'd Be the will of my frinds that I shoud hear from them I should Be glad to hear.

Sir you must Excuse my Not writing for it is Now 9 oclock in the Eavning & the Candel is out I have Not an other mill in the world. I am Sir with Evry Sentiment your Duty full sone

N Emerson

Sir I send you a fine Doge I Should be glad if their mite Be a grate deale of pains with him for he is apt to follow Strangers & Bite hogs very Bad.

ALS, Pepperrell Papers, Massachusetts Historical Society, Boston.

[1] Lieutenant Joseph Raymond of the Tenth Massachusetts Regiment.

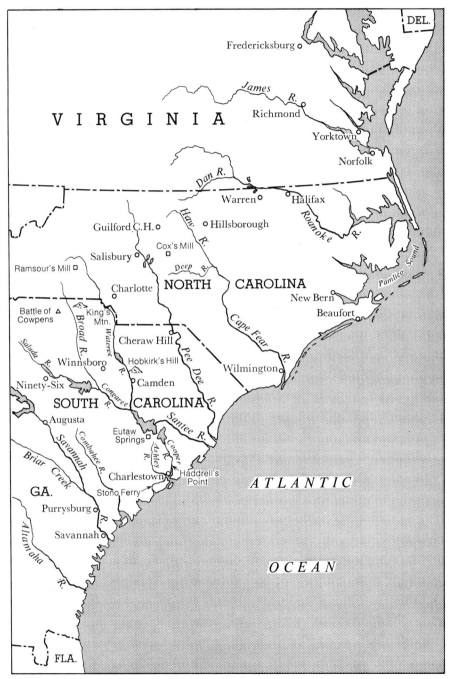

THE WAR IN THE SOUTH

# CHAPTER FOUR

# The War in the South, the End of the War

❧❧❧❧❧❧❧❧❧❧❧❧❧❧❧❧❧

## 1778–1783

THE DECISION of the British high command to shift the focus of their operations to the south in 1778 placed a severe burden on the American forces in Georgia and South Carolina. The first year of British invasion saw the seizure of Savannah and Charleston, with the capture of thousands of American soldiers, who had to endure the rigors of prison or the frustration of parole. The army's desperate attempts to send relief to Charleston were hindered by supply problems. The defeat at Camden reduced the American army to a force of less than one thousand men, an insufficient number to defend the region. The replacement of Horatio Gates by Nathanael Greene spurred the army to new action, resulting in both victories and defeats for the Americans, all at the expense of heavy losses for Lord Cornwallis, whose ever-weakening army was not reinforced.

The Yorktown campaign was a brilliant maneuver by Washington, who capitalized on Cornwallis' error of placing himself in an exposed position. For the first time the French-American alliance worked to gain numerical superiority on land and control of the sea. The brutal siege and trench warfare at Yorktown ended with the surrender of a major British army in October 1781. This one victorious campaign lessened the brunt of the many bitter defeats in the south.

The Revolutionary War did not end, however, with the victory at Yorktown. Indian attacks, naval engagements, and short but violent skirmishes remained to keep the army alert. Soldiers in north and south faced an ever-increasing need for vigilance and patience. The American army under Nathanael Greene stayed in the Charleston area and endured the persistent problems of inadequate supplies, discontent, and fatigue. The British evacuation of Charleston, and then their final exodus from New York City in November 1783, brought the war to an end. The last two years of the war had been times of exhaustion, loneliness, boredom, and restlessness for both soldier and officer. Peace was the ultimate reward for service faithfully rendered.

# OWEN ROBERTS MEMORIAL POEM

## July 16, 1779

THE SOUTHERN CAMPAIGN began in December 1778 when 3,500 British soldiers and Loyalist retainers led by Lieutenant Colonel Archibald Campbell landed near Savannah, Georgia. The British general staff had hoped that southerners would join them in their effort to restore the region to British control. The defeat of Major General Robert Howe at Savannah on December 29, 1778, which cost 83 lives and 413 prisoners, and the timely reinforcements under General Augustine Prevost (1723–86), who had moved north from Florida, seemed to insure the success of the new amphibious campaign. Major General Benjamin Lincoln was given command of the southern forces in September 1778. He arrived at Charleston, South Carolina, on December 19, 1778. By May 1779, General Prevost withdrew his British forces to Savannah after threatening Charleston, leaving Lieutenant Colonel John Maitland in command of the rear guard at Stono Ferry. On June 20, 1779, Benjamin Lincoln ordered an attack on Maitland's garrison at Stono Ferry. The American assault resulted in the loss of 147 men who were killed or missing in action. These casualties included Colonel Owen Roberts (1720–79) of the Fourth South Carolina Regiment of Artillery. His death is touchingly remembered in this memorial poem.

*To the Memory of*
*Owen Roberts Esq.*
*Colonel of the Continental Corps of Artillery,*
*Raised by the State of South-Carolina;*
*Who was slain in the attack of the British lines at Stono-Ferry*
*June 20th, 1779.*

To worth approv'd, at merits honou'd shrine,
The muse that tribute pays so justly thine,
Lamented Roberts! whose virtues great and good,
Were, for thy country's safety, sealed in blood.
If sorrowing friendship could that worth display,
Which would have grac'd the Greeks heroick lay;
Thy memory should to future ages dear,
Be ever honour'd with a grateful tear.
In every act thy patriot spirit shown,
But most in *that* when Freedom called for one,
Whose generous soul would every danger brave,
Her wrongs to right, her right from wrong to save.
For this, her soldier, thou her cause embrac'd,

Thy country happy in a choice well plac'd;
For this, thou brav'd grim war's terrifick low'r,
And mov'd undaunted through the deathful show'r.
But here, alas! how shall my muse relate?
The cruel mandate of relentless fate
Arrests the good, the valient and the just,
And bids him mingle with his native dust;
His soul, serenely great, attends the call,
Nor seeks to shun, but glories in his fall,
Your praises then, O Carolinians, give,
And in your annals, let him ever live;
Let every honour be bestow'd by fame.
For sure such merit must deserve a name.

*South Carolina Historical and Genealogical Magazine* (1914), 17:154–55.

# JOHN BAKER TO RICHARD CASWELL

THE RIGORS of combat affected the ability of many men to continue in active military service. In the following letter, John Baker (c.1726–91), a captain in the Third North Carolina Militia Regiment, advises Governor Richard Caswell of North Carolina that he is unable to serve despite his vigorous efforts to recruit troops and lead them in the field. His tenacity and patriotism compelled him to remain in the service for a year after he was wounded.

*Gates County,[1] August 1, 1779*

Sir,

When I saw you at the last assembly at Smithfield, I was desirous of resigning my commission you did not seem inclined to recieve it at that time, but refered me to Col: Meleane who I applied to when I got to Halifax[2] he told me he did not think he was empowered to recieve it. I still continued to do my duty, and was ordered by Col: Lamb to recieve the Recruits raised in the County where I live, and to repair to Kingston.[3] I accordingly recd. the Men and marched them to Halifax where I met with Major Hogg, and delivered him the men and desired he would accept of my resignation. He told me he did not think I could resign 'till I had settled my account with the public and advised me to march as far as Kingston. I obtained leave to return home to equip myself and should have joined them at Kingston or before but was prevented by some thing rising on my thigh which rendered me incapable of riding. I should be fond of continuing in the service if I was able to discharge my duty as I ought, but a wound I recieved some time past renders me unfit, as I am not able to walk any distance and should be very willing to settle my accounts with the public, and resign my commission.

I sincerely believe a few of the State Regiment might be of infinite service here, you may rely that 'Ill use every means in my power to have them secured. Let me know your pleasure with regard to my Regiment as soon as possible. I am dear Sir, with due respect, your Mo. ob. huml. Servt.

JNO. BAKER
*Capt. 3d. No. Ca. Regiment*

Richard Caswell Letterbook, North Carolina Archives, Raleigh.

[1] Gates County, N.C.
[2] Colonel Robert Mebane of the Third North Carolina Regiment of militia.
[3] Colonel Gideon Lamb (1740–81).

# JOSEPH HABERSHAM TO ISABELLA HABERSHAM

GENERAL PREVOST'S return to Savannah, Georgia, presaged the attack on that city by General Lincoln from land and Count d'Estaing by sea. Prevost, consequently, prepared for a long siege. He employed slaves to construct fortifications and held the population hostage to prevent the besieging allies from burning the town. The American demand for surrender went unanswered, because Prevost was reinforced with Maitland's troops. Colonel Joseph Habersham (1751–1815) participated in the American assault, although he had resigned his commission as commander of the First Georgia Regiment more than one year earlier. Colonel Habersham describes the opening stages of the French-American siege to his wife, Isabella. The siege ended violently on October 9, 1779, when an attack by d'Estaing's and Lincoln's forces was fiercely beaten back. The allies suffered heavy casualties. Approximately 457 Americans and 637 Frenchmen were killed or wounded in the

**Joseph Habersham**

battle. General Lincoln urged d'Estaing to continue the naval siege, but the French were unwilling. Lincoln's ravaged army then retreated to Charleston.

*Camp near Savannah Tuesday 5th Octr 1779*

My dear Bella

I wrote you some days ago which was to have gone by Titus Hollinger but thro' some Mistake it was not delivered to him.

The French open'd their Batterys Yesterday Morning and a very heavy Canonade ensued for an Hour which we are told did great Mischeif both in Town and in the Enemys Lines, they are now busy in throwing up some new Works. I am in hopes the allied Army will be in possession of Savannah in a very few days.

Pray inform Colonel Rae that the Doctors,[1] some of them very eminent in their Profession, held a Consultation this day on this Case and that Doctor Bagbie will set off in a few days on his Return with their Opinion and Recommendation I am hopeful it will be attended with great Releif to him.

General McIntosh sent in to Prevost requesting Liberty for his Wife & family to come out of Town,[2] he returned for Answer that he would not permit it, that there are none but Women & Children in the Town and those our friends and that if we chose to burn the Town & destroy them we might begin as soon as we pleased. They say most of the Tory family are on the Island opposite town.

I have been pretty well since I have been in Camp. My Brother James arrived a few days ago and John has gone back to Sunbury.[3]

Col: Kirkland his Son and 142 Prisoners mostly sick were taken a few days ago or rather surrenderd themselves to White who without any Power granted them Terms, which General Lincoln refused to comply with and Kirkland is now closely confined.

I wish you would write to me by every Conveyance make best Regards acceptable to Col Rae and Mrs. Rae and communicate the Contents of the Letters to them. My Compliments to Miss Somerville and a Kiss to Miss Polly. I am my Dear Bella Yours Affecty.

Jos Habersham

P.S. I am informd the French have sent for Carcases to set the Town on fire with. If so, adieu to our Savannah home and the Country House cannot be finishd just now, so that you may at any Rate expect to be an Inhabitant of the back Country, I have offerd Pinckney the Price he asks for a Tract of Land above Augusta Col: Rae knows.

ALS, Habersham Family Papers, Duke University, Durham, N.C.

[1] Colonel Robert Rae of the First Georgia Regiment.
[2] Brigadier General Lachlan McIntosh (1725–1806) of the Continental army.
[3] Major John Habersham (1754–99) of the First Georgia Regiment.

# JOHN HABERSHAM TO [BENJAMIN LINCOLN]

THE SOUTHERN CAMPAIGN was costly for both sides. Major John Habersham, of Colonel Robert Rae's First Georgia Regiment, was imprisoned by the British after the Battle of Briar Creek on March 3, 1779. Brigadier General John Ashe (1720–81) had ordered the rebuilding of the bridge at Briar Creek so that his North Carolina state troops could join the army of General Lincoln, who was preparing to wrest Georgia from the British. A well-executed British operation, however, routed the Continental and militia forces at Briar Creek. One hundred and fifty Americans were killed or drowned in the action, and 227 were captured. Habersham had been a prisoner previously, having been captured in the fall of Savannah. Writing from Belfast, a plantation south of Savannah, he explains the details of a proposed exchange of captured officers. Major Habersham was exchanged and served until the war's conclusion. His eagerness to serve despite being captured twice illustrates well his outstanding patriotism.

**John Habersham**
ARTIST: JEREMIAH THEUS

*Belfast, the 16th: October, 1779*

Sir,

I do myself the honor to inclose your Excellency the two Certificates of Exchange you sent Colonel Walton.[1] Those names which were not inserted by the British Commissary are now filled up with those of the officers whose right it is to be exchanged.

Lieutenant Colonel Munro is a Prisoner to the United States. I flatter myself if he was offered for me, that General Prevost would not hesitate at accepting the proposal; tho if the difference of rank is considered too great, it is not my wish to injure the Army. Forgive me, Sir, for troubling you at this critical moment with business relating only to myself, and attribute it to the earnest desire I have to share the fate of my bleeding Countrymen.[2] I am, with perfect respect, Sir, Your Excellency's very obedient Servant.

JOHN HABERSHAM

ALS, in the possession of G. Noble Jones.

[1] Colonel George Walton (1740–1804), of the Georgia militia, was taken prisoner at Savannah, December 29, 1778, and was exchanged in September 1779.

[2] Eagerness to serve was a trait of many Continental army officers. Captain Theodosius Fowler (1752–1841), of New York, requested appointment to a peacetime army in a letter to George Washington of December 3, 1783.

# LACHLAN McINTOSH TO BENJAMIN LINCOLN

THE AMERICANS' disorderly retreat from Savannah to Charleston in October 1779 required bridges and boats to transport the tired and wounded American army. Brigadier General Lachlan McIntosh, of Georgia, supervised the several crossing points of the Savannah River. His efforts to repair bridges and to deploy men to guard the route were essential to the survival of Lincoln's force. In the following letter, McIntosh gives his commander a description of these endeavors to safeguard the southern army.

*Lubly Ferry* [1] *Monday 18th Octob: 1779*

Dear Sir,

I rec'd your Letter of this Morning upon the Causway & altho I could get but five work men upon it, I hope to have it & the Bridge in tollerable order this Night.

I could not get all the Stores at Purysburg, nor all the Sick away Yet for want of waggons but hope to accomplish it this Night.

I am informed there are but seventeen Men (Privates) Remaining here of Eight Companys which are barely enough for a Centinel on the Boats, & one on the Bridge on their Rear, but I have picked up a few Stragglers, Deserters Servants and Convalescents from the Sick of the Horse & Foot to make small Piquetts upon the Landings below Purysburgh, & a Centinel upon the Stores, so that it is impossible for me to Send any Men to the Georgia side of the River—and I apprehend it Needless as you have a Pickett at Grahams fifteen Miles below this the only Landing upon the So. side of the River from that plantation to this Ferry.

I will apply to Colo. [Garden] for asistance who Lives 40 miles from here,[2] but have Little expectation of asistance in time if at all. I am Dr. Genl. Your most obt. Hble Servt.

LACHN. McINTOSH

ALS, Miscellaneous Manuscripts, New-York Historical Society, New York City.
[1] On the Savannah River.
[2] Probably Lieutenant Colonel Benjamin Garden of South Carolina.

# Samuel Hopkins to Benjamin Lincoln

After the siege of Savannah, Lincoln's tired army returned to Charleston. Years of service had created many financial, physical, and psychological problems for the Continental soldier in the south. The desire to serve was often offset by the pressing demands of personal life. Reluctance to leave the service of his country is very evident in this letter of Samuel Hopkins (1753–1819), a lieutenant colonel in the Tenth Virginia Regiment, to General Benjamin Lincoln. Ultimately, Hopkins did not leave his command; he was taken prisoner, exchanged twice while imprisoned, and served until the end of the war.

**Samuel Hopkins**

*Augusta, October 26, 1779*

Sir:

    I address you on a subject, not more disagreable to You 'than it gives me pain; to make requests that may be deem'd prejudicial to the Service I have studiously avoided as well as reason for the most distant reflection on my character as an officer, by imprudently absenting myself, when an active part of the Campaign might not have justify'd it. I have served in the army four years, in which time I have never (but in one Instance) been indulged with a furlough, or any kind of absence, and in that only for a few Weeks; previous to my entering into the army I had long Been Engaged in the Mercantile Business, which I had not time to settle then, & from my [Const.?] residence in the army since, I also have been prevented from accomplishing; added to this, is the Care & disposition of a small fortune my Expectations for a future Subsistance, as well as that of four orphans left to my patronage, all of which must particularly suffer without my presence; Some other Reasons of less Weight might be urged to prove the Necissity of my Absence, but these I omit, & have Troubled you with Those inserted, merely because I might not be thought Childish in my request, as well as to justify my Conduct as an officer. I Well know a Winter Campaign is expected in this Country; shoud it take place, I wou'd Risque every other Consequence & resign any pretention to leaving the army at that Period; It is only on a presumption that nothing will be attempted by the enemy this Winter, which Various Causes may forbid—and which shou'd it take place at all, may be delay'd till Very late;—the 1st of December Sir I wish to set out from this Place & shou'd any thing turn up after my absence, I would most Chearfully return on the shortest notice.

The Diminish'd Strength of the Corps I serve in at present, and the Number of Officers, will Very much favour my request.

You will receive this by Lt. Hogg, by whom I shall Expect your Determination;[1] Should you think Sir, that the service will be less injured by my Resignation, than Indulgence on the Terms I ask it, please signify it by Mr. Hogg—but as I have ever Execrated the Idea of leaving the service (without the Consent of the Commander in chief), as dishonourable, I entirely rely on you to decide that.

I beg your pardon for Troubling you on this Occasion; but I hope you will think with me it is justify'd by necessity—should Capt. Watts of Blands Dragoons,[2] return or any other oppery present itself before Lt. Hogg, I request the favor of your answer. I have the Honour to be, with the most Perfect Regard & Esteem, Sir Your mo. obt. Hble. Servn.

SAM HOPKINS

ALS, Emmet Collection, New York Public Library, New York City.
[1] Lieutenant Samuel Hogg of the First Virginia Regiment.
[2] Colonel Theoderick Bland (1708–84) of the First Continental Dragoons.

# WILLIAM CROGHAN DIARY

DURING THE COLD WINTER of 1779 Major William Croghan (1752–1822) was encamped with his Fourth Virginia Regiment at Stony Point, New York. Croghan's diary records the difficult journey of two brigades of Virginia Continental soldiers to Charleston, South Carolina, by way of Philadelphia. They had been ordered south with North Carolina units to reinforce General Benjamin Lincoln's troops. Braving extreme cold, deep snow, frozen rivers, and inadequate supplies, they arrived at their destination early in 1780, in time to be involved in General Sir Henry Clinton's attack on that city. The British expeditionary convoy had arrived from New York on February 10, intending to capture Charleston, a feat which they had been unable to accomplish in 1776. After a long and effective British siege from land and sea, Lincoln was forced to accept Clinton's terms of surrender on May 12. The Americans lost not only the city but also over 3,500 troops from the town's garrison. Among the Continental soldiers taken prisoner by the British was Major Croghan, who was eventually paroled until the end of the war.

General Woodfords & Muhlenburg's Brigades March from Stony point on the North River in the State of New York.[1] The tents were wet when put in the Waggons, Owing to Snow that fell last Night which with its Continuing to Snow . . . all day made this days March Very Disagreeable. . . . The Troops were Billeted on the Inhabitants, which was very Inconvenient both to them & us, making the line of March Very long & Deep, & Many of the Soldiary Under the Necessity of pitching their tents to Stay in; not having Room in the Houses. . . . Decr. 2 & 3rd About Eight oClock began the March . . . came in Sight of Morristown, where haulted untill the Straglers came up—then got in good Order & Marched through Morristown (Where General Washington had taken up his Winter Quarters) to our Intended Winter Quarters about two Miles from Town, where we was Shewn Our Grounds on a high Narrow Disagreeable Ridge, on which there was no Water Nor a Sufficiency of Wood to build Hutts to Winter in. Decr. 4th. . . . All this day the Soldiary were Very Busy Building Chimneys to their officers & Their Own Tents, on the above bleak hill, not knowing we would be allowed Any Other Ground & Determined to live in the tents untill Our Hutts were Finished—It Snowed all Night. . . . December 8th. Officers & Soldiers Very attentive to the Building their Hutts; about three oClock in the afternoon when Near All the Virginia Hutts were Raised. Orders Came for us to get in readiness to March to philadelphia. The Orders had Different Effects, both on Officers & Soldiers, Some wish Much to go to philadelphia while Others were Sorry for leaving their New Town, which they had so Much trouble with And the Whole Seemed to dread their being Moved from Philadelphia in the Extream Cold Season to the Intemperate Climes of Georgia, or South Carolina—Others flatter'd themselves with being Stationed in their Native Clime Virginia for Some time etc. etc. December 7th. All the Officers Ordered to philadelphia. . . . General Muhlenburg's Brigade Mustered by Colonel Cabell[2] & General Woodfords by Mr. . . . December 16. Settout on our Journey towards Coopers Ferry opposite philadelphia, Very Disagreeable & Dangerous riding on acc't of a few Inches Snow falling last Night, which Covered the Ice & Made the Horses Clogg, Slip, & Fall Frequently. . . . About Sun Sett Arrived at Coopers Ferry, where taking advantage of the Flowing of the Tide we Crossed the Delaware to philadelphia. December 23rd: . . . When the River Delaware froze so hard as to Carry the Troops & Baggage over on from Trenton, Colonel Russell's Detachment march'd for Philada as Did the Other two within two or three days of Each other. . . . The Extream Cold weather during their Continuance here & the frequent heavy Snow & high Winds prevented the City being Supply'd as Usual with Fire Wood, Vegetables, etc., for which articles both Inhabitants & Soldiars Suffered Very Much Especially for Wood which was at the Extravigant price of $40 per Cord. On their March through Philadelphia it was generally Agreed they Made the Most Martial & Soldiar like appearance of any Troops that ever went through that City. The Drummers & Fifers far Excelled, both as to Judgment & Numbers, Especially those of Russells & Nevilles.[3] (middle of January) . . . We being pretty well furnished to go by Land, proceeded but with inexpressable Difficulty. The Snow being three Foot Deep on a levell & Drifted so high, as to Cover the Tops of the Fences a great part of the Road—Several Empty Waggons sent in front to open or beat the Road, but to little Effect, The Cold North West Winds Blue so hard as fill up the Tracts with Snow almost as Soon as the Waggons had left them. . . . January 13th. After riding afew Miles find it Very Difficult to Travell owing to the Snow being so deep & drifted so as to prevent our knowing where the road is, Not notwithstanding its being as publish a Road as any on the Continent—in the Evening we Arrived at Downingtown, where Colonel Nevills Detachment was Detained, on Account of the Difficulty of Marching, & Breaking the Road through the Deep Snow—Almost all the Horses he Took from philada. Tired out, drawing the Waggons & Artillery through the Snow. The Commissary Informs the Colonel that he Can't get provision . . . Hall'd on account of the Snow, & presses him to March, Saying if he does not that he will have no provision for the Other Detachment which he Expects toMorrow. The Troops Are Billeted in the most Convenient houses on & Near the road. January 14th: . . . Several have their Hands Feet & other parts of their Bodys Frozen.

William Croghan Diary, Historical Society of Wisconsin, Madison.

[1] Brigadier General William Woodford of the Continental army; Brigadier General John Peter Gabriel Muhlenberg of the Continental army. North River: the Hudson River.

[2] Lieutenant Colonel Samuel Jordan Cabell (1756–1818) of the Fourth Virginia Regiment.

[3] Colonel William Russell; Colonel John Neville (1731–1803) of the Fourth Virginia Regiment.

# JAMES FRANCIS ARMSTRONG TO WILLIAM C. HOUSTON

AFTER THE FALL of Charleston, the Continental Congress authorized a force of Maryland, Delaware, and New Jersey units led by Baron de Kalb to proceed south. James Francis Armstrong (1750–1816) was a chaplain assigned to these men. In this letter to William Churchill Houston (1746–88), a member of the New Jersey delegation to the Continental Congress, Armstrong decries the lack of support and food that the soldiers were forced to endure. The fatigued relief expedition rested in North Carolina.

**James Francis Armstrong**
COURTESY OF THE SOCIETY OF THE CINCINNATI,
ANDERSON HOUSE, WASHINGTON, D.C.

*Wilcock's Iron Works, Deep River, North Carolina,*[1] *July 8, 1780*

. . . We have marched five hundred miles from Philadelphia, ignorant as the Hottentot of the situation or numbers of the enemy. Though it was long known that we were marching to the assistance of the South, not the least provision was made to hasten or encourage our march. Wagons to transport the baggage, and provisions to subsist the troops, have both been wanting. We have for some time depended upon the precarious and cruel practice of impressing horses from post to post. We have also been driven to the disagreeable alternative of permitting the men to murmur and languish for the want of meat, or seizing cattle on the march; not knowing whose property they were unless the owners came to camp to complain of the injury. Horrid war! Heaven's greatest curse to mankind! We are told things will grow better, the further we proceed south; but the hope must be precariously founded which depends upon the complaisance of Gen. Lord Cornwallis. I would not write such plain truths, did you not know that I am not given to despondency; and I have the same providence to call forth my hopes, which exerted itself so miraculously when Howe was in New Jersey. . . .

John Hall, *History of the Presbyterian Church in Trenton,* 2d ed. (Trenton, N.J., 1912), p. 183.

[1] Deep River is at the junction of the Haw and Deep rivers.

# MORGAN BROWN, JR., TO HORATIO GATES

ORGAN BROWN, JR. (1758–1840), was commissioned assistant commissary of purchases for the Southern Department on July 20, 1780. He wrote this letter concerning supplies to Major General Horatio Gates just two weeks after the latter was appointed commander of the Southern Department by the Continental Congress. Gates was appointed in the hope that he could turn the unfavor-able tide of the war in the south. The army was severely disheartened by the continued inadequacy of supplies and the shortage of men. Despite the army's problems, Gates decided to confront quickly the British army. The Battle of Camden on August 16, 1780, was an American disaster, with 1,050 casualties, leaving Gates' ragged army with only 700 men.

*Guilford County August 2d. 1780*

Sir,

I received your instructions dated at Coxes July 20th.,[1] by Genl. Harrington,[2] and have purchesed about 400 Bushels of Wheat and 25 Steers. The wheat I shall have manufactured as soon as posable; and wate your Orders what to do with the beef. I have agreed with a Gentleman who lives in Virginia for 130 Bushels of Salt, 65 of which is ready to be delivered at this Magazin on the payment of the Continental Money; and the remainder by the last of this Month.

I could Purchas much larger quantities of Provision if I could have money to pay the people immediately, for they depend on their Crops to purches salt and other Nesserys for their family's. I shal remain in this place and Purchis what I can on credit until I Receive further Orders. I have nothing more to inform you but that I am Sir your most Obedient Humbl. Servt.

MORGAN BROWN JUNR.

ALS, Horatio Gates Papers, New-York Historical Society, New York City.
[1] Cox's Mill, N.C.
[2] Brigadier General William Henry Harrington of the North Carolina militia.

# WILLIAM CAMPBELL TO ARTHUR CAMPBELL

FTER THE CRUSHING DEFEAT of General Horatio Gates's forces at Camden, Major Patrick Ferguson was selected to lead an army of Loyalist militiamen and British regulars into North Carolina and Virginia. A makeshift army of patriot militia and "Over Mountain Men" (frontiersmen from beyond the Blue Ridge Mountains) resisted their advance. The leader of the Virginia contingent was Colonel William Campbell (1745–81), a frontiersman and patriot from the King's Mountain region of the border of North and South Carolina. Colonel Campbell's 400 Virginians combined with the remainder of the southern army in a series of raids and skirmishes against the British, culminating on October 7, 1780, with the Battle of King's Mountain, South Carolina. Ferguson and over 150 of his men were killed. This signal victory was a turning point in the southern theater. Campbell reported the battle in this letter to Colonel Arthur Campbell (1743–1811).

*Wilkes County, Camp on Brier Creek, Oct. 20th, 1780*

Dear Sir:

Ferguson and his party are no more in circumstances to injure the citizens of America. We came up with him in Craven County, South Carolina, posted on a height, called King's Mountain, about twelve miles north of the Cherokee Ford of Broad river, about two o'clock in the evening of the 7th inst., we having marched the whole night before.

Col. Shelby's regiment and mine began the attack,[1] and sustained the whole fire of the enemy for about ten minutes, while the other troops were forming around the height upon which the enemy were posted. The firing then became general, and as heavy as you can conceive for the number of men. The advantageous situation of the enemy, being the top of a steep ridge, obliged us to expose ourselves exceedingly; and the dislodging of them was almost equal to driving men from strong breast-works; though in the end we gained the point of the ridge, where my regiment fought, and drove them along the summit of it nearly to the other end, where Col. Cleveland and his countrymen were. They were driven in a huddle, and the greatest confusion; the flag for a surrender was immediately hoisted, and as soon as our troops could be notified of it, the firing ceased, and the survivors surrendered themselves prisoners at discretion.

We fought an hour and five minutes, in which time two hundred and twenty-five of the enemy were killed, and one hundred and thirty wounded; the rest, making about seven hundred regulars and Tories, were taken prisoners. Ferguson was killed near the close of the action. The victory was complete to a wish; and I think it was won by about seven hundred men, who fought bravely. I have lost several of my brave friends, whose death I much lament. Maj. Edmondson will give you their names, though I must myself mention Capt. Edmondson, his two brothers, and Lieut. Bowen.[2] My regiment has suffered more than any other in the action. Our loss in the field was, altogether, about thirty killed, and sixty wounded. I must proceed on with the prisoners until I can in some way dispose of them. Probably I may go on to Richmond, in Virginia.

Lyman C. Draper, *King's Mountain and its Heroes* (Cincinnati, 1881), p. 526.

[1] Colonel Isaac Shelby (1750–1826) of the Virginia militia.

[2] Major William Edmondson (1734–1822) of the Virginia Rangers; Lieutenant Robert Edmondson, Sr. (d. 1780), Lieutenant Robert Edmondson, Jr. (1753–1816), and Ensign Andrew Edmondson (c. 1750–80), of the Virginia Rangers were all either killed or wounded in the battle; Ensign Reese Bowen (1742–80).

# Adam Jamison to Nathanael Greene

After the american victory at the Battle of King's Mountain, Lord Cornwallis withdrew his army to Winnsboro, South Carolina, and General Horatio Gates moved the remainder of his army from Hillsboro to Charlotte, North Carolina. Writing from the Continental army's new camp, Adam Jamison (1752–95), a lieutenant in the Fifth Maryland Regiment and commissary general of issues for the Continental army in the Southern Department, suggests to Major General Nathanael Greene, who assumed command of the Southern Department on December 3, 1780, that a commissary of hides be appointed. Shortage of hides for shoes and harnesses was just one supply problem facing Greene's army. In his army of 2,500 men, fewer than one-third were properly clothed and equipped. Greene, who had served as quartermaster general of the Continental army, was familiar with the persistent supply problem.

*Charlotte Decr. 15th. 1780*

Sir

I am persauded the Public has Suffer'd not a little, in the Southern Army, for want of a Commisary of Hides and with regret I have frequently observd it. There has not yet any Person been appointed, by proper Authority to Act in that Capacity, that might become subject to be call'd on for the produce of the Property intrusted in their hands; For want of which the Hides have been frequently, and commonly, left in the Encampment and carry'd off by the Inhabitants at their Discretion. Since my appointment in the Issuing Department I have been particular in directing the Commisary to take care of them and I believe the Chief part of the Hides Northerly of Salisbury, have been Deliver'd to some person that affected to act for the Public, but than Slaughter'd since that time are lying at different places, to the amount of near four hundred, expos'd to the averice of the Inhabitants without any person to look after them. If the Hides were Sav'd, and Exchang'd for Leather or otherwise dispos'd of, they would go a great length in furnishing the Army with Shoes and Harness, which is much wanted. I have Yesterday engag'd a young Gentleman Volunteer in the Maryd. Line to enter in the Business, and will if aggreeable to you, appoint him to that Duty and for the present Superintend the Business myself till such time, as matters can be better Regulated, and endeavour to have the Hides Sav'd. I am Sir, your Obt. Humble Servant

Adam Jamison *C. G. Issus sct*

ALS, Nathanael Greene Papers, William L. Clements Library, Ann Arbor, Mich.

# JOHN W. WILLIS TO
# THE VIRGINIA HOUSE OF DELEGATES

## December 21, 1780

MAJOR JOHN W. WILLIS (1740–1816) of the Fifth Virginia Regiment was exchanged on November 8, 1780, after almost three years as a prisoner of war. On December 21, 1780, he successfully petitioned the Virginia legislature for compensation for personal financial losses caused by his prolonged captivity. He was awarded financial relief the next day and resumed service in the Fifth Virginia Regiment until his retirement on January 1, 1783. Such tenacious patriots as Willis were needed in the south to counteract the large number of Loyalists in the region.

To the Honble the speaker & Gentlemen of the House of Delegates. The Memorial of Major John Willis Humbly Sheweth

That your Memorealist, being Now discharged from a Captivity of near three years as a Prisoner of war, & having During his Captivity supported himself from his own private fortune, without the Aid of Government, finds that He Cannot, without the utmost Difficulty, now join the army without receiving from Govement a Sum of money to enable him so to do. He therefore prays, that the same advance may be made him as have been to other officers in Simular Circumstances he thinking himself equally entitled Thereto & your Memorialist as in Duty bound Shall pray.

ALS, Willis Family Papers, Virginia State Library, Richmond.

# WILLIAM RUSSELL TO NATHANAEL GREENE

COLONEL WILLIAM RUSSELL commanded the Fifth Virginia Regiment between September 14, 1778, and his capture by the British on May 12, 1780, during the fall of Charleston. He spent the remainder of the year at the Haddrell's Point prison camp in Charleston harbor. Colonel Russell asks General Greene to seek from Cornwallis an extension of his parole so that Russell can protect his family on the Indian-infested southwestern border of Virginia. Russell did not know that his exchange had been arranged in November 1780. He then served until November 3, 1783.

*Hadrills Point 31st. December 1780*

Sir,

I beg leave to trouble you with the within contents by favour of Colonel Ball, who, in his way to Virginia will wait upon you.[1] I was favoured to day with the perusal of your letter to Brigadier General Moultrie;[2] am happy to find your good state of health still enables you to perform the duties of your station; and sincerely congratulate you on your safe arrival to command in the southern department. It is now almost eight months since the fortune of war placed us here in a state of captivity; in no which time, we have received no supplies either from Congress or the State of Virginia: consequently, our wants are considerable of which, you will most likely be informed by Genl. Moultrie. Ever since the fall of Charles Town, I have been very apprehensive the indians wood commit hostilities on the southwestern frontier of Virginia, where, my family is situated; and by recent accounts from the New York and Charles Town Gazette, find my fears verified; whence, I have reason to expect my family may be of the sufferers. Anxiety for the wellfare of nine (motherless) children many of them very small, withall exposed to a savage enemy, urge me at present to entreat your humanity and interest, to solicit the Earl Cornwallace, for the extension of my parole six or eight months to go to Virginia for their security: no object less interesting could induce me to add to your present weight of business, and am persuaded of your friendly office to effect the indulgence: any necessary and usual restriction on the occasion shall be carefully observed.

Please make my respectfull compliments to General Smallwood, and Colonel Morgan, and other gentlemen of my acquaintance in your army. That you may enjoy health and prosperity, is the real wish of sir, your most obedt. Humble Servt.

W RUSSELL
*prisoner of war*

N.B. Since I wrote the within letter, a flag has arrived from Virginia.

ALS, Nathanael Greene Papers, William L. Clements Library, Ann Arbor, Mich.
[1] Lieutenant Colonel Burgess Ball (1749–1800) of the First Virginia Regiment.
[2] Brigadier General William Moultrie (1730–1805) of the Continental army.

# JOSEPH CLAY TO NATHANAEL GREENE

INSUFFICIENT CLOTHING for the soldiers seriously hampered the effectiveness of Greene's southern army. This problem was sometimes alleviated by the efforts of private contractors. Lieutenant Colonel Joseph Clay (1741–1804) had served as deputy paymaster general of the Southern Department from August 6, 1777, until his election to the Continental Congress on February 26, 1778. Clay, a merchant in the port town of New Bern, North Carolina, writes to General Nathanael Greene about his purchases for the army. Supplies were often ordered through Clay, but high prices, poor credit, and meager financial resources were persistent problems that made his task difficult. Although not in uniform, Clay showed his continued patriotism in his efforts to win the war with his attempts to supply the army.

**Joseph Clay**
PHOTO: WILLIAMS STUDIO, SAVANNAH, GA.

*Camden 1st: January 1781*

Sir,

I reached this place last Night, after a very tedious & disagreable Journey from the excessive bad Weather we have had for some time past. I wrote you from Beaufort, Newbern, Washington & Halifax, informing you of the few purchases I had made, & of the little prospect I had of increasing them. I returned by way of Newbern where I procured 26 doz. more of Thread Hose 50 Yds Irish Linnen, 10 Ld Thread, 1 doz. common Knives & Forks & 3 doz. Military Shirts, all of which except the Shirts I purchased on the same terms. I got the other Articles 5 for 1, & for the Shirts 5 1/2 for 1. I paid for the Salt & every thing else I purchased in Bills on France a 6/ Pensylva: Curry: per Dollar, so that I had no occasion to draw on any of the States. Before I left Newbern I sent away for Salisbury a Case wth. Hatts, Military Shirts & 3 1/2 Reams writing Paper, a Trunk with some Hosiery, a little Blue broad Cloth & Buff Casimire, 1/2 Ream Gilt Paper & a few Articles for myself & the Gentlemen of your Family &c. large Hhd wth. Saddles Bridles & Military Shoes &c. a Cask containing 7 doz. Bottled Port 1 Cask Rum & 4 Kegs Barley. The other Articles were on board a Vessel wch. had been on her way from Beaufort to Newbern near a Month, owing to bad Weather & contrary Winds & as 'twas very uncertain when she might get up, I Empower'd a Friend to receive them & deliver them to the Q: M: there & directed him to have them forwarded to Salisbury.

Mr. Bankes a partner in the House who were among the Principal owners of one of the Privateers (and from whom I expected to have been furnish'd with a large quantity of Linnens Hatts & Hosiery & under the Encouragement he gave me, I took the Journey to St. Quay in hopes of receiving them) put on board a Vessel at Beaufort bound for Newbern 53 doz. Military Shoes & 2 Hhds Sadlery. The latter were not fit for Dragoons, therefore as I had before purchas'd as many as wou'd supply our Officers & some very common ones fit for Servants, I did not think it material to purchase them for the Army, & as I was likewise well convinced the intention of sending them up was rather to push them on me than to serve the Public, as I have every reason to suppose they withheld many other Articles wch. I wanted (particularly Linnens) on an expectation that they cou'd dispose of them to more advantage in a retail way, & I am the more confirmed in this opinion because when I was at Beaufort they denied having any more even of these Articles then they then let me have, especially Shoes, this with the excessive high price of the Shoes operated wth. me to decline taking them unless he wou'd let me have them on more reasonable terms, if he had furnish'd me generally wth. such Articles as I wanted taking the one with the other I shou'd have made no objection. The Shoes cost or are charg'd by him at upwards of 52/ Sterlg: per doz., wch. with 5 for 1 Adve. brings them to near 3 Dollars per pair, wch. is 1 Dollar more than they sell out of the Stores (even at Newbern) by the single pair. I waited at Newbern near a fortnight in expectation of seeing Mr. Bankes & perhaps getting them on more moderate Terms, being told that he wou'd be up from Day to Day, at length being wearied with waiting there on such an uncertainty, I wrote him on the Subject offering him 100 per Sterling on the Cost & to take the Sadlery for this State, as I knew 'twou'd not suit the Army. I have reason to believe he will accept these terms as I do not think while they sell from 14/ to 16/ No: Car. Curry. per the single pair (& which they now do) that any one can afford or will give him more. However on reflecting on the Season of the Year & the great Consumption of this Article & how necessary they were for our Soldiery, I have Empower'd a Friend in Newbern (Mr. James Green) by letter I wrote him from X Creek on my way here, to inquire whether he (Mr. Bankes) accepts my offer, & if he will not, to engage him on the lowest Terms he can, & go as far as the Advance he Asked 5 for 1 provided he will not take less; these if we get them will also be delivered to the Q: M: there & forwarded by him to Salisbury.

These Prizes were by no means so Valuable as we were inform'd £17,000 Sterlg. was the outside of their cost in Great Britain, & they were divided among so many hands there was no doing any thing among them. If I cou'd have paid down Specie I cou'd have collected from individuals a very considerable quantity of usefull Articles and on very reasonable terms, but Bills were no inducement to Seamen or Officers or to few of the Owners, even these latter were numerous. The Prizes were taken by two Privateers & each of them had several Owners, & the Cargoes were not sold but divided among all the Claimants (Owners, Officers & Seamen) so that it became difficult to find a large Quantity of any Article in the possession of any one of them. I do assure you my ill success has given me great anxiety especially when I reflect on the wants & necessities of our Army, however I am conscious of having Spared no trouble or pains in my power that cou'd have tended to promote the business I went on.

I will send you down in a few Days a particular Account of every thing I have purchas'd or perhaps bring it myself as I propose as soon as myself & Horses are recruited to come to Camp & from thence if you have no occasion to detain me proceed to Georgia. I wou'd beg leave to trouble you relative to Forage for my Horses, the Q:M: here thinks he is not Empower'd to furnish me with more than for one Horse, & I am now, & have been during the whole time I have been here oblig'd to purchase what more I had occasion for, indeed at present & for some time before I went away I have received none, not choosing to receive for one only. I have never had less than three in Use ever since we were drove from this place (in May 1780) & them my own, nor have I ever had a Waggon, wch. I am intitled to, nor any means to convey the Public Money or Papers &c since I have been in the Office, wch. is now going on five Years, during which time I have always transported them at my own Expence both as to Horses & Servants. If you think it proper & consistent that I shou'd be furnish'd with Forage for all my Horses I will be oblig'd to you to furnish me wth. an Order to Mr. Saml. Matthews Q:M: to that purpose, & that he shou'd receive my Returns for the time past (I mean while here) as well as for the future.

I had forgot to notice that I cou'd not get any Madera Wine, wch. was the reason of my taking the Cask Bottled Port. Cou'd I have got 3 or 4 Casks I shou'd have sent them on, but I was too late; Mr. Green of Newbern told me he had sent away for the Army three or four Pipes tolerable Wine a few Days before I got there, under the direction of Major Forsyth,[1] and while I was there two more wch. Dr. Oliphant had engaged in Phila. of Mr. Stanley (Mr. Greens Partner) one of these he told me was exceedingly good Old Wine & intended for their own Use. The Pipe was near half out, but as they had no other they were oblig'd to send it as it was. I mention this Circumstance as possibly it may be intended for the Hospital, where Wine of an inferior Quality wou'd answer the Hospital purpose equally as well & that might be reserved for drinking. The Cask of Rum is but of a midling Quality though the best I cou'd meet with. I am wth. Regard & great respect Sir Your most Obedt. humble Servt.

JOSEPH CLAY

ALS, Nathanael Greene Papers, William L. Clements Library, Ann Arbor, Mich.
[1] Major Robert Forsyth of the Virginia militia.

# THOMAS NELSON, JR., TO BARON VON STEUBEN

LORD CORNWALLIS' efforts in the Carolinas were considered successful, but the British generals assumed that the key to the southern campaign would be control and occupation of Virginia. General Sir Henry Clinton sent Brigadier General Benedict Arnold on an extensive raid in Virginia to complement the British activities in North Carolina. Sailing from New York on December 20, 1780, the forces led by Arnold moved up the James River toward Richmond to destroy American stores and supplies. Despite continual threats of attack, Governor Thomas Jefferson (1743–1826) was unprepared for this raid. Arnold's 1,600-man force occupied Richmond on January 5, destroying warehouses and many other buildings before withdrawing to Portsmouth. Brigadier General Thomas Nelson, Jr. (1738–89), who had served in the Continental army and was in command of Virginia state troops, was given the hopeless task of rousing the militia to repel the invasion. His outmanned force was routed on January 8 at Charles City Courthouse. In a letter to Baron von Steuben, Nelson shows his tireless energy and determina-

**Thomas Nelson, Jr.**
ARTIST: MASON CHAMBERLIN

tion and describes enemy movements and the lack of men and arms to resist invasion.

*Long Bridges Jany. 7. 1781. 4 oClock PM*

Dear General

My not knowing where you had taken your Quarters, & the Difficulty of conveying Intelligence across the River while the Enemy were in Richmond, have prevented your being more frequently informed of the different movements I have made, & those of the Enemy. They are now moving down with the utmost Rapidity to their Shipping; having marched this Morning from Hudson's ordinary, which is 12 Miles below Richmond. Major Dick[1] is in their Rear with a few tired Militia. It was my Intention to have put myself in Motion immediately on receiving Intelligence of their leaving Richmond; & orders were issued for that Purpose, when the violent Rains set in last Night, which for the want of Covering, rendered the Troops with me incapable of immediate Action. Their arms are unfit for Service, & the little Ammunition they had

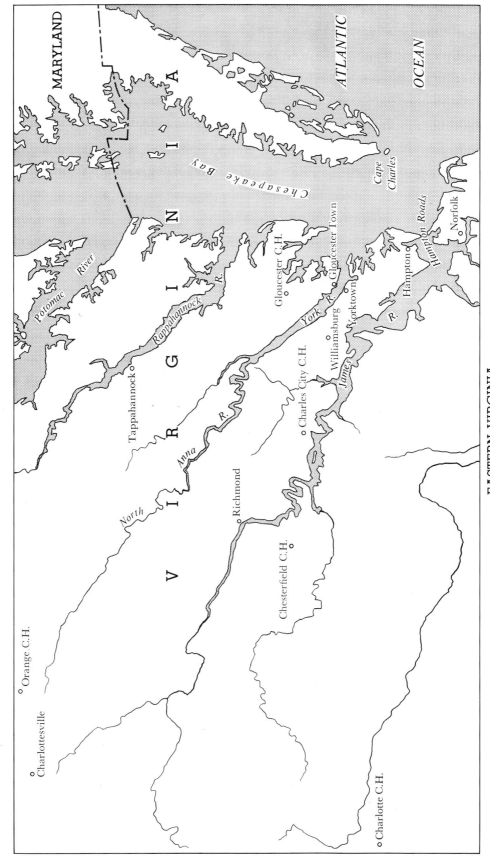

EASTERN VIRGINIA

is almost destroyed. Major Dick is nearly in the same Circumstances. Before I received your orders I had determined to proceed down on this Side of the River with the Troops under my Command. I am, Dear General, with great Esteem, your Obedt. Servt.

Thos Nelson Jr. *B.G.*

ALS, von Steuben Papers, New-York Historical Society, New York City.
[1] Major Alexander Dick of the Virginia state troops.

# John Spotswood to Baron von Steuben

General benedict arnold's raid on Richmond found the Continental army in a state of unpreparedness. Troops in Virginia were under the command of Baron von Steuben, who had moved south with General Nathanael Greene in 1780. His urgent request for men reached the home of Captain John Spotswood (c.1748–1800) in Orange, Virginia, near Fredericksburg.

Spotswood had served since 1776 and was wounded at Brandywine and Germantown in 1777. He was captured at the latter and not exchanged until November 1780. His answer to von Steuben is a reminder that the gallantry of men in battle was often touched with human tragedy with many men crippled, blinded, or lamed.

*Orange, Jany 10, 1781*

Sir

Haveing seen your Excellencys Orders for all Continental Officers to repair to Chesterfield Court House, by the 10th. of Feby. take this method of informing your Excellency, that I was Among the Unfortunate that fell the 4 of October 1777 at the Acction of German Town haveing my thigh Broke, by which Misfortune I have been renderd a Criple ever since, and as my Wounds frequently break out from useing much Exersises, hope my not appearing in person will be no Obstical in the Appointment of my Rank. The date of my Commission I am at a Loss to know it being taken from me when I was stript in the field, by the Enemy. I Bore a Captancy in the Tenth Virginia Regt. I am one of those Officers who have been Lately Exchanged. I have the honour to be Respetfull Your Excellencys most Obt Servt.

John Spotswood

ALS, von Steuben Papers, New-York Historical Society, New York City.

# Burgess Ball to George Washington

Burgess Ball of the First Virginia Regiment was among those imprisoned by the British after the surrender of Charleston. He was released on parole after eight months of captivity. Ball informs George Washington of his imminent trip to the Mississippi River, planned because he could not return to active duty until exchanged. He was destined to remain on parole until February 12, 1781, despite his earnest desire to rejoin the military effort. He, however, refused to violate the terms of parole and showed himself to be in the truest sense both a patriot officer and a gentleman.

*Fredericksburg. Jany. 30th. 1781*

Sir,

Having been indulg'd with a Parole, unsolicitted and unexpected, thro the Interest of Genl. Phillips (as I'm inform'd) for Virginia or elsewhere,[1] and, ever desireous to conduct myself so as to avoid any reproach from Your Excellency, I have thought it expedient thus to write to you.

It being, in my present situation, improper and out of my power to take any active part in a military capacity, I think of taking an excursion to the Waters of the Mississippi, there to make some provision for a future day, having greatly impair'd my hereditary possessions. This I think it necessary to inform Your Excellency of, least I shd. be wanting when an Exchange shd. take place, it being my uniform intention to continue my services to my Country as long as they may be wanting. If an Exchange is like to happen in any short time, it is far from my desire to evade any dangers or hardship which my attendance might present. I am, Your Excellencys most Obedient & very Hbl. Servt.

B: Ball

ALS, George Washington Papers, Library of Congress, Washington, D.C.
[1] Major General William Phillips (1731–81) of the British army.

# Thomas Polk to Nathanael Greene

Colonel thomas polk (1732–94) had commanded the Fourth North Carolina Regiment from its creation on April 16, 1776, until his resignation from the Continental army on June 28, 1778. In this letter, he thanks General Nathanael Greene for recommending him to be commissary of purchases for the southern army. His patriotic dedication moved him to vow to sell his slaves to pay his public debt. Part of Greene's army had defeated Lieutenant Colonel Banastre Tarleton's (1754–1833) British forces at Cowpens, South Carolina, on January 17, 1781, but the whole army was then obliged to conduct a rapid retreat 200 miles to the Dan River in Virginia. Polk's knowledge of enemy movements and concern for the war effort are emphasized in this letter. Greene's men reached their destination on February 15, 1781.

*March 1st, 1781*

Sir

I Recevd. yours of the 16th. on satrday the 24th. & am much distrd. for your being obligd. to Retreat as fare as you have but it cartainly is the salvation of our Countrey for you Not to Run any Risqus With your armey, for while your safe the British Cannot oceppy Nor possess any Part of our Countrey but What is inside of thir sentreys on Lines. Sir I thank you for the Honor you Intend me by a Recomandaton to the asembly & was Such an apintment to take Place Wood with the greatest Chearfullness draw all the men Posable into the feld & Nothing at Present discoredges me only the backwardness of the People. Our Members of asembly has ben at home this four days & I have Never heard aney thing of my appintment and supose they had maid other appintments befour your Letter Rechd. them. Genl. Sumter has movd. to the Congree & has taken a small Number of British that Lay ther With about 500 Negros & a deal of Stores it is Reported the Militia all turn out Wherever he Goes.[1] Conl. Jack Informs me he waited on you with my Letter Respecting a draft but did not Receve any. I shall be obliged to sell sum of My Negros to Pay Publick debt as I Cannot bear to be doond. for Money.

I this Moment Rd. Notice that Lord Raden had gone in Pursute of Sumter & had left Camden almost without a Gard. I am Sir with Great esteem, your Huml. Sarvt.

THOS. POLK

ALS, Nathanael Greene Papers, William L. Clements Library, Ann Arbor, Mich.
[1] Brigadier General Thomas Sumter (1734–1832) of the South Carolina state troops.

# CHARLES MAGILL TO THOMAS JEFFERSON

CHARLES MAGILL (1760–1827) had served as a second lieutenant and regimental adjutant in the Eleventh Virginia Regiment until his resignation on April 18, 1778. Subsequently, he served as a major and aide-de-camp to Brigadier General Isaac Huger (1743–97), who commanded a brigade consisting of the Fourth and Fifth Virginia Continental Regiments, at the Battle of Guilford Courthouse, North Carolina, on March 15, 1781. Magill reports this hollow British victory to Thomas Jefferson. Greene's army positioned itself at Guilford Courthouse and awaited Lord Cornwallis' attack. The British forced Greene to retreat to avoid further losses. Cornwallis was left in possession of the battlefield but with one-third of his men killed or wounded. He was soon compelled to retreat to Wilmington, North Carolina.

*Camp at the Iron Works Gilford County March 16th 1781*

Sir

On the 15 Lord Cornwallis anticipated the design of General Greene (whose intentions were to Attack the British Army, the same day) by advancing his main Body to Gilford Court House, where the Army had taken post the day before. On the advance Colo. Lee charged Tarltons Legion who were some distance in front of the Enemys main Body, cut thro them and put them to the Rout with very considerable loss.[1] The British then moved on with the utmost rapidity, and whilst displaying their Column kept up a heavy Cannonade with four Field Pieces upon two posted in the Road under the command of Capt. Singleton who returned it with considerable damage.

Immediately on the display of their Column an Attack was made on our Front line composed entirely by Militia, who returned their Fire, and the greater number from Virginia behaved in such a manner as would do honor to Veterans, but were at last compell'd to give way by Superior numbers. The Virginia and Maryland Brigades that composed the Second Line immediately Engaged and after some time the left of the Maryland Troops gave way. This and other concurrences gave the Enemy possession of the ground and four Field Pieces all that were in the Action. Never was ground contested for with greater Obstinacy and never were Troops drawn off in better order. Such another dear bought day must effectually ruin the British Army. From the nicest calculation Seven hundred of the Enemy were killd and Wounded. Their best Troops the Guards and 33d. Regiment suffer'd most. The loss on our side is inconsiderable when put in a comparison, and the Troops now breathe nothing but a desire for a second Action. My Duty as Aid De Camp to Genl. Huger, who commanded the Virga. Brigade, prevents my being so particular as I would wish, the whole of my attention being confined to that Line. The Virginia Regulars with a sufficient number of Officers would have done honor to themselves, that deficiency frequently created confusion.

An account is circulating in Camp pretty well Authenticated that General Marian has repuls'd Lord Raddon who attackd him some place near the River Santee, with a very considerable loss,[2] further that Genl. Sumpter has taken a post upon the same River where a Magazine of Stores were laid up.[3]

I have the honor to be Yr. Excellencys Most Obedt. Humble Servt.

CHAS MAGILL

ALS, Executive Papers, Virginia State Library, Richmond.

[1] Lieutenant Colonel Henry Lee.

[2] Brigadier General Francis Marion (c.1732–95), of the South Carolina state troops and Second South Carolina Regiment, clashed with British troops near Wiboo Swamp, South Carolina, on March 6, 1781. Lieutenant Colonel Francis Rawdon-Hastings (1754–1826) of the British army.

[3] Thomas Sumter.

# READING BLOUNT TO [JETHRO SUMNER]

CAPTAIN READING BLOUNT (1757–1807) served in Colonel Thomas Clark's First North Carolina Regiment from January 1, 1781, until discharged at the end of the American Revolution. His regiment was temporarily immobilized in Salisbury, North Carolina, because the men had no shoes for marching. Blount's experience with inadequate supplies was common at all times and in all theaters for all participants in the conflict. The main part of General Nathanael Greene's southern forces was then resting from combat and the oppressive summer heat in the hills above the Santee River. After six weeks of recuperation in South Carolina, the southern army resumed its campaign on August 22, 1781. On September 8, Greene's army, with Brigadier General Jethro Sumner's North Carolina Brigade on the right flank, met the British at the Battle of Eutaw Springs, South Carolina. The British won a hard-fought victory but suffered devastating, heavy losses. Such losses soon became intolerable to the British effort, for their forces lacked reinforcements.

**Reading Blount**

*Salesburg Augt 9th 1781*

I have the pleasure to inform you that Capt Goodman arrive at this post on the Eigth with about one hundred & twenty Men, on the same day the Armes arrive from Virgt[1]—which I shall take on to you, as they are, unless ordered to the Contrary, I shall be able to leave this in about five days & not sooner as many of the Soldiers are Barfooted & cant March without shoes. I have percurr'd an Order from the Cloathes Genrl for as many shoes as well doe them by sending to Davidsons for them.

You should of been furnish'd with a Genrl Return of what men there is at this post, but Capt Goodman has not had time to make me one since he arrive—if you have any Orders relative to the armes or Trupes I shall be happy to receive them as soon as possle. I am Sir Yours

READING BLOUNT

P S No stores for our Brigadere not as much as will serve one Officer

R B

P.S. We shall have upwards of one hundred stand of armes that has been refited which I shall bring on as Colo. Wotten has no armes they will answer him very well.

Alice Barnwell Keith, ed., *The John Gray Blount Papers* (Raleigh, N.C., 1952), I, 17.
[1] Captain William Goodman of the North Carolina militia was killed on September 8, 1781.

# CHARLES HARRISON TO NATHANAEL GREENE

No MAJOR ACTION occurred in the early summer of 1781 in the Carolinas. What seemed to be a time for rest for the weary soldiers and for replenishing supplies and munitions proved deceptive. Clothing and weapons were either unavailable or in poor condition. In this letter to Nathanael Greene, Colonel Charles Harrison (1742–96), of the First Continental Artillery, informs his commander of the problems encountered in collecting serviceable weapons. In addition, manpower problems often required that the sick be employed in noncombatant positions.

*Charlotte 20th. Augt 1781*

Dr Sir

Agreeable to your instructions have inspected the Arms at this post; & 'am sorry to inform you, that out of 375, there are very few fit for repair; at Olliphants 330, also in want of repair, the whole have order'd to Salsbury, from whence will inform your Excellency more particularly what number can be made fit for the field.

I have been detain'd here some days by indisposition; & 'am now waiting the arrival of 300 stand of Arms, & fifty thousand musket Cartridges, at present, betwixt this & Salsbury, shall order them on to Camp immediately.

I have taken the liberty of makeing application to Doctor Read, for such of the invalids, as, (will answer the purpose of working in the Laboratory, &) are render'd unfit for the field,[1] I flatter myself it will meet with your approbation. 'Am Dr Sir Your Affte & Huml Sert

CHA HARRISON
*Comdt Arty*

ALS, Nathanael Greene Papers, William L. Clements Library, Ann Arbor, Mich.
[1] William Read (1754–1845), hospital physician and surgeon in the Southern Department. The laboratory was an arsenal for the storing and manufacture of ammunition. Many officers and men in the southern campaign suffered permanent injury and death. In the American siege of Ninety-Six, S.C., May 22-June 19, 1781, Lieutenant Isaac Duval (1757–81) was severely wounded. Colonel Otho Holland Williams (d. 1794) described the casualties to his brother: "Captain Armstrong of the Maryland Line killd. Capt. Benson Dangerously wounded & Lt Duvall also wounded." (Williams to Elie Williams, June 23, 1781, Otho Holland Williams Papers, Maryland Historical Society, Baltimore.) Duvall survived his wounds from that siege but was killed in the Battle of Eutaw Springs on September 8, 1781.

# FRANCIS JOHNSTON TO NATHANAEL GREENE

CONTINENTAL OFFICERS often encountered elements of dissension within their ranks. Personal ambition, avarice, and rivalry all added to the many problems faced by the army. The dismissal of Benjamin Lincoln, the assignment of Horatio Gates, and his replacement by Nathanael Greene were all tainted not only by defeats on the battlefield but also by politics in the high command and in the Continental Congress. Most high-ranking officers were often compelled to support their fellow officers against criticism of their actions on the field of battle. Francis Johnston (1748–1815), a retired colonel of the Fifth Pennsylvania Regiment, had written a complimentary and flattering letter to General Greene that was intercepted. Greene commanded troops that had suffered several bloody defeats at Guilford Courthouse, North Carolina, on March 15, 1781, Hobkirk's Hill, South Carolina, on April 25, 1781, and Eutaw Springs, South Carolina, on September 8, 1781. The tension among those officers who equated victory with patriotism is clearly evident in the worried tone of Johnston's letter.

*Philadelphia, September 11, 1781*

Dear General

Some Weeks ago I wrote you a long & circumstantial Letter, giving you an account of the situation of our Affairs in this quarter, and I am sorry to inform you, that in consequence of the Mail being robb'd between this place and Wilmington, my Letter with many others were (I believe) taken in to N. York. However, it matters not, as my information to you was dictated by a pure and unsullied Spirit of Whiggism, containing such matter as wou'd prove very injurious to the delicate feelings of the present Possessors of N. York. I pass'd many Eulogiums on the exertions, the military Abilities and the fervent Zeal for this Country, evidently discovered by our faithful Allies. I likewise applauded the virtue the perseverance and fortitude of the American Soldiery, inspired by the brilliant Example of our Illustrious Chief. Nor did I forget to give my tribute of praise to my ever esteemed friend General Greene, but here Sir I shall stop, least the honest frustrations of a Heart truely grateful for the various blessings wh. my Countrymen experience from your Zeal & military Talents, shou'd involuntarily draw from my Pen aught that shou'd be deem'd adulation.

Inclos'd I take the liberty of sending you a News paper, in wh. you will find that notwithstanding the depravity of the times & the undue authority wh. sordid pity hath gain'd over the Minds of men, yet you are not forgotten by your Country, nor are your Services concealed.

My Dear General I have no News to communicate wh. the bearer cannot inform you of *viva Voce.* Therefore shall conclude with sincerely wishing you a continuation of your Health and Successes, and that indulgent Heaven may shield you till you behold your Country free. I am Dr. General most sincerely, Your's

F. JOHNSTON

ALS, Nathanael Greene Papers, William L. Clements Library, Ann Arbor, Mich.

# HENRY KNOX TO MRS. BAXTER HOWE

CORNWALLIS' DECISION to leave his base at Wilmington, North Carolina, in 1781 was a major tactical error. He and his forces wandered about Virginia without directly attacking any major American force. By June 25, 1781, he had reached Williamsburg, Virginia. There he refused General Sir Henry Clinton's advice to march toward Baltimore and remained in the Tidewater region. He fortified Yorktown, Virginia, a base that was particularly vulnerable by sea. Cornwallis' strategic blunders were soon exploited by George Washington. The commander in chief prepared for a combined French-American expedition to prevent Cornwallis' escape. Forces led by the Marquis de Lafayette positioned themselves to oppose British flight by land until the northern armies under Washington and Comte de Rochambeau had marched southward. By September 2, 1781, they had reached Philadelphia.

Baxter Howe (1748–81), a captain-lieutenant in the Continental artillery, died on September 20, 1781, en route to aid in the siege of Yorktown. Mrs. Howe received the news in this emotional letter from Brigadier General Henry Knox.

*Camp before York in Virginia, October 2, 1781*

It is with great pain madam, that I find myself under the disagreable necessity of informing you that [the?] partner of your Life, was oblig'd to pay his last Debt to nature, on the 20th of last month in James River, where his body lies buried at a place call'd Newport News. His death was very sudden, finding a [    ] on his Stomach he took an emetic & died under the operations of it in about two hours. This afflictive dispensation of divine providence robs you of an affectionate husband & the public of a faithful servant. Heaven I hope will furnish you with a sufficient degree of fortitude to sustain the severity of its decree & certainly you will not want some means of consolation. The rectitude and amiableness of his [    ], by which he acquired the love of all his brother soldiers, and the lively Zeal in the cause of his country are subjects which will give you a satisfaction in reflecting upon, & a melancholy pleasure which may be soothing to your wounds.

Captain Lt. Hubbill Paymaster of the regt.[1] has taken charge of the effects of Capt Howe, and according to the custom of the Army to prevent loss sold them to his brother officers who were eager to have some token of remembrance. He will transmit to you as soon as possible an account of them, with the proceeds & a certificate the pay which is still due to him from the public.

I am madam with, every sentiment of sympathy your, Humble sert.

H KNOX

Contemporary draft, Henry Knox Papers, Massachusetts Historical Society, Boston.
[1] Isaac Hubbell (d. 1842) was a regimental paymaster.

# John Davis Journal

## September 28–October 25, 1781

Between september 14 and 24, 1781, the allied force of 16,000 men had reached Williamsburg. The American and French armies had taken up their siege positions at Yorktown by September 28. The French fleet, led by Comte de Grasse (1722–88), entered the Chesapeake Bay and blocked the entrance to the York River, preventing Cornwallis' escape. For the next three weeks the besieging forces pressed closer to Cornwallis' men huddled in the town. Artillery from the French batteries destroyed British ships and redoubts. The journal kept by Captain John Davis of the First Pennsylvania Regiment describes the siege. He narrates the relentless bombardment, slow advance of the allied forces, and the final surrender of Lord Cornwallis at the Moore House.

*28th.* Camp: before York. Army march'd this morning at 5, by the right for York. On ariving on its environs the British horse appear'd. The French open'd some Fild pices & they retreated in their works.—lay on our arms.

*29th.* This morning form'd a compleat investment round the Town and pitch'd our Camp. The Enemy retreated this night in their contacted works.

*30th.* Took possession of their out lines.

*Oct'r 1st.* A warm fire continued all this day, about 40 Guns to the hour, on an average & 10 by night to the hour 2 men kill'd one of them in the works.

*2d, 81.* Camp before York. A continual firing from the Enemys Batteries all this day. Our works goes on rapidly.

*3d.* A continual firing was kept up all this day. A deserter went in who inform'd them where our covering parties lay. They directed their shot for them the first kill'd 3 men & mortally wounded a fourth. Our works go on rapidly.

*4th.* Camp before York. Our cannon and mortars now arived. This day Col'l Tarlton made a charge on Duke Luzerne's Legionary Corps, on Glochester side,[1] and was repuls'd with the loss of his commaning off'r of Infantry kill'd and Tarlton badly wounded with 50 privates kill'd on the spot.

*5th.* Our works go on day and night some chance Men kill'd with the incessant fire kept up on our works.

*6th.* A rainy day. 3000, fatigued this night, a making lines for our covering parties.

*7th.* The first paralel finish'd carrying on the Batteries an incessant firing Day & Night.

*8th.* Our heavy artilery taken up 10 pieces this night.

*9th.* Camp before York. A heavy cannonnade kept up from us, which dismounted all their pieces.

*10th.* A Mr. Nelson came this day out who say our shells do much execution.

*11th.* Continual firing kept up, this night we broke ground & form'd 2d paralel with the loss of 2 millita men kill'd.

*12th.* The Enemy kept up a very hot fire all this day.

*13th.* This morning 2 Hessian deserters came in who says our shells do much execution.

*14th.* Camp before York. This morning a deserter says the Infantry refus'd doing duty, that Cornwallis flatters them they shall be reliv'd in a few days & gave each reg't a pipe of wine. This night the Marquis took their river Battery with very inconsiderable loss, and Maj'r Gen. Virmiuel[2] took another on their extreme to the left, with little loss likewise, & run our second paralel compleat.

*17th.* Lord Cornwallis proposes deputies from Each Army to meet at Moores House to agree on terms for the Surrender of the garrison at York & Gloucester. An answer sent by 3 oClock when a cessation of arms took place.

*18th.* Flags passing this day alternately.

*19th.* At 1 oClock this day our troops march'd in & took possession of their batteries, and the British Army march'd Out & Grounded their Arms. Our Army drew up for them to march through French on one side & American on the other.

*20th.* Camp York. Lay quiet in Our Camp cleaning Ourselves.

*21st.* British Army march'd out for their cantoonments under Militia G'ds.

*22d.* Brgade on duty.

*23d.* Orders for the troops to hold themselves in readiness to march at the shortest notice.

*24th.* Marquis de St. Simons troops embarking their Cannon.[3]

*25th.* Camp York. Orders for Brigades daily to be on duty to demollish our works.

"The Yorktown Campaign: Journal of Captain John Davis of the Pennsylvania Line," *Pennsylvania Magazine of History and Biography* (1881), 5:303–4.

[1] Gloucester County, Va.

[2] Chevalier de Vioménil.

[3] Claude Anne, Marquis de St. Simon, a lieutenant general, was wounded at Yorktown.

# MATTHEW GREGORY DIARY

## *September 30—November 6, 1781*

ENSIGN MATTHEW GREGORY (1757–1848), of the Fifth Connecticut Regiment, was a youthful participant in the siege of Yorktown. His diary vividly describes the bitter conflict in the attempt to attain a closer vantage point for men and artillery. Men were killed to gain vital yards. On October 17, 1781, Lord Cornwallis capitulated to the

Americans and French. With this surrender of over 8,000 men, the major battles of the southern campaign ended with a great victory for the dedicated and tenacious patriots.

The courage that had sustained them in battle would soon be challenged by the need for patience and endurance, because peace was not achieved until 1783.

*Camp before York 30 Sept.* We were alarmed last night at one o'clock. A fatigue party men paraded at 7 o'clock in the morning for the purpose of cutting Gabions etc etc.[1] At 12 o'clock 400 of the fatigue party was ordered to be furnished with spades, picks, axes, etc. and pressed up to our Light Infantry and waited for orders.

The enemy left their outworks last night, consisting of three small redoubts without cannon, and three or four Batteries. Their works are about half a mile from the Town. Our Troops marched up about 9 o'clock and took possession of them. Some cannonade but no one hurt during the day except Col. Scammell who was unfortunately wounded and taken prisoner in the morning reconoitering near the Enemy.[2] Our engineers laid out two Redoubts near the Enemy's abandoned works, which were begun about dark by the 400 men who soon covered themselves from any shot. Some musquetry was fired last night. I was upon fatigue, was relieved in the morning. No cannon was fired. The Light Troops lay upon their arms all night in the field.

N.B. The French had two officers wounded and six men killed and wounded. We had one man deserted.

*Octr. 1st.* A considerable cannonade by the enemy during the day and night following. We continued in building our works. Two men killed by cannon balls.

The Enemy was at work day and night in pulling down houses to fortify their works. I mounted Camp Guard. . . .

*Saturday 6th.* Tis reported this morning that our patrols alarmed a Captain's piquet of the enemie's which occasioned a considerable firing of musquetry and Grape Shot etc. Drove them into their works. A regiment from every Brigade paraded this afternoon at five o'clock, commanded by Major General Lincoln, and as many from the French, commanded by Baron Viomenil, for the purpose of opening a parallel line within six or seven hundred yards of the enemy's works and two miles in length, which completely hems the enemy in upon this side of the River. This parallel is ten feet wide and four deep, which made a sufficient cover for our men, in the course of one night. Not more than five or six shot were fired upon the Americans—but a very considerable upon the French—I believe near a thousand shot.

*Sunday 7th.* The Light Infantry mounted the Trenches at 12 o'clock with drums beating and colours flying. A considerable number of shot at our approach near the works. No man hurt except one that was wounded in the foot. Began several Redoubts and Batteries a little in front of the Parallel Line. We were alarmed several times during the course of the night. Captain Weed who was upon piquet in front near drove into the French.[3] He said he was pursued by 200 of the enemy and two Field pieces; but they did not come within musquet shot of our Lines. Our Orders were if the enemy should make a Sally, to give them our fire, then charge Bayonets and meet them. Captain Weed had one man killed who belonged to Captain Harnbranch's Company. A very severe cold night.

*Monday 8th.* Were relieved by Baron Steuben's Division. A very little cannonade this night.

*Tuesday 9th.* Lincoln's Division mounted the trenches. Two Batteries were opened, one upon the left of the French, the other upon our right. American flag was hoisted upon our Right Battery about 3 o'clock, and immediately began the firing which was very hot for some time, 5 10 pounders, three 24 and Hoets in one night. A constant firing all night.

*Wednesday 10th.* Three more Batteries were opened and a constant fire kept up day and night. Some small arms were fired in the night. Two of the enemy's shipping were set on fire by some of our Shells.[4] The Light Troops mounted the trenches. We expected to begin the second parallel but some circumstances prevented. A great number of shell were hove this night.

*Thursday 11th.* A flag came out this morning reports that four officers were dining at the table, there came a shot thro the ruff of the house killed three and wounded the fourth. A vast many of the inhabitants and soldiers were killed and wounded. They keep their men constantly in their works. One ship was set on fire this morning. Scarcely a man of the enemy is to be seen, neither a shot from them.

*Friday 12th.* The second Parallel was opened last night 300 yards in front of the first, and 300 yards from the enemy's works. It extends from the left of the French to their right. Two men killed. A severe cannonade the whole day. I was upon fatigue with 60 men made 42 Sausongs 42 Gabions, 140 Fasheins, 420 Pickets.

*Saturday 13th.* The Light Troops mounted the Trenches. Tis said our allyd Army lost 30 men killed and wounded last night and this day.

*Sunday 14th.* Captain White Col. Vose's Regt. was killed last night with a cannon ball which took him by the side of the head,[5] also killed one man and wounded two more with the same shots. A new battery was begun upon the second Parallel. Capt. Gosselen of Genl. Hazen's Regt. was wounded.[6] 25 men of the Americans were killed and wounded last night and this day by 12 o'clock.

*Monday 15th.* Last evening Col. Hamilton's Battalion and Col. Gimat's Regiment under the command of Col. Hamilton and four companies of French Grenadiers, under the command of Count William Depong, took two important posts from the enemy by storm.[7] Won without returning a single shot. The Gallantry and Bravery of the troops upon this occasion deserves the highest praise of everyone who is a friend of his country. Took and killed of the enemy 7 Majors, 2 Captains, 3 subalterns, and about 90 men. Our loss is about 60 killed and wounded. Laurens attacked the redoubt from the rear. Capt. Stephen Betts was wounded.[8]

*Tuesday 16th.* N.B. The enemy sallied last night when upon our lines spiked up some cannon. Took one French officer. The enemy had 20 killed and 8 taken prisoner. Mounted the Trenches. A severe Cannonade kept up on the enemy. Received but very little damage on our side. The troops employed in compleating the Batteries with all possible dispatch.

*Wednesday 17th.* An incessant Cannonade of shells and shot kept up on the enemy. A flag sent from his Lordship this morning at 10 o'clock with the proposals for a Capitulation, on which the Cannonade ceased for about one hour, then it began more severe than ever, on which the enemy Immediately beat a parley but had little or no attention taken of them till about four o'clock when we again ceased firing. Colonel Lawrence and Count Noill were appointed to meet two British officers of the same rank to agree upon the articles of Capitulation.[9]

*Thursday 18th.* Last night and this day spent in agreeing upon the articles and terms of the Surrendery of Lord Cornwallis' Army.

*Friday 19th.* Cornwallis' Army marched out of York and grounded their arms. A Detachment of the Americans and some part of the French Grenadiers took possession of York.

*The 20th–31st.* The army was employed in leveling our works, gathering the stores in town and putting the Ordinance on Board etc. etc.

*Nov. 1st–6th.* The troops spent their time in putting stores and embarking for the Head of Elk. The Penna Line Maryland Troops go to the northward. The French fleet sailed for the West Indies.

Typescript copy, Wilton Historical Society, Wilton, Conn. Original manuscript in private hands.

[1] Gabion: a wicker basket used in entrenchments. Both ends were to be cut off, and the basket was to be filled with dirt.

[2] Colonel Alexander Scammell (d. 1781) of the First New Hampshire Regiment.

[3] Captain Thaddeus Weed of the Second Connecticut Regiment.

[4] H.M.S. *Charon* and some transports.

[5] Adjutant William White (c.1750–81) of the Seventh Massachusetts Regiment.

[6] Captain Clement Gosselin (1747–1816) of Hazen's Canadian Regiment.

[7] Colonel de Gimat, aide-de-camp to Lafayette; Lieutenant Colonel Christian Marquis des Deux Ponts.

[8] Colonel John Laurens (c.1756–82); Captain Stephen Betts (1756–82) of the Third Connecticut Regiment.

[9] Louis Marie (Viscount) de Noialles (c.1756–c.1804).

# LOUIS MARIE (VISCOUNT) DE NOAILLES TO GEORGE WASHINGTON

THE AID OF the French on land and sea was crucial to the American victory at Yorktown. The French fleet became a major factor in American strategy and negated British superiority on the rivers and the sea. In addition, the troops of Louis XVI provided the decisive superiority in numbers required to surround Cornwallis. Lafayette, de Grasse, Rochambeau, and many other brave Frenchmen, contributed their unique qualities of leadership to the American cause. An equally enthusiastic supporter of American independence was Louis Marie (Viscount) de Noailles. In this parting letter to George Washington, de Noailles displays the spirit of camaraderie that typified the French-American alliance during the American Revolution.

*Boston the 15th. of December [1781]*

General

When I went away from york town I expected to See your excellency in Philadelphia. I desired before my departure for france to express to you my gratitude and ardent wishes to be led again on the glorious Sceenes of war by the same commander. The reputation of a chief is divided with his Soldiers and my attachment for the officers of your Army will not permit me to remain long in france. I hope your excellency will receive with Kindness the assurance of my most respectful Sentiments. I have the honour to be your excellency Most obedient humble Servant.

VISCOUNT DE NOAILLES

ALS, George Washington Papers, Library of Congress, Washington, D.C.

# ELIAS DAYTON TO GEORGE WASHINGTON

THE WAR IN THE NORTH became one of vigilance and minor raids as the American forces surrounded the British in New York City following Lord Cornwallis' surrender. Colonel Elias Dayton, commander of the Second New Jersey Regiment, had impressed General Washington when he effectively led a brigade of 1,300 New Jersey and Rhode Island troops during the Yorktown campaign. Following the victory there, most of Dayton's men encamped for the winter in Chatham, six miles southeast of Morristown, New Jersey. A detachment of approximately 100 men were dispatched from Chatham to Elizabethtown and Newark to suppress Loyalist depredations there against civilians. Dayton's regiment remained in the Morristown area for five more months before assuming its new post in the Hudson Highlands. Dayton's letter emphasizes the many local problems confronting the Continental army.

*Chatham Feb'y 8th. 1782*

Sir

I have received the letter which contained your Excellencys orders for the releif of the garrison at Wyoming, I expected the N. York line would have been ordered to releive them, but as your Excellency is pleased to order it other ways I would ask permission to releive the officers only as the men at that place are fit for garrison duty, and no other, I have therefore delayed the marching of the men until further orders. I have reason to beleive the men at Wyoming will be contented to remain with a new set of officers, I have at this time about one hundred men at Eliz. Town and Newark which number I thought necessary (during the severe frost) to prevent the robers from the other side plundering & abuseing the friends to the states. They have had a very good effect, we have made prisoners one Doctor two Negroes & four privates, & killed one. I have had one rase after a party of them on the salt marsh for two Miles I got one black & 1 white prisoner & took from them eight sleds loaded with hay. The matter with respect to flags I expect will be settled at least so far as respects Mr. Skiners negotiation, but Skinner has been absent at Goshen this week or more, enclosed is the particular cantonment of the troops in N.Y. & vicinity, handed me by [      ]. I have also an accurate map of the fortifications at Brooklyn given me by the same person but will take a safer opportunity of conveyance. We have had from three to six deserters from the enemy every day since the river has been froze.

Autograph copy, Ely Collection, New Jersey Historical Society, Newark.

# JOHN LAMB AND EBENEZER STEVENS TO GEORGE WASHINGTON

THE YORKTOWN VICTORY ended the prospect of a British victory. The king's soldiers, however, remained in large numbers in New York City and in Georgia and South Carolina. While American citizens hoped for peace, the Continental army prepared for continued warfare. The significant decrease in combat, however, brought no relief to the ever-impoverished officers and men. This persistent problem is discussed in this letter to General Washington from Colonel John Lamb and Lieutenant Colonel Ebenezer Stevens, both of whom had been praised by General Henry Knox for their marksmanship and skill during the siege of Yorktown. Lamb and Stevens detail the problems of discipline and of jealousies created by the pay inequities.

*Burlington 13 Febry. 1782*

Sir,

We have been informed, that it is in Contemplation to advance the officers of the Army, two Months Pay, to be received in Notes from the Financier, payable the first of August next.[1] Supposing the Information to be good, we take the Liberty of addressing your Excellency, upon the Subject, and do beg the favor of you, to lay our Sentiments before the Financier.

We conceive that the full Confidence of the Men under our Command, is not only necessary to preserve good Order and harmony in our Regiment, but that the Service, which we have so much at heart, must be injured whenever that Confidence is withdrawn. That the Sure way to preserve it, is to Share with our Men, the Rewards and Benefits, as well as the Toils and Difficulties, and dangers of Service. That this happy and equal communion of Services and Rewards, forms in the Minds of Soldiers, and most when in difficult Services, a pleasing Coalition of Affections upon which that Service materially depends. We think also, that the present measure, if adopted, will produce in the Minds of our Men, Jealousy and discontent; or at least will be opening a wound, already too much irritated, without much administering a Cure.

From these Considerations, and from a Sincere desire not to receive a Single exclusive Benefit, which shall not be received on a due proportion by those under our Command, we pray that the benefit now intended the Officers, may be extended to the Soldiers also, or if from the peculiar Situation of our Finances, this may not be in the power of the Financier to grant, we beg that the partial Payment may be made to the Soldiers, in preference to ourselves.

Though we have already felt too Sensibly the Painfulness of our Situation, The want of Money, and with many, of Credit, under which, may generally be comprised the want of every thing else, Tho' our prospects are far from flattering us with a Change in our Circumstances Yet, Such is our desire to cultivate the Affections and Confidence of our Men—to preserve Harmony and order in our Regiment, that we beg, that if our Requests cannot be granted, that our Renunciation of the partial Payment intended, may be accepted, and that no Payment may be made to the Regt. unless extended to the Soldiers, as well as to the Officers.

We beg leave to assure your Excellency, that we wish not to embarrass the Affairs of Government, by asking for more than can be conveniently granted, but that we are induced to make this Address, from the purest motives, a Love of the Service, and a desire to promote it.

Signed at the unanimous Request, in behalf of the officers present, of the 2d. Regt. of Artillery.

JOHN LAMB, *Colo. 2nd. Regt. Artillery*
E. STEVENS *Lt. Colo. 2 Regt. Art.*

ALS, George Washington Papers, Library of Congress, Washington, D.C.
[1] Robert Morris (1734–1804), superintendent of finances.

# THOMAS POSEY TO NATHANAEL GREENE

GENERAL NATHANAEL GREENE'S southern army, reinforced by detachments from Washington's army, continued to sweep the British from the south. On January 12, 1782, General Anthony Wayne, who had marched from Yorktown with reinforcements, began his Georgia expedition. Lieutenant Colonel Thomas Posey (1750–1818), commanding a Virginia battalion of 379 men, explains to Greene his inability to reach Wayne's forces because of serious shortages of supplies.

**Thomas Posey**
PHOTO: MENASCO STUDIO, SHREVEPORT, LA.

*Charlotte 16th March 1782*

Dr. Sir

With much fatigue and difficulty I have arriv'd at this place, I need not inform you how distressing it is to me and fatigueing to both officers and men to be under the necessity of procuring provision by impress, as I know you have experienced in a much greater degree like circumstances. When I received my orders to join you I was informed that a sufficientcy of provision was laid in at every post, but insted of that I verily beleave there has no manner of pains been taken to procure any, altho' being repeatedly inform'd of my march this route; I can assure you I have not drawn more than ten days including the whole that I have drawn from every post; upon my arrival here I was inform'd there was no provision which of course detaind me to impress, similar circumstancus detains me one in every three or four, exclusive of maney dais that the badness of roades bad weather, and the breaking of waggons geirs &c takes up; a great deal of which I have experienced upon the march.[1]

I mentioned to you in my last the situation the men were in for the want of shoes, and hearing there was some at Charlotte I observ'd to you that I was in hopes to be able to procure a few, since my arrival here I understand there is shoes in the hands of the Quarter Master, but none can be delivered without your order; I am sencible of the propriety and being situated as I am am intirely at a loss to know in what manner to procure shoes; I have alwais indeavoured to adhear strictly to orders, and should be exceeding loth to infringe in the smalest degree upon yours; was you present to see the men you would not hesitate a moment to grant an order, I have been carefull to examine into the necessity that every man is in and find near one hundred to be realy barefooted, and a number of others in a few dais will be in the same situation. Mr. Russell Quarter Master at this post agrees to send one hundred pair by my Pay Master, to be deliver'd to the cloathier of your Army or to your order; the shoes I have directed to be issued to the men realy in want, in hopes to obtain your order to Lt. Jones the Pay master for the delivery of them, that he may hereafter be able to account with the cloathier.[2]

You will please to excuse me in taking up your attention so frequently with a detail of my circumstances, I am exceeding anxious to join you with all possible expedition and am afraid of being sensur'd for a tadious march. I hope to meet your orders at Camden should I not receive them before, in six dais I expect to be there. I am with much respect Your obt. Sert.

THOMAS POSEY

ALS, Nathanael Greene Papers, William L. Clements Library, Ann Arbor, Mich.

[1] The condition of roads for the transportation of men and supplies was a constant problem in all theaters of the war. Thomas Shubrick (1756–1810), an aide-de-camp to General Greene, wrote to Wood Furman on November 19, 1781: "The General has been informed that you intend immediately upon the removal of this Army to destroy the bridges thro' the Swamp at your plantation. He has directed me to acquaint you that the publick service requires that a good road be kept constantly in repair there and to forbid your injuring it in any manner whatever as you may depend upon being severely punished should you presume to do it." (Nathanael Greene Papers, William L. Clements Library, Ann Arbor, Mich.)

[2] Lieutenant Charles Jones (1754–95) of the Sixth Virginia Regiment.

# Joshua Barney's "Song"

## *April 26, 1782*

Two years after joining the infant American navy in 1777 as an eighteen-year-old officer, Joshua Barney (1759–1818), of Pennsylvania, boarded an armed merchant ship and quickly became one of the best-known American privateers. In 1782 Barney was engaged by a group of Philadelphia merchants to captain the privateer *Hyder Ally,* which was to protect American shipping from British depredations in Delaware Bay. On or about April 8, 1782, Captain Barney's privateer, heading a convoy of merchant ships, was engaged at the mouth of the Delaware River by the British brig-sloop H.M.S. *General Monk.* Captain Barney's brilliant maneuvers led to the capture of the larger British vessel. The *General Monk* was renamed the *General Washington* and joined the American navy. Captain Barney received a sword from Pennsylvania in recognition of his prowess in this engagement. Barney's triumph was soon celebrated in a "Song," penned on April 26, 1782, by Philip Morin Freneau (1752–1832) and published in the newspaper *Freeman's Journal* on May 8.

**Joshua Barney**

SONG

*On Captain Barney's Victory over the Ship* General Monk

O'er the waste of waters cruising,
Long the *General Monk* had reigned;
All subduing, all reducing,
None her lawless rage restrained:
Many a brave and hearty fellow
Yielding to this warlike foe,
When her guns began to bellow
Struck his humbled colours low.

But grown bold with long successes,
Leaving the wide watery way,

She, a stranger to distresses
Came to cruise within Cape May:
"Now we soon (said captain Rogers)
"Shall their men of commerce meet;
"In our hold we'll have them lodgers,
"We shall capture half their fleet.

"Lo! I see their van appearing—
"Back our topsails to the mast—
"They toward us full are steering
"With a gentle western blast:
"I've a list of all their cargoes,
"All their guns, and all their men:
"I am sure these modern Argos
"Cant escape us one in ten:

"Yonder comes the *Charming Sally* ¹
"Sailing with the *General Greene* ²—
"First we'll fight the *Hyder Ali,*
"Taking her is taking them:
"She intends to give us battle,
"Bearing down with all her sail—
"Now boys, let our cannon rattle!
"To take her we cannot fail.

"Our eighteen guns, each a nine pounder,
"Soon shall terrify this foe;
"We shall maul her, we shall wound her,
"Bringing rebel colours low."—
While he thus anticipated
Conquests that he could not gain,
He in the Cape May channel waited
For the ship that caused his pain.

Captain Barney then preparing,
Thus addressed his gallant crew—
"Now, brave lads, be bold and daring,
"Let your hearts be firm and true;
"This is a proud English cruiser,
"Roving up and down the main,
"We must fight her—must reduce her,
"Though our decks be strewed with slain.

"Let who will be the survivor,
"We must conquer or must die,
"We must take her up the river,
"Whate'er comes of you or I:

"Though she shews most formidable
"With her eighteen pointed nines,
"And her quarters clad in sable,
"Let us baulk her proud designs.

"With four nine pounders, and twelve sixes
"We will face that daring band;
"Let no dangers damp your courage,
"Nothing can the brave withstand.
"Fighting for your country's honour,
"Now to gallant deeds aspire;
"Helmsman, bear us down upon her,
"Gunner, give the word to fire!"

Then yard arm and yard arm meeting,
Strait began the dismal fray,
Cannon mouths, each other greeting,
Belched their smoky flames away:
Soon the langrage, grape and chain shot,
That from Barney's cannons flew,
Swept the *Monk,* and cleared each round top,
Killed and wounded half her crew.[3]

Captain Rogers strove to rally
But they from their quarters fled,
While the roaring *Hyder Ali*
Covered o'er his decks with dead.
When from their tops their dead men tumbled,
And the streams of blood did flow,
Then their proudest hopes were humbled
By their brave inferior foe.

All aghast, and all confounded,
They beheld their champions fall,
And their captain, sorely wounded,
Bade them quick for quarters call.
Then the *Monk's* proud flag descended,
And her cannon ceased to roar;
By her crew no more defended,
She confessed the contest o'er.

Come, brave boys, and fill your glasses,
You have humbled one proud foe,
No brave action this surpasses,
Fame shall tell the nations so—
Thus be Britain's woes completed,
Thus abridged her cruel reign,

'Till she ever, thus defeated,
Yields the sceptre of the main.

Reprinted in Frederick Lewis Pattie, ed., *The Poems of Philip Freneau, Poet of the American Revolution* (Princeton, N.J., 1903), II, 149–53.

[1] A British ship.
[2] An American privateer captured by the British.
[3] British casualties: 20 killed, 33 wounded.

# HENRY BROCKHOLST LIVINGSTON TO WILLIAM LIVINGSTON

PROVOST JAIL was the most dreaded British prison in New York City. Henry Brockholst Livingston found himself there briefly in 1782. After serving as an aide-de-camp to major generals Philip Schuyler and Arthur St. Clair, Livingston accepted a position as private secretary to John Jay, his brother-in-law, minister plenipotentiary to Spain, in 1779. While en route home from the Spanish port Cadiz, he was captured by the British and held in Provost jail. General Sir Guy Carleton, who had just become the British commander in New York City, soon ordered Livingston's release on parole. Livingston relates details of his imprisonment in this letter to his father, Governor William Livingston (1723–90) of New Jersey, and displays his courage and determination.

*3 May 82*

My dear Sir,

If You have received my letter by the Commerce you already know of my leaving Cadiz on the 11th of March last. The 25th of the month following I was taken by the Quebec frigate & yesterday by General Robertson's order committed to the Provost of this City.[1] I have taken the liberty to remonstrate with that Gentleman on this measure. Enclosed You have a Copy of my letter to him. I hope you will think it conceived in spirited & at the same time in decent terms. Whether it will work out my release I cannot tell. It has been hinted to me by the Provost Martial, and perhaps you will hear it, that I shall not be set at liberty, untill Lippincott's affair be settled, and that if General Washington puts his threat into Execution, I may be thought a proper subject for retaliation.[2] I laugh at this Insinuation, and am so fully persuaded of the justice of our General's conduct on this occasion, that I did believe any thing of the kind would be mentioned to him, I would entreat him myself to pay no attention to it. On this I am determined, that let what will happen, I will never stoop so low as to ask the smallest favor at their hands, and could I believe that my letter to General Robertson could be considered in that light, I would rather have burnt than sent it. Pray give yourself no uneasiness on my account. I must do Capt. Cunningham the Justice to say that he does every Thing in his power to render my situation comfortable.[3]

Mr. & Mrs. Jay are well. Sally had another daughter in february. I am dear Sir Your dutiful Son

HENRY B. LIVINGSTON

ALS, George Washington Papers, Library of Congress, Washington, D.C.

[1] Lieutenant General James Robertson of the British army.

[2] For a complete account of the death of Joshua Huddy at the hands of Richard Lippincott, a Loyalist captain, see the Benjamin Mooers Memoir below.

[3] William Cunningham.

# DAVID TOWNSEND TO WILLIAM HEATH

DR. DAVID TOWNSEND (1753–1829) served as a hospital physician and surgeon in the Continental army from October 6, 1780, until the close of the American Revolution. After being ordered to stop smallpox inoculations of the fifteen Connecticut and Massachusetts regiments in the West Point area, he wrote to General William Heath requesting that soldiers not be quartered in infected barracks. Humanitarian concern was the hallmark of the physician using his specialized talents in the cause of liberty.

*West Point May 6th 1782*

Sir

As by the inclosed I am directed to stop the inoculation, it becomes my duty to acquaint you of the circumstance, that should you think proper it might be made known to the Army in Orders to prevent any more recruits being sent to the hampshire huts, or to barracks that are infectious.

I should have done myself the honor to have waited on you with this information, but for indisposition.

As the purpose of sending the inclosed will be fully answered when you have seen it, I shall be obliged if you will send it back by the return of the soldier. I am Sir with great respect Your very humble Servt.

D TOWNSEND *hospl Surgeon*

ALS, William Heath Papers, Massachusetts Historical Society, Boston.

# Benjamin Mooers Memoir

## *1782*

THE REVOLUTIONARY WAR was also a civil war. Captain Joshua Huddy (1735–82), of the New Jersey militia, was captured by Loyalists at Toms River, New Jersey, on March 24, 1782. Loyalist Captain Richard Lippincott arranged to have Huddy released from prison and then supervised his hanging on April 12, 1782, at Gravelly Point, Monmouth County, New Jersey. This atrocity was committed in retaliation for the killing of a Monmouth County Loyalist. Because Huddy was a militia officer, not a spy or civilian, there were many calls for protest and reprisal. Lippincott was court-martialed and acquitted. George Washington took decisive action on May 3, 1782, when he ordered Brigadier General Moses Hazen to select for possible execution a British officer from those confined in Pennsylvania. Benjamin Mooers (1758–1838) was a lieutenant and regimental adjutant to Hazen. He describes the tense moments at Lancaster, Pennsylvania, when the random selection of British Captain Charles Asgill (c.1762–1823) was made. Humanitarian concern and diplomatic pressure resulted in the release of the young

**Benjamin Mooers**

officer from his subsequent confinement at Chatham, New Jersey, on July 29, 1782.

The Brittish had taken a Militia Capt.—gave him a short trial—& *hung him for a spy* on Staten Island—this was intended to retaliate but no officer of this description was found!

Than came an order to assemble all the Captains—at the several Posts at Lancaster—York, & Reading—& that a lot be cast amongst them. The number was 13 assembled, & a Major Gordan, Gen. Hazen—the Commissary of Prisoners (Capt. White Myself, & I believe some other officers present.

Gen. Hazen made known to them, for what purpose they were called together. They were extremely agitated that they should be called on, as they were taken by capitulation—& mentioned that a Refugee ought to be taken if any.

There were 12 blank pieces of paper, & one wrote on *unfortunate!!* put into a

Hat—& then each of their names written on 13 pieces of paper & put into another Hat. They were asked if they would draw out a paper? They all declined.

One or two small Drummers was called in—One drew from one, the other from the other Hat. The names when drawn out, was handed to the commissary of Prisoners I think, & when a paper was drawn from the other Hat—was handed to Capt. White—if a blank so declared—& so it continued until the 11th name came out and against that was drawn "unfortunate" which fell on Capt. Asgill a young man about 20 years old—a son Sir Charles Asgill, an only Son! At the time they were all seated, but arose, & were much affected, perhaps not a dry eye in the Room. . . .

Typescript copy, Benjamin F. Feinberg Library, State University of New York at Plattsburgh, N.Y.

# NICHOLAS LONG TO NATHANAEL GREENE

COLONEL NICHOLAS LONG (1728–1819), deputy quartermaster general of the Southern Department, spent most of his years of service attempting to procure wagons, arms, and other vital supplies from reluctant farmers and state governments. In this letter to General Nathanael Greene, Long provides an account of the dismal state of finances and the hardships in provisioning soldiers in North Carolina.

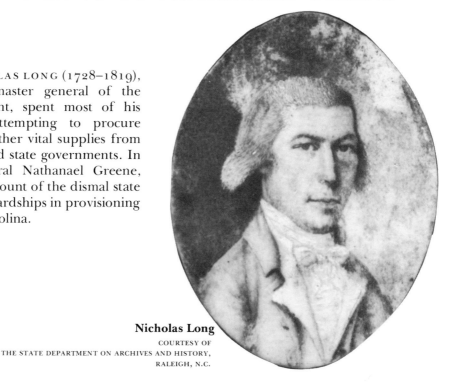

**Nicholas Long**
COURTESY OF
THE STATE DEPARTMENT ON ARCHIVES AND HISTORY,
RALEIGH, N.C.

*Halifax 20 June 1782*

Sir

By Enclosed you will be informed of the unfavourable Cercumstances into which the Quarter Master's Department, in this State is involved, by Means of the Exhausted

Condition of Public Funds & Stores of Specific Supplies. It is impossible, therefore, that I can longer answer the various Demands which will be expected in sundry Branches, unless some plan be adopted whereby success in those Attempts may ensue.

I therefore humbly submit my Case to your Consideration. Should you devise any Method for effectually furnishing me with Means, either by a Warrant or otherwise, All Commands consistent with my Duty shall be punctually & faithfully Executed, by, Sir Your most Obedient, humble Servant,

NICHOLAS LONG *D Q M*

ALS, Nathanael Greene Papers, William L. Clements Library, Ann Arbor, Mich.

# HENRY COLLINS FLAGG TO NATHANAEL GREENE

Dr. HENRY COLLINS FLAGG (1742–1801), apothecary general of the Southern Department, had as much difficulty securing medical supplies as the quartermaster corps had with less-specialized provisions. Writing from a hospital in South Carolina, Dr. Flagg expresses his intention to secure British medical supplies for the army after Savannah's expected liberation from the British. General Anthony Wayne had begun a sweep through Georgia that culminated five months later in the British evacuation of Savannah by sea on July 12.

*Gen. Hospital. 26th. June 1782*

Sir,

I will set out for Georgia as soon as you shall honor me with a letter to General Wayne which I request for an introduction as well as to enable me upon the evacuation of Savannah to secure for the Army any Medicines which may either be confiscated or for sale. I am extremely mortify'd at the necessity of refusing almost daily demands for Meds. which I know not how to procure otherwise than by the means I have propos'd or from Charlestown. As ineligible as this method is I am oblig'd to have recourse to it for a few articles which are immediately wanted. I have the honor to be very respectfull, Sir, your most obedt. hum. servt.

HENRY COLLINS FLAGG

ALS, Nathanael Greene Papers, William L. Clements Library, Ann Arbor, Mich.

# SILAS TALBOT TO GEORGE WASHINGTON

SILAS TALBOT had been commissioned a captain in the Continental navy on September 17, 1779. Within a year he was captured at sea by the H.M.S. *Colloden* and imprisoned in New York City's Provost jail. Captain Talbot was released by the British in 1781. He had received a discharge from Continental service during his imprisonment.

The disappointed naval officer in this letter to General Washington requests a certificate to use to acquire back wages and expresses his earnest desire to serve again. His request was granted, and despite his previous imprisonment and injury, Talbot served his country until the end of the American Revolution.

*Providence July 8th. 1782*

Sir

Doubtless Your Excellency will remmember that in February eighty, I did myself the Honour to wait on You (in Company with Coll. Barton)[1] at your Quarters in Morristown New Jersey. The motives that induced us to trouble your Excellency at that time, was a hope we Entertaind that Your Honour would be pleas'd to Appoint us to some command in the Army, by which means We might have it in our power to gratify the great desire we had of further serving our Country in So Glorious a Cause. Your Excellency manifested a desire to comply with our Request, but at the same time told us that it was impossible to annex us to any Regiment Without giveing offence, and as thier was a greater Porportion of Officers than men, you could not give us any Employ agreeable to our Rank, and Concluded with Observing that it was possible I might have some offers of an Armed Ship Either in publick or Private Employ, and if such should be the Case, You Rather advised me to imbrace the opportunity, I then took my leave of Your Excellency and went on to Phileadelphia, and as Humbly as Respectfully Petition'd Congress and the Board of Admiralty to give me Employ in the Navy, but was Very Politely informed that they should be happy to have me in their service, but they had no Ships but ware Officerd, and they were too poor to build more—being then disappointed in every expectation, I resolved to return to my Famely, and on my way I took the Liberty to call at your Quarters with an intent to Request a Written Furlow, but Your Honour was absent on Some occation, and the scarsity of Forage compeled me to leave Camp; and in August Following I excepted of the Command of the private armed Ship Genl. Washington, as a means to avoid the bad consequences and Shame which attends an Idle life, but unfortunately for me I was soon Captured by his Majestys Ship the Colloden, and after being confined for a While in the Provost New York, I was sent to England where I Was closely confined in Prison till last Decr., on my Return to this place I was inform'd that my self and many Other Supernumerary officers were discharged from their Appointments in the Army. I must Confess I think there was a degree of Propriety in the Order, but I could not see the Reason why a Very few inferior officers should be pointed out and dismist from pay especially as their are some (my self for one being wounded and have a ball in my body and another through my left Rist Which I Recd. at Mud Island) who must Remain Crippld till death puts a final Period to their existence, and so many superior officers Retaind eaqually unservisable to the army and at home about their Necessary Employ, However I dont pretend to say it is wrong.

The motives that induced me to Trouble Your Excellency with this, is to Request that you will be pleas'd to indulge me with the Favor of a certificate amounting in Substance that You did Verbally give me liberty to gow into Sea Employ, but not till after I had made Frequent Applications to be Employd in the Army, this I want to make use of in acquireing my Wages, perhaps your Honour will Remmember that I made application For Employ accompanied by Genl. Greene when head Quarters was at White marsh, and again in Jersey the Second day after the action of monmouth, as well as at Morristown, I have allso to beg that your Excellency will pardon the Liberty I have taken in Troubleing you with this long and Tedious appistle, and which I am induced to hope will be the Case, when you Reflect that this is the only time that I ever made use of simelar fredom during the present war. I beg your Excellency will favour me with a letter, and the certificate which will be esteemd a Great Honour Done on Sir Your Excellency's most Obedient And most humble Servt.

SILAS TALBOT

ALS, George Washington Papers, Library of Congress, Washington, D.C.
[1] Possibly Colonel William Barton (1748–1831) of Rhode Island.

# ALEXANDER BREVARD TO JETHRO SUMNER

WITH THE BRITISH ARMY restricted by the American forces to the southern coastal towns, the militia and a few Continental units were required to keep order in the extensive back country of the Carolinas. Captain Alexander Brevard (1755–1829), of the Third North Carolina Regiment, and a small contingent of his men were often compelled to defend themselves against Loyalists and Indians in the western counties of North Carolina. His bravery was shown in his service in that region until January 1, 1783. This letter to Brigadier General Jethro Sumner describes some of the conditions he faced.

*Rowan County 16th. July 1782*

Sir

I Received your Orders Dated Warren the 25th. June 1782 By the hand of his Excellency the Governor & shall attend either at Burk Court House or at Ramsours Mill for the Reception of the Troops of Morgan District (Ramsours is the place pointed out by the assembly for the Rendevous of the Troops of Morgan District).[1] I am very unhappy in not being able to Command One officer to my assistance. Lieut. Alexander is under Orders from Major Armstrong Posted at Charlotte.[2] I will shew Mr. Alexander your Letter to me & if he will March with me it is the only help I expect. If he Insists on waiting Major Armstrongs further Orders its likely I shall be alone untill I Receive assistance from your Orders. I have wrote Major Armstrong on the Occation. I am affraid I shall not be able to March any Considerable Number of Troops as soon as you expected as I am Informed that some of the Counties have not yet Classed their Men. However You may Depend on my Industry & good Intentions, as far in my power. I am much affraid of being lonesome while Imployed in this Business. Pray Order me on some Company. It is a wild young Country. I am Sir with all Possible Esteem & Respect Your Friend & Humble Servant

ALEXR. BREVARD *Capt*
*3rd N C Regt*

ALS, Preston Davie Collection, Southern Historical Collection, University of North Carolina, Chape Hill.

[1] Burk Court House, now Morganton, N.C.
[2] First Lieutenant Charles Alexander; probably Thomas Armstrong, aide-de-camp to Sumner.

# John Hutchinson Buell Diary

## *August 10, 1782*

THE EXTENDED STALEMATE between the American army in the Hudson Highlands and the British in New York City helped initiate many letters between the British commander General Sir Guy Carleton and George Washington, who was headquartered at Newburgh. The Huddy-Asgill affair was only one of many incidents that were subjects of this correspondence. Carleton and Washington developed a relationship of mutual trust that was evidenced by Carleton's letter of August 2, 1782, implying the possibility of prisoner exchange and negotiations. The prospect of peace alarmed the Loyalists in New York City. This incident is described in the diary of Major John Hutchinson Buell (1753–1813) of the First Connecticut Regiment. Buell served from the first engagement at Lexington in April 1775 and continued in service until June 1783.

**John Hutchinson Buell**

*10th Augt.* In the morning we relived the Command. The same day was sent out from New York a Coppy of a Letter sent from Sr. Giy Carleton to Genl Washington in which Carleton informd the Genl. that comissionors were appointed by the Court of Great Brittan to settle Peace between all Nations at War, and that the first proposition was the Independance of America, and than an Exchange of Prisoners was to take place offering to exchange Soldiers of equal Condition, man for man. Then they, (the Enemy,) offerd to Exchange seaman for soldiers on this Condition, that the Seamen so Exchangd should be at Liberty to enter immediately service, and that the Soldiers so recd by them should not enter into any service short of one year; at the Above inteligence we Recd a great share of satisfaction and waited with impatience to hear further of the matter. This acct was first published by Sr. Giy Carleton at the request of the Refugees in N. York which shew a Vary great dislike and disapprobation at it. . . .

John Hutchinson Buell Diary, original in private hands.

# WILLIAM MCKENNAN TO NATHANAEL GREENE

## *August 24, 1782*

CAPTAIN WILLIAM MCKENNAN (1758–1810) served with the Delaware Regiment, which was assigned on June 13, 1782, to Lieutenant Colonel John Laurens' Light Infantry Corps. In the following letter, McKennan transmits to General Greene military intelligence of the movements of a British naval squadron that was foraging on the Combahee River, some fifty miles southwest of Charleston, South Carolina. Major General Alexander Leslie (c.1740–94) who commanded a garrison of 3,000 British regulars in Charleston, the last major British garrison in the south, had ordered light infantry on armed vessels to secure and transport essential provisions. This foraging expedition was attacked on August 27, 1782, by a force led by Brigadier General Mordecai Gist (1742–92). The Americans seized one of the British ships returning to Charleston. In this engagement, John Laurens lost his life. The American action on the Combahee River forced the British to confine their foraging expeditions to coastal islands and the countryside closer to Charleston.

*Chehaw Neck Saturday 10 oClock*

Sir,

I have just received Intelligence of the Arrival of Eighteen Sail of Schooners, and Sloops, in the Combahee River, with Troops on board, supposed to be a foraging Party; This Information comes by several Gentleman, the last of whom Captn: Fields, who left them at his Point, near Twenty Miles from the ferry, at dusk. Several Men were landed there, and fired on him; After staying a while on Shore, they went on board, and its supposed, they entered higher up. In Consequence of this, I have ordered my Party, (who march'd Yesterday Evening to the ferry) to proceed by the nearest Rout to the above Place, where every Opposition in the Power of the Subaltern, (I make no doubt) will be made; I have been extremely ill with a fever, these five days, Scarcly able to cross my Room; also eight of my Men are laid down with the same disease. I have directed the Officers of the Militia, to be busy in collecting as many Men as possible, but am afraid their Numbers will be Small, as they appear much discontented. I can't learn their Intentions, there being no Rice on Cambachee; but imagine, they are in pursuit of Negroes, and Corn, as there are great Quantities of the latter planted on the River Swamps.

Agreeable to a letter sent me by Major Burnet,[1] I appointed Wednesday Afternoon, to put the Men on board the Vessels loaded in Ashepoo, but as they are still in security, thirty Miles up the River, shall direct their remaining there, until the present fleet disappears, from the other River. I am sir, with every Mark of Respect your Mo. Obt. Humble Servt.

W MCKENNAN

Mr Hoit will please to forward this with speed.

W McKennan

ALS, Nathanael Greene Papers, William L. Clements Library, Ann Arbor, Mich.
[1] Major Robert Burnett (1762–1854), aide-de-camp to Greene.

# Samuel Cogswell to Mason Cogswell

The tiresome drudgery that replaced the serious activities of battles and maneuvers provided, at times, humorous interludes for the Continental officer. Lieutenant Samuel Cogswell of the Fourth Massachusetts Regiment, in this letter to his brother, narrates satirically the endless inspections and parades that in 1782 kept the tired soldiers occupied until peace finally came one year later.

*Camp Nelson's point, 29th August 82*

Dear Mason,

Was I in almost any other situation than what I am, you might, with a great deal of justice, complain of my neglect. So soon as the day peeps, the long roll thundered from twenty Drums, announces the necessity of my immediate attendance on the parade. In ten minutes the platoons are formed, and away marches the regiment for a three hours exercise. This is scarcely over, when roll call drags me out of my tent to the parade again. Are your men all present? cries the Adjutant. Are their arms all clean? can the men see their faces in them? have they a speck of dirt on any of their clothes? bawls the Major. These matters properly attended to, the parade is dismissed—breakfast brought in—the Barber called—the hair is put in queue—and the Lieutenant rigged for the day. Enter Pay Master with a face as long as my arm. "Pray Sir have you completed your return for hats, stocks, Coats, Vests, Shirts, overalls, Shoes, and Buckles?" No Sir, but you shall have it immediately. "Pray be very particular about it, and let me have it as quick as you can, for I am in the greatest hurry that ever I was in, in my life. 'Not in a bit greater hurry Mr W. than you always are—triffles always disconcert you, therefore haste and confusion always attend you, but you shall have my returns soon." Enter Quarter Master with a countenance full of chearfulness—as easy and unconcerned as if he had no business to do, but such as afforded him the highest satisfaction. "I wish for a return of all the Arms, Ammunition, Canteens, Knapsacks, Camp-kettles, axes, barrels, dishes, tents &c, that you have in your Company—how long before I can have it?" As soon as I get rid of the Pay-Master"—Very well sir—Don't hurry yourself too much"—Servant Sir" Out comes my Company Book—my paper pens, ink, rule, and plummset, are paraded—everything ready for *returns-making*. Enter the Major shewing a whip—his brow knit into as many wrinkles as were ever seen upon a face of three score years standing—his temper perfectly soured by six years continual fretting, flashing from every feature in his face—"Have you given orders that none of your Company wear any of their new clothes except on parade?" "Yes Sir" and Then why does that black rascal wear his hat?" Tie him up instantly; order your drummer to give him thirty nine. Are your half gaiters finished? Have you taken care to provide every man in your company with a red stopper?" "Yes, yes, yes" "Such a regiment I never saw—the officers so inattentive—I am obliged to see to every thing myself." No Major you are not obliged to, but your piddling, fretting, disposition leads you to peep into matters which you ought to be above meddling with; and to scold at every thing that is done whether right or wrong. And by these means, give me leave to tell you, you are ruining your reputation in the regiment—Farewell. By this time the drum calls me to twelve o'clock exercise—then comes our dinner. My returns must next be finished—and at four o'clock the regiment again turns out to be disciplined. So that my duty is almost as constant as the moments of my life—for all which I have no pay from my country—no thanks—no hopes of promotion—and am constantly obliged to put up with the whim & caprice of a man, who suffers his passions to do with him as they please—who possesses all the bad qualities of a tyrant, without a single good one—and who hates or fears everybody but himself. Such my dear brother is my situation, and I assure you I am tired of it. I have been long enough a slave to a week, fretful unprincipled creature. And if I cannot change my situation no other way I will leave the army. Make my love and compliments to all your and my friends with you. Last month I had four shirts stolen from me. Can you replace them from the store without injury to yourself. Mr Sands—who by the way, I believe to be a very clever fellow—will tell you what I want. I am, dear Mason, your friend & Brother

SAM: COGSWELL

My whole stock of shirts amounts to 2.

ALS, Beinecke Library, Yale University, New Haven, Conn.

# TENCH TILGHMAN TO "MOLLY" TILGHMAN

THE FATIGUE of the Continental officers and their longing to see families, friends, and lovers are much in evidence in this letter from Lieutenant Colonel Tench Tilghman to his sister, Ann Maria (Molly) Tilghman, of Chestertown, Maryland. His letter from headquarters at Verplanck's Point, New York, reflects the rigors of prolonged duty as well as the desire for personal contact and news of loved ones and the hope for peace. All his wishes were fulfilled in 1783, for he was married on June 9, and the final treaty of peace was signed on September 3, 1783.

*Head Quarters, September 7, 1782*

I am infinitely obliged to my dear Molly, for her letter of the 18h. of Septembr. She has accounted to me for that Silence of which I so justly complained in my last, and I beg she will look upon herself as exculpated from the general charge, I made, of neglect. I will just add, that you need not be in want of opportunities of writing whenever you find inclination. No conveyance can be safer than the post—address my letters to the care of Mr. Morris, but let the postage be paid to Philade.—from thence they come free.

I am more sorry on your account than my own, for the miscarriage of the packet by Colo. Graves. There was nothing in my letter, but what I would take pride in shewing to all the World. A certain Lady has had her palpitations on the occasion, but I suppose they are now pretty well over.

What would I not give to be of the Bay Side party. To make me amends, you must write me from thence by every post, not in general, but journalwise. Was I there, I would set you all at defiance. I would convince you, that lovers who have settled matters between themselves and perfectly understand each other, (mark that) behave before Company just like other well bred people. I would not be that cold-oyster like thing, that would not let it be discovered by my behaviour that there was a load Stone in the room, but I would not, by my particularity, embarrass the Lady and make myself ridiculous. I speak from experience, having come very honorably off, when all the Eyes of prying curiosity were staring wide to make discoveries. I do not take all the credit to my self, much is due to the discretion and propriety of conduct of a lady who is deservedly esteemed an ornament to her Sex.

Were I to believe what I wish, I should tell you that we should certainly have peace this Winter. I do not however tell you that we shall not. I think the contrary, provided the British do not gain some advantage this Summer. The expected packet will enable me to form a better judgment after her arrival.

I have no hopes of putting on those pleasing Badges which you mention, so soon as you imagine. After I have put off the gay Blue and Buff, I must put on a Brown or some good hard working colour and must endeavour to make up in substantials, what I have lost in seeking "that bubble reputation at the Cannons mouth." I have however the pleasing consolation of knowing, that a moderate share of the goods of this world will satisfy her at whose feet I would wish to lay the whole World.

After my love to all at home, remember me affectionately to both Mrs. Ringgolds and Mr. and Mrs. Forman, if they are at Chester town. I am my dear Sister Your most affect. Brother

TENCH TILGHMAN

ALS, in the possession of Tench Frazer, Philadelphia, Pa.

# STEPHEN SOUTHALL TO ROBERT BURNETT

Lieutenant stephen southall, regimental paymaster of the First Continental Artillery Battalion commanded by Colonel Charles Harrison, writes Major Robert Burnett about current supply problems. During 1782, Greene's main army slowly closed in on Charleston. British Major General Alexander Leslie was finally forced to evacuate the city by sea on December 14, 1782. Despite this victory, the Americans still faced grave inadequacy of provisions. Southall's gallant efforts as paymaster were severely hindered by the critical shortage of funds.

*Camp. 2nd. Octr. 1782*

Dear Sir

In my general return of Clothing, Captain McClure's Company were mention'd which clothing I drew and have it now in my possession,[1] but as now Application has been made for them, & as an Escort is to go there to morrow, I should be glad to be informed whither I shall send his propotion up. As I observe by Genl Orders that the paymasters are to send the clothing to there men who are Absent, but are responcible for defficiencies shou'd there be any. But as the pay that is promised us is by no means Adequate (Shou'd we Obtain it) to the risk of Clothes being pilliaged on the way, I cannot think of sending them unless I have orders from head Quarters. I will get an Officer to se them packed & also that the Invoice agree, I woud have done myself the honor to have waited on the General personally, but am much indisposed. I am, very respectfully, Your H Servant

STEPHEN SOUTHALL *Lt & p m Arty.*

ALS, Nathanael Greene Papers, William L. Clements Library, Ann Arbor, Mich.
[1] Captain James McClure of the Fourth Continental Artillery.

# EPHRAIM KIRBY TO RUTH MARVIN

IN CAMPS encircling New York City, the Continental army awaited the peace agreement and the end of British and Loyalist activity. Ephraim Kirby (1757–1804) had risen from the position of private in December 1776 to ensign in Jeremiah Olney's Rhode Island Battalion. From Verplanck's Point, near Peekskill, New York, Kirby wrote this poignant letter to his future wife, Ruth Marvin, in Litchfield, Connecticut. The inadequate provisions and quarters added to his loneliness but did not dampen his devotion to duty as the war lingered on.

**Ephraim Kirby**

*Camp Var-Planks Point, October 18, 1782*

My Dear Ruthy,

I am in a tent, destitute of any fire, (except a little at some distance where my servant cooks my victuals) and a violent cold northeast storm of rain, (which has raged two days and nights) beats about my ears, & still appears to encrease. I am so chill'd with the cold, that I now write you with my gloves on. I find myself in a very suitable situation for reflection. I immagine you cannot be ignorant of the principal object of my contemplation. The following lines of Dr. Goldsmith frequently occur to my mind with peculiar force.

> "Thou source of all my bliss, & all my woe
> "That found'st me poor at first & keep'st me so"

All the inconveniences & distresses which I now suffer not in the least damp me in the ardour of my pursuits. The motives which first induced me to give up the means of acquireing a good estate for my present mode of life, (altho' they were perhaps founded upon mistaken conceptions) still enable me to suffer with pleasure; and consider every hardship as a favourable smile of fortune. One circumstance however comes frequently across my mind, & brings with it a pang hardly to be bourn. I was going on, but Capt. Beach has just arrived which will take up my time until tomorrow when I am appointed for duty. If you are able to study out my meaning from the uninteligible [      ] I have given I shall be glad. Make my most respectful compliments to your Father & Mother and write me, my dearest Ruthy, if you regard the happiness of your most faithful Friend

E. KIRBY

I wrote you the other [      ] immagine this will reach you as soon.

ALS, Edmund Kirby-Smith Papers, Southern Historical Collection, University of North Carolina, Chapel Hill.

# PETER FAYSSOUX TO NATHANAEL GREENE

THE CONTINUED PRESENCE of British soldiers in Charleston created many hardships for the American army and southern civilians. Passports or flags were required for passage through the British lines to family and friends. Peter Fayssoux (c.1744–95), chief physician and surgeon of hospitals in the Southern Department, wrote to Nathanael Greene to have his ailing wife transported out from British-controlled territory. In all of the American states, citizens and soldiers were exhausted by the war's duration and the British occupation of major port cities.

*Stono Novr. 11th. 1782*

Dear General

Mrs. Fayssoux has been obligd to goe to Charlestowne for the benefit of her Health. She has been there for some time past & is very anxious to get back, particularly as there is reason to believe the British will evacuate the Town by the next spring tides which will be at their Height next Monday. I & my two children are all sick, it is out of my power to goe for her, & her situation does not admit of her travelling by land. I will esteem it a particular favor if you will grant me a flag, for Mr. John Willson (a Brother in law of mine) to goe down with a Boat & hands & bring her up. I will be answerable for the flag equally as if I went myself. I am with great respect Sir yr. obliged hble. Servant

P. FAYSSOUX

ALS, Nathanael Greene Papers, William L. Clements Library, Ann Arbor, Mich.

# PHILIP HILL TO EDWARD CARRINGTON

LIEUTENANT PHILIP HILL (C. 1740–1800), of the Second Maryland Regiment, had been securing supplies for the Southern Department as Greene's quartermaster general. Lieutenant Hill explains to Colonel Edward Carrington (1749–1810) his reluctance to leave Greene's staff and join the First Maryland Regiment, because of the "confused state" of his own regiment's finances. These common complaints of unsettled accounts for food and clothing were among the grievances voiced by many frustrated officers.

*17th Novr 82*

Dr Colo

By the inclosd you'l find I am ordered to give up my post in the Staff & Join the 1st Mayd Rege Emedeately. This order I am Obligd to Obey or lay myself open to an Arrest. I informd Major Eccleston the confusd state of my Accts.[1] & that I could not quit the Department with any propriety untill they are setteld (but would Render the company all the Services in my power in the Absence of the Other two Officers Arrang to it. I am still willing to fulfill my engagements [    ] provided Generall Greene will Issue such an Order as will secure to me my command in the Rege whenever I give up my post in this Dept. The six months Mr Fraser agreed to Stay with Cap Dyer is now expired[2] & I expect him to leave me every Day, so you will perceive it Nessesary for something to be done Emediately. I am Sir your Mo. Obd. Sert.

P HILL *D Colo*

ALS, Nathanael Greene Papers, William L. Clements Library, Ann Arbor, Mich.

[1] Major John Eccleston (1750–98) of the First Maryland Regiment.

[2] Captain Lieutenant Edward Dyer of the Second Maryland Regiment.

# LEWIS MORRIS, JR., TO NANCY ELLIOTT

THE BRITISH PRESENCE in the South had ended by December 1782. Many of Nathanael Greene's men and officers had found the long period of inactivity during the British occupation of the several coastal towns almost beyond endurance. For many, including his aide-de-camp, Lieutenant Colonel Lewis Morris, Jr. (1752–1824), their homes and farms were hundreds of miles away. Lewis Morris, Jr., writes to his fianceé about the lack of news, expresses concern for his family and friends, and describes rumors of the British departure from their coastal enclave. The day after Morris' letter, the British left Charleston and sailed for New York City.

**Lewis Morris, Jr.**
COURTESY OF THE CAROLINA ART ASSOCIATION,
CHARLESTON, S.C.

*Dec. 13th 1782*

Our prospects brighten, my spirits revive, and in a little time I expect to congratulate you on the departure of the Enemy. O my soul! How exquisite will be the pleasure of that moment to me; to realize what we could scarcely believe, to enjoy in peace the sweet society of my dearest friend, will be a sensation unknown to me before. From that period I shall date my happiness, and Heaven grant me a completion of my wishes, and make me worthy of the heart I love.

Never was there such a thirst for news. Head Quarters is crowded with inquisitors. Every ear is open, and every horse that gallops at a distance, is an express. Have you heard from Gen. Wayne, or has Colonel Kosciuszkio returned from below? I am told he says the fleet is in motion, and that he saw a man, who heard another say, that the troops would embark this night. I listen attentively to all, and in the warmth of my wishes, believe the whole. Strange credulity; but how can I help it. A mind so sanguine, is easily seduced. I will shun the temptation for a time. I will join the circle of my friends, and in fancy, partake of the joy which they feel in living once more together. Recommend me to the esteem of your Sister—assure her that I am solicitous of that honor, and proud that my small attentions, should meet with her approbation.

Have you heard from your dear Mamma? I am ever anxious about her; and in the general confusion, most fervently hope she may not suffer.

I have sent you a faithful fellow as a safeguard, and by next Sunday, perhaps I may be with you in that capacity myself. Adieu my dearest girl and believe me with sincerity Your faithful and most affect. friend

AL, Miscellaneous Manuscripts, New-York Historical Society, New York City.

# BENJAMIN TUTT TO BENJAMIN GUERARD

AN EXTENDED PERIOD of military service often resulted in financial problems that would plague many patriots at the conclusion of the war. Because of his years of service since September 1776, Captain Benjamin Tutt (1740–c.1800), of South Carolina, was well qualified to report on the many incidents in which he and his men served with little or no compensation, such as those described in this letter to Governor Benjamin Guerard.

*Charles Town, February 17, 1783*

Sir

I have the honour to Address your Excellency in behalf of myself & the other Officers and Soldiers of the Independent Company formerly in the Service of the State under my Command.

About the time of the Surrender of this Capital to the British, the time of the Inlistments of most of the Men was near expired, that Event and the amazing depreciation of our Currency put it out of my power to continue them in the Service or to Inlist others. I was therefore induced to discharge those whose times had expired, the remainder about forty whose times were almost nearly out, remained at Fort Rutledge until that Post was delivered up to the British in consequence of Orders from the then Brigdr. Genl. Williamson who had always the direction of that Post and its Garrison in Consequence of Powers vested in him by the Governor or Legislature.[1]

Myself, the other Officers and Soldiers surrendered Prisoners of War and obtained Paroles, the Stores were delivered to a party of the Enemy detached by Colo. Brown from Augusta,[2] which Party remained a few weeks at the Fort and then distroyed it and returned to Augusta.

There are accounts for building that Fort, Waggoning Provisions etc. due myself to a considerable amount, also Pay due to the Officers and Men for about sixteen months, some of the pay Bills are attested and there is authentic vouchers ready to be produced for the whole. The hardships the Officers and Men suffered by receiving part of their pay at a very depreciated rate, and the not receiving a great part of it at all will be so obvious to your Excellency, that I need not observe any further on that occasion.

The Officers had also the promise of Cloathing from the Public which they never received.

I had been lately applied to by the Officers and some of the Men to obtain relief in their different circumstances and have promised to do every thing in my power to have them done Justice. I must therefore beg leave to submit the matter to your Excellency not doubting but so soon as provision can possibly be made for the purpose the money will be paid or the account put on such a footing as will render the matter upon a certainty. I have the honour to be, Sir, Your Excellency's most Obt. humble Serv.

BENJA. TUTT

To His Excellency Benjamin Guerard Esquire, Governor and Commander in Chief of the State of South Carolina.

Letterbook copy, South Carolina Archives, Columbia.

[1] Fort Rutledge was at Clemson, S.C. Brigadier General Andrew Williamson of the Georgia militia betrayed his troops in July 1780.

[2] Lieutenant Colonel Thomas Brown of the Georgia Loyalists.

# ALEXANDER THOMPSON DIARY

## *January–April 20, 1783*

FOR THE MEN serving on the northern and southern frontiers, the war between Great Britain and the United States did not end with the withdrawal of all British forces to New York City. As the diary of Alexander Thompson (1759–1809), a second lieutenant in the Continental artillery, shows, even carrying news of the cessation of hostilities to a British garrison at Oswego, New York, was exhausting and hazardous. On his journey he often passed poignant evidence of the protracted war between Indians and whites, British soldiers and American patriots.

**Alexander Thompson**

In the begining of the Month of January One thousand seven hundred and Eighty three, I was appointed to the Command of the Artillery, at the several Posts on the Mohawk River, Namely—Fort Rensselear being the Head Quarters of these detachments on the River, I thought proper to have my quarters near the Commanding Officer, that I might be enabled the more expeditiously to furnish detachments from my own Corps, as circumstances might require.

*On the 17th:* of April following an Express arrived from the HeadQuarters of His Excellency General Washington, to dispatch an Officer To the British Garrison at Oswago To announce a Cessation of Hostilities and deliver the inclosed dispatches directed "To the Commanding Officer of Oswago." Major Andrew Finck the then Commanding Officer,[1] sent for me immediately after the express arrived, and desired to know wether I wou'd perform the duty: that I shou'd have a sufficient party, and that every assistance shou'd be afforded me that I might require. I accordingly accepted the Majors proposal, and Orders were immediately given for such persons as I shou'd nominate, to hold themselves in Readyness to march the Next Morning. I then selected one Bombardier of my own detachment, one Serjeant of Willetts Levies,[2] and one of the Chief Stockbridge Indians, My Chief Guide and Interpreter I was to take at Fort Herkermer on my way up the River. These being deemed sufficient to make rafts and help me across the Rivers and Creeks, that I must necessarily have to pass, and being so few in Number might be able to do our duty with greater fecility. . . .

*Sunday, 20th:* The sun rose clear and pleasant, about which time I left my place of encampment, and took the path for *Fort Stanwix,* two hours on my march the weather became cloudy and Cold, but no rain. I pass'd by Old *Fort Schuyler* about ten oClock, and about three Miles beyond which after passing over the low grounds, I enter'd a second difficult swamp. And on the Creeks of *Seekaquate,* which is about the middle, I found the bridges entirely distroy'd, which made some difficulty in crossing. The Swamp was not so large as the One I had pass'd through the Afternoon before, but in many places equally as difficult, immediately after I assended *Ariska Hill* and arrived on its Summit about one oClock, which is generally allowed to be the highest piece of ground from Schennectandy to *Fort Stanwix,* I halted one hour, the weather begining to be clear and pleasant, I then proceeded for *Ariska Creek* and between the Summit of the Hill and the Creek, I went over the ground where General Herkermer fought Sir John Johnson,[3] This allow'd likewise to one of the most desperate engagements that has ever been fought by the militia. I saw a vast number of human skulls and bones scattered through the woods. . . .

Alexander Thompson Diary, Society of the Cincinnati, Washington, D.C.

[1] Major Andrew Fincke (1751–1820) of New York.
[2] Colonel Marinus Willett (1740–1830) of New York.
[3] The Battle of Oriskany on August 6, 1777.

# ISAAC CRAIG TO WILLIAM IRVINE

WITH THE ADVENT of peace in 1783, the hostilities in the settled areas of the east subsided. British forces under General Sir Guy Carleton remained relatively inactive in their enclave of New York City. On the frontier of Pennsylvania the British aided and abetted the Indians in disturbing settlers and the string of forts in the western part of the state. Major Isaac Craig (1746–1826), stationed at Fort Pitt, describes the interminable viciousness of the Indian warfare.

*Fort Pitt 5th April 1783*

Dr General,

Notwithstanding General Carletons assurance of the Savages being Restrained and the Indian Partisans Called in, we have almost every day accounts of Famileys being murdered or carreyed off the Frontier Inhabitants of Washington & Ohio Counties are moving into the Interior Settlements, the Inhabitants of Westmoreland it is said will follow their Example and we have Reason to believe that the Post of Wheeling is or will Shortly be Evacuated it appears there are several Partys of the Enemy or Detachments of Some Large Party as they are Ravaging the County in Several Places at the same time Col Byards Letter will further Inform You Applications and Petitions for Ammunition from Assistance have come in from all Quarters.

Prospects of Peac on this side of the Mountains seems to Vanish; the British Either have very little influence over their Savage Allies, or they are acting a most deceitfull Part. I hope however that the Assurance we have of the Pacefick Deposition of England will give Congress an Oppertunity of Sending a Sufficient Force to Exterpiate or at least Properly Chastise these murdering Rascals.

Should an Expedition be Determined on, in which Artillery is to be Employed I hope it will be remembered that there is not a three Pdr fit to be Carreyed into the Field at this Place and that at least two of that Caleba will be wanted according to my Opinion. I hope I shall have the Pleasure of Battering the Wyandot Block Houses in the Course of the Ensuing Summer and Perhaps of taking Possession of Detroit. I am Dr General Your Obt & Hebl Servt.

ISAAC CRAIG

"Letter of Major Isaac Craig to Gen. William Irvine, 1783," *Pennsylvania Magazine of History and Biography* (1912), 36:507.

# JAMES NICHOLSON TO NATHANAEL GREENE

CAPTAIN JAMES NICHOLSON (1737–1804) had commanded the British ship *Defence* in 1775, before he joined the infant American navy. During the American Revolution, Nicholson commanded several warships and was the senior officer in the Continental navy by 1783. Two months after the last naval engagement of the war on March 10, 1783, Captain Nicholson writes to Nathanael Greene about procuring a fleet of ships to transport troops from Charleston to Chesapeake Bay. Greene's army remained at Charleston until transported north to a location more suitable for discharge.

*New York 30th. May 1783*

Sir,

Agreeable to my Instructions, I do myself the honor of Enclosing you a Copy of an Agreement between the Superantendant of Finance & Mr. Danl. Parker & Comp: from which you will find the latter are to procure 1500 Tons of shipping for the purpose of bringing the Troops under your command to the Bay of Chesapeack. In behalf of the United States I have been ordered to this place to assist Mr. Parker in procuring & forwarding the Transports. It has been, & is still, attended with difficulty to get the quantity of Tons specified. I suppose without a great detention we shall not exceed 13 or 1400 Tons, and as I find it necessary to continue here a few days after the sailing of this first Transport in order to foward the remainder, I beg leave to Point out the necessity of puting as many Troops as can stow with any conveniency in each Vessel so as not greatly to incommode the men. At any rate not less than one man to each Ton of the Vessel agreeable to the Enclosed list of Tonnage.

In order to prevent any Demurrage, I have no doubt your Excellency will be of oppinion with myself, That the Transports ought to sail immediately. The Troops are Embarked without waiting for each other. If so you will please to give the Capts. of the Vessels the necessary orders in my absence.

Your Excellency will also please to be particular in your orders to the Commanding officer onboard each seperate Transport to attend to the Mustering of the Troops & giving the Cap. a Cirtificate which will determine the Pay of the Vessel agreeable to the Charter. Also that he may suffer no Demurrage from a Detention in Embarking & Debarking the Troops. I am Sir with the greatest respect your Excellencys most Obedt. Humbl. Servt. &c.

JAMES NICHOLSON

PS. I expect the last Vessel will Sail in 4 or 5 days from this Docke.

ALS, Nathanael Greene Papers, William L. Clements Library, Ann Arbor, Mich.

# Nathanael Greene General Orders

After years of conflict, the men in the southern army were eager to go home. General Nathanael Greene's general orders to his troops, recorded by his aide-de-camp, Captain Nathaniel Pendleton (1746–1821), mirror the fatigue of the two officers and of their restless men. Both officers had served their country through the northern campaigns and the battles in the south. Both knew the harsh environment of winter encampment, the trauma of battle, the frustrations and vexations of supply, and finally the sullen resentment and impatience at remaining in the field after 1782. The orders extol the virtues of the men and caution them to behave as disciplined soldiers. The unrelenting faith in their cause and the tireless effort to affirm their independence are major elements of this last communication from the patriot leaders to their exhausted and warweary men.

*June, 1783*

The conclusion of a general peace having occasioned a cessation of all Hostility, nothing is left to complete your Character as soldiers, but that you leave it with dignity. To quit those fields, whereon you have been so emminently distinguished, as soldiers; and retire to the less splended, but not less honorable character of private citizens, will be an illustrious proof of the greatness of your Souls, and the humility of your desires.

Nothing can be more interesting to the feelings of a soldier than the remembrances of those incidents of danger, and affliction he has suffered in the pursuit of honors, and in the service of his Country; and no Army can indulge those delightfull feelings with so much justice, as that which it has been the Generals good fortune to command. He esteems it a peculiar felicity, that having tasted the bitterness of adversity together with the Army, they have been also destined to enjoy together the sweets of peace—the complete reward of all their Toils.

The Contrast between your circumstances, when he took the Command in the Southern Department, and at the present moment, excite emotions in his bosom, which he cannot forbear to cherish with a mixture of pleasure and of pride. Then You were overwhelmed with want, your Spirits broken by misfortunes, your hopes extinguished by defeat: Now, He can dismiss you crowned with Success, with the applause of a grateful people. And what perhaps is still more desireable to a Soldier, the unwilling respect and admiration of defeated enemies. Then, the inhabitants of this Country were subjected to intolerable oppressions, or wandered in a voluntary exile. Now, they possess their Country, and enjoy it with freedom. The occasion was pressing, the attempt was noble, and your Success has been Answerable. The General claims an equal share of the happiness, but no part of the honors of Success. He only pointed to the object, which that generous confidence, and those persevering exertions, so peculiarly and so justly your distinction, only accomplished. The happiness and freedom of your

Country is the foundation of your glory. Laurels planted in such a soil will acquire fresh verdure, but will never be deminished by length of time.

Your operations in these States are marked by circumstances, that will tender the Story of them interesting to mankind. You found a Country wasted by war, and subjected to an Army three times your number, and completely appointed. The spirits of your friends were subdued by miseries, and those of your enemies rendered insolent by success. But the Soul of liberty is superior to fortune, your Enemies are defeated, and the Country restored to Peace and freedom. To effect this you have indeed suffered the keenest extremities of cold and hunger, and every species of severe Affliction, and it was the Generals peculiar misfortune to see and to deplore, while he could not relieve you. That you sustained these unexampled sufferings with patience and even with chearfulness, while it excites the astonishment of mankind will be now matter of uxultation to yourselves, while you exhibit to the World the singular and striking instance of military perfection. The American Army is doubly illustrious, but the Southern Army is more peculiarly so; No Army ever displayed so much Obedient fortitude, because no Army ever suffered such variety of distresses; Nor can any Army discover more humility, because no Army ever had more glorious causes of tryumph. Nevertheless the General has the consolation to reflect that every thing was attempted—every Expedient applied to relieve you in those trying moments of adversity. His measures to effect this has some times excited mean Jealousies and low suspicions, but prompted by duty, and the affection he bears his Army, he reviews them with a very sensible pleasure. Indeed, it was then your misfortune, tho' it now exalts your Character, that no measures could be adopted, which your peculiar sufferings would not have justified, and the General has nothing to regret, except that he was not more successfull.

Peace which was the object, must now be the period of our military connexion. The same necessity which called us together, requires us now to be seperated. It will be some alleviation to the pain of parting after having seen the vicissitudes of good and ill Fortune together, that the same love and veneration for our Country which then compelled us to abandon the peacefull habitudes of private life, now require us to abandon the splendor of Arms and return again to obscurity; if indeed that person can be vieled in obscurity, whose actions have been celebrated through so many Countries and Nations of the earth. But tho Submission to the Laws of our Country oblige us to be seperated, nothing will lessen those lively sentiments of affectionate gratitude he feels for the Army, nor extinguish those impressions their generous confidence, chearfull obedience and noble exertions have made in his mind, and it will afford him the highest satisfaction if he can promote the interest of any Soldier who has been his partner in all the changes of the Southern War, and who serves out his time with Fidelity.

The General cannot take leave of the Army without assuring them, that he has the most perfect confidence in the gratitude, honor, and justice of his Country, and he is entirely convinced that every Soldier who serves out his time with Fidelity, will be paid with Justice, if not rewarded with liberallity and that this will be done as soon as the nature of our unsettled Country, and the State of its Finances will admit.

The General expects the Army will not relax its discipline, for the little time it will probably remain in the field. He is anxious that so bright a character should not be stained by a single instance of licenciousness. If this should happen, he is determined to punish it with severity.

Autograph draft in Pendleton's hand, Pendleton Papers, New-York Historical Society, New York City.

# The Final Days

❧❧❧❧❧❧❧❧❧❧❧❧❧❧

## GEORGE WASHINGTON'S
## CIRCULAR TO THE STATE GOVERNORS

By JUNE 1783 the war was not yet over. Some men would still be killed in service, and not until late November would the last British troops evacuate New York City. George Washington wrote a circular letter to the executives of the thirteen states from his headquarters at Newburgh, New York, on June 8, 1783. Much has been said and written about George Washington's inspired leadership. It does not need repeti-

tion here except to ask from whence came this extraordinary quality. Washington was a spiritual man and his faith was a significant factor in his greatness. Throughout the war his orders and dispatches directed his men to worship and to ask for God's protection. Such religious values are evident in the following excerpts from this lengthy and memorable message.

*Head Quarters, Newburgh, June 8, 1783*

Sir: The great object for which I had the honor to hold an appointment in the Service of my Country, being accomplished, I am now preparing to resign it into the hands of Congress, and to return to that domestic retirement, which, it is well known, I left with the greatest reluctance, a Retirement, for which I have never ceased to sigh through a long and painful absence, and in which (remote from the noise and trouble of the World) I meditate to pass the remainder of life in a state of undisturbed repose; But before I carry this resolution into effect, I think it a duty incumbent on me, to make this my last official communication, to congratulate you on the glorious events which Heaven has been pleased to produce in our favor, to offer my sentiments respecting some important subjects, which appear to me, to be intimately connected with the tranquility of the United States, to take my leave of your Excellency as a public Character, and to give my final blessing to that Country, in whose service I have spent the prime of my life, for whose sake I have consumed so many anxious days and watchfull nights, and whose happiness being extremely dear to me, will always constitute no inconsiderable part of my own. . . . I now make it my earnest prayer, that God would have you, and the State over which you preside, in his holy protection, that he would incline the hearts of the Citizens to cultivate a spirit of subordination and obedience to Government, to entertain a brotherly affection and love for one another, for their fellow Citizens of the United States at large, and particularly for their brethren who have served in the Field, and finally, that he would most graciously be pleased to dispose us all, to do Justice, to love mercy, and to demean ourselves with that Charity, humility and pacific temper of mind, which were the Characteristicks of the Divine Author of our blessed Religion, and without an humble imitation of whose example in these things, we can never hope to be a happy Nation.

John C. Fitzpatrick, ed., *The Writings of George Washington from the Original Manuscript Sources, 1745–1799* (Washington, D.C., 1931–44), XXVI, 483–84, 496.

# Benjamin Tallmadge Memoir

## *November–December 1783*

On NOVEMBER 25 the triumphant Americans, led by George Washington and George Clinton, governor of New York, entered New York City in a ceremonial parade, marching past cheering crowds. Nine days later, on December 4 in Fraunces Tavern,[1] General Washington bade a sad farewell to his officers who were in the city at that time. Among those officers was Major Benjamin Tallmadge, the senior officer of the Second Continental Dragoons, who later described this emotional scene. Except for the wounded soldiers who could not be moved, most of the troops, having been discharged, rode or walked their weary but triumphant way home after Washington's departure. What possessions they still had were piled into wagons and sent ahead, but what they carried with them was the memory of that rare combination of respect, admiration, and affection that they felt for the general who had kept them together during the long years of combat.

Having accomplished all my business in New York, I returned again to the army, and made my report to the Commander-in-Chief. The troops now began to be impatient to return to their respective homes, and those that were destined for that purpose, to take possession of the city. Gen. Washington now dismissed the greater part of the army in so judicious a way, that no unpleasant circumstances occurred. The 25th of November, 1783, was appointed for the British troops to evacuate the city, and for the American troops to take possession of it. Gen. Knox, at the head of a select corps of American troops, entered the city as the rear of the British troops embarked; soon after which the Commander-in-Chief, accompanied by Gov. Clinton and their respective suites, made their public entry into the city on horseback, followed by the Lieut.-Governor and members of the Council. The officers of the army, eight abreast, and citizens on horseback, eight abreast, accompanied by the Speaker of the Assembly, and citizens on foot eight abreast, followed after the Commander-in-Chief and Gov.

Clinton. So perfect was the order of march, that entire tranquility prevailed, and nothing occurred to mar the general joy. Every countenance seemed to express the triumph of republican principles over the military despotism which had so long pervaded this now happy city. Most of the refugees had embarked for Nova Scotia, and the few who remained, were too insignificant to be noticed in the crowd. It was indeed a joyful day to the officers and soldiers of our army, and to all the friends of American independence, while the troops of the enemy, still in our waters, and the host of tories and refugees, were sorely mortified. The joy of meeting friends, who had long been separated by the cruel rigors of war, cannot be described.

Gov. Clinton gave a public dinner, at which Gen. Washington and the principal officers of the army, citizens, etc., were present. On the Tuesday evening following, there was a most splendid display of fireworks, at the lower end of Broadway, near the Bowling Green. It far exceeded anything I had ever seen in my life.

The time now drew near when the Commander-in-Chief intended to leave this part of the country for his beloved retreat at Mount Vernon. On Tuesday, the 4th of December, it was made known to the officers then in New York, that Gen. Washington intended to commence his journey on that day. At 12 o'clock the officers repaired to Francis' Tavern, in Pearl Street, where Gen. Washington had appointed to meet them, and to take his final leave of them. We had been assembled but a few moments, when His Excellency entered the room. His emotion, too strong to be concealed, seemed to be reciprocated by every officer present. After partaking of a slight refreshment, in almost breathless silence, the General filled his glass with wine, and turning to the officers, he said: "With a heart full of love and gratitude, I now take leave of you. I most devoutly wish that your latter days may be as prosperous and happy as your former ones have been glorious and honorable."

After the officers had taken a glass of wine, Gen. Washington said: "I cannot come to each of you, but shall feel obliged if each of you will come and take me by the hand."

Gen. Knox being nearest to him, turned to the Commander-in-Chief, who, suffused in tears, was incapable of utterance, but grasped his hand; when they embraced each other in silence. In the same affectionate manner, every officer in the room marched up to, kissed, and parted with his General-in-Chief. Such a scene of sorrow and weeping I had never before witnessed, and hope I may never be called upon to witness again. It was indeed too affecting to be of long continuance—for tears of deep sensibility filled every eye—and the heart seemed so full, that it was ready to burst from its wonted abode. Not a word was uttered to break the solemn silence that prevailed, or to interrupt the tenderness of the interesting scene. The *simple thought* that we were then about to part from the man who had conducted us through a long and bloody war, and under whose conduct the glory and independence of our country had been achieved, and that we should see his face no more in this world, seemed to me utterly insupportable. But the time of separation had come, and waiving his hand to his *grieving children* around him, he walked silently on to Whitehall, where a barge was in waiting. We all followed in mournful silence to the wharf, where a prodigious crowd had assembled to witness the departure of the man, who, under God, had been the great agent in establishing the glory and independence of these United States. As soon as he was seated, the barge put off into the river, and when out in the stream, our great and beloved General waived his hat, and bid us a silent adieu.

We paid him the same affectionate compliment, and then returned to the same hotel whence Gen. Washington had so recently departed. Thus closed one of the most interesting and affecting scenes that I ever witnessed—a scene so fraught with feeling, that it seemed for a time as if it never could be erased from vivid and constant reflection. But, such is the wise constitution of human nature, that other objects and pursuits occupy the mind and engross the attention, or life would become a burden too heavy to bear.

In a few days, all the officers who had assembled at New York to participate in the foregoing heartrending scene, departed to their several places of abode, to commence anew their avocations for life.

Henry Phelps Johnston, ed., *Memoir of Colonel Benjamin Tallmadge* (New York, 1904), pp. 94–98.

[1] Fraunces Tavern, 54 Pearl Street, New York City, built in 1719, is designated a New York Historic Landmark. Purchased in 1904 by the New York State Society of the Sons of the Revolution, it has been restored by that Society and is maintained as a museum.

# George Washington's Address to Congress

In ANNAPOLIS, nineteen days after his farewell in New York City, George Washington, at a special session of the Continental Congress, resigned his commission as commander in chief. This episode brought to a close the eight-year struggle dating from the April 1775 battles of Lexington and Concord. The young nation's hard-won War for Independence had taken an inestimable toll in human suffering. The recovery would be long and painful. The Continental Congress, assembled on December 23 for the express purpose of conveying its gratitude to Washington, received a message as humble as it was impressive, a message to be long remembered.

**George Washington at Valley Forge**
BAS RELIEF: EDWARD JAMES KELLY
(FROM A PAINTING BY J. C. LEYENDEKER)
COURTESY OF THE NATIONAL PARK SERVICE, FEDERAL HALL
NATIONAL MEMORIAL, NEW YORK CITY

*Annapolis, December 23, 1783*

Mr. President:

The great events on which my resignation depended having at length taken place; I have now the honor of offering my sincere Congratulations to Congress and of presenting myself before them to surrender into their hands the trust committed to me, and to claim the indulgence of retiring from the Service of my Country.

Happy in the confirmation of our Independence and Sovereignty, and pleased with the oppertunity afforded the United States of becoming a respectable Nation, I resign with satisfaction an Appointment I accepted with diffidence. A diffidence in my abilities to accomplish so arduous a task, which however was superseded by a confidence in the rectitude of our Cause, the support of the Supreme Power of the Union, and the patronage of Heaven.

The Successful termination of the War has verified the most sanguine expectations, and my gratitude for the interposition of Providence, and the assistance I have received from my Countrymen, encreases with every review of the momentous Contest.

While I repeat my obligations to the Army in general, I should do injustice to my own feelings not to acknowledge in this place the peculiar Services and distinguished merits of the Gentlemen who have been attached to my person during the War. It was impossible the choice of confidential Officers to compose my family should have been more fortunate. Permit me Sir, to recommend in particular those, who have continued in Service to the present moment, as worthy of the favorable notice and patronage of Congress.

I consider it an indispensable duty to close this last solemn act of my Official life, by commending the Interests of our dearest Country to the protection of Almighty God, and those who have the superintendence of them, to his holy Keeping. Having now finished the work assigned me, I retire from the great theatre of Action; and bidding an Affectionate farewell to this August body under whose orders I have so long acted, I here offer my Commission, and take my leave of all the employments of public life.

John C. Fitzpatrick, ed., *The Writings of George Washington, from the Original Manuscript Sources, 1745–1799* (Washington, D.C., 1931–44), XXVII, 284–85.

THE BOOK COMMITEE
Daughters of the Cincinnati

**Benjamin Bartholomew**
PHOTO: GEOFFREY A. HALL, PINEHURST, N.C.

**John Berrien**
PHOTO: STERLING, MELBOURNE, FLA.

**Charles-Louis-Victor Broglie**
COURTESY OF THE NEW-YORK HISTORICAL SOCIETY

**Francis Taliafero Brooke**
COURTESY OF THE SOCIETY OF THE CINCINNATI, ANDERSON HOUSE,
WASHINGTON, D.C.

**Edward Butler**

**Jonathan Cass**

ARTIST: W. B. COOPER (AFTER A PORTRAIT PROBABLY BY TRUMBULL)

**The Death of General Montgomery at Quebec. (Jacob Cheesman and John Macpherson were also killed in the same battle.)**

COURTESY OF YALE UNIVERSITY, NEW HAVEN, CONN.
ARTIST: JOHN TRUMBULL

**John Chew**
PHOTO: BOURGEOIS, BRUSSELS

**Matthew Clarkson**

**Lemuel Clift**

**Ebenezer Crosby**
ARTIST: R. O'BRIEN
COURTESY OF THE NEW-YORK HISTORICAL SOCIETY

**Daniel Deniston**

COURTESY OF THE FRICK ART REFERENCE LIBRARY, NEW YORK CITY

**Edward Eells**

**Moses Este**

**James Ewing**

**Francois-Joseph-Paul de Grasse**
COURTESY OF THE NEW-YORK HISTORICAL SOCIETY

**George Gray**
COURTESY OF THE FILSON CLUB, LEXINGTON, KY.

**Abijah Hammond**

**Thomas Hunt**

**Amasa Jackson**

**Allen Jones**
COURTESY OF THE STATE DEPARTMENT OF ARCHIVES AND HISTORY,
RALEIGH, N.C.

**James McCubbin Lingan**
ARTIST: ROBERT FIELDS
PHOTO: MUSEUM OF HISTORY
COURTESY OF THE SMITHSONIAN INSTITUTION, WASHINGTON, D.C.

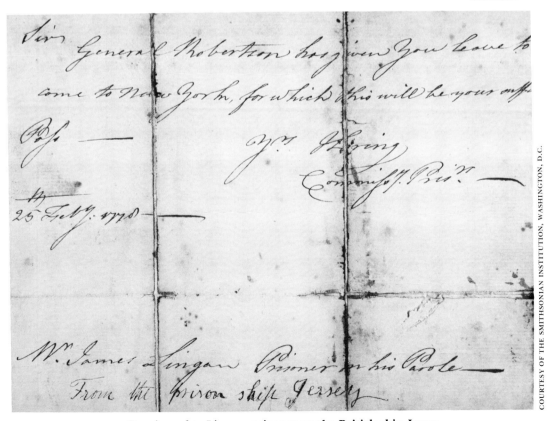

**Pass issued to Lingan, prisoner on the British ship *Jersey***

William Lytle

301

Samuel Alexander McCoskry

Charles McKnight

COURTESY OF THE NATIONAL LIBRARY OF MEDICINE, WASHINGTON, D.C.

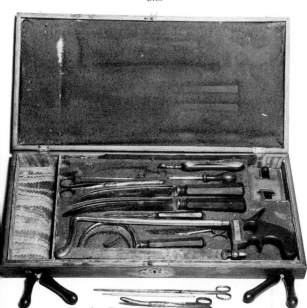

Surgical instruments belonging to Charles McKnight

**Gabriel Maupin**

PHOTO: FRED HABIT STUDIOS, NORFOLK, VA.

**Henry Miller**

COURTESY OF THE HISTORICAL SOCIETY OF PENNSYLVANIA, PHILADELPHIA

**Aeneas Munson, Jr.**

PHOTO: E. IRVING BLOMSTRANN, NEW BRITAIN, CONN.

**William North**

ARTIST: RALPH EARLE

**Martin Phifer**

**Timothy Pickering**
COURTESY OF DIPLOMATIC RECEPTION ROOMS,
DEPARTMENT OF STATE, WASHINGTON, D. C.
ARTIST: ARTHUR S. CONRAD (AFTER A PORTRAIT BY GILBERT STUART

**William Polk**
COURTESY OF THE STATE DEPARTMENT OF ARCHIVES AND HISTORY,
RALEIGH, N.C.

**Charles Pope**

**Thomas Shubrick**
PHOTO: DUNLOP
COURTESY OF THE SOCIETY OF THE CINCINNATI, ANDERSON HOUSE,
WASHINGTON, D.C.

**William Sproat**
COURTESY OF THE PENNSYLVANIA SOCIETY OF THE CINCINNATI

**John Stricker**
ARTIST: CHARLES KING BIRD
COURTESY OF THE MARYLAND HISTORICAL SOCIETY, BALTIMORE

**Joseph Thomas**

**Tench Tilghman bringing the news of Washington's victory at Yorktown, Va., to the Continental Congress in Philadelphia**

ARTIST: JOHN WARD DUNSMORE
COURTESY OF THE NEW-YORK HISTORICAL SOCIETY

John Francis Vacher

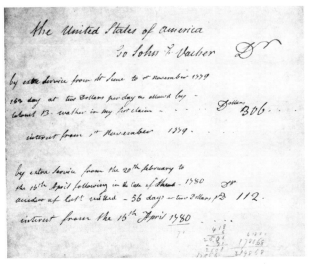

**Voucher made out to John Vacher**

**Robert White**

**Jacob Wright**

COURTESY OF THE DUTCHESS COUNTY HISTORICAL SOCIETY, POUGHKEEPSIE, N. Y.

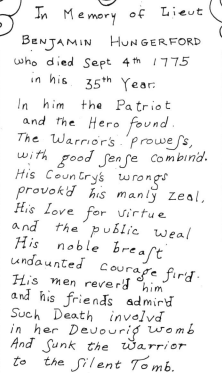

In Memory of Lieut

BENJAMIN HUNGERFORD
who died Sept 4th 1775
in his 35th Year.

In him the Patriot
and the Hero found.
The Warrior's prowess,
with good sense combin'd.
His Country's wrongs
provok'd his manly zeal,
His Love for virtue
and the public weal
His noble breast
undaunted courage fir'd.
His men reverd him
and his friends admir'd
Such Death involvd
in her Devourig womb
And sunk the Warrior
to the silent Tomb.

**Tombstone of Benjamin Hungerford, Woodbury, Conn.**

REDRAWING: LAIYING CHONG

# Roster of Ancestors of
# The Daughters of the Cincinnati

Alexander, William, Maj. Gen., N.J. (Earl of Stirling); *b* Dec. 27/29, 1725, New York, N.Y.; *d* Jan. 15, 1783, Albany, N.Y.; *m* Sarah Livingston (1725–1804) on Nov. 1, 1748/54, New York, N.Y.

Amis, William, Lt., N.C.; *b* 1756; will probated March 1824; *b* & *d* Northampton Co., N.C.; *m* Susan Welbourne.

Anderson, Richard, Capt., Md.; *b* Jan. 16, 1752, St. Mary's Co., Md.; *d* June 22, 1835, Philadelphia, Pa.; *m* Ann Wallace, July 31, 1787.

Anderson, Richard Clough, Lt. Col., Va.; *b* Jan. 12, 1750, Hanover Co., Va.; *d* Oct. 16, 1826, "Soldiers Retreat," Jefferson Co., Ky.; *m* Sarah Marshall (Nov. 20, 1779–Aug. 25, 1854), Sept. 17, 1797.

Angell, Israel, Col., R.I.; *b* Aug. 24, 1740, Providence, R.I.; *d* May 4, 1832, Johnston (or Smithfield), R.I.; *m* Martha Angell, Feb. 20, 1765.

Antill, Edward, Lt. Col., N.Y.; *b* April 11, 1742, Piscataway, Middlesex Co., N.J.; *d* May 21, 1787/89, St. Johns, Canada; *m* Charlotte Riverain (Riverin?), May 4, 1764, Quebec, Canada.

Aorson, Aaron, Capt., N.Y.; *b* 1741(?); *d?*; *m* Aaltje Quakhenboss, April 14, 1768, New York, N.Y.

Armstrong, James Francis, Brig. Chap., Md.; *b* April 3, 1750, West Nottingham, Md.; *d* Jan. 19, 1816, Trenton, N.J.; *m* Susannah Livingston, Aug. 22, 1782.

Armstrong, William, Capt., N.C.; *b* c.1745, Cumberland Co., Pa.; *d* Nov. 30, 1814, Orange Co., N.C.; *m* Nancy (Ann) Gibson, 1767, Cumberland Co., N.C.

Avery, Ebenezer, Lt., Conn.; *b* March 7, 1732, Groton, Conn.; *d* Sept. 6, 1781, Fort Griswold, Groton Hill, Conn.; *m* Phoebe Denison (1743–1818), dau. Daniel & Rachel Starr Denison, June 11, 1761, New London, Conn.

Baker, John, Capt., N.C.; *b* c.1726; *d* after May 23, 1791; *b* & *b* Bertie, Hertford Co., N.C.; *m* Elizabeth Wilson, dau. James Wilson, Sept. 5, 1754, Hertford Co., N.C.

Baldwin, Henry, Lt., Md.; *b* 1754, Anne Arundel Co., Md.; *d* 1792/93; *m* Maria Graham Woodward, Jan. 25, 1790.

Ball, Burgess, Lt. Col., Va.; *b* July 28, 1749, Lancaster Co., Va.; *d* March 7, 1800, "Springwood" near Leesburg, Loudoun Co., Va.; *m* Mary Chichester (1753–1775), dau. John & Jane (Smith) Chichester, July 2, 1770, St. James Northan Parish, Goochland Co., Va.

Barbour, James, Lt., Va.; *b* c.1763, Culpeper, Va.; *d* 1782 in service; unmarried; line went to brother.

Barnard, John, Capt., Conn.; *b* Dec. 25, 1732; *d* Dec. 28, 1813; *b* & *d* Hartford, Conn.; *m* Hannah Bigelow, Dec. 2, 1757.

Barney, Joshua, Lt., Pa.; *b* July 6, 1759, Baltimore, Md.; *d* Dec. 1, 1818, Pittsburgh,

Pa.; *m* Anne Bedford, March 16, 1780, Philadelphia, Pa.

Barret, William, Capt., Va. (and N.C.); *b* Jan. 2, 1756, Richmond, Va.; *d* Feb. 16, 1815, Green Co.(?), Ky.; *m* Dorothea Winston, 1784.

Bartholomew, Benjamin, Capt., Pa.; *b* Feb. 16, 1752; *d* March 31, 1812; *b* & *d* Chester Co., Pa.; *m* Rachel Dewees (March 7, 1765–Dec. 4, 1848), Feb. 16, 1782, Philadelphia, Pa.

Beale, Robert, Capt., Va.; *b* Jan. 30, 1759, Chestnut Hill, Richmond Co., Va.; *d* Sept. 1, 1843, Hickory Hill, Westmoreland Co., Va.; *m* Martha Felicia Turbeville/Tuberville (1786–1822), dau. Major George Lee & Elizabeth Tayloe (Corbin) Turbeville, Aug. 1, 1802, Hickory Hill, Va.

Beall, Lloyd, Capt., Md.; *b* Aug. 9, 1756, Prince Georges Co., Md.; *d* Oct. 5, 1817, Harpers Ferry, Va.; *m* Elizabeth Waugh Jones, May 1, 1785.

Beall, Samuel Brooke, 2d Lt., Md.; *b* 1762, Georgetown (now D.C.); *d* March 28, 1842, Amherst Co., Va.; *m* Elinor Berry, Nov. 3, 1785, Prince Georges Co., Md.

Beaumont, William, Lt., Conn.; *b* May 25/26, 1753, Lebanon, Conn., *d* Oct. 7, 1807, Champlain, N.Y.; *m* Polly Wright of Fishkill, N.Y., Aug. 1782.

Bedinger, Henry, Capt., Va.; *b* Oct. 16, 1753, York Co., Pa.; *d* May 14, 1843, near Charles Town, Jefferson Co., Va. (now W.Va.); *m* Rachel Strode (Oct. 19, 1762–Oct. 17, 1839), Dec. 22, 1784.

Beekman, Tjerck, 2d Lt., N.Y.; *b* Dec. 30, 1754; *d* Dec. 25, 1791; *b* & *d* Kingston, Ulster Co., N.Y.; *m* Rachel Dumont, Oct. 16, 1783, Kingston, N.Y.

Beers, Nathan, Lt., Conn.; *b* Feb. 24, 1753, Stratford, Conn.; *d* Feb. 10, 1849, New Haven, Conn.; *m* Mary Phelps of Stafford Springs, Conn., dau. Judge John & Abigail Richardson Phelps, May 26, 1781.

Bell, Jesse, Capt., Conn.; *b* March 6, 1745/46, Stamford, Conn.; *d* Oct. 20, 1834, Saratoga, N.Y.; *m* Comfort Garnsey, Nov. 8, 1767.

Bennett, Caleb Prew, 1st Lt., Del.; *b* Nov. 11, 1758, Kennett Township, Chester Co., Pa.; *d* May 9, 1836, Wilmington, Del.; *m* Catharine Britton, April 5, 1792, Linicorn Island, Delaware Co., Pa.

Berrien, John, Capt., Ga.; *b* 1760, Rock Hill, Somerset Co., N.J.; *d* Nov. 6, 1815, Savannah, Ga.; *m* Margaret MacPherson, Nov. 9, 1780, Philadelphia, Pa.

Biggs, Benjamin, Capt., Va.; *b* January 31, 1753, Md.; *d* Dec. 2, 1823, West Liberty, Va. (later W.Va.); *m* Priscilla Metcalf, Md.

Birge, Jonathan, Capt., Conn.; *b* Aug. 1734, New Windsor, Conn.; *d* Nov. 8, 1776, Stamford, Conn.; *m* Priscilla Hammond, March 24, 1763, Bolton, Conn.

Blackwell, Joseph, Capt., Va.; *b* 1775; *d* Sept. 8, 1823; *b* & *d* Fauquier Co., Va.; *m* Ann Grayson Gibson, dau. Col. Jonathan Gibson, Aug. 14, 1787, Fauquier Co., Va.

Blount, Jacob, Col., N.C.; *b* 1726; *d* Aug. 17, 1789; *b* & *d* Blount Hall, Lenoir Co., N.C.; *m* Barbara Gray (May 31, 1726–April 8, 1763), 1748, N.C.

Blount, Reading, Maj., N.C.; *b* Feb. 22, 1757, Blount Hall, Lenoir Co., N.C.; *d* Oct. 13, 1807, Washington, D.C.; *m* Lucy Harvey, Feb. 4, 1794.

Bond, William, Col., Mass.; *b* Feb. 17, 1734, Watertown, Mass.; *d* Aug. 30, 1776, Camp Mt. Independence; *m* Lucy Brown, dau. Jonathan & Elizabeth (Simonds) Brown, Feb. 7, 175?.

Bowen, Reese, Ens., Va.; *b* c.1742, Md.; killed Oct. 7, 1780, Battle of King's Mt., N.C.; *m* Lauisa (or Louisa) Levicie Smith (*d* Feb. 15, 1834, age 84 yrs.), 1768.

Bowie, Daniel, Capt., Md.; *b* 1754, Prince Georges Co., Md.; *d* 1777, prisoner of war; unmarried; line went to cousin.

Bradford, Samuel Killett, Capt. Lt., Va.; *b* in England; *d* 1793, buried at sea; *m* Jane Carter of "Blenheim," Albemarle Co., Va., 1781.

Bradley, James, Capt., Va.; *b* 1753; *d* 1828; *m* Caroline Everett.

Breckenridge, Alexander, Capt., Va.; *b* Va.; *d*

Feb. 1801, Ky.; *m* Jane Buchanan Floyd, Dec. 9, 1784; line went to brother.

Breckenridge, Robert, Lt., Va.; *b* Augusta Co., Va.; *d* Sept. 11, 1833, Ky.; unmarried; line went to a collateral heir.

Brevard, Alexander, Capt., N.C.; *b* April 1755, Iredell Co., N.C.; *d* Nov. 1, 1829, Lincoln Co., N.C.; *m* Rebecca Davidson, April 27, 1784, Mecklenburg Co., N.C.

Brodhead, Daniel, Col., Pa.; *b* Marbletown, Ulster Co., N.Y.; baptized Oct. 17, 1736, Kingston, N.Y.; *d* Nov. 15, 1809, Milford, Pa.; *m* Elizabeth DePuy, Ulster Co.

Brodhead, Luke, Capt., N.J. (Pa.); *b* 1737 Pa.; *d* June 19, 1806, Stroudsburg, Pa.; *m* Elizabeth Harrison, 1765, Pa.

Broglie, Charles-Louis-Victor, Prince de, Maréchal, France; *b* Sept. 22, 1756, Paris; *d* (guillotined) July 10, 1794, Paris; *m* Sophie-Rose, Comtesse de Rosen, Feb. 3, 1779.

Brooke, Francis Taliafero, Lt., Va.; *b* Aug. 27, 1763, Smithfield, Va.; *d* March 3, 1851, St. Julien near Fredericks, Md.; *m* Mary Champe Carter, Feb. 14, 1804.

Brooke, George, Col., Va.; *b* before Sept. 28, 1728/38, King and Queen Co., Va.; *d* April 7, 1782, Richmond, Va.; *m* Anna Tunstall.

Brown, Morgan, 1st Lt., N.C.; *b* Jan. 13, 1758, Anson Co., N.C.; *d* Feb. 23, 1840, Nashville, Tenn.; *m* Elizabeth Little (Nov. 24, 1765, S.C.), Jan. 22, 1784, Cheraw, S.C.

Browne, Joseph, Surg., N.J.; *b* 1758, Bridgeport, Dorset Co., England; *d* Jan. 1810, New Diggings, Mo. (Louisiana Purchase); *m* Catharine De Visme, dau. Philip & Ann Bartow De Visme, July 6, 1782, Hermitage, Hohokus, Bergen Co., N.J.

Buell, John Hutchinson, Capt , Conn.; *b* Nov. 21, 1753; *d* Sept. 19, 1813; *b* & *d* Hebron, Conn.; *m* Sarah Taylor Metcalf, Nov. 4, 1800.

Bulkeley, Charles, Capt., Conn.; *b* Dec. 19, 1752/53, Colchester, Conn.; *d* 1848, New London, Conn.; *m* Elizabeth Hallam, Dec. 14, 1779. All children died without issue. Line went to first cousin.

Bulkelly, Charles, Capt., Conn.; *b* May 22, 1752, Colchester, Conn.; *d* Jan. 12, 1824, Granville, N.Y.; *m* Betsy Taintor (1st wife), c.1770.

Burbeck, Henry, Capt., Mass.; *b* Jan. 8, 1754, Boston, Mass.; *d* Oct. 2, 1848, New London, Conn.; *m* Lucy Elizabeth Rudd, Dec. 15, 1813.

Burgess, Basil, 2d Lt., Md.; *b* Anne Arundel Co., Md.; *d* March 30, 1824; *m* Eleanor Dorsey; line went to second cousin.

Burnet, William, Surg. Gen., N.J.; *b* Dec. 2, 1730, Lyons Farms, N.J.; *d* Oct. 7, 1791, Newark, N.J.; *m* Mary Camp (1st wife), dau. Capt. Nathaniel Camp, Jan. 23, 1754, Newark, N.J.

Burnley, Garland, Capt., Va.; *b* Jan. 12, 1753; *d* Aug. 17, 1793; *b* & *d* Orange Co., Va.; *m* Frances Taylor on Nov. 8, 1779.

Burwell, Nathaniel, Maj., Va.; *b* 1750, "Kings Mill," James City Co., Va.; *d* 1802, "Vermont Place," Va.; *m* Martha Digges, March 11, 1780.

Bushnell, David, Capt., Conn.; *b* Aug. 30, 1740, Westbrook (West Parish of Saybrook), Conn.; *d* 1826, near Warrenton, Ga.; unmarried; line went to brother.

Butler, Edward, Lt., Pa.; *b* March 20, 1762, "Mount Pleasant," Cumberland Co., Pa.; *d* May 6, 1803, Springfield, Tenn.; *m* Isabella Fowler, July 14, 1787, near Pittsburgh, Pa.

Butler, Zebulon, Col., Conn.; *b* Jan. 23, 1730/31, Ipswich, Mass.; *d* July 28, 1795, Wilkes-Barre, Pa.; *m* Lydia Johnson (2d wife), 1775, Wyoming, Pa.

Cabell, Nicholas, Col., Va.; *b* Oct. 29, 1750, Warminster, Va.; *d* Aug. 18, 1803, Virginia Springs, Va.; *m* Hannah Carrington, April 16, 1772, Cumberland Co., Va.

Cadwalader, Lambert, Col., N.J. (Pa.); *b* Dec. 1742; *d* Sept. 13, 1823; *b* & *d* Trenton, N.J.; *m* Mary McCall, 1793.

Callis, William Overton, 2d Lt., Va.; *b* March 4, 1756/March 23, 1757, Urbana, Louisa Co., Va.; *d* March 14/30, 1814, "Cuckoo," Louisa Co., Va.; *m* Martha Winston (June 21, 1765– April 29, 1788) (1st wife), Oct. 24, 1782.

Campbell, William, Brig. Gen., Va.; *b* 1745,

Augusta Co., Va.; *d* Aug. 22, 1781, Rocky Mills, Hanover Co., Va.; *m* Elizabeth Henry, April 2, 1776, Hanover Co., Va.

Capers, William, Capt., S.C.; *b* Oct. 13, 1758, St. Thomas Parish, S.C.; *d* Dec. 8, 1812, Woodland, Sumter Parish, S.C.; *m* Mary Singletary, Sept. 10, 1783; line went to cousin once removed.

Carrington, Clement, Cornet, Va.; *b* Nov. 22, 1762; *d* Nov. 28, 1847; *b* & *d* Charlotte Co., Va.; *m* Jane (Watkins) Poage c.1803, Charlotte Co., Va.

Carrington, George, Jr., Lt., Va.; *b* June 21, 1758, Va.; *d* May 27, 1809, Halifax Co., Va.; *m* Sarah Coles Tucker (1765–1812), April 8, 1784.

Cass, Jonathan, Capt., N.H.; *b* Exeter, N.H.; *d* Wapetrika, Ohio; *m* Mary (Mollie) Gilman, Dec. 20, 1781.

Chadwick, Edmund, Surg., N.H.; *b* Feb. 6, 1751, Boxford, Mass.; *d* Nov. 8, 1826, Deerfield Center, N.H.; *m* Elizabeth Gookin, Oct. 3, 1779.

Chambers, James, Col., Pa.; *b* June 5, 1743, Chambersburg, Pa.; *d* April 25, 1805, Loudon Forge, Pa.; *m* Katharine Hamilton, Feb. 16, 1763.

Channing, Walter, 2d Lt., R.I.: baptized Sept. 11, 1757, Newport, R.I.; *d* c.Feb. 8, 1827, Boston, Mass.; *m* Hannah Smith of Charleston, S.C., June 3, 1798.

Chapin, Nathaniel, Ens., N.H.; *b* Dec. 31, 1738; *d* Feb. 10, 1831; *b* & *d* Enfield, Conn.; *m* Sybil Terry (Aug. 8, 1740–June 26, 1775), Dec. 10, 1761, Enfield, Conn.

Chapman, Elijah, Capt., Conn.; *b* Feb. 3, 1753; *d* Dec. 17, 1825; *b* & *d* Tolland, Conn.; *m* Sarah Keeler of Ridgefield, Conn., Oct. 20, 1783.

Chapman, Henry Henley, Lt., Md.; *b* June 9, 1764, Charles Co., Md.; *d* Dec. 5, 1821, Georgetown, Md.; *m* Mary Davidson, dau. John Davidson of Annapolis, Md., Jan. 7, 1799.

Cheesman, Jacob, Capt., N.Y.; *b*?; *d* (killed) Dec. 31, 1775; unmarried; line went to brother.

Chester, John, Col., Conn.; *b* Jan. 18,

1748/49; *d* Nov. 4/5, 1809; *b* & *d* Wethersfield, Conn.; *m* Elizabeth Huntington, Nov. 25, 1773.

Chew, John, 1st Lt., Va.; *b* 1753, Va.; *d* Feb. 19, 1806, Fredericksburg, Va.; *m* Elizabeth Smith.

Chrystie, James, Capt., Pa.; *b* Jan. 13, 1750, Hailes/Hales Quarry near Edinburgh, Scotland; *d* June 1807, New York, N.Y.; *m* Mary Wygandt, dau. Rev. John Albert Wygandt, 1781.

Church, Thomas, Maj., Va.; *b* c.1743, Ireland; *d* Sept. 1812, buried St. James-Perkiomen, Pa.; *m* Ann Lane.

Cilley, Joseph, Col., N.H.; *b* 1734; Aug. 25, 1799; *b* & *d* Nottingham, N.H.; *m* Sarah Longfellow, Nov. 4, 1756, Nottingham, N.H.

Clark, Joseph, Rev. & Dep. Muster-Master, N.J.; *b* Oct. 21, 1751, Elizabethtown, N.J.; *d* Oct. 20, 1813, New Brunswick, N.J.; *m* Margaret Imlay, 1783, Allentown, N.J.

Clark, Thomas, Col., N.C.; *b* ?; *d* Dec. 25, 1792; line went to brother.

Clark, William, Lt., Va.; *b*?, Caroline Co., Va.; *d* Sept. 1, 1838, St. Louis, Mo.; *m* Julia Hancock, Jan. 5, 1808, Fincastle, Va.

Clarkson, Matthew, Maj., N.Y.; *b* Oct. 17, 1758; *d* April 25/26, 1825; *b* & *d* New York, N.Y.; *m* Mary Rutherfurd, May 24, 1785.

Clay, Joseph, Lt. Col., Ga.; *b* Yorkshire, England, Oct. 16, 1741; *d* Nov. 15, 1804, Savannah, Ga.; *m* Ann Legardere, Jan. 2, 1763, Savannah, Ga.

Claypoole, Abraham George, Capt., Pa.; *b* 1756; *d* Feb. 11, 1827; *b* & *d* Philadelphia, Pa.; *m* Elizabeth Steele (2d wife), Nov. 23, 1795, Philadelphia, Pa.

Clements, Henry, Lt., Md.; *b* c.1751/53; *d* after 1790 intestate; *b* & *d* Charles Co., Md.; unmarried; line went to sister.

Cleveland, Aaron, Lt., Conn.; *b* June 29, 1750, Canterbury, Conn.; *d* Sept. 19, 1818, Lebanon, N.H.; *m* Jemima Robinson (Oct. 13, 1750–March 12, 1826), June 12, 1777, Canterbury, Conn.

Clift, Lemuel, Capt., Conn.; *b* Oct. 10, 1755, Plainfield, Conn.; *d* Sept. 13, 1821, Poughkeepsie, N.Y.; *m* Sarah Hall, Dec. 6, 1778, Plainfield, Conn.

Clinton, George, Brig. Gen., N.Y.; *b* July 26, 1739, Little Britain, Orange Co., N.Y.; *d* April 12, 1812, Washington, D.C.; *m* Cornelia Tappan, Feb. 7, 1770.

Clinton, James, Brig. Gen., N.Y.; *b* Aug. 18, 1736; *d* Dec. 22, 1812; *b* & *d* Little Britain, N.Y.; *m* Mary DeWitt, Feb. 18, 1765, Neponach, N.Y.

Cochran, John, Surg. Gen., N.Y.; *b* Sept. 11, 1730, Sadsbury, Fallowfield Township, Chester Co., Pa.; *d* April 6, 1807, Palatine, N.Y.; *m* Gertrude (Schuyler) Schuyler, widow of Peter Schuyler, Dec. 4, 1760.

Cogswell, Amos, Capt., Mass.; *b* Oct. 2/4, 1752, Haverhill, Mass.; *d* Jan. 28, 1826, Dover, N.H.; *m* Lydia (Baker) Wallingford, widow of S. Wallingford, Nov. 13/20, 1785.

Cogswell, Samuel, 1st Lt., Mass. (Conn.); *b* May 23, 1754, Canterbury, Conn.; *d* Aug. 20, 1790, Lansingburgh, N.Y.; *m* Mary Backus (March 18, 1767–Nov. 21, 1834, *b* Windham, Conn.) before 1785.

Cogswell, Thomas, Lt. Col., Mass.; *b* Aug. 4, 1746, Haverhill, Mass.; *d* Sept. 3, 1810, Gilmanton, N.H.; *m* Ruth Badger, Feb. 26, 1770.

Coleman, John, Lt., Va.; *b* 1720, England; *d* c.1781/82, Halifax Co., Va.; *m* Sarah Embry, 1765, Gloucester Co., Va.

Colt, Peter, Lt., Conn.; *b* March 28, 1744, Lyme, Conn.; *d* March 17, 1824, Paterson, N.J.; *m* Sarah Lyman of New Haven, Conn., Oct. 19, 1776.

Comstock, John, 1st Lt., Conn.; *b* June 24, 1734, Montville, Conn.; *d* Sept. 15, 1776; *m* Eunice Stoddard.

Comstock, Samuel, Capt., Conn.; *b* 1747, Montville, Conn.; *d* 1827, Lyme, Conn.; *m* Ester Lee, Feb. 2, 1769.

Cooke, John, 2d Lt., R.I.; *b* 1745, Tiverton, R.I.; *d* Dec. 17, 1812, Newport, R.I.; *m* Sarah Gray.

Cornish, Joseph, Lt., Conn.; *b* June 13, 1729, *d* Dec. 29, 1776, in service; *m* Elizabeth Morton (*d* Nov. 14, 1792); line went to a cousin.

Cox, Joseph, 2d Lt., Pa.; *b* c.1742, New York, N.Y.; *d* unknown (taken prisoner, exchanged Jan. 29, 1781); *m* Susan Ann Haywood, dau. John Johnson and Jane Haywood Johnson, July 31, 1761.

Craig, Isaac, Maj., Pa.; *b* Ireland near Hillsborough, County Down; *d* near Pittsburgh, Pa.; *m* Amelia Neville (*b* April 4, 1763, Winchester, Va.; *d* Feb. 17, 1849), dau. John Neville & Winifred Oldham, Feb. 1, 1785.

Craik, James, Surg., Md.; *b* 1730, Orbigland near Dumfries, Scotland; *d* Feb. 6, 1814, Vaucluse, Fairfax Co., Va.; *m* Marianne Ewell, Nov. 13, 1760.

Cresap, Michael, Capt., Md.; *b* June 29, 1742, Oldtown, Md.; *d* Oct. 18, 1775, New York, N.Y.; *m* Sarah Whitehead of Philadelphia Oldtown, Frederick Co. (renamed Allegheny Co.), Aug. 4, 1764.

Crittenden, John Capt. Lt., Va.; *b* 175?; *d* 1805, Woodford Co., Ky.; *m* Judith Harris.

Croghan, William, Maj., Va.; *b* c.1752; *d* Sept. 1822, Locust Grove, near Louisville, Ky.; *m* Lucy Clark, dau. John & Ann Rogers Clark, 1784/88, Mulberry Hill, Ky.

Cropper, John, Jr., Lt. Col., Va.; *b* Dec. 23, 1755; *d* Jan. 15, 1821; *b* & *d* "Bowman's Folly," Accomac Co., Va.; *m* Margaret Fettitt, June 1776.

Crosby, Ebenezer, Surg., N.Y.; *b* Sept. 30, 1753, Braintree, Mass.; *d* July 16, 1788, New York, N.Y.; *m* Catherine Bedloe, Oct. 11, 1781, Clinton House, New Windsor, N.Y.

Curtiss, Agur, Capt., Conn.; *b* Sept. 11, 1730, Stratford, Conn.; *d* Feb. 8, 1784, Southbury, Conn.; *m* Mercy Hinman, dau. Capt. Wait Hinman, Jan. 30, 1755, Woodbury, Conn.

Davies, William Col., Va.; *b* Hanover Co., Va.; *d* "Millbank," Mecklenburg, Va.; *m* Mary Murray (Gordon), *b* 1754; her mother, Anne Bolling, was a great-great-granddaughter of Pocahontas.

Davis, John, Capt., Pa.; *b* 1732; *d* July 10, 1827; *b* & *d* near Paoli, Tredyfferin Township, Chester Co., Pa.; *m* Anne Morton, 1784.

Dayton, Elias, Brig. Gen. N.J.; *b* July 1737, Elizabeth, N.J.; *d* July 17, 1807; *m* Hannah Rolfe

DeGroot, William, Lt., N.J.; *b* June 7, 1751, Bound Brook, Somerset Co., N.J.; *d* Aug. 28, 1840/41, Middlessex Co., N.J.; *m* Anne La Tourette, Dec. 30, 1780, Bound Brook, N.J.

Deming, Pownal, 1st Lt., Conn.; *b* Sept. 30, 1749, Lyme, Conn., *d* April 9, 1795, Hartford, Conn., *m* Abigail Hubbell, Feb. 19, 1784, New Fairfield, Conn.

Deniston, Daniel, Lt., N.Y.; *b* Feb. 3, 1758; *d* Feb. 3, 1824, New York, N.Y.; *m* Elisabeth Kierstead (1769–1861), May 25, 1784.

de Treville, John La Boularderie, Capt., S.C.; *b* Jan. 26, 1742, Louisbourg, N.S. (New France); *d* Jan. 26, 1791, Port Royal, S.C.; *m* Sarah Julia Wilkinson, Dec. 27, 1778, Beaufort, S.C.

Dodge, Samuel, 1st Lt., N.Y.; *b* 1749, Cow Neck; *d* October 27, 1795/97, N.Y.; *m* Mary Forbes, 1784.

Douglas, Richard, Capt., Conn.; *b* June 25, 1750; *d* March 1, 1816; *b* & *d* New London, Conn.; *m* Lucy Way, Sept. 2, 1804.

DuBois, Henry, Capt., N.Y.; *b* July 26, 1755; *d* May 25, 1794; *b* & *d* Poughkeepsie, N.Y.; *m* Eleanor (Nellie) Terbash, Orange Co., N.Y., June 24, 1780.

Dunn, Abner Martin, Lt., Pa.; *b* c.1755, Middlesex Co., N.J.; *d* July 18, 1795, Cincinnati, Ohio; *m* Priscilla Tyler, Dec. 29, 1787.

Dunscomb, Edward, Capt., N.Y.; *b* May 23, 1754; *d* Nov. 12, 1814, *b* & *d* New York, N.Y.; *m* Mary (Elsworth) Whitehead, June 14, 1786.

Duval, Edward, 1st Lt., Md.; *b* 1755, Prince Georges Co., Md.; *d* Aug. 16, 1780, Battle of Camden, S.C.; unmarried; line went to brother.

Duval, Isaac, Lt., Md.; *b* 1757, Prince Georges Co., Md.; *d* Sept. 8, 1781, in action; unmarried; line went to brother.

Earle, John, Capt., S.C.; *b* June 5, 1737, Frederick Co., Va.; *d* 1815, Spartanburg, S.C.; *m*

Thomassine Prince (1746–1784) (1st wife), 1765, Spartanburg, S.C.

Edwards, Leroy, Capt., Va.; *b* Feb. 9, 1754, Northumberland Co., Va.; *d* April 2, 1800, Naddy Point Plantation, Va.; *m* Mary Glasscock, Northumberland Co., Va.

Eells, Edward, Jr., Capt., Conn.; *b* Aug. 11, 1741; *d* Dec. 8, 1787; *b* & *d* Middletown, Conn.; *m* Abigail (Dunham) Brandegee (widow), April 26, 1770, Middletown, Conn.

Ellis, John, Brig. Chaplain, Conn.; *b* 1727, Cambridge, Mass.; *d* Oct. 20, 1805, Franklin, Conn.; *m* Bethiah Palmer, Oct. 24, 1749.

Elmer, Ebenezer, Surg., N.J.; *b* Aug. 23, 1752; *d* Oct. 18, 1843; *b* & *d* Bridgeton, N.J.; *m* Hannah Seeley, Sept. 9, 1784; line went to brother.

Ely, John, Col., Conn.; *b* Sept. 24, 1737, Lyme, Conn.; *d* Oct. 3, 1800, Pachog (now Westbrook), Conn.; *m* Sarah Worthington, July 15, 1759.

Emerson, Nehemiah, Capt., Mass.; *b* Jan. 20, 1749; *d* Dec. 11, 1832; *b* & *d* Haverhill, Mass.; *m* Polly (Mary) Whittier (1739–1835), Jan. 24, 1784, Haverhill, Mass.

Este, Moses, Capt., N.J.; *b* Jan. 18, 1752, Enfield, Conn.; *d* Feb. 4, 1836, Philadelphia, Pa.; *m* Anne Kirkpatrick (1764–1811), sister of Chief Justice Andrew Kirkpatrick of N.J., 1784.

Ewing, James, Capt., Md.; *b* Somerset Co., Md.; *m* Elizabeth Griffith (March 30, 1770–Sept. 29, 1841), Feb. 15, 1792.

Fairlie, James, Maj., N.Y.; *b* 1757, baptized Nov. 22, 1758, Hempstead, N.Y.; *d* Oct. 10/11, 1830, New York, N.Y.; *m* Maria Yates, dau. Chief Justice Robert & Jane Van Ness Yates, c.1788–90, Kinderhook, N.Y.

Fay, Joseph, Ens., N.H.; *b* Sept. 27, 1738, Westborough, Mass.; *d* Nov. 2, 1777, in service, Albany, N.Y.; *m* Lucy Warren, July 24, 1762.

Fayssoux, Peter, Surg., Ga.; *b* 1744/45, France; *d* Feb. 1, 1795, Charleston, S.C.; *m* Mrs. Ann Smith Johnston (nee Bulline), March 20, 1777.

Fish, Nicholas, Maj., N.Y.; *b* Aug. 28, 1758; *d* June 20, 1833; *b* & *d* New York, N.Y.; *m* Elizabeth Stuyvesant, dau. Petrus Stuyvesant & Margaret Livingston, April 30, 1803, New York, N.Y.

Fitzhugh, Peregrine, Lt. Col., Md.; *b* May 10, 1759, Calvert Co., Md.; *d* Oct. 23, 1810, Sodus Point, N.Y.; *m* Elizabeth Chew (1765, Anne Arundel Co., Md.–June 4, 1854, Sodus Point, N.Y.), dau. Samuel & Elizabeth (Crowley) Chew, Dec. 11, 1781.

Flagg, Henry Collins, Surg., S.C.; *b* Aug. 21, 1742, Newport, R.I., *d* April 1, 1801, St. Thomas Parish, in or near Charleston, S.C.; *m* Rachel Moore (widow of Capt. William Allston), Dec. 5, 1784.

Forman, Jonathan, Lt. Col., N.J.; *b* Oct. 16, 1755, Middletown Point (now Matawan), N.J.; *b* May 25, 1809, Pompey Hill, Cazenovia, Onondaga Co., N.Y.; *m* Mary Ledyard, dau. Young Ledyard, April 2, 1781, Groton, Conn.

Forrest, Uriah, Lt., Col., Md.; *b* 1756, St. Mary's Co., Md.; *d* July 6, 1805, Rosedale, near Georgetown, D.C.; *m* Rebecca Plater, Oct. 11, 1789.

Foster, Thomas, Lt., Mass.; *b* Feb. 18, 1759, Gloucester, Mass.; *d* Dec. 15, 1793, West Indies; *m* Lucy Sayward, May 24, 1785.

Fowler, Theodosius, Capt., N.Y.; *b* 1752, *d* Oct. 16, 1841; *b* & *d* New York, N.Y.; *m* Mary Steele, 1782.

Fox, Joseph, Capt., Conn.; *b* Nov. 10, 1749; *d* March 24, 1820, Hurley (Woodstock), Ulster Co., N.Y.; *m* Sophia Marcy/Marey, Aug. 1, 1783.

Fox, Nathaniel, Maj., Va.; *b* c.1750, King William Co., Va.; *d* 1825, Hanover Co., Va.; *m* Mary Carver King, dau. Robert & Mary (Bailey) King, before 1789.

Frothingham, Benjamin, Capt., Mass.; *b* April 6, 1734, Boston, Mass.; *d* Aug. 19, 1809, Charlestown, Mass.; *m* Mary Deland, May 4, 1762.

Gansevoort, Peter, Col., N.Y.; *b* July 17, 1749, Albany, N.Y.; *d* July 2, 1812; *m* Catherine Van Schaick.

Gardner, Caleb, Lt. Col., R.I.; *b* 1728, Mass.; *d* Oct. 23, 1801, Providence, R.I.; *m* Eleanor Phillips, Aug. 1752.

Gibson, George, Maj., Va.; *b* c.1732, probably Ireland; *d* April 3, 1819, Lee Co., Va.; *m* Elizabeth Smith, probably Augusta Co., Va.

Gilchrist, James, Lt., Pa.; *b* ?, Dauphin Co., Pa.; *d* March 1791, Fayette Co., Pa.; unmarried; line went to brother.

Gildersleeve, Finch, 1st Lt., N.Y.; *b* Sept. 17, 1750, Northport, L.I., N.Y.; *d* March 2, 1812, South East N.Y.; *m* Mary (Polly) Seymour (2d wife), Nov. 2, 1782.

Giles, Aquila, Maj., N.Y.; *b* 1758, Baltimore, Md.; *d* April 8, 1822, New York, N.Y.; *m* Elizabeth Shipton, Oct. 30, 1780.

Giles, James, 2d Lt., N.Y. (N.J.); *b* March 8, 1759, New York, *d* will proved July 30, 1825, Bridgeton, N.J.; *m* Hannah Bloomfield (1768–1823), May 23, 1784.

Glenney, William, 2d Lt., Conn.; *b* Aug. 18, 1759, Westford, Mass.; *d* Nov. 26, 1801, at sea, buried in Milford, Conn.; *m* Mary Green, June 28, 1785.

Glentworth, James, 1st Lt., Pa.; *b* March 15, 1747; *d* Jan. 18, 1839, Philadelphia, Pa.; *m* Elizabeth Granbury, March 12, 1782.

Goldsborough, William, 2d Lt., Md.; *b* Aug. 5, 1763, Talbot Co., Md.; *d* May 22, 1826, Frederick Co., Md.; *m* Sarah Worthington, dau. Col. Nicholas & Catherine Griffith Worthington, Nov. 18, 1792.

Goodale, Nathan, Capt., Mass.; *b* Nov. 11, 1743/44, Brookfield, Mass.; *d* March 1, 1793, captured by the Indians at Sandusky, fell sick and died; *m* Elizabeth Phelps, Sept. 11, 1763/ Nov. 28, 1765, Rutland, Mass.(?)

Goodrich, Isaac, Lt., Conn.; *b* March 23, 1752, Wethersfield, Conn.; *d* Sept. 27, 1813, Waterford, New London, Conn.; *m* Elizabeth Raymond of New London, Feb. 15, 1784.

Gould, Abraham, Col., Conn.; *b* May 10, 1732, Fairfield, Conn.; *d* April 27, 1777, in Danbury Raid; *m* Elizabeth Burr on Jan. 1, 1754.

Gould, Benjamin, Capt., Mass.; *b* May 15, 1751, probably Topsfield, Mass.; *d* May 30,

1841, Newburyport, Mass.; *m* Grizzel (Griselda) Apthorpe Flagg, July 19, 1781.

Graham, John, Maj., N.Y.; *b* ?; *d* May 7, 1832, Schuyler, N.Y.; *m* Julia Ogden.

Grasse, Francois-Joseph-Paul, Comte de, Admiral, France; *b* Sept. 13, 1722, Chateau du Bas, France; *d* Jan. 11, 1788; *m* Antoinette Rosalie Allason, Jan. 28, 1764.

Gray, George, Capt., Va.; *b* 1740/41, Culpeper Co., Va.; *d* Dec. 3, 1823, Louisville, Ky.; *m* Mildred Thompson

Grayson, William, Col., Va.; *b* 1735, Dumphries, Va.; *d* ?; *m* Elenor Smallwood.

Green, John, Col., Va.; *b* 1730, *d* 1793; *b* & *d* Culpeper Co., Va.; *m* Susanna Blackwell (1739–?), dau. William & Elizabeth (Crump) Blackwell.

Green, John, 1st Lt., Va.; *b* ?, Va.; *d* in service Feb. 1, 1783; unmarried; line went to brother.

Greenleaf, William, Lt., Mass.; *b* Jan. 10, 1724, Yarmouth, Mass.; *d* July 21, 1803, New Bedford, Mass., *m* Mary Brown, dau. Judge Robert Brown, June 3, 1747, Plymouth, Mass.

Gregory, Matthew, Lt., Conn.; *b* Aug. 1, 1757, Wilton, Conn., *d* June 4, 1848; *m* Mary DeForest; line went to brother.

Griffith, Charles, 2d Lt., Md.; *b* Dec. 16, 1758, Anne Arundel Co., Md.; *d* prior to 1794, Montgomery Co., Md.; unmarried; line went to brother.

Griffith, Philemon, Capt. (Maj.), Md.; *b* Aug. 29, 1756, Anne Arundel Co., Md.; *d* April 29, 1838, Frederick Co., Md.; unmarried; line went to brother.

Grout, Daniel, 1st Lt., N.H.; *b* 1737, Westborough, Mass.; *d* 1809, Acworth, N.H.; unmarried; line went to brother.

Grubb, Peter, Capt., N.J.; *b* Sept. 8, 1740, Cornwall, Pa.; *d* Jan. 17, 1786, Hopewell Forge, Pa.; *m* Mary Shippen Burd (Jan. 13, 1753–Feb. 23, 1774), Nov. 28, 1771.

Habersham, John, Maj., Ga.; *b* Dec. 23, 1754, Beverly Plantation; *d* Nov. 19, 1799; *b* & *d* Savannah, Ga.; *m* Ann Sarah Camber, dau. Thomas Camber, March 19, 1783, Bryan Co., Ga.

Habersham, Joseph, Col., Ga.; *b* July 28, 1751; *d* Nov. 17, 1815; *b* & *d* Savannah, Ga.; *m* Isabella Rae, dau. John Rae, May 19, 1776, at Brampton Plantation, Ga.

Hackley, John, Lt., Va.; *b* ? King George Co., Va.; *d* will dated March 1799, proved June 15, 1801, Culpeper Co., Va.; unmarried; line went to sister.

Hale, Jonathan, Capt., Conn.; *b* Feb. 1/7, 1720/21, Glastonbury, Conn.; *d* March 7, 1776, Jamaica Plains, Mass.; *m* Elizabeth Welles, Jan. 18, 1743.

Hamilton, Alexander, Lt. Col., N.Y.; *b* Jan. 11, 1757, Nevis, BWI; *d* July 12, 1804, New York; *m* Elizabeth Schuyler, Dec. 17, 1780, Albany, N.Y.

Hammond, Abijah, 1st Lt., N.Y.; *b* Feb. 22, 1757, Cambridge, Mass.; *d* Dec. 30, 1832, Westchester, N.Y.; *m* Catharine Ludlow Ogden in 1791.

Hammond, Thomas, Capt. Md.; *b* 1745, Anne Arundel Co., Md.; *d* Oct. 1776, N.Y., in battle; *m* Elizabeth Jacob c.1770, Anne Arundel Co., Md.; line went to a cousin.

Hand, Abraham, Lt., Conn.; *b* Oct. 17, 1751, Durham, Conn.; *d* 1813, New Lebanon, N.Y.; *m* Ruth Southworth in 1772, Durham, Conn.

Handy, George, Capt., Md.; *b* Nov. 23, 1756, Somerset Co., Md.; *d* July 19, 1820, Princess Anne, Md.; *m* Elizabeth Wilson, March 21, 1787.

Hardin, John, 1st Lt., Va.; *b* Oct. 1, 1753, Fauquier Co., Va.; *d* April 1792, killed by Indians in Ohio; *m* Jane Daviess.

Harris, Arthur, Lt., Md.; *b* 1730, Calvert Co., Md.; *d* 1800; *m* Elizabeth Green, 1750.

Harris, Jacob, Surg., N.J.; *b* probably in N.J.; *d* after Nov. 1783, Long Island, N.Y.; no record of marriage; line went to brother.

Harris, John, 2d Lt., Va.; *b* Oct. 13, 1758; *d* Dec. 4, 1815; *b* & *d* in Va.; *m* Rebecca Britton, May 24, 1794.

Harris, Jordan, Lt., Va.; *b* May 20, 1763, Powhatan Co., Va.; *d* Oct. 7, 1826, Princeton, Ky.; *m* Elizabeth Mosby Cannon, April 2, 1789, Mt. Ida, Buckingham Co., Va.

Harris, West, Lt., N.C.; *b* 1756, Isle of Wight

Co., Va.; *d* July 19, 1826, Montgomery Co., N.C.; *m* Edith Ledbetter, dau. Charles & Mary (Randal) Ledbetter, 1786, Montgomery Co., N.C.

Harrison, Charles, Col., Va.; *b* Sept. 30, 1742, "Berkeley," Charles City Co., Va.; *d* 1794/96, Chesterfield Co., Va.; *m* Mary Herbert Claiborne (1745–July 25, 1775), 1761.

Hawkins, Philemon, Col., N.C.; *b* Dec. 3, 1752, Granville Co., N.C.; *d* Jan. 28, 1833, Pleasant Hill, Warren Co., N.C.; *m* Lucy Davis, Aug. 31, 1775.

Heard, John, Capt., N.J.; *b* Dec. 1742/52, near Woodbridge, N.J.; *d* Feb. 16, 1826, New Brunswick, N.J.; *m* Mary Sargant/Sariant/Sargent, dau. Samuel Sargent (c.1762–1812), Dec. 11, 1783.

Henry, John, Capt., Md.; *b* c.1715, Rehoboth, Md.; *d* 1781; *m* Dorothy Rider.

Heron, James Gordon, Capt., Md.; *b* ?; Dumfries, Scotland; *d* Dec. 30, 1809, Franklin, Pa.; *m* Eleanor Evans, dau. James and Eleanor Kirkpatrick Evans, March 1777, "Evans' Choice," Cecil Co., Md.

Hill, Philip, Lt., Md.; *b* 1740; *d* unknown, living in 1800 or 1805; unmarried; line went to first cousin.

Hinman, Benjamin, Col., Conn.; *b* Jan. 22, 1720, Woodbury (now Southbury) Conn.; *d* March 22, 1810, Southbury, Conn.; *m* Mollie/Mary Stiles, dau. Lt. Francis Stiles, 1744.

Holden, Abel, Capt., Mass.; *b* Oct. 2. 1752, Sudbury, Mass.; *d* Aug. 3, 1818, New York, N.Y.; *m* Thankful Cutting, July 23, 1777, Waltham, Mass.

Holmes, Hardy, Capt., N.C.; no information; line went to brother, Owen Holmes, *b* 1762, Duplin Co., N.C.; *d* July 17, 1814, Sampson Co., N.C.; *m* Ann Clinton, Duplin Co., N.C.

Hopkins, Samuel, Lt. Col., Va.; *b* April 19, 1753, Albermarle Co., Va.; *d* Sept. 16, 1819, Henderson Co., Ky.; *m* Elizabeth Bugg, marriage bond dated Jan. 10, 1783.

Hoppin, Benjamin, Capt., R.I., *b* May 12, 1747, Attleboro, Mass.; *d* Nov. 30, 1809, Providence, R.I.; *m* Anna Rawson, Jan. 25, 1770.

Howard, Vachel (Vashel) Denton, Capt., Md.; *b* 1751, Elkridge Hundred, Md.; *d* March 15, 1778, N.J.; unmarried; line went to first cousin.

Howe, Baxter, Capt. Lt., N.Y.; *b* Sept. 11, 1748, Marlborough, Mass.; *d* Sept. 20, 1781, Ethton (Elkton), Md.; *m* Mary Moone (Oct. 15, 1748–March 14, 1819), May 13, 1779.

Howell, Joseph, Capt., Pa.; *b* June 30, 1750, *d* Aug. 8, 1798; *b* & *d* Philadelphia, Pa.; *m* Rebecca Betterton, 1785.

Hubbard, Elijah, Lt., Conn.; *b* baptized Aug. 18, 1745, Middletown, Conn., *d* May 30, 1808, Hartford, Conn.; *m* Hannah Kent, Jan. 5, 1772.

Hubbard, Hezekiah, Lt., Conn.; *b* 1742; *d* Nov. 30, 1804; *b* & *d* Middletown, Conn.; *m* Esther Foster, Oct. 8, 1764, Middletown, Conn.

Hubbard, Jonas, Capt., Mass.; *b* May 21, 1739, Worcester, Mass.; *d* Jan. 1, 1776, of wounds and exposure, Quebec, Canada; *m* Mary Stevens, March 7, 1759, Worcester, Mass.

Hubley, Adam, Jr., Lt. Col., Pa.; *b* Jan. 9, 1752, Lancaster, Pa.; *d* March 4, 1798, Philadelphia, Pa.; *m* Lydia Field, April 10, 1783.

Hull, Joseph, Lt., Conn. (N.J.); *b* Oct. 27, 1750, Derby, Conn.; *d* Jan. 1825/26; *m* Sarah Bennett of Derby, Conn.

Hume, Francis, Capt., Va.; *b* c.1730, Spotsylvania Co., Va.; *d* (Administrator of estate) 1813, Culpeper Co., Va.; *m* Elizabeth Duncan, Aug. 30, 1763, Fauquier Co., Va.

Hungerford, Benjamin, 2d Lt., Conn.; *b* June 1741, Bristol, Conn.; *d* Sept. 4, 1775, Woodbury, Conn.; *m* Keziah Walker.

Hunt, Abraham, Capt., Mass.; *b* June 2, 1748, Braintree, Mass.; buried Boston, Mass.; *m* Mary St. Leger, Sept. 19, 1771.

Hunt, Thomas, Capt., Mass.; *b* Sept. 17, 1754, Watertown, Mass.; *d* Aug. 18, 1808, Bellefontaine, Mo.; *m* Eunice Wellington of Waltham, dau. Samuel & Abigail Wellington, Aug. 16, 1784.

Hunter, Andrew, Brig. Chaplain, N.J.; *b* April 30, 1750, Little York, Pa.; *d* Feb. 24,

1823, Washington, D.C.; *m* Anna Riddell (1st wife), Oct. 2, 1775.

Huntington, Jedediah, Brig. Gen., Conn.; *b* Aug. 4, 1743, Norwich, Conn.; *d* Sept. 25, 1818, New London, Conn.; *m* Ann Moore, dau. Thomas Moore of New York City, 1777.

Hyatt, Abraham, 1st Lt., N.Y.; *b* June 17, 1747; *d* June 30/Aug. 3, 1820; *m* Sarah Ryder/Rider.

Hyde, James, Lt., Conn.; *b* July 17, 1752; *d* April 9, 1809, Bean Hill; *b* & *d* Norwich, Conn.; *m* Martha Nevins (1756–1823), dau. David & Mary (Lathrop) Nevins, April 5, 1774, Norwich, Conn.

Hyer, Jacob, Ens., N.J.; *b* Sept. 5, 1763, New Brunswick, N.J.; *d* Feb. 23, 1812, Trenton, N.J.; unmarried; line descends through William Hyer.

Irvine, William, Brig. Gen., Pa.; *b* Nov. 3, 1741, near Erniskillen, Fermanagh Co., Ireland; *d* July 30, 1804, Philadelphia, Pa.; *m* Ann Callender, c.1772, Carlisle, Pa.

Jackson, Amasa, Ens., Mass.; *b* June 5, 1765, Newtown, Mass.; *d* March 24/25, 1824, New York, N.Y.; *m* Mary Phelps (Sept. 5, 1778–Sept. 11, 1859, Canandaigua, N.Y.), dau. Oliver & Mary Seymour Phelps, Jan. 10, 1798.

Jackson, Michael, Col., Mass.; *b* Dec. 18, 1734; *d* April 10, 1801; *b* & *d* Newtown, Mass.; *m* Ruth Parker (*d* 1810), dau. Ebenezer & Sarah (Seavers) Parker, Jan. 31, 1759.

Jameson, John, Lt. Col., Conn. (and Va.); *b* 1751; *d* Nov. 20, 1810; *b* & *d* Culpeper Co., Va.; *m* Rachel Berrim (1st wife), dau. John & Sarah Fish Berrim of N.Y., Feb. 25, 1785, Va.; *m* Elizabeth Davenport (2d wife), dau. Col. Burkett & ? Brown Davenport of Culpeper; line went to brother.

Jamison, Adam, Lt., Md.; *b* 1752; *d* March 16, 1795; *b* & *d* Baltimore Co., Md.; *m* Mary Johnson, Sept. 10, 1786, in Baltimore Co., Md.

Jaquett, Joseph, 2d Lt., Pa.; *b* New Castle, Del.; *d* Aug. 27, 1776, killed in Battle of Long Island; *m* Susanna Jaquet, April 17, 1750.

Johnson (Johnston), George, Lt. Col., Va.; *b* c.1738; *d* April 18, 1828; *b* & *d* Fauquier Co., Va.; *m* Elizabeth Blakemore, Feb. 1, 1786, Lancaster Co., Va.

Johnston, Francis, Col., Pa.; *b* Oct. 17, 1748, New London Cross Roads, Pa.; *d* 1815, Philadelphia, Pa.; *m* Alice Erwin, Dec. 13, 1775, Philadelphia, Pa.

Jones, Allen, Brig. Gen., N.C.; *b* Dec. 24, 1739, Halifax Co., N.C.; *d* Nov. 10, 1798, "Mt. Gallant," North Hampton Co., N.C.; *m* Rebecca Edwards, Sept. 3, 1768, Brunswick Co., Va.

King, Rufus, Capt., Mass.; *b* March 24, 1755, Scarborough, Me.; *d* April 29, 1827, Jamaica, N.Y.; *m* Mary Alsop, dau. John & Mary (Frogat) Alsop, March 30/31, 1786.

Kirby, Ephraim, Ens., R.I. (Conn.); *b* Feb. 23, 1757, Judea Society, Ancient Woodbury, Conn.; *d* Oct. 20, 1804, Fort Stoddard, Ala. (Mississippi Territory); *m* Ruth Marvin, dau. Judge Reynold & Ruth Welsh Marvin, March 17, 1784.

Kirkwood, Robert, Capt., Del.; *b* 1756, Mill Creek Hundred, Newcastle Co., Del.; *d* Nov. 4, 1791, near Ft. Recovery in St. Clair's defeat, Ohio Territory; *m* Sarah England, White Clay Creek Hundred, Del.

Knox, Henry, Maj. Gen., Mass.; *b* July 25, 1750, Boston, Mass.; *d* Oct. 25, 1806, Thomaston, Maine; *m* Lucy Flucker, dau. Thomas Flucker, last royal secretary of colony, June 16, 1774, Boston, Mass.

Kollock, Shepard (also Shephard), 1st Lt., N.J.; *b* 1750/51?, Lewes, Del.; *d* July 28, 1839, Philadelphia, Pa.; *m* Susan Arnett, June 5, 1777, Essex Co., N.J.

Lamar, William, Capt., Md.; *b* 1755, Frederick Co., Md.; *d* Jan. 8, 1838, Cumberland, Alleghany Co., Md.; *m* Margaret Worthington (1767–March 17, 1821), dau. John & Mary Todd Worthington, 1784, Baltimore, Md.

Lamb, John, Col., N.Y.; *b* Jan. 1, 1735; *d* May 31, 1800; *b* & *d* New York, N.Y. (buried Trinity Church); *m* Catherine Jandine (1733–1807), dau. Charles Jandine, Nov. 13, 1755, New York.

Lane, Derick, Capt., N.J.; *b* April 30, 1755,

Somerset Co., Bedminster Township, N.J.; *d* March 26, 1831, Troy, N.Y.; *m* Engelthe/Angelica/Engeltie Van Rensselaer (2d wife), July 14, 1805, Troy, N.Y.

Lansdale, Thomas Lancaster, Maj., Md.; *b* Nov. 10, 1748, Prince Georges Co., Md.; *d* Jan. 19, 1803, Md.; *m* Cornelia Van Horne (2d wife), Feb. 12, 1782.

Lasher, John, Col., N.Y.; *b* March 4, 1724; *d* Feb. 22, 1806, New York, N.Y.; *m* Catharine Ernest (2d wife), June 21, 1763, New York, N.Y.

Lawrence, John, Capt., Pa.; *b* Sept. 15, 1751; *d* Nov. 15, 1796; *b* & *d* Philadelphia, Pa.; *m* Elizabeth St. Clair, dau. Gen. & Gov. Arthur St. Clair, 1782, Pottsgrove (now Pottstown), Pa.

Lawrence, Nathaniel, Lt., N.C. (and N.Y.); *b* July 11, 1761, Newtown, L.I., N.Y.; *d* July 5, 1797, Hampstead, N.Y.: *m* Elizabeth (Eliza) Berrien, April 14, 1787.

Lawton (Laughton), William, Surg. Mate., Mass.; *b* April 9, 1759, Leicester, Mass.; *d* 1800, Flushing, N.Y.; *m* Abigail Farrington, dau. John Farrington & Mary Bowne Farrington (Dec. 12, 1763–Feb. 26, 1858), March 27, 1784, Flushing, N.Y.

Lay, Asa, Capt., Conn; *b* 1749; *d* Feb. 23, 1813; *m* Sarah Wolcott, April 18, 1770.

Leavenworth, Elia, Maj., Conn.; *b* Dec. 10, 1748, Huntington, Conn.; *d* 1790, Savannah, Ga.; *m* Sarah (Sally) Eliot, Dec. 23, 1778.

Ledyard, Benjamin, Maj., N.Y. (and N.J.); *b* March 5, 1753, Groton, Conn.; *d* Nov. 9, 1803, Aurora, Cayuga Co., N.Y.; *m* Catherine Forman of Pennsylvania, Jan. 22, 1775.

Ledyard, Isaac, Surg. Mate, N.Y.; *b* Nov. 5, 1754, Ledyard (Groton) Conn.; *d* Aug. 28, 1803, Staten Island, N.Y.; *m* Ann McArthur, March 13, 1785.

Lee, Elisha, Capt., Conn.; *b* ?; *d* Oct. 15, 1815; *m* Abigail Murdock, 1761.

Lee, Henry, Lt. Col., Va.; *b* Jan. 29, 1756, Leesylvania, Va.; *d* March 25, 1818, Cumberland Island, Ga.; *m* Matilda Lee (*d* May 1790), dau. Philip Ludwell & Elizabeth Steptoe Lee, spring 1782, Va.

Lee, Noah, Capt., Conn.; *b* Oct. 15, 1743, Norwalk, Conn.; *d* May 5, 1840, Castleton, Vt.; *m* Dorcas Bird, 1770.

Lee, William Raymond, Col., Mass.; *b* 1744, Manchester, Mass.; *d* Oct. 1824, Salem, Mass.; *m* Mary Lemmon.

Leighton, Samuel, Capt., N.H.; *b* March 16, 1740, Eliot, Me.; *d* Feb. 27, 1802, Kittery, Me.; *m* Abigail Frost, Oct. 1767, Eliot, Me.; line went to cousin.

Lenox, David, Capt., N.J.; baptized Oct. 14, 1753, Kirkudbright, Scotland; *d* April 10, 1828; unmarried; line went to brother.

Lewis, Archilaus, 2d Lt., Mass.; *b* Feb. 15, 1753, Berwick, Me. (then Mass.); *d* Jan. 2, 1834, Westbrook, Me.; *m* Elizabeth Brown (2d wife), Sept. 18, 1791.

Lewis, George, Capt., Va.; *b* March 14, 1757, Fredericksburg, Va., at "Kenmore"; *d* 1821, at "Marmion," King George Co., Va.; line went to Robert Lewis.

Lewis, Morgan, Col., New York; *b* Oct. 16, 1754; *d* April 7, 1844; *b* & *d* New York, N.Y.; *m* Gertrude Livingston, May 11, 1779, "Clermont," N.Y.

Lewis, Samuel, Lt., N.Y.: *b* Sept. 29, 1754, New York, N.Y.; *d* Sept. 20, 1822, Lancaster, Pa.; *m* Elizabeth Anne Godfrey, 1778.

Lightfoot, Philip, Lt., Va.; *b* 1750; *d* 1786; *b* & *d* Caroline Co., Va.; *m* Mary Warner Lewis; line went to sister.

Lighthall, William, Lt., N.Y.; *b* 1759; *d* Oct. 5, 1822; *b* & *d* Schenectady, N.Y.; *m* Sarah Mersalis, Oct. 9, 1793.

Lingan, James McCubbin, Capt., Md.; *b* May 31, 1751, Harford Co., Md.; *d* killed July 28, 1812, Baltimore, Md.; *m* Janet Henderson (*b* Sept. 2, 1765).

Livingston, Henry Beekman, Col., N.Y.; *b* Nov. 9, 1750, Clermont Manor, N.Y.; *d* Nov. 5, 1831, Columbia or Dutchess Co., N.Y.; *m* Ann Harris Shippen, March 1781.

Livingston, Henry Brockholst, Lt. Col., N.Y.; *b* Nov. 25, 1757, New York, N.Y.; *d* Washington, D.C., March 18, 1823; *m* Catharine Keteltas (?), Dec. 2, 1784.

Logan, Samuel, Maj., N.Y.; *b* 1730, Dublin, Ireland; *d* 1825, New Windsor, N.Y.; *m* Abigail Clark.

Long, Nicholas, Col., N.C.; *b* Eastern Shore of Va., "came to N.C. 1750"; *d* Aug. 22, 1819, Ga.; *m* Mary McKinnie, Aug. 24, 1761, Roanoke River, N.C.

Long, William, Capt., Va.; *b* Oct. 1755, Augusta Co., Va.; *d* 1822, Grayson Co., Va.; *m* Catherine Surface, 1778, Augusta Co., Va.

Lyman, Daniel, Brig. Maj., R.I. (Conn.); *b* Jan. 27, 1756, Durham, Conn.; *d* Oct. 16/Dec. 16, 1830, Providence, R.I.; *m* Mary Wanton, January 10/20, 1782.

Lytle, William, Capt., N.C.; *b* Feb. 17, 1755, Pa.; *d* Sept. 4, 1829, Murfreesboro, Tenn.; *m* Nancy Taylor, c.1787.

McCoskry, Samuel Alexander, Surg., Pa.; *b* Aug. 1751; *d* Sept. 4, 1814; *b* & *d* Carlisle, Pa.; *m* Alison Nisbet, dau. Rev. Charles & Anne Tweedie Nisbet, Carlisle, Pa.

McCullen, James, Capt., R.I.; *b* 1753, County Atrim, Ireland; *d* Dec. 5, 1788, New York, N.Y.; *m* Mary Curry, Oct. 28, 1773, First Presbyterian Church, New York, N.Y.

McDougall, Alexander, Maj. Gen., N.Y.; *b* 1732, Island of Islay, Hebrides, Scotland (at Toradale, parish Kildalton (?)); *d* 1786 New York, N.Y.; *m* Nancy McDougall, dau. Stephen McDougall, 1751.

McDowell, John, Surg., Pa.; *b* 1748, Lancaster Co., Pa.; *d* Feb. 21, 1814, "Troy Farm," Allegheny Co., Pa.; *m* Margaret Sanderson Lukens.

McHenry, James, Maj., Md.; *b* Nov. 16, 1752, Ballymena, Ireland; *d* May 3, 1816, Baltimore, Md.; *m* Margaret Caldwell, dau. David & Grace Caldwell, Jan. 8, 1784, Philadelphia, Pa.

McIntosh, Lachlan, Brig. Gen., Ga.; *b* March 17, 1725, Raits, Scotland; *d* Feb. 20, 1806, Savannah, Ga.; *m* Sarah Threadcraft.

McKennan, William, Capt., Del.; *b* May 8, 1758, Christiana Hundred, Newcastle Co., Del.; *d* Jan. 14, 1810, Washington, Pa.; *m* Elizabeth Thompson, 1781, Newcastle, Del.

McKinley, John, Lt., Va.; *b* ?; killed in action June 1782; *m* Mary Connolly, Oct. 10, 1763.

McKnight, Charles, Surg., N.Y.; *b* Oct. 10, 1750, Cranbury, Middlesex Co., N.J.; *d* Nov. 16, 1791, New York, N.Y.; *m* Mary Morin Scott Litchfield (widow) (July 17, 1753– Sept. 19, 1796), dau. John Morin Scott, April 22, 1778.

McPherson, Samuel, Capt., Md.; *b* 1754; *d* after 1800; *b* & *d* Charles Co., Md.; *m* Elizabeth Goldsmith, 1775, Charles Co., Md.

Magill, Charles, Col., Va.; *b* July 10, 1760, near Belfast, Ireland; *d.* late March or early April 1827, "The Meadows," near Winchester, Va.; *m* Mary Buckner Thruston, May 24, 1792, "Mount Zion," near Winchester, Frederick Co., Va.

Malcom, William, Col., N.Y.; *b* 1745, Scotland; *d* Sept. 1, 1791, New York, N.Y.; *m* Ann Ayscouth, Feb. 3, 1772.

Maltbie (Maltby), Jonathan, Lt., Conn.; *b* Dec. 17, 1744, Stamford, Conn.; buried Feb. 11, 1798, Fairfield, Conn.; *d* while in command of the *Argus;* *m* Elizabeth Allen, Oct. 23, 1768.

Marshall, Elihu, Capt., N.Y.; *b* Jan. 18, 1750, Nantucket, R.I.; *d* April 18, 1806, New York, N.Y.; *m* Susanna Brown, Sept. 12, 1775.

Marshall, Thomas, Col., Va.; *b* April 2, 1730, Westmoreland Co., Va.; *d* June 22, 1802, Mason Co. (or Woodford Co.), Ky., or Westmoreland Co., Va.; *m* Mary Randolph Keith, dau. Rev. James & Mary Isham (Randolph) Keith, 1754, prob. Prince William Co. (later Fauquier Co.), Va.

Martin, Thomas, Capt., Va.; *b* 1752, Abermarle, Va.; *d* 1818, Newport, Ky.; *m* Susan W. Ledbetter, 1790, Washington, Ga.

Massie, Thomas, Maj., Va.; *b* Aug. 11/22, 1747; New Kent Co., Va.; *d* Feb. 2, 1834, Nelson Co., Va.; *m* Sally Cocke (1760–1836), April 11, 1781.

Maupin, Gabriel, Capt., Va.; *b* Feb. 12, 1737; *d* Nov. 10, 1800; *b* & *d* Williamsburg, Va.; *m* Dorcas Allen (2d wife), Oct. 20, 1768, Williamsburg, Va.

Mead, Jasper, 2d Lt., Conn.; *b* 1755; *d* 1830; *m* Elizabeth Benedict, April 8, 1779.

Meigs, John, 1st Lt., Conn.; *b* Nov. 21, 1753;

Middletown, Conn.; *d* Nov. 24, 1826, New Hartford, Conn.; *m* Elizabeth Henshaw, Jan. 18, 1781, Middletown, Conn.; line went to brother.

Mercer, Hugh, Brig. Gen., Va.; baptized Jan. 1725/26, Aberdeen, Scotland; *d* Jan. 12, 1777, Princeton, N.J.; wounded at Princeton; *m* Isabella Gordon.

Miller, Henry, Lt. Col., Pa.; *b* Feb. 13, 1751, Lancaster Co., Pa.; *d* April 5, 1824, Carlisle, Pa.; *m* Sarah Ann Ursula Rose, June 26, 1770/71.

Milliken, James, Capt., R.I.; *b* near Montgomery, Orange Co., N.Y.; killed in action at Fort Clinton/Montgomery, Orange Co., N.Y., Oct. 6, 1777; *m* Mary ?

Milling, Hugh, Capt., S.C.; *b* Feb. 19, 1752, Drumbo, County Down, Ireland; *d* May 7, 1837, Fairfield Co., S.C.; *m* Elizabeth Burney, June 8, 1780.

Milton, John, Capt., Ga.; *b* c.1740, Halifax Co., N.C.; *d* Oct. 17, 1803/c.1804, Louisville/Burke Co., Ga.; *m* Hannah Spencer/Spenser of South Carolina.

Minnis, Callohill/Callowhill, Capt., Va.; *b* c.1749, Yorktown, Va.; *d* Sept. 2, 1812, Campbell Co., Va.; *m* (Mrs.) Mary (Mason) Aylett, c.1782, King William Co., Va.; line went to niece.

Mitchell, John, 1st Lt., Ga.; *b* Aug. 25, 1748, Va.; *d* Jan. 3, 1804, Hancock Co., Ga.; *m* Sarah Thweatt, dau. James & Sarah Sturdevant Thweatt.

Mooers, Benjamin, Lt. Col., Mass.; *b* April 1, 1758, Haverhill, Essex Co., Mass.; *d* Feb. 23, 1838, Plattsburgh, N.Y.; *m* Hannah Platt, April 24, 1791.

Moore, James, Brig. Gen., N.C.; *b* Jan. 15, 1737; *d* April 9, 1777, N.C.; *m* Ann Ivey.

Moore, John, Lt., N.C.; *b* no record; line went to Robert Moore, Va., *b* c.1758; *d* 1815; *m* Elizabeth McGehee (2d wife), dau. Capt. Mumford McGhee, 1784, Caswell Co., N.C.

Moorehead, James, Lt., N.C.; *b* 1750, Pittsylvania Co., (or Fauquier Co.) Va.; *d* will probated 1815, Richmond Co., N.C.; unmarried; line went to brother.

Morris, James, Capt., Conn.; *b* Jan. 19, 1752; *d* April 2, 1820; *m* Elizabeth Hubbard (1st wife), Rhoda Farnham (2d wife); line went to sister.

Morris, Lewis, Maj., S.C.; *b* 1752, "Morrisania," Westchester Co., N.Y.; *d* Nov. 22, 1824, Charleston, S.C.; *m* Ann Elliott, Jan. 23, 1783, Charleston, S.C.

Mortemart, Victurnien-Henri-Elezear/Elzéar/Eleazar de Rochechouart, Vicomte de, Capitaine, France; *b* Jan. 11, 1757, Paris; *d* at sea March 17, 1783, in service of his country; line went to brother.

Moylan, Stephen, Col., Pa.; *b* 1732, Cork, Ireland; *d* April 13, 1811, Philadelphia, Pa.; *m* Mary Ricketts Van Horn, Sept. 12, 1778.

Munson, Aeneas, Jr., Surg. Mate, Conn.; *b* Sept. 11, 1763; *d* Aug. 22, 1852; *b* & *d* New Haven, Conn.; *m* Mary Shepherd (1772–1848), dau. Levi Shepherd, May 6, 1754, Northampton, Mass.

Murdock, William, Cornet, Md.; *b* c.1748, Frederick Co., Md.; *d* Feb. 22, 1791, Georgetown, Md.; *m* Jane Contee Harrison, May 27, 1793, Prince Georges Co., Md.; line went to first cousin.

Murray, Francis, Maj., Pa.; *b* 1731, Ireland; *d* Nov. 13, 1816, New Town, Pa.; *m* Martha Gamble c.1768, probably Westmoreland City, Pa.

Mytinger, Jacob, 1st Lt., Pa.; *b* Sept. 19, 1750, Brettach (now Brettin), Baden, Germany; *d* 1793, Philadelphia, Pa.; *m* Elizabeth Matthieu/Matthien, Oct. 1778/79, near Pottsgrove, Pa.

Nazro, Nathaniel, Capt. Lt., Mass.; baptized Feb. 21, 1754, Boston, Mass.; *d* c. 1781/82. Mill Prison, Plymouth, England; unmarried; line went to brother.

Neale, Francis, Surg., Md.; *b* 1750, St. Mary's Co., Md.; *d* on active duty 1781; unmarried; line went to cousin.

Nelson, John, Capt., Va.; *b* 1761 Va.; *d* 1845, Louisville, Ky.; *m* Martha Patton c. 1793, Louisville, Ky.

Nelson, Thomas, Brig. Gen., Va.; *b* Dec. 26, 1738, Yorktown, Va.; *d* Jan. 4, 1789,

Mount Air, Hanover Co., Va.; *m* Lucy Grymes, July 29, 1762.

Neville, John. Col., Va. (Penn.); *b* near headwaters of Occoquan Creek, July 26, 1721/31; *d* July 29, 1803, Montour's Island, Allegheny Co., Pa.; *m* Winifred Oldham, Aug. 24, 1754.

Nicholas, Samuel, Maj., Pa.; *b* 1750; *d* Sept. 9, 1790; *b* & *d* Philadelphia, Pa.; *m* Mary Jenkins (*b* 1752), 1778.

Nichols, Francis, Maj., Pa.; *b* 1737, Enniskillen, Ireland; *d* Feb. 13, 1812, Potts Grove, in Pottstown, Pa.; *m* Elizabeth Strombourg.

Nicholson, James, Capt., Pa.; *b* Dec. 5, 1734, Chestertown, Md.; *d* Sept. 2, 1804, Greenwich Village, New York, N.Y.; *m* Frances Witter, dau. Thomas & Mary Lewis Witter of Bermuda, May 1/2, 1763, New York, N.Y.

Nixon, Thomas, Col., Mass.; *b* April 27/May 7, 1736; *d* Aug. 12, 1800, in passage from Boston, Mass., to Portland, Maine; *m* Bethiah Stearns, 1757.

Noailles, Louis-Marie, Vicomte de Mestre de Camp, France; *b* probably April 17, 1756, probably Paris, France; *d* probably Jan. 5, 1804, probably Havana, Cuba; *m* Anne Jeanne Bonne Pauline de Noailles, dau. duc d'Ayen, Sept. 19, 1773.

North, William, Capt., Mass.; *b* 1755, Fort Frederick, Pemaquid, Maine; *d* Jan. 3, 1836, New York, N.Y.; *m* Mary Livingston Duane, dau. Hon. James Duane, Oct. 14, 1787.

Ogden, Moses, Ens., N.J.; *b* Aug. 25, 1760; *d* killed June 7, 1780, Battle of Connecticut Farms, N.J.

Oldham, George, 1st Lt., Va.; *b* c.1750, probably Northumberland Co., Va.; *d* c.1789/90, St. George's Parish, Accomac Co., Va.; *m* twice; line went to first wife's daughter, Elizabeth (Oldham) Jones.

Page, Carter, Capt., Va.; *b* 1758, "North End," Gloucester (now Mathews) Co., Va.; *d* April 8/9, 1825, Cumberland Co., Va.; *m* Mary Cary (1st wife), dau. Col. Archibald and Mary Randolph Cary, April 12, 1783, "Tuckahoe," Goochland Co., Va.

Pange, Marie-Louis-Thomas, Marquis de, Col., France; *b* May 11, 1763/68; *d* Jan. 29, 1796, *b* & *d* Vendée au Pin; *m* Marie Felicité Victoire Josephine de Valincourt, Aug. 24, 1784, Paris, France; line went to brother.

Pannill, Joseph, Lt. Col., Ga.; *b* c.1747, Culpeper Co./ Orange Co., Va.; *d* 1811, Adams Co., Miss.; *m* Agnes ?; line went to brother.

Parker, William Harwar, Capt., Va.; *b* Jan. 13, c.1752, Westmoreland Co./Essex Co., Va.; *d* Dec. 1815, Westmoreland Co., Va.; *m* Mary Sturman, Westmoreland Co., Va., 1783.

Parsons, Samuel Holden, Maj. Gen., Conn.; *b* May 14, 1737, Lyme, Conn.; *d* Dec. 17, 1789, Marietta, Ohio; *m* Mehitabel/Mehetabel Mather, Sept. 10, 1761.

Peaslee, Zacheus, Lt., Pa.; *b* 1765, Haverhill, Mass.; *d* July 12, 1810, Burlington, Vt.; *m* Sally Stanton, Aug. 1, 1796.

Pemberton, Thomas, Capt., Va.; *b* ?, King William Co., Va.; *d* ? Goochland Co., Va.; *m* Dice (called Dicey) King, Dec. 15, 1791, Va.

Pendleton, Nathaniel, Capt., Va.; *b* 1746, Martinsburg, Va.; *d* Oct. 20, 1821, Hyde Park, N.Y.; *m* Susan Bard, Sept. 22, 1785, Savannah, Ga.

Pettibone, Jonathan, Col., Conn.; *b* 1709, Simsbury, Conn.; *d* Sept. 26, 1776, in service, Rye, N.Y.; *m* Martha Humphry.

Phelps, Thomas, Lt., Conn.; *b* July 17, 1741; *d* Feb. 28, 1789, *b* & *d* Simsbury, Conn.; *m* Dorothy Lamb Woodbridge.

Phifer, Martin, Capt., N.C.; *b* March 25, 1756; *d* Nov. 12, 1837; *b* & *d* Cabarrus Co., N.C.; *m* Elizabeth Locke (Dec. 22, 1758, Rowan Co., N.C.–June 1, 1791), 1778.

Phillips, Jonathan, Capt., N.J.; *b.* Dec. 16, 1744; *d* June 29, 1801; *b* & *d* Maidenhead (now Lawrenceville), N.J.; *m* Mary Foreman, Aug. 1781.

Piatt, Jacob, Capt., N.J.; *b* May 17, 1747, Six Mile Run (now Franklin Park) near New

Brunswick, N.J.; *d* Aug. 14, 1834, "Federal Hall," Boone Co., Ky.; *m* Hannah Cook McCullough, 1779.

Pickering, Timothy, Col., Pa. (Mass.); *b* July 17, 1745; *d* Jan. 29, 1829; *b* & *d* Salem, Mass.; *m* Rebecca White.

Pierce, Benjamin, Lt., Mass.; *b* Dec. 25, 1757, Chelsmford, Mass.; *d* April 1, 1839, Hillsboro, N.H.; *m* Anna Kendrick 1789.

Platt, John, Surg.'s Mate, Del.; *b* Aug. 13, 1749, New Hanover Township, Burlington Co., N.J.; *d* Dec. 31, 1823, Chatham, near Wilmington, Del; *m* Mary Conrow (2d wife), Sept. 1808, Burlington Co., N.J.

Polhemus, John, Maj., N.J.; *b* May 25, 1738, Hopewell, N.J.; *d* May 25, 1834, Philadelphia, Pa.; *m* Susannah Hart, Nov. 23, 1766, Hopewell, N.J.

Polk, Thomas, Brig. Gen., N.C.; *b* 1732 near Carlisle, Cumberland Co., Pa.; *d* June 26, 1794, Charlotte, N.C.; *m* Susan Spratt, 1755, Mecklenburg Co., N.C.

Polk, William, Maj., N.C.; *b* July 9, 1758, Charlotte, N.C.; *d* Jan. 4/14, 1834, Raleigh, N.C.; *m* Grizelda Gilchrist (1st wife), Oct. 15, 1789, N.C.

Poor, Enoch, Brig. Gen., N.H.; *b* June 21, 1736, Andover, Mass.; *d* Sept. 8, 1780, Paramus, N.J.; *m* Martha Osgood.

Pope, Charles, Lt. Col., Del.; *b* 1748, Del.; *d* Feb. 16, 1803, Columbia Co., Ga.; *m* Jane Stokesly, 1772.

Popham, William, Capt., N.Y; *b* Sept./Oct. 19, 1750, Brandon, County Cork, Ireland; *d* Sept. 25/27, 1845/47, New York, N.Y.; *m* Mary Morris, dau. Richard Morris, Oct. 19, 1783.

Porter, Phineas, Col., Conn.; *b* Dec. 1, 1739; *d* March 9, 1804, *b* & *d* Waterbury, Conn.; *m* Melicent Baldwin Lewis (2d wife), Dec. 23, 1778.

Posey, Thomas, Lt. Col., Va.; *b* July 9, 1750, near Alexandria, Va.; *d* March 18, 1818, Shawneetown, Ill.; *m* Mary Alexander Thornton (widow), Jan. 22, 1783.

Potts, Jonathan, Surg., Pa.; *b* April 1, 1745, Popodicon, Pa.; *d* Oct. 1781, Reading, Pa.; *m* Grace Richardson, May 5, 1766, Philadelphia, Pa.; line went to brother.

Pratt, William, Lt., R.I.; *b* Sept. 30, 1759, Bristol, R.I.; *d* Feb. 6, 1845, Freetown, Mass.; *m* Mary (Polly) Lawton, dau. Capt. Elisha Lawton, Jan. 6, 1785.

Prentice (Prentiss), Samuel, Lt. Col., Conn.; *b* Oct. 4, 1736; *d* July 1807; *b* & *d* Stonington, Conn.; *m* Phoebe Billings (1738–1829).

Price, Thomas, Col., Md.; *b* Sept. 15, 1732, Philadelphia, Pa.; *d* 1795, Frederick Co., Md. (will probated May 20, 1795); *m* Mary (Beatty?) before 1752.

Proctor, Thomas, Col., Pa.; *b* 1739, Ireland; *d* March 16, 1806, Philadelphia, Pa.; *m* Anna Maria Fox, Jan. 1, 1767, Philadelphia, Pa.

Putnam, Daniel, Maj., Conn.; *b* Nov. 18, 1757, Pomfret, Conn.; *d* April 30, 1831, Brooklyn, Conn.; *m* Catherine Hutchinson, dau. Shrimpton & Elizabeth Malbone Hutchinson, Sept. 2, 1782, Brooklyn, Conn.

Putnam, Israel, Maj. Gen., Conn.; *b* Jan. 7, 1717/18, Salem Village, Mass.; *d* May 29, 1790, Brooklyn, Conn.; *m* Hannah Pope, July 19, 1739.

Quarles, Robert, Lt., Va.; *b* July 26, 1763, Va.; *d* Aug. 23, 1827, San Fernando Township (now St. Louis), Mo.; *m* Martha ("Patsy") Minor (Feb. 6, 1770–April 26, 1855), Nov. 16, 1791.

Quarles, William P., 2d Lt., Va.; *b* 1752, Va.; *d* 1814, White Plains, White Co., Tenn.; *m* Nancy Ann Hawes, c.1783.

Randolph, Robert, Lt., Va.; *b* 1760, Va.; *d* Sept. 12/25, 1825, Va.; *m* Elizabeth/Eliza Carter (1764–1832).

Ransom, Samuel, probably Capt., Conn.; *b* c.1737, at or near Ipswich, England; *d* July 3, 1778, Battle of Wyoming Valley, Pa.; *m* Esther Laurence, May 6, 1756, Canaan Township, Conn.

Reed, James, Brig. Gen., N.H.; *b* Jan. 8, 1723/24, Sudbury, Mass.; *d* Feb. 13, 1807, Keene, N.H.; *m* Abigail Hinds.

Reed, John, 1st Lt., N.J.; *b* July 6, 1742; *d* 1829; *b* & *d* Hopewell Township, Mercer Co., N.J.; *m* Leah Golden, 1776.

Reeves, Enos, 1st Lt., Pa. (S.C.); *b* Feb. 4, 1753, Greenwich, Cumberland Co., N.J.; *d* June 23, 1807, Charleston, S.C.; *m* Amey Legaré, dau. Daniel Legaré Jr. Esq., Dec. 21, 1784, Charleston, S.C.

Riddick, Willis, Capt., Va.; *b* June 25, 1725; *d* Oct. 12, 1800; *b* & *d* Nansemond Co., Va; *m* Mary Folke/Foulke (1731–1801), Nansemond Co., Va.

Riker, John Berrien, Surg., N.J.; *b* 1737/38, Newton, N.Y.; *d* Sept. 5, 1794; *m* Susannah Fish, Nov. 19, 1771; line went to nephew.

Roberts, Owen, Col., S.C.; *b* 1720; *d* June 20, 1779, Battle of Stono Ferry; *m* Ann Fraser, widow of William Cattell, July 2, 1775, Charleston, S.C.

Roberts, Richard Brooke, Capt., S.C.; *b* Jan. 1, 1758, Charleston, S.C.; *d* Jan. 19, 1797, Burlington, N.J.; *m* Everarda Catharina Sophia Van Braam Houckgust, Jan. 10, 1785.

Ross, John, Maj., N.J.; *b* March 2, 1752, Mount Holly, N.J.; *d* Sept. 7, 1796; *m* Mary Brainerd, July 8, 1778.

Roy, Beverley, Capt., S.C.; *b* 1750/60, Port Royal, Va.; *d* Oct. 8, 1820, Poplar Grove, King & Queen Co., Va.; *m* Janet Dickie Byrd/Bird (2d wife), 1801, Poplar Grove, Va.

Russell, William, Col., Va.; *b* 1735, Culpeper Co., Va.; *d* 1793, near Abingdon, Va.; *m* Tabitha Adams.

Rutledge, Joshua, 2d Lt., Md.; *b* April 3, 1759, Harford Co., Md.; *d* Sept. 26, 1825, Baltimore Co., Md.; *m* Augustine Biddle of Delaware, Nov. 10, 1792, Annapolis, Md.

St. Clair, Arthur, Maj. Gen., Pa.; *b* March 23, 1734, Thurso, Scotland; *d* Aug. 31, 1818, Westmoreland Co., Pa.; buried Greensburg, Pa.; *m* Phoebe Bayard, dau. Balthazar & Mary Bowdin Bayard, May 1760, Boston, Mass.

Schott, John Paul, Capt., Pa.; *b* Oct. 15, 1744, Berlin, Prussia; *d* July 18, 1829, Philadelphia, Pa.; *m* Naomi Sill, Oct. 18, 1780, Wyoming, Pa.

Schuyler. Philip, Maj. Gen., N.Y.: *b* Nov. 20/22, 1733; *d* Nov. 18, 1804; *b* & *d* Albany, N.Y.; *m* Catharine Van Rensselaer, Sept. 17, 1755, Albany, N.Y.

Scott, John Baytop, Ens., Va.; *b* Sept. 26, 1761, Prince Edward Co., Va.; *d* Feb. 26, 1814, Scottsburg, Halifax Co., Va.; *m* Martha (Patsy) Thompson (2d wife), 1785, Halifax Co., Va.

Scott, Joseph, Sr., Capt., Va.; *b* c.1760, Cumberland, Va.; *d* Nov. 20, 1810, Richmond, Va.; *m* unknown.

Scott, Joseph, Jr., Capt., Va.; *b* 1752, Amelia Co., Va.; *d*?; *m* Elizabeth Booker, 1778.

Scott, Moses, Surg., N.J.; *b* 1737, Bucks Co., Pa.; *d* Dec. 21/28, 1821, New Brunswick, N.J.; *m* Anna Johnson.

Selden, Samuel, Col., Conn.; *b* Jan. 11, 1723, North Lyme or Hadlyme, Conn.; wounded and taken prisoner Sept. 15, 1776; *d* Oct. 11, 1776, in prison; *m* Elizabeth Ely (Oct. 11, 1724–Feb. 2, 1802) May 23, 1745.

Sevier, Robert, Capt., N.C.; *b* c.1747, Rockingham Co., Va.; *d* Oct. 7, 1780, King's Mountain, N.C.; *m* Keziah Robertson; line went to brother.

Shearman, Henry, Lt. R.I.; *b* March 31, 1759, South Kingstown, R.I.; *d* April 8, 1829, North Kingstown, R.I.; *m* Mary Gardner, North Kingstown, R.I.

Sheldon, Elisha, Col., Conn.; *b* March 3/6, 1739, Lyme, Conn.; *d* 1805, Franklin Co., Vt.; *m* Sarah Bellows (or Whiting), Dec. 30, 1759.

Sherman, John, 1st Lt., Conn.; *b* July 8/9, 1750, New Milford, Conn.; *d* Aug. 8, 1802, Canton, Mass.; *m* Rebecca Austin, Aug. 28, 1771.

Sherman, Josiah, Chap., Conn.; *b* April 2, 1729, Woodbury Conn.; *d* Nov. 24, 1789, Woodbridge, Conn.; *m* Martha Minott, dau. Hon. James Minott, Jan. 24, 1757, Durham, N.Y.

Shubrick, Thomas, Capt., S.C.; *b* Dec. 27, 1756; *d* March 4, 1810; *b* & *d* Charleston, S.C.; *m* Mary Branford on April 9, 1778, Charleston, S.C.

Shute, William, Capt., N.J.; *b* March 9, 1760, Elizabethtown, N.J.; *d* Aug. 12, 1841, New

York, N.Y.; *m* Ann Hatfield Blanchard (June 12, 1764–Oct. 26, 1843), Dec. 5, 1784.

Slade, William, 2d Lt., N.C.; *b* c.1740, Hyde Co., N.C.; *d* c.1791, Martin Co., N.C.; *m* Anne Gainou, c.1765.

Slaughter, Lawrence, Lt., Va.; *b* 1735, Culpeper Co., Va.; *d* 1806, Spotsylvania Co., Va.; *m* Elizabeth Field.

Slaughter, Robert, Lt., Va.; *b* April 16, 1758, Culpeper Co., Va.; *d* Dec. 1826, Mercer Co., Ky.; *m* Lucy Harrison (1st wife), dau. Robert & Susannah Harrison, Va.

Smaw, Henry, Sr., Capt., N.C.; *b* ?, Northampton Co., Va.; *d* will dated April 30, 1775, Beaufort Co., N.C.; *m* Mary Respass before 1730.

Smith, Larkin, Capt., Va.; *b* c.1757, "Rickahock," King & Queen Co., Va.; *d* Sept. 28, 1813, Fredericksburg, Va.; *m* Mary Eleanor Hill (176?–Feb. 10, 1797), dau. John & Eleanor (Roy) Hill, April 21, 1781, in Fredericksburg, Va.

Somervell, James, Capt., Md.; *b* April 19, 1758, Prince Georges Co., Md.; *d* May 4, 1815, Md.; *m* Ann Magruder Trueman (1st wife).

Southall, Stephen, 1st Lt., Va.; *b* ?; *d* ?; *m* Martha Wood.

Spencer, Joseph, Maj. Gen., Conn.; *b* Oct. 3, 1714; *d* Jan. 13, 1789, *b* & *d* East Haddam, Conn.; *m* Martha Brainerd (1st wife), Aug. 2, 1738.

Spencer, Oliver, Col., N.J.; *b* Oct. 6, 1736, East Haddam, Conn.; *d* Jan. 22, 1811, Columbus or Cincinnati, Ohio; *m* Anna Ogden, dau. Robert & Phoebe (Hatfield) Ogden, Jan. 22, 1758, Elizabethtown, N.J.

Spotswood/Spottswood, John, Capt., Va.; *b* c.1748/49, Germanna, Spotsylvania Co., Va.; *d* between Oct. 23, 1800 and May 9, 1801, Orange Co., Va.; *m* Sarah Rowsie (Rowzie/Rowzee/Rouze), Sept. 19, 1771, probably "Farmers Hall," Essex Co., Va.

Sproat, William, Capt., Pa.; *b* 1757, Guilford, Conn.; *d* Oct. 11, 1793; *m* Maria Thompson, Oct. 11, 1792, Philadelphia, Pa.

Stanton, Ebenezer, 2d Lt., Conn.; baptized 1758; line went to nephew.

Steddiford, Gerard, 1st Lt., N.Y.; *b* 1752; *d* April 3, 1820, N.Y.; *m* Jane Bicker on Nov. 10, 1774.

Steele, John, Capt., Pa.; *b* June 5, 1758, Drumore Township, Pa.; *d* Feb. 27, 1827, Philadelphia, Pa.; *m* Abigail Bailey on March 4, 1784.

Stevens, Ebenezer, Lt. Col., N.Y.; *b* Aug. 11/12, 1751, Boston, Mass.; *d* Sept. 2, 1823/24, Rockaway, N.Y.; *m* Rebecca Hodgson (1st wife), dau. Benjamin Hodgson, Oct. 11, 1774; *m* Lucretia Ledyard Sands (widow) (2d wife), on May 4, 1784.

Stevenson, George, Hosp. Mate, Pa.; *b* Oct. 22, 1759, York, Pa.; *d* May 1829, Wilmington, Del.; *m* Mary Holmes.

Stricker, John, Capt. Lt., Pa.; *b* Feb. 15, 1759, Fredericktown, Md.; *d* June 23, 1825, Baltimore, Md.; *m* Miss Bedford, dau. G. Bedford, a Signer, Oct. 10, 17??, Baltimore, Md.

Strong, Adonijah, Lt., Conn.; *b* July 5, 1743, Coventry, Conn.; *d* Feb. 12, 1813, Salisbury, Conn.; *m* Abigail Bates (*b* 1750, Hanover, Morris Co., N.J.), July 28, 1777.

Strong, Nathan, Capt., N.Y.; *b* Nov. 1, 1751, Blooming Grove, N.Y.; *d* July 17, 1796, New York, N.Y.; *m* Ruth Brewster (c.1755–Sept. 17, 1796), dau. John Brewster, Jan. 13, 1777.

Stuart, William, Lt., Pa. (N.Y.); *b* c.1738, Green Hill, Letterkenny, County Donegal, Ireland; *d* 1831, Mercer Co., Pa.; *m* Mary Gass, 1760.

Sullivan, John, Brig. Gen., N.H.; *b* Feb. 17, 1740, Somersworth, N.H.; *d* Jan. 28, 1795, Durham, N.H.; line went to brother.

Talbot, Silas, Capt., N.Y.; *b* Dec. 11, 1751, Dighton, Bristol Co., Mass.; *d* June 30/July 1, 1813, New York, N.Y.; *m* Anna Richmond (1st wife), March 1, 1772.

Tallmadge, Benjamin, Maj., Conn.; *b* Feb. 25, 1754, Brookhaven, Suffolk Co., N.Y.; *d* March 7, 1835, Litchfield, Conn.; *m* Mary Floyd, March 18, 1784, Mastic, N.Y.

Taylor, Othniel, Capt., Mass.; *b* Jan. 10, 1753, Charlemont, Mass.; *d* Aug. 15, 1819, Canandaigua, N.Y.; *m* Dorothy Wilder, Feb. 6, 1785, Leominster, Mass.; line went to brother.

Taylor, William, Maj., Va.; *b* Jan. 23, 1753, Orange Co., Va.; *d* April 14, 1830; line went to brother.

Ten Broeck, John Cornelius, Capt., N.Y.; *b* March 15, 1755, Claverack, N.Y.; *d* Aug. 10, 1835, Water Vleit (or Watervliet), N.Y.; *m* Antje Ten Broeck, Dec. 30, 1784.

Tennille (Tannell), Francis, Capt., Ga.; *b* 1747, Va.; *d* Dec. 1812, Ga.; *m* Mary Bacon Dixon (1774–1848) (2d wife), Ga.

Thomas, Charles, Capt., Va.; *b* ?; *d* between May 24, 1785 and June 11, 1787; will probated June 11, 1787, Nansemond Co.; *m* Ann ?

Thomas, Joseph, Capt., Mass.; *b* Jan. 8, 1755; *d* Aug. 10, 1838; *b* & *d* Plymouth, Mass.; unmarried; line went to brother.

Thompson, Alexander, 2d Lt., N.Y.; *b* Aug. 17, 1759, New York, N.Y.; *d* Sept. 28, 1809, West Point, N.Y.; *m* Abigail Amelia Christina De Hart, March 4, 1784.

Thompson, William, Lt., Conn.; *b* Oct. 29, 1742, Stratford, Conn.; *d* April 27, 1777, killed in action, Ridgefield, Conn.; *m* Mehitable Ufford (*b* March 16, 1745), Oct. 14, 1762.

Thruston, Charles Mynn, Col., Va.; *b* Nov. 6, 1738, Gloucester Co., Va.; *d* March 28, 1812, near New Orleans, La.; *m* Mary Buckner, 1760.

Tilghman, Tench, Lt. Col., Md.; *b* Dec. 25, 1744, Francis Estate, "Fausley," Talbot Co., Md.; *d* April 18, 1786, Baltimore, Md.; *m* Anna Maria Tilghman (July 17, 1755–Jan. 13, 1843), June 9, 1783, St. Michael's Parish, Talbot Co., Md.

Tillotson, Thomas, Surg., N.Y.; *b* 1751, Md.; *d* May 5, 1832, Rhinebeck, N.Y.; *m* Mary Livingston (1749–March 1823), dau. Robert R. & Margaret Beekman Livingston, on Feb. 22, 1779, "Clermont," Rhinebeck, N.Y.

Tousard, Anne-Louis, Chevalier de, Lt. Col., France; *b* March 12, 1749; *d* May 4, 1817; *b* & *d* Paris, France (or *b* Burgundy); *m* Marie Françoise Reine Joubert (1764–July 1794, Wilmington, Del.) (widow of M. de St. Martin), Feb. 19, 1788, Danto Domingo.

Townsend, David, Surg., Mass.; *b* Jan. 7, 1753; *d* April 13, 1829; *m* Elizabeth Davis, May 24, 1785, Boston, Mass.

Triplett, William, Lt., Va.; *b* 1730; *d* 1802/03; *b* & *d* Fairfax Co. (then Prince William Co.), Va.; *m* Sarah Peake, dau. William Peake of Truro Parish, Va., 1760.

Troup, Robert, Lt. Col., N.Y.; *b* Aug. 19, 1756, Morris, N.J.; *d* Jan. 14, 1832, New York, N.Y.; *m* Janet Goelet, May 23, 1787.

Tuberville/Turberville, George Lee, Maj., Va.; *b* Sept. 7, 1760, "Hickory Hill," Westmoreland Co., Va.; *d* March 26, 1798, "Epping Forest," Richmond Co., Va.; *m* Elizabeth Tayloe Corbin, dau. Hon. Gawin & Joanna (Tucker) Corbin, Jan. 4, 1782, probably "Buckingham," Middlesex Co., Va.

Tupper, Benjamin, Col., Mass.; *b* March 11, 1738, Stoughton (now Sharon), Mass.; *d* June 7, 1792, Campus Martius Fort, Marietta, Ohio; *m* Huldah White, dau. Edward White, Nov. 18, 1762, Bridgewater, Mass.

Turnbull, Charles, Capt., Pa.; *b* Sept. 4, 1753, Kingston, Surrey Co., England; *d* Dec. 19, 1795, Pelham, Westchester Co., N.Y.; *m* Phebe Bloom on Feb. 1, 1781, Bedford, N.Y. (?)

Tutt, Benjamin, Capt., S.C.; *b* 1740; *d* after 1800; *b* & *d* S.C.; *m* Barbara Stallnaker, c.1770, S.C.

Tutt, Charles, Lt., Va.; *b* ? (under age in 1766), Va.; *d* Sept. 11, 1777, Battle of Brandywine; unmarried; line went to heir, James Tutt.

Tuttle, William, Ens., N.J.; *b* Nov. 5, 1760, N.J.; *d* Jan. 11, 1836, N.J.; *m* Tempe Wickham (Oct. 30, 1758–April 28, 1822), April 3, 1788; line went to brother.

Upshaw, James, Capt., Va.; *b* c.1756, Va.; *d* July 1806/07/08, Essex Co., Va.; *m* Mary Martin.

Vacher, John Francis, Surg., N.Y.; *b* 1751,

Toulon, France; *d* Dec. 4, 1807/09, New York, N.Y.; *m* Sarah Potter of Madison, N.J., 1783.

Van Cortlandt, Nicholas Bayard, Maj., N.Y.; *b* March 1756, New York, N.Y.; *d* May 1, 1782, Parsippany, N.J.; unmarried; line went to brother.

Van Horne, Isaac, Capt., Pa.; *b* Jan. 13, 1754, Bucks Co., Pa.; *d* Feb. 2, 1834, Zanesville, Ohio; *m* Dorothy John Marple (widow of Isaac Marple), 1783, Bucks Co., Pa.

Van Rensselaer, James, Capt., Conn.; *b* Feb. 1, 1747, Fort Crailo, Greenbush, N.Y.; *d* Feb. 1, 1827, "Crystal Hill," Albany, N.Y.; *m* Catharine Van Cortlandt, Oct. 10, 1782.

Van Rensselaer, Jeremiah, Lt., N.Y.; *b* July 15, 1740; *d* Feb. 19, 1810; *b* & *d* Albany, N.Y.; *m* Helen Lansing, July 3, 1760; line went to cousin.

Van Schaick, Goose/Gozen, Col., N.Y.; *b* Sept. 5, 1736; *d* July 4, 1789; *b* & *d* Albany, N.Y.; *m* Maria Ten Broeck, Nov. 15, 1770.

Vose, Joseph, Col., Mass.; *b* Dec. 7, 1739/29; *d* May 22, 1816; *b* & *d* Milton, Mass.; *m* Sara Howe, Nov. 5/Dec. 27, 1761.

Wadsworth, Jeremiah, Col., Conn.; *b* July 12, 1743; *d* April 30, 1804; *b* & *d* Hartford, Conn.; *m* Mehitable Russell, Nov. 19, 1764.

Walker, Timothy, Col., Mass.; *b* July 18, 1718; *d* Dec. 26, 1796; *b* & *d* Rehoboth, Mass., *m* Elizabeth Carpenter (1st wife), Dec. 10, 1741.

Wallace, Gustavus Brown, Lt. Col., Va.; *b* Nov. 9, 1751, "Ellerslie," King George Co., Va.; *d* Aug. 17, 1802, Fredericksburg, Va.; unmarried; line went to brother.

Wallace, William Brown, 2d Lt., Va.; *b* July 26, 1757, "Ellerslie," King George Co., Va.; *d* summer of 1833, Lawrenceburg, Ky.; *m* Barbara Tunstall Fox (Feb. 1766–1833), March 22, 1787.

Waller, Allen, Ens., Va.; *b* Stafford Co., Va.; *d* Aug. 1, 1776; line went to brother.

Ward, Joseph, Col., Mass.; *b* July 2, 1737, Newton, Mass.; *d* Feb. 14, 1812, Boston, Mass.; *m* Prudence Bird, Nov. 30, 1784.

Ward, Samuel, Jr., Lt. Col., R.I.; *b* Nov. 17, 1756, Westerly Colony, R.I.; *d* Aug. 16, 1832, New York, N.Y.; *m* Phoebe Greene, dau. Gov. W. Greene of Rhode Island, March 8, 1778.

Washington, George, Gen., Va.; *b* Feb. 22, 1732, Bridge's Creek, Va.; *d* Dec. 14, 1799, Mount Vernon, Va.; *m* Martha (Dandridge) Custis (widow of Daniel Parke Custis), Jan. 6, 1759; line went to brother.

Waterman, Jedediah, Ens., Mass. & N.Y.; *b* June 8, 1759, Conn.; *d* Sept. 25, 1828, New York, N.Y.; *m* Elizabeth Plummer, Feb. 8, 1801.

Waters, Richard, Capt., Md.,; *b* c1759/60, Prince Georges Co., Md.; *d* April 28, 1810, Montgomery Co., Md.; *m* Margaret Hamilton Smith, dau. Philemon Hamilton & Betsy Rawlins Smith, June 2, 1785, Calvert Co., Md.

Watkins, Gassaway, Capt., Md.; *b* 1752, Anne Arundel Co., Md.; *d* July 14, 1840, Howard Co., Md.; *m* Ellen Bowie Claggett on April 26, 1803.

Watson, James, Capt., Conn.; *b* 1750, Woodbury, Conn.; *d* May 15, 1806; *m* Mary Talcott; line went to brother,

Webb, Nathaniel, Capt., Conn.; *b* 1737; *d* 1814; *m* Zerviah Abbe in 1767.

Webb, Samuel Blachley, Col., Conn.; *b* Dec. 15, 1753, Wethersfield, Conn.; *d* Dec. 3, 1807, Claverack, N.Y.; *m* Catherine Hogeboom (2d wife) of Claverack, N.Y., Sept. 3, 1790.

Weeks, John, Lt., N.H.; *b* Feb. 17, 1749, Hampton, N.H.; *d* Sept. 10, 1818, Wakefield, N.H.; *m* Deborah Brackett, Dec. 27, 1770.

White, James, Capt., N.C.; *b* 1747, Rowan Co., N.C.; *d* Aug. 14, 1821, Knoxville, Tenn.; *m* Mary Lawson, April 14, 1770, Iredell Co., N.C.

White, Moses, Capt., Mass.; *b* June 29, 1756, Dracut, Mass.; *d* Dec. 7, 1833, Springfield, Mass.; *m* Elizabeth Amelia Atlee, Dec. 7, 1786.

White, Robert, Capt., Va.; *b* March 29, 1759, Frederick Co., Va.; *d* March 9/Nov. 2, 1831, Winchester, Va., *m* Arabella Baker.

White, William, 2d Lt., Va.; *b* May 24, 1743; *d* July 27, 1814; *b* & *d* Louisa Co., Va.; *m* Catharine (Chapman) Smith Pendleton (*d* Jan. 15, 1829) (widow, her 3d marriage), c.1770.

Whiting, John, Lt., Mass.; *b* Feb. 24, 1760, Lancaster, Mass.; *d* Sept. 3, 1810, Washington, D.C.; *m* Orplia Danforth, May 24, 1784.

Whiting, Samuel, Lt., Conn.; *b* 1744, Stratford, Conn.; *d* 1816, Riverside, Conn.; *m* Abigail Ferris, 1769.

Whitlock, Ephraim Lockhart, 1st Lt., N.J.; *b* Sept. 22, 1755, Monmouth Co., N.J.; *d* Sept. 22, 1825, Elizabethtown, N.J.; *m* Anna Tiebout, 1778, Monmouth, N.J.

Wigton, John, Lt., Pa.; *b* 1742, probably Philadelphia, Pa.; *d* Sept. 13, 1793, Philadelphia, Pa.; *m* Margaret Cochran (Coughlan), April 14, 1766.

Williams, Abraham, Capt., Mass.; *b* Feb. 10, 1754; *d* Feb. 22, 1796; *b* & *d* Sandwich, Mass.; *m* Abigail Freeman on Jan. 4, 1786, Sandwich, Mass.

Williams, John 1st Lt., N.C.; *b* 1745, Hanover Co., Va.; *d* Oct. 1799, Orange Co., N.C.; *m* Elizabeth White (Williamson).

Williams, Joseph, Col., N.C.; *b* March 27, 1748, Hanover Co., Va.; *d* Aug. 11, 1827, Surry Co., N.C. *m* Rebeckah Lanier, Sept. 16, 1772, Granville Co., N.C.

Willis, John W., Maj., Va.; *b* 1740, "Willis Hill," Spotsylvania Co., Va.; *d* 1816, Spotsylvania Co., Va.; *m* Ann; line went to brother.

Wilmot/Wilmott, Robert, 1st Lt., Md.; *b* Dec. 25, 1757, Baltimore Co., Md.; *d* Aug. 5, 1839, Bourbon Co., Ky.; *m* Priscilla Ridgely Dorsey (*b* 1762, Baltimore Co., Md; *d* 1814, Bourbon Co., Ky), Oct. 8, 1781, Baltimore Co., Md.

Winchester, George, 1st Lt., Md.; *b* March 6, 1757, White Level, Md.; *d* killed by Indians July 9, 1794, Gallatin, Tenn.; unmarried; line went to brother.

Winslow, John, Capt., Mass.; *b* Sept. 29, 1753; *d* Nov. 29, 1819; *b* & *d* Boston, Mass.; *m* Ann Gardner (July 26, 1755–Nov. 12, 1836), May 21, 1782.

Withers, Enoch Keene, Ens., Va.; *b* Oct. 14, 1760; *d* July 26, 1813; *b* & *d* Fauquier Co., Va.; *m* Jannett Chinn on May 15, 1786, Fauquier Co., Va.

Wolcott, Oliver, Maj. Gen., Mass. (Conn.); *b* Nov. 20, 1726, East Windsor, Conn.; *d* Dec. 1, 1797, Litchfield, Conn.; *m* Laura (or Lorraine) Collins, on Jan. 21, 1755.

Wooster, David, Brig. Gen., Conn.; *b* March 2, 1710, Stratford, Conn.: *d* May 2, 1777, Danbury, Conn., of wounds; *m* Mary Clapp, March 6, 1746, Conn.; line went to cousin.

Wright, Jacob, Capt., N.Y.; *b* ? Oyster Bay, N.Y.; *d* after 1810; *m* Catherine Pell/Pells (2d wife), Dec. 10, 1736; *m* Margaret Moffat (3d wife) (1757–1826), dau. Rev. John and Margaret Little Moffat.

Young, John, Capt., Va.; *b* March 25, 1737; *d* Dec. 5, 1824; *b* & *d* Augusta Co., Va.; *m* Mary White (1st wife), dau. Isaac and Jean Gordon White II, Sept. 13, 1763, Augusta Co., Va.

Zane, Ebenezer, Lt., Va.; *b* Oct. 7, 1747 (what is now) Moorefield, Hardy Co., Va. (now W.Va.); *d* buried Nov. 19, 1812, Martin's Ferry, Ohio; *m* Elizabeth McCulloch c.1768, Potomac Valley, Va.

The Book Committee

# Index